NEW YORK FIELD CODES SERIES

Volume I

NEW YORK FIELD CODES SERIES

Volume I. The Code of Civil Procedure of the State of New-York (1850)

Volume II. The Code of Criminal Procedure of the State of New York (1850)

Volume III. The Civil Code of the State of New York (1865)

Volume IV. The Penal Code of the State of New York (1865)

Volume V. The Political Code of the State of New York (1860)

NEW YORK FIELD CODES SERIES

VOLUME I

THE CODE

OF

CIVIL PROCEDURE

OF THE

STATE OF NEW-YORK.

REPORTED COMPLETE

BY THE

COMMISSIONERS ON PRACTICE AND PLEADINGS.

General Introduction to the Series
by Michael Weber

THE LAWBOOK EXCHANGE, LTD.
Clark, New Jersey

New York Field Codes Series
ISBN 978-1-886363-40-3

Vol. I. The Code of Civil Procedure of the State of New-York
ISBN 978-1-886363-34-2

Vol. II. The Code of Criminal Procedure of the State of New York
ISBN 978-1-886363-35-9

Vol. III. The Civil Code of the State of New York
ISBN 978-1-886363-38-0

Vol. IV. The Penal Code of the State of New York
ISBN 978-1-886363-36-6

Vol. V. The Political Code of the State of New York
ISBN 978-1-886363-37-3

Lawbook Exchange edition 2011

The quality of this reprint is equivalent to the quality of the original work.

THE LAWBOOK EXCHANGE, LTD.
33 Terminal Avenue
Clark, New Jersey 07066-1321

Please see our website for a selection of our other publications and fine facsimile reprints of classic works of legal history:
www.lawbookexchange.com

Library of Congress Cataloging-in-Publication Data

New York (State). Commissioners on Practice and Pleadings.
The code of civil procedure of the State of New-York / reported complete by the Commissioners on Practice and Pleadings.
p. cm. (New York Field codes, 1850-1865)
Originally published: Albany : Weed, Parsons, public printers, 1850.
ISBN 1-886363-34-X (alk. paper)
1. Civil procedure—New York (State) I. Title. II. Series.
KFN5990.A2 1997
347.747'05—dc21 97-42137
CIP

Printed in the United States of America on acid-free paper

GENERAL INTRODUCTION
TO THE SERIES

These five volumes (of which this is Volume I) contain the complete texts of the law codes drafted for New York State by David Dudley Field, and his colleagues during the years 1847 to 1865. They include Field's two procedural codes—Civil Procedure and Criminal Procedure—and three substantive codes—Political, Penal, and Civil. The two procedural codes were drafted first, pursuant to Article VI, Section 24, of the 1846 New York State Constitution, which stated:

> The Legislature at its first session after the adoption of the Constitution, shall provide for the appointment of three commissioners, whose duty it shall be to revise, reform, simplify, and abridge the rules and practice, pleadings, forms, and proceedings of the courts of record of this State, and to report thereon to the Legislature, subject to their adoption and modification from time to time.[1]

A separate provision of the Constitution called for commissioners "to reduce into a written and systematic code the whole body of the law of this state, or so much and such parts thereof as to the said commissioners shall seem practicable and expedient." This provision eventually resulted in the substantive political, penal, and civil codes.[2]

Field was perhaps the leading American proponent of codification. He served with both groups of commissioners.

---

[1] Quoted in Mildred V. Coe and Lewis W. Morse, "Chronology of the Development of the David Dudley Field Code," *Cornell Law Quarterly* 27 (1942): 238.

[2] Alison Reppy, "The Field Codification Concept," in *David Dudley Field: Centenary Essays Celebrating One Hundred Years of Legal Reform,* ed. Alison Reppy (New York: New York University School of Law, 1949), 37. Reppy's chapter is very useful for untangling the convoluted history of the commissions, the writing of the codes, and the fates of the codes in the New York legislature.

More than any other individual, Field was responsible for the drafting of all the codes. (He has been called "an inexhaustible one man codifying machine."[3])

New York, however, enacted only three: the Code of Civil Procedure—which is often referred to simply as "the Field Code"—and, after many years, the Code of Criminal Procedure and the Penal Code. But the significance of Field's work extended far beyond New York State. As one legal scholar has observed, Field's efforts changed how lawyers and judges do their work and led to "new ways of understanding the law itself."[4]

The Codification Movement

Field's codes were part of a wider codification movement in the United States in the first half of the nineteenth century.[5] In the 1830s, for example, a few years before Field's work began in New York, U.S. Supreme Court Justice Joseph Story was active in attempting to codify the Massachusetts law. The codification movement was an attempt to clarify the law and remove obsolete rules so that the law could be intelligible to ordinary citizens. Its proponents considered the existing body of law, based as it was on English common law, "inaccessible and uncertain . . . unnecessarily mysterious, complex, and overly technical."[6] Field remarked:

> The common law of New York, like the common law of England, from which it is in great part derived, consists of a vast number of rules of property and of conduct, which have been applied by the judicial tribunals, and which had their origin either in legislative enactments, now forgotten, or in

---

[3] Robert W. Gordon, review of *The American Codification Movement: A Study of Antebellum Legal Reform,* by Charles C. Cook, *Vanderbilt Law Review* 36 (1983): 435.

[4] William P. LaPiana, "Just the Facts: The Field Code and the Case Method," *New York Law School Law Review* 36 (1991): 304.

[5] See Charles C. Cook, *The American Codification Movement: A Study of Antebellum Legal Reform* (Westport, Conn.: Greenwood, 1981).

[6] Ibid., 5.

> traditions from ancient times, or in the consciences of the judges, as the cases came before them.[7]

Proponents of codification took to heart the critical observation of the great English reformer Jeremy Bentham that common law judges made law "as a man makes laws for his dog. When your dog does anything you want to break him of, you wait till he does it, and then you beat him for it."[8] They wanted more system, more precision, and more simplicity in the law. Many were impressed by France's Civil Code, established by Napoleon in 1804, which Edward Livingston had applied to Louisiana in the 1820s.

For some American codifiers, flushed by post-Revolutionary War patriotism, the great weight of the English common law was seen as an alien, un-American presence. A few wanted to go so far as to abolish the common law entirely. Most of the reformers, however, including Field, were not so radical. Their goal was to reduce the common law power of judges and give state legislators the chance to shape the law by reducing to statutory form those parts of the common law that could be plainly stated in a concise book of statutes.

Field's Range of Influence

David Dudley Field (1805–1894) was born in Haddam, Connecticut, into a family of high achievers.[9] Both his father, a minister, and mother were the children of Revolutionary War officers. Among his siblings were Stephen Johnson Field (1816–1899), who was appointed by President Lincoln to the United

---

[7] Introduction to *The Civil Code of the State of New York* (1865), in vol. III of this series, xiv.

[8] Quoted in Lawrence M. Friedman, *American Law* (New York: Norton, 1984), 92.

[9] Useful biographical sources are Helen K. Hoy, "David Dudley Field," in *Great American Lawyers,* ed. William Draper Lewis, vol. 5 (Philadelphia: Winston, 1908; reprint, South Hackensack, N.J.: Rothman, 1971); and the biography written by Field's younger brother, Henry M. Field, *The Life of David Dudley Field* (New York: Scribner's, 1898).

States Supreme Court in 1863, and Cyrus West Field, who laid the first transatlantic cable in 1866. While Field had extra ordinary intelligence, ability, and diligence, he was also competitive, cantankerous, and stubborn. He outlived three wives. (His childhood nurse called him "a most determined fellow."[10]) Not everyone felt affection for him, but very few questioned his legal skill. A colleague, subsequently dean of New York University's Law School, said, "For at least a third of a century, David Dudley Field was the most commanding figure at the American bar."[11]

After attending Williams College, Field studied law in Albany and New York City and was admitted to the New York Bar in 1828. He was active in politics as a Democrat but broke with the party over the Mexican War and slavery and in the 1850s became one of the founders of the Republican Party. Field played an important role in securing Abraham Lincoln's nomination as the Republican candidate for president in 1860. After the Civil War, however, he returned to the Democratic fold and was a close associate of Samuel J. Tilden.

Field was active as a lawyer for 60 years and participated in many notable cases heard by the Supreme Court, including *Ex parte Milligan* (1866), *Cummings* v. *Missouri* (1867), *Ex parte McArdle* (1868), and *United States* v. *Cruikshank* (1876). He provoked considerable controversy in the late 1860s and 1870s by serving as counsel to Jay Gould and James Fisk during the scandal involving the Erie Railroad and by defending New York's notorious William Marcy "Boss" Tweed.

The Origin of the Codes

Field valued precision and clarity. He greatly admired the sciences and mathematics, saying of the latter, "Its superiority over every other department of learning . . . is to be ascribed, I fancy, to the precision of its language."[12] No doubt this penchant

---

[10] Quoted in Stephen N. Subrin, "David Dudley Field and the Field Code: A Historical Analysis of an Earlier Procedural Vision," *Law and History Review* 6 (Fall 1988): 314.
[11] Austin Abbot, quoted in Field, *Life,* vii.
[12] Subrin, "David Dudley Field and the Field Code," 315.

contributed to Field's interest in the movement for codification of the law. He began working for codification in the late 1830s and was instrumental in having the provisions mandating commissions to reform the law of the state written into the 1846 New York Constitution.

Field's goal was to put all of New York's law into written form and to combine in one set of procedures the whole of actions in both law and equity. He wanted to reform the procedural law so that a legal dispute could be started with pleadings that clearly related what happened and settled in one court in one action. In his 1847 essay "What Shall Be Done with the Practice of the Courts?" Field wrote:

> What I propose, then, in respect to cases of legal cognizance, is this: that the present forms of action be abolished, and in their stead a complaint and answer required, each setting forth the real claim and defense of the parties. Such pleadings would be precisely similar to those proposed for equity cases, and we should thus have a uniform course of pleading for all cases, legal and equitable.
>
> . . .
>
> Let the plaintiff set forth his cause of action in his complaint briefly, in ordinary language, and without repetition; and let the defendant make his answer in the same way. Let each party verify his allegation by making oath that he believes it to be true. The complaint will then acquaint the defendant with the real charge, while the answer will inform the plaintiff of the real defense. The disputed facts will be sifted from the undisputed, and the parties will go to trial knowing what they have to answer. The plaintiff will state his case as he believes it, and as he expects to prove it. The defendant, for his part, will set forth what he believes and expects to establish . . . He will not be perplexed with questions of double pleading, nor shackled by ancient technical rules.[13]

---

[13] Quoted in Kermit L. Hall, William M. Wiecek, and Paul Finkelman, eds., *American Legal History: Cases and Materials,* 2nd ed. (New York: Oxford University Press, 1996), 323.

In September 1847 Field became one of the three commissioners—the other two were Arphaxad Loomis and David Graham—appointed by the New York legislature to reform legal procedures as mandated by the Constitution.[14] He replaced Nicholas Hill, who resigned because he was appalled that his colleagues were contemplating changes "so purely experimental, so sudden and general, and so perilous."[15] Field dominated the commission's work, which proceeded swiftly. The commission presented a draft of a Code of Civil Procedure to the legislature on February 29, 1848. The draft was enacted into law on April 12 of that year and has become known as the "Field Code." Subsequently the commission presented additional reports, proposing amendments to the code, some of which the legislature enacted. On December 31, 1849, the commission completed its work by presenting two complete codes: Civil Procedure and Criminal Procedure. Published in 1850, these codes are reprinted as volumes I and II of the present series. Years later, on July 1, 1881, an amended version of the Code of Criminal Procedure was enacted.[16]

Meanwhile, a separate commission also created in 1847 and charged with codifying the substantive law had made little progress, and it was abolished in 1850. But after intense effort Field in 1857 persuaded the legislature to set up a new commission empowered to fulfill the Constitution's mandate "to reduce into a written and systematic code the whole body of the law of the state of New York." Field, William Curtis Noyes, and Alexander W. Bradford were selected as the commissioners.[17] Over the next eight years they labored on three codes: a Political Code, embracing "the laws respecting the government of the state, its civil polity, the functions of its public officers, and the political rights and duties of its citizens"; a Civil Code, covering "the laws of personal rights and relations of property, and of obligations"; and a Penal Code, defining "all the crimes for which persons can be punished and the punishment for the

---

[14] Coe and Morse, "Chronology," 238.

[15] Lawrence M. Friedman, *A History of American Law,* 2nd ed. (New York: Simon & Schuster, 1986), 391.

[16] Reppy, "The Field Codification Concept," 33–8.

[17] Ibid., 38.

crime."[18] Field himself personally prepared the civil code. The entire scheme roughly paralleled the France's Code Napoleon. The Political Code was submitted to the legislature and published in 1860, the final version of the Penal Code was submitted in 1864 and published in 1865, and the final version of the Civil Code was submitted and published in 1865.[19] We reprint them in volumes III-V of the present series.

Field remained devoted to the cause of codification for the rest of his life. His interest even extended to the codification to international law, and in the 1870s he prepared a draft outline for a code of international law. He traveled to both Europe and Asia and was gratified to see the influence his New York codification work was having in Great Britain as well as in India and other British colonies.

When Field died in 1894 at the age of 89, a member of the New York Bar paid him this tribute:

> The magnitude of the results of his labors can scarcely be overestimated. . . . That he exerted a greater influence in modifying and simplifying the judicial systems of the United States and England than any other man of his time will hardly be denied. The world over, wherever the prevailing jurisprudence has had its origin in the English common law, the form and manner of conducting litigations and transacting the business of the courts are due to the influence of David Dudley Field.[20]

The Reception and Significance of the Field Codes

As we have seen, the New York legislature quickly passed Field's Code of Civil Procedure. The legislature later amended the code several times, however, and considerably diluted its concision and weakened the force of Field's reforms.

The other codes encountered much more difficulty in New York. Only two were enacted and both not until 1881: the Code of Criminal Procedure, which had been submitted initially in late

---

[18] Coe and Morse, "Chronology," 244–5.
[19] Ibid., 245.
[20] Quoted in Hoy, "David Dudley Field," 128.

1849, and the Penal Code of 1865. The New York Assembly passed the Civil Code four times, and the entire legislature did so twice—only to have it vetoed each time by the governor.[21] The Civil Code, which the commissioners claimed made important changes in "the rights of married women, the adoption of children, and the assimilation of the laws of real and personal by politicians. James C. Carter, a prominent property,"[22] sparked particularly intense debate. Opposition within the legal profession was intense, and the New York City Bar Association in 1883 unanimously passed a resolution against it.[23]

Opposition to the Civil Code—and to the codification movement in general—centered around two general points. The first was that no code, however skillfully prepared, could encompass all the wealth of experience embodied in the common law. The second was that codification would take control of the law away from the courts, where it belonged, and give it to legislatures run by politicians. James C. Carter. A prominent New York lawyer and a leading opponent of codification—he termed Field's work "grossly defective"[24]—wrote in essays in the 1880s:

> The question is [whether the] growth, development and improvement of the law [should] remain under the guidance of men selected by the people on account of their special qualifications for the work [or] be transferred to a numerous legislative body, disqualified by the nature of their duties for the discharge of this supreme function . . . [Courts apply] "a social standard of justice[,] . . . the product of the combined operation of the thought, the morality, the intellectual and moral culture of the time."[25]

These arguments carried the day in New York.

---

[21] Reppy, "The Field Codification Concept," 46.
[22] *Civil Code,* vol. III of this series, xxxi.
[23] Morton J. Horwitz, *The Transformation of American Law: 1870-1960* (Cambridge: Harvard University Press, 1977), 118.
[24] Quoted in Hoy, "David Dudley Field," 165.
[25] Quoted in Friedman, *A History of American Law,* 404.

But outside New York, especially in the newer western states and territories that did not have an inherited body of law, Field's codes enjoyed considerably more success. The Code of Civil Procedure—the "Field Code"—was adopted in Missouri as early as 1849. California, newly admitted to the Union, followed in 1851 with the help of Field's brother Stephen, who had been elected to the California legislature in 1850 after moving from New York the previous year. By 1862 ten more states and territories had adopted the Code of Civil Procedure, and by 1900 another 12 had done so.[26] In addition several states adopted a procedural criminal code and substantive penal, political, and civil codes based on Field's work. Indeed California enacted adaptations of all five of Field's codes. Portions of these codes are still in effect today.[27]

Ironically Field's attempts through codification to limit the role in America of English-derived common law had consequences for legal reform in Great Britain itself. The authors and proponents of the English Judicature Acts of 1873 and 1875, many of whom knew Field personally, were influenced by his work. Field's codes inspired lawmakers in the British colonies of India, Singapore, and Hong Kong as well.[28]

Field's codes, then, had great impact both in the United States and internationally and clearly are worthy of study today. Scholars agree, however, that Field's outstanding achievement remains the New York Code of Civil Procedure, the "Field Code." That code and the 1938 Federal Rules of Civil Procedure, which it influenced, remain the two most fundamental sets of

---

[26] The states and territories that adopted the Code of Civil Procedure by 1862 were, in addition to Missouri, California, Iowa, Indiana, Kansas, Minnesota, Nebraska, Nevada, Ohio, and Washington. By 1900 they had been joined by Arizona, Colorado, Idaho, Montana, New Mexico, North Carolina, North and South Dakota, Oklahoma, South Carolina, Utah, and Wyoming. Ibid., 394.

[27] See E. Allan Farnsworth, *An Introduction to the Legal System of the United States,* 2nd ed. (New York: Oceana, 1983); Friedman, *A History of American Law,* 405; and Horwitz, *The Transformation of American Law,* 117–8.

[28] Reppy, "The Field Codification Concept," 48.

rules in American civil procedure."[29] Section 554 of the Code of Civil Procedure contained the following revolutionary declaration:

> The distinction between actions at law and suits in equity, and for the forms of all such actions and suits heretofore existing, are abolished; and, there shall be in this state, hereafter, but one form of action, for the enforcement or protection of private rights and the redress or prevention of private wrongs, which shall be denominated a civil action.[30]

As Field intended, the code simplified the pleadings of plaintiff and defendant, limiting the former to a concise factual complaint, demurrer, and reply and the latter to a concise factual answer and demurrer. It adopted the rules of equity for the application of relief.[31] In the words of the great legal scholar Roscoe Pound:

> No treatises on the theory of legislation and no polemical tracts on law reform have led to such far-reaching concrete results. It [the Code of Civil Procedure] stands toward procedure in the world of the common law where Beccaria's treatise on Crimes and Punishments stood toward the nineteenth-century criminal law. It showed the way.[32]

Michael Weber

---

[29] Roscoe Pound, "David Dudley Field: An Appraisal," in *David Dudley Field: Centenary Essays Celebrating One Hundred Years of Legal Reform,* ed. Alison Reppy (New York: New York University School of Law, 1949), 11; Suprin, "David Dudley Field and the Field Code," 312.

[30] See page 225 of volume I of this series.

[31] Reppy, "The Field Codification Concept," 49–51.

[32] Roscoe Pound, "David Dudley Field: An Appraisal," 8.

THE CODE

OF

CIVIL PROCEDURE

OF THE

STATE OF NEW-YORK.

REPORTED COMPLETE

BY THE

COMMISSIONERS ON PRACTICE AND PLEADINGS.

ALBANY:

WEED, PARSONS & CO., PUBLIC PRINTERS.

1850.

REPORT.

TO THE LEGISLATURE OF THE STATE OF NEW-YORK.

THE COMMISSIONERS ON PRACTICE AND PLEADINGS have the honor to submit herewith, their complete Report of a CODE OF CIVIL PROCEDURE.

This Code is intended to embody the whole law of the state, concerning judicial remedies in civil cases, and to supersede the third part of the Revised Statutes, a portion of the first and second, a large number of subsequent statutes, and all of the common law, on the subject of civil remedies.

Having entered upon the duties of their commission, with an earnest conviction that the time had arrived, when great changes in judicial procedure ought to be made; charged by the constitution and the statute, under which they were appointed, with an entire revision of the existing system; and specially enjoined to make changes which struck at its foundation, it can excite no surprise, that the reforms they have proposed are comprehensive and fundamental. In bringing their labors to a conclusion, it is their highest hope, that the favorable opinions which have encouraged them so far, may not be forfeited upon maturer experience.

It was a question with the commissioners of some embarrassment, how far it was wise to go into details. There were two opposite difficulties to be avoided; on one hand was the danger, by provisions too general, of leaving a wide space for judicial discretion; on the other, equal danger, by going into minute details, of making the practice inflexible and intricate, increasing the risks of mischance, and leaving unprovided for whatever particulars were unforseen. Whether they have succeeded in finding, what they desired, a middle path between a judicial discretion, too wide for safety on the one hand, and too narrow for convenience on the other, can only be known by the result.

It is impossible, within the compass of this communication, to give any other than the most general account of the Code, as it is now presented. It is divided into four parts. The first relates to the courts of justice, their organization and jurisdiction, and the functions and duties of all judicial and ministerial officers, connected with them. The second embraces the subject of civil actions, with all their incidents; the third relates to special proceedings; and the fourth to evidence.

The essential features of the original code remain of course unchanged by the present report. Every day's experience adds new testimony to the soundness of its theory, and to the beneficial effects of its reduction to practice. The system which it traced out, and which is now filled up, will, it is hoped and believed, remain the settled policy of the state, for it is founded upon just and immutable principles.

In completing the system, and adapting to each other the parts already enacted and those which are now for the first time submitted, changes of minor details were of course necessary; the addition of new provisions affected to some degree the previous ones; and the frequent references to the old law, which the existing code contains, are in the present report generally omitted as unnecessary, because it is proposed that the old shall be superseded. With these exceptions, and a few other changes in-details, which experience has shown to be desirable, such as a modification of the reply in pleading, and a reduction of costs in certain cases, the present complete report will be found not to depart, in any essential respect, from that which was enacted as a part of the system.

The purpose of the constitutional provision and of the statute under which this code is prepared, was to make legal proceedings more intelligible, more certain, more speedy, and less expensive. Heretofore the records of the courts, have been sealed books to the mass of the people. Though concerned in them as suitors, and participating in them as jurors, they were repulsed by strange forms, and technical language. If the law could have been administered with absolute certainty, without delay, and without expense, yet if it had been unintelligible to them, it would not have been satisfactory. In a country where the people are sovereign, where they elect all officers, even the judges themselves, where education is nearly universal, it was not long possible, to keep the practice of the courts enveloped in mystery.

The Commissioners have never lost sight of these considerations. In aiming at directness and efficiency, they have aimed also at diffusing a knowledge of legal proceedings; and there is, they trust, nothing in this code, which any person of ordinary intelligence and education cannot understand. And although the law of rights is a vast science, the accumulation of numerous countries and ages, which it requires study and patience to comprehend, yet it is believed, that the practice of the courts is here set forth in such a manner, that no person need have occasion to witness a legal proceeding, read a pleading, or render a verdict, the meaning of which, he does not comprehend.

That the expense of legal proceedings has been greatly diminished by the existing code, is generally admitted; it will be diminished still more by the present. That certainty is promoted by the abolition of needless distinctions, the disuse of technical forms, and a free use of the power of amending errors and defects, and despatch by frequent courts, and the directness and simplicity of their operations, should seem to be unquestionable.

That there are great delays in some of the districts, is too evident; but they arise from the accumulation of business, devolved upon the new courts by the old supreme court and court of chancery, and also from the habits of business in some of these courts. If the old cases were now disposed of, the Commissioners are persuaded, that, under proper regulations for the despatch of business, no court need ever adjourn, until it had disposed of all the cases upon its calendar. Indeed it ought to be held a cardinal rule, that, at each session of a court, every case ready for its action, should be acted upon; and if that does not happen, there is a defect somewhere, which requires the immediate interposition of the government.

Under any system, from which the trial by jury is inseparable, as it is in ours, there must be some delay. Juries cannot be assembled for particular cases as they arise; they must be drawn periodically, and in large or thinly populated counties, at considerable intervals. So much the more reason is there, that when the court does meet, and the jury are called together from different parts of the county, all the business waiting for them should be dispatched.

The Commissioners have inserted in their report, for the purpose of carrying out this principle, a provision requiring the judges of the supreme court in any district, whenever a court adjourns leaving business undone, to request the Governor to assign other judges for it, and giving power to him, to appoint extraordinary terms and circuits, as well as to assign judges to hold them. Is is quite certain, that the present delays in certain districts ought not to be longer endured. Should these provisions, for any cause, fail of securing the end in view, after the lapse of a suitable time, the Commissioners recommend, that the Legislature appoint a committee to investigate the cause of the delays, particularly in the first district.

Among other provisions of the code, will be found a chapter designed to furnish a summary remedy in a certain class of contracts, where the defendant has liquidated the demand, and given an ununconditional promise to pay it, or where it has been already settled by a judgment in a sister state. Thus upon a bond, promissory note, bill of exchange, or judgment of another state, the plaintiff may give notice, with his complaint, of application for judgment to a judge out of court, at any time not less than forty-eight hours afterwards, and if a sufficient answer be not then made, summary judgment must be given, and even if an answer be made, the plaintiff, on indemnifying the defendant, may have an attachment to secure his debt. So, upon a mortgage, there is provided a summary foreclosure, without action, more comprehensive and safe than the present proceeding by advertisement, and at small expense. Provisions are inserted, for the purpose of applying a remedy to the abuses in assessments, so far as can be done by the action of the courts. There are also chapters, for the discharge of insolvents in certain cases, and for a compulsory cession of their property, for the payment of their debts.

By means of the courts of conciliation, for which, in accordance with the constitution, provision has been made, many of the actions now brought for slander, assault, and others of the like kind, may be avoided, and by extending the inducements to a compromise during a litigation, actions commenced may often be settled before a trial. Thus it is to be hoped, there will be fewer cases, requiring the decision of the courts, and not more than they can readily despatch, as fast as they are brought before them.

Upon the subject of evidence, the change of the name of the writ of *habeas corpus*, and the organization and functions of the courts of conciliation, as reported, one of the Commissioners, (Mr. Graham), dissents: a dissent which his colleagues regret, but to which their views of their duty will not permit them to yield.

If the time given to the Commissioners, for the completion of their work, had permitted it, they would have introduced more detailed provisions for certain proceedings in surrogate's courts, and would also have prepared a book of forms to accompany the code.

The Commissioners are constrained to bespeak beforehand the indulgence of the Legislature and the People, for the errors and imperfections, which will doubtless be discovered in their work. When it is considered, that the two codes of procedure, civil and criminal, cover the whole ground of remedial law, and are intended to dispense with all previous statute and common law in that department, that they together constitute an entire code of remedies, the complement of the code of rights, and designed in connection with it to unite, as the constitution contemplates, in "a written and systematic code, the whole body of the law of this state," the magnitude and difficulty of the work, and the need of the amplest indulgence towards its authors, will be admitted.

In laying down at last the great trust, with which they have been clothed, the Commissioners take this occasion, to make their most grateful acknowledgments to the People of the state, for that generous confidence and support, which could alone have sustained them.

All which is respecfully submitted.

ARPHAXED LOOMIS,
DAVID GRAHAM,
DAVID DUDLEY FIELD.

Albany, December 31, 1849.

TABLE OF CONTENTS.

PART I.

TITLE I.

CHAPTER I.

CHAPTER II.

CHAPTER III.

CHAPTER IV.

CHAPTER V.

CHAPTER VI.

CHAPTER VII.

CHAPTER VIII.

CHAPTER IX.

CHAPTER X.

ARTICLE I.

ARTICLE II.

ARTICLE III.

CHAPTER XI.

ARTICLE III.

ARTICLE IV.

CHAPTER XIII.

CHAPTER XIV.

CHAPTER XV.

CHAPTER XVI.

ARTICLE I.

ARTICLE II.

ARTICLE III.

ARTICLE IV.

ARTICLE V.

ARTICLE VI.

ARTICLE VII.

TITLE II.

CHAPTER I.

CHAPTER II.

CHAPTER III.

CHAPTER IV.

CHAPTER V.

CHAPTER VI.

CHAPTER VII.

TITLE III.

CHAPTER I.

ARTICLE I.

ARTICLE II.

ARTICLE III.

ARTICLE IV.

ARTICLE V.

ARTICLE VI.

ARTICLE VII.

ARTICLE VIII.

ARTICLE IX.

ARTICLE X.

CHAPTER II.

CHAPTER III.

CHAPTER IV.

TITLE IV.

CHAPTER I.

CHAPTER II.

CHAPTER III.

CHAPTER IV.

ARTICLE I.

ARTICLE II.

ARTICLE III.

ARTICLE IV.

ARTICLE V.

ARTICLE VI.

CHAPTER V.

ARTICLE I.

ARTICLE II.

ARTICLE III.

ARTICLE IV.

ARTICLE V.

ARTICLE VI.

ARTICLE VII.

ARTICLE VIII.

ARTICLE IX.

ARTICLE X.

ARTICLE XI.

ARTICLE XII.

CHAPTER VI.

ARTICLE I.

ARTICLE II.

CHAPTER VII.

CHAPTER VIII.

TITLE V.

CHAPTER I.

ARTICLE I.

ARTICLE II.

ARTICLE III.

ARTICLE IV.

ARTICLE V.

ARTICLE VI.

ARTICLE VII.

ARTICLE VIII.

ARTICLE IX.

CHAPTER II.

CHAPTER III.

CHAPTER IV.

CHAPTER V.

PART II.

TITLE I.

TITLE II.

CHAPTER I.

CHAPTER II.

CHAPTER III.

CHAPTER IV.

TITLE III.

TITLE IV.

TITLE V.

TITLE VI.

CHAPTER I.

CHAPTER II.

CHAPTER III.

CHAPTER IV.

CHAPTER V.

CHAPTER VI.

CHAPTER VII.

TITLE VII.

CHAPTER I.

CHAPTER II.

CHAPTER III.

CHAPTER IV.

CHAPTER V.

CHAPTER VI.

TITLE VIII.

CHAPTER I.

CHAPTER II,

CHAPTER III.

CHAPTER IV.

ARTICLE I.

ARTICLE II.

ARTICLE III.

CHAPTER V.

CHAPTER VI.

CHAPTER VII.

ARTICLE I.

ARTICLE II.

ARTICLE III.

CHAPTER VIII.

TITLE IX.

CHAPTER I.

CHAPTER II.

TITLE X.

TITLE XI.

CHAPTER I.

CHAPTER II.

CHAPTER III.

CHAPTER IV.

CHAPTER V.

CHAPTER VI

CHAPTER VII.

CHAPTER VIII.

CHAPTER IX.

CHAPTER X.

ARTICLE I.

ARTICLE II.

ARTICLE III.

ARTICLE IV.

TITLE XII.

CHAPTER I.

CHAPTER II.

CHAPTER III.

CHAPTER IV.

CHAPTER V.

TITLE XIII.

CHAPTER I.

CHAPTER II.

CHAPTER III.

CHAPTER IV.

CHAPTER V.

CHAPTER VI.

TITLE XIV.

PART III.

TITLE I.

CHAPTER I.

CHAPTER II.

CHAPTER III.

CHAPTER IV.

CHAPTER V.

CHAPTER VI.

TITLE II.

CHAPTER I.

CHAPTER II.

CHAPTER III.

CHAPTER IV.

CHAPTER V.

TITLE III.

CHAPTER I.

CHAPTER II.

CHAPTER III.

CHAPTER IV.

CHAPTER V.

CHAPTER VI.

TITLE IV.

TITLE V.

CHAPTER I.

CHAPTER II.

TITLE VI.

TITLE VII.

TITLE VIII.

TITLE IX.

CHAPTER I.

CHAPTER II.

CHAPTER III.

TITLE X.

CHAPTER I.

CHAPTER II.

CHAPTER III.

TITLE XI.

TITLE XII.

CHAPTER I.

CHAPTER II.

CHAPTER III.

CHAPTER IV.

PART IV.

TITLE I.

TITLE II.

CHAPTER I.

CHAPTER II.

CHAPTER III.

ARTICLE I.

ARTICLE II.

ARTICLE III.

CHAPTER IV.

CHAPTER V.

CHAPTER VI.

CHAPTER VII.

TITLE III.

CHAPTER I.

CHAPTER II.

CHAPTER III.

ARTICLE I.

ARTICLE II.

ARTICLE III.

ARTICLE IV.

ARTICLE V.

ARTICLE VI.

TITLE IV.

TITLE V.

TITLE VI.

CHAPTER I.

CHAPTER II.

CHAPTER III.

CHAPTER IV.

CODE OF CIVIL PROCEDURE.

THE CODE

OF

CIVIL PROCEDURE.

AN ACT

To Establish a Code of Civil Procedure.

The People of the State of New-York, represented in Senate and Assembly, do enact as follows:

PRELIMINARY PROVISIONS.

SECTION 1. This act shall be known as the Code of Civil Procedure of the State of New York.

§ 2. This Code is divided into four parts:

The first relates to the courts of justice:

The second relates to civil actions:

The third relates to special proceedings of a civil nature:

The fourth relates to evidence.

The Commissioners have unanimously agreed upon the division of the Code, as provided in this section, except as to the fourth part,—that relating to evidence.

From the introduction of that part, Mr. Graham dissents.

§ 3. The rule of the common law, that statutes in derogation thereof are to be strictly construed, has no application to this Code. The Code establishes the law of this state, respecting the subjects to which it relates; and its provisions, and all proceedings under it, are to be liberally construed, with a view to promote its objects, and to assist the parties in obtaining justice.

The rules of statutory construction present one of the widest fields of learning known to the lawyer. While it is a general principle, that the will of the legislature, as expressed in a statute, is to be carried into full effect, and that, for the purpose of ascertaining it, every source of information is to be resorted to, such as its title, its preamble, its history and attendant circumstances, and above all, the evil aimed at and the remedy intended to be applied, it is equally well settled that a more stringent rule is applicable to a certain class of statutes —namely, to those of a penal nature, and those which are, as it is termed, in derogation of the common law. Within this latter category, have been classed, statutes prescribing the practice of the courts; in respect to which it was remarked by the supreme court, in *Jackson v. Wiseburn*, 5 Wend. 137, that "the rules and practice of the court, being established by the court, may be made to yield to circumstances to promote the ends of justice. Not so, as to a statute; it is unbending, requiring implicit obedience as well from the court as from its suitors."

Without stopping to inquire how far this principle is applicable to statutory provisions, prescribing, for example, the time within which a particular act must be done, (which was the case in the instance referred to,) the Commissioners suppose that it does not apply in all its severity to a system of regulation, having in view, as its sole object, the furtherance of justice and a disregard of technical strictness. This is the great principle, running through all the provisions which the Commissioners have hitherto reported, and which marks the complete code they have now the honor to report. Regarding the code in this light, not merely from its general spirit, as deducible from all its provisions, but from express declarations to this effect throughout, they had supposed that the courts would have felt themselves bound to apply to it a liberal construction, according to its spirit and objects. While many of the judges have done so, others have taken a different view. By them the severe test above referred to has been applied, and the code has been considered an inflexible statutory rule, admitting of but little, if any, relaxation in furtherance of the great object for which it was designed.

Of the many instances of this nature, to be found in the reports of decisions upon the code, a case recently decided in New-York, illustrates these remarks. The action was on a promissory note, of which the plaintiffs were the endorsers, and the defendants the makers. The complaint alleged "that the defendants made their promissory note in writing, bearing date on a day mentioned, by which they promised to pay to S. K. Saxton or bearer, eighteen months after date, six hundred dollars; that the plaintiffs are now the lawful holders of said note, and there is now due thereon six hundred dollars and interest." This complaint was demurred to, on the ground "that it did not state facts sufficient to constitute a cause of action, in that it does not state that the note therein mentioned, had been assigned or transferred to the plaintiffs, or that they were the *owners* thereof." On a motion to set aside the demurrer as frivolous, the judge, in denying the motion, remarked: "It is the duty of the plaintiff, to show a prima facie cause of action; and to do this, he must show he is the party in interest; in such a case as this, that he is the "owner" of the note, the subject of the action. I do not think he has done this, for I am not prepared to say that the words "*lawful holder*" impart "ownership." I do not think the defendant was bound to raise the question of ownership, by answer; the plaintiff must allege an interest. I cannot say that this demurrer is frivolous, and I shall therefore deny this motion," *Beach* v. *Gallup*, 2 Code Rep. 66.

If this be a sound interpretation of the rules of pleading as prescribed by the code, the Commissioners are obliged to admit, that they have entirely failed of the object they had in view, in the section which provides, that the complaint must contain, among other things, "a statement of the facts constituting the cause of action, in ordinary and concise language, without repetition, and in such a manner as to enable a person of common understanding to know what is intended;" *Amended code, sec.* 142, *subd.* 2; and in the general rule of pleading, that, "in the construction of a pleading, for the purpose of determining its effect, its allegations shall be liberally construed, with a view to substantial justice between the parties." *Ibid. sec.* 159.

Another case, in which the application of the ancient strictness in the construction of statutes, has resulted in embarrassing the practice under the Code, is reported in reference to the provision which declares, that "the report of the referees upon the whole issue shall stand as the judgment of the court; and judgment may be entered thereon in the same manner as if the action had been tried by the court." *Amended code, sec.* 272. A reference of the whole issue, as defined in sec. 272, means where the referees are "directed to hear and decide the whole issue;" and a trial by the court is, as defined in previous provisions, a trial by a single judge, without a jury. The plain sense of the provision as to a judgment, as intended by the Commissioners, and as they supposed they had distinctly presented in terms, is that this judgment, where the whole issue is decided by the referees, is to be entered precisely as upon a trial by the court.

And yet, out of this provision, a variety of interpretation has arisen. In *Clark* v. *Andrews*, 1 Code Rep. 4, it is reported to have been decided, that judgment cannot be entered until the report has been confirmed at a special term. This case arose under the similar provision of *sec.* 5, of the supplementary act, that "the report of the referee or referees upon the whole cause, or upon the whole of any issue therein, shall stand as the decision of the court, in the same manner as if the cause or issue had been determined by the court at a special term, and may be reviewed in like manner."

In *Doke* v. *Peck*, 1 Code Rep. 54, a report had been made, finding a certain sum due to the plaintiff. On a motion to set it aside, on the ground, among others, that it was irregular in not setting out the facts proved before the referee, the judge, after remarking that "it is exceedingly difficult to ascertain from the Code, what is the practice in such a case as the present," ordered that the report be set aside, and that the referee make a new one, on the ground that the referee must set out the facts proved by the evidence, and the conclusions of law upon them.

In the case of *Renouil* v. *Harris*, 1 Code Rep. 125, however, the New-York Superior Court, followed the true meaning of the Code, in this respect; and held, in accordance with the views of the Commissioners, that a party in whose favor a referee reports, may thereupon enter up judgment, without any further notice to the adverse party, than the notice of adjusting the costs; and that it is not necessary that he should obtain the assent of the judge to enter up judgment.

Again.—Under the provision of the *code of* 1848, *sec.* 2, which defined an action to be "a regular judicial proceeding, in which a party prosecutes another party, for the enforcement or protection of a right, the redress or prevention of a wrong, or the punishment of a public offence," different constructions have been given upon the question whether an action can be commenced for the partition of lands. Independently of the fact, that an action for the partition of lands is expressly mentioned in several portions of the code, the Commissioners, after a very careful consideration of this definition, supposed that it was clearly comprehended within its terms. In accordance with this view, it was held by Mr. Justice *Harris*, in *Backus v. Stilwell*, 3 Howard's Pr. Rep., 318, to be clear that such an action was maintainable. A contrary opinion, however, founded upon a critical examination of the language of the code, was strongly expressed by Mr. Justice *Barculo*, in *Traver v. Traver*, 3 Howard's Pr. Rep., 351-357; which, it is stated, in a subsequent part of the same volume *p.* 368, was unanimously affirmed, Mr. Justice *M'Coun* delivering the opinion of affirmance.

The provisions as to amendments, also, which were designed by the Commissioners, to extend the power of the court, for this purpose, to every conceivable case, in furtherance of justice, have been the subject of different interpretations. The provision more especially referred to, is that contained in section 149, of the *code of* 1848, and is as follows:—

"The court may, at any time, in furtherance of justice, and on such terms as may be proper, amend any pleading or proceeding, by adding or striking out the name of any party, or a mistake in any other respect, or by inserting other allegations, material to the case, or by conforming the pleading or proceeding to the facts proved, whenever the amendment shall not change substantially the cause of action or defence."

In the case of *Spalding v. Spalding*, 3 Howard's Pr. Rep., 297, the facts, as set out in the complaint, constituted a caus of action, either in trespass or replevin under the old practice, and prayed for damages instead of the possession or return of the property. An amendment of the prayer, in this respect, was held inadmissible. In *Dows v. Green*, 3 Howard's Pr. Rep, 377, however, Mr. Justice *Parker* took a different view of the question; holding, that it being in furtherance of justice, the court had the power, under the section referred to, to allow an amendment of the complaint, by altering the prayer for relief contained in it, so as to claim the property itself, and damages for its detention, it being originally for the value of the property only; and that, although the amendment would change the form of the action, or rather, the class to which it belonged, it did not change the cause of action in the sense in which those terms are used in this section.

Other instances might be adduced, if it were necessary, of similar differences of construction. Enough, however, has been presented, to show that the application of the strict rule in this respect, applicable to statutes generally, cannot but be productive of great injustice, when made to a system, whose chief design and whose great merit, if it have any, is its attempt to make the attainment of justice the paramount object, and the use of forms mere auxiliaries, which, when they come in conflict with the ends of justice, are to be relaxed. A careful examination of the cases already referred to, will show, moreover, that these differences of opinion result from the adoption of different tests as to the meaning of the code. The one class proceeding upon the principle of a strict statutory construction, the other based upon a liberal and benign interpretation of the provisions to which they refer.

This section, in the opinion of the Commissioners, will obviate much of the difficulty under which the courts have labored, and will render the code, instead of a rigid and unbending statute, as construed by some, a rule of procedure susceptible of easy adaptation to the purposes of justice, which it alone has in view.

The further attainment of this object is also sought by a subsequent provision of the code, *sec.* 42, which gives an appeal to the supreme court, from an order affecting a substantial right, made in a civil action, involving the construction of the constitution or of a provision of this code. This provision is introduced after mature consideration, and from a conviction of its necessity. So far as it relates to questions affecting the construction of the code, the Commissioners beleive that it is important to the successful operation of the reforms already introduced, and which this report proposes further to introduce into the practice.

§ 4. No part of this code is retroactive, unless expressly so declared.

§ 5. Judicial remedies are such as are administered by the courts of justice, or by judicial officers empowered for that purpose, by the constitution and statutes of this state.

This definition was not contained in the code of 1848, or in the amended code. It is here introduced as a concise and convenient definition of judicial remedies.

§ 6. These remedies are divided into two classes:

1. Actions: and
2. Special proceedings.

Same as *amended code, sec.* 1.

§ 7. An action is an ordinary proceeding in a court of justice, by which one party prosecutes another, for the enforcement or protection of a right, the redress or prevention of a wrong, or the punishment of a public offence.

Same as *amended code, sec.* 2.

§ 8. Every other remedy is a special proceeding.

Same as *amended code, sec.* 3.

§ 9. Actions are of two kinds:

1. Civil: and

2. Criminal.

Same as *amended code, sec.* 4.

§ 10. A civil action arises out of,

1. An obligation:

2. An injury.

§ 11. An obligation is a legal duty, by which one person is bound to the performance of an act towards another, and arises from,

1. The contract of the parties; or

2. The operation of law, as in the case of a statute or judgment.

§ 12. An injury is of two kinds:

1. To the person: and

2. To property.

§ 13. An injury to property consists in depriving its owner of the benefit of it, which is done by taking, withholding, deteriorating, or destroying it.

§ 14. Every other injury is an injury to the person.

§ 15. A criminal action arises out of an act or omission forbidden by law, and to which is annexed, upon conviction, either of the following punishments:

1. Death:

2. Imprisonment:

3. Fine:

4. Removal from office: or

5. Disqualification to hold and enjoy any office of honor, trust or profit under this state.

§ 16. A civil action is prosecuted by one party against another, for the enforcement or protection of a right, or the redress or prevention of a wrong.

§ 17. A criminal action is prosecuted by the state, as a party, against a person charged with a public offence, for the punishment thereof.

The last two sections are more distinct than sections 5 and 6 of the amended code, for which they are substituted.

§ 18. When the violation of a right admits of both a civil and criminal remedy, the right to prosecute the one is not merged in the other.

Same as *amended code, sec.* 7. This section is taken substantially from 2 *R. S.* 3*d ed.* 390, *sec.* 2.

PART I.

PART I.

OF THE COURTS OF JUSTICE.

TITLE I.

OF THE ORGANIZATION AND JURISDICTION OF THE COURTS OF JUSTICE.

CHAPTER I.

THE COURTS OF JUSTICE, IN GENERAL.

SECTION 19. The several courts of this state.
20. They are courts of record, except that some of them are courts not of record for certain purposes.

§ 19. The following are the courts of justice of this state:

1. The court for the trial of impeachments:
2. The court of appeals:
3. The supreme court, including the circuits:
4. The superior court of the city of New-York:
5. The court of common pleas of the city of New-York:
6. The courts of oyer and terminer:
7. The county courts:
8. The surrogates' courts:
9. The courts of sessions:
10. The city courts of the cities of Albany, Brooklyn, Buffalo, Hudson, Oswego, Troy and Utica:
11. The justices' courts:
12. The marine court of the city of New-York:
13. The police courts:
14. The courts of conciliation.

§ 20. These courts are courts of record; except that the justices' and police courts are deemed inferior courts not of record, within the section of the constitution providing for the removal of justices of the peace and judges or justices of inferior courts not of record, and their clerks, by such county, city or state courts as may be prescribed by law, but for no other purpose.

This section abolishes the distinction between courts of record and courts not of record ;—a distinction which is of no practical utility, and which has introduced much confusion, in the attempt to ascertain its precise meaning.

It is thus defined by Blackstone. "A court of record is that, where the acts and judicial proceedings are enrolled in parchment, for a perpetual memorial and testimony: which rolls are called the records of the conrt, and are of such high and supereminent authority, that their truth is not to be called in question. For it is a settled rule and maxim, that nothing shall be averred against a record, nor shall any plea, or even proof, be admitted to the contrary. And if the existence of a record be denied, it shall be tried by nothing but itself; that is, upon bare inspection whether there be any such record or no; else there would be no end of disputes. But if there appear any mistake of the clerk in making up such record, the court will direct him to amend it. All courts of record are the king's courts, in right of his crown and royal dignity, and therefore no other court hath authority to fine or imprison; so that the very erection of a new jurisdiction with power of fine or imprisonment, makes it instantly a court of record. A court not of record is the court of a private man, whom the law will not intrust with any discretionary power over the fortune or liberty of his fellow subjects. Such are the courts-baron, incident to every manor, and other inferior jurisdictions, where the proceedings are not enrolled or recorded; but, as well their existence as the truth of the matters therein contained shall, if disputed, be tried and determined by a jury. These courts can hold no plea of matters cognizable by the common law, unless under the value of 40 *s.;* nor of any forcible injury whatsoever, not having any process to arrest the person of the defendant. 3 *Bl. Com.*, 24, 25.

In view of this definition of the distinction between courts of record and courts not of record, which was recognised by the supreme court, as late as 1840, in *Wheaton v. Fellows*, 23 Wend. 377, the statutes of this state have at various times declared certain inferior courts, such as the marine court of the city of New-York, the late municipal court of the city of Brooklyn, and some of the justices' courts in cities, in express terms to be courts of record. And yet, notwithstanding this declaration, the courts have held that, while for certain purposes they are deemed courts of record, they are not such, as between party and party. For example, it was held in *The People v. The Marine Court of the city of New-York*, 12 Wend. 220, that the marine court had not the power, incident to a court of record, to set aside a judgment and grant a new trial. Though in the subsequent case of *Watson v. Smith*, 13 Wend. 51, it was held, that, being a court of record, it has power to issue a commission to examine witnesses residing abroad. More recently it has been held, both by the court of errors and by the superior court of the city of New-York, that it is not a court of record for the purpose of appointing a crier, a power incident to courts of record, as that term is understood at common law; and in *Wheaton v. Fellows*, 23 Wend. 377, already referred to, it was held, that the justices' court of the city of Albany, which is declared in terms, by the statute creating it, to be a court of record, though a court of record for some purposes, is not such in the exercise of its jurisdiction between party and party.

The practical result of these decisions is, that the attributes of courts of record are entirely wanting in these courts, in the powers and forms of proceeding with which they are invested, and that they exercise this jurisdiction only in reference to the right of naturalization, which is conferred by Congress upon every state court of record having a clerk and seal.

From the brief review thus given, it will be readily perceived that the distinction is one in name only. If we recur to the definition given by Blackstone, there is no court in this state, which is not in reality a court of record. For there is none, of which it may not be said, that its records cannot be called in question. Nothing is better settled, than that the record of every court in this state imports absolute verity, and is conclusive upon the parties as to the matter which it contains. To preserve the distinction, therefore, prolific as it is, of difficulties and embarrassments, is not only unnecessary, but useless. Its only practical importance, as has been already remarked, grows out of the investment of courts of record with the power of naturalization; but the difficulty in this respect is readily obviated, by withholding, as is done in a subsequent portion of the code, from inferior courts, to which this power should not be intrusted, the attributes of a clerk and seal, both of which must be added to their functions as courts of record, to enable them to exercise this power.

While this general distinction is abolished, however, the section under consideration provides that justices' and police courts are deemed inferior courts not of record, within the section of the constitution providing for the removal of justices of the peace, and judges or justices of inferior courts not of record, and their clerks, by such county, city or state courts as may be prescribed by law, but for no other purpose.

CHAPTER II.

THE COURT FOR THE TRIAL OF IMPEACHMENTS.

§ 21. The court for the trial of impeachments has power to try impeachments, when presented by the assembly, of all civil officers of the state, except justices of the peace, justices of justices' courts, police justices, and their clerks, for wilful and corrupt misconduct in office.

§ 22. The court is composed of the president of the senate, the senators, or a majority of them, and the judges of the court of appeals, or a majority of them. But on the trial of an impeachment against the governor, the lieutenant-governor cannot act as a member of the court.

§ 23. The president of the senate, or in case of his impeachment, death or absence, the chief judge of the court of appeals, or in the absence of both, such other member as the court may elect, is the presiding judge of the court.

§ 24. The clerk and officers of the senate, are the clerk and officers of the court for the trial of impeachments

§ 25. There are no stated terms of this court; but upon the delivery of an impeachment from the assembly, the president of the senate must cause the court to be summoned to meet at the capitol in the city of Albany, on a day not less that thirty nor more than sixty days from the day of the delivery of the articles of impeachment.

§ 26. At the time and place appointed, and before the court proceeds to act on the impeachment, the clerk must administer to the presiding judge, and the presiding judge to each of the members of the court then present, an oath or affirmation truly and impartially to hear, try and determine the impeachment; and no member of the court can act or vote upon the impeachment or any question arising thereon, without having taken such oath or affirmation.

The preceding sections of this chapter, are the same as are contained in the Code of Criminal Procedure, *sec.* 17—22. They are explained in the notes to that code, *p.* 12—14.

§ 27. When the court is held during the recesso f the legislature, the president of the senate, the senators, and the clerk and officers of the court are entitled to the same compensation for their attendance thereon, and for travelling to and from the place where it is held, as is allowed them at a meeting of the senate.

Substantially the same as 2 *R. S*, 3*d ed.* 224, *sec.* 13.

CHAPTER III.

THE COURT OF APPEALS.

§ 28. The court of appeals has exclusive jurisdiction to review, upon appeal, every actual determination hereafter made, at a general term, by the supreme court, by the superior court or court of common pleas of the city of New-York, in the following cases, and no other:

1. In a judgment in an action commenced therein, or brought there from another court; and upon the appeal from that judgment, to review any intermediate order involving the merits, and necessarily affecting the judgment:

2. In an crder affecting a substantial right, made in such action, when such order in effect determines the

action, and prevents a judgment, from which an appeal might be taken:

3. In a final order, affecting a substantial right, made in a special proceeding, or upon a summary application in an action, after judgment:

But the appeal given by this section is not allowed in an action originally commenced in a justice's court, or in the marine court of the city of New-York.

This section, with the exception of the second subdivision, is the same as presented by the Commissioners in their first report, and retained by the legislature in the amended code, *sec.* 11. The second subdivision, which provides for an appeal from an order, in certain cases, appears proper.

§ 29. In addition to the jurisdiction conferred by the last section, this court has jurisdiction of all cases pending in the late court for the correction of errors, on the first Monday of July, 1847, and on that day transferred to this court by the constitution, and now remaining undetermined.

Taken from the judiciary act, *Laws of* 1847, *p.* 322, *sec.* 12.

§ 30. This court may reverse, affirm, or modify the judgment or order appealed from; and its judgment must be remitted to the court below, to be enforced according to law.

Same as the *code of* 1848, *sec.* 12. This section was altered in the *amended code, sec.* 12, by authorising the court to reverse, affirm, or modify the order, "in whole or in part, and as to any or all of the parties." This alteration is wholly unnecessary, being included in the power to *modify* the judgment or order.

§ 31. This court is composed of eight judges, of whom four are elected by the electors of the state for eight years, and four selected from the class of judges of the supreme court having the shortest time to serve, as prescribed by special statutes.

Conformable to the Constitution, *art.* 6, *sec.* 2.

§ 32. The judge elected by the electors of the state, and having the shortest time to serve, is for the time being the chief judge.

The constitution, *art.* 6, *sec.* 2, prescribes that provision shall be made by law, for designating one of the number of the judges of the court of appeals elected by the electors of the state, as chief judge. This section does so, in conformity with the judiciary act. *Laws of* 1847, *p.* 320, *sec.* 5.

§ 33. The presence of six judges is necessary for the transaction of business; but any one or more of the judges may adjourn the court from day to day or for the term, with the same effect as if all were present.

The constitution, *art.* 6, *sec.* 2, provides, that this court shall be "composed of eight judges," omitting to declare that a less number is competent for the transaction of business. The judiciary act, however, provided that "six judges of the court of appeals shall be necessary to constitute a quorum for holding any term of said court." *Laws of* 1847, *p.* 321, *sec.* 6.

The constitutionality of this provision having been virtually affirmed by the action of the court under it, it is retained in this section.

§ 34. The concurrence of five judges is necessary, to pronounce a judgment. If five do not concur, the case must be reheard.

This section is the same as section 14, of the *code of* 1848. It was altered in the *amended code, sec.* 14, so as to read as follows: "The concurrence of five judges shall be necessary to pronounce a judgment. If five do not concur, the judgment or order appealed from shall be affirmed, unless the court order a rehearing."

The reason for this alteration does not appear in the repor of the committee by which it was made, nor was it, that the Commissioners are aware, the subject of discussion in the legislature. It departs from a principle which was maturely considered by the Commissioners, and which the legislature itself, by which the alteration was made, retained in section 19, of the *amended code*, in respect to the supreme court. The reasons, as stated by the Commissioners in their first report, *p.* 24, 25, and which subsequent reflection has convinced them are unanswerable, they deem it proper here to repeat.

By the present practice, upon an equal division of the court the judgment below is affirmed. But it is well settled, that such an affirmance merely determines the particular case, and leaves the questions involved in it, open for consideration in any future case in which they may arise. *Bridge v. Johnson*, 5 Wend. 342; *The People v. The Mayor and Aldermen of the city of New-York*, 25 Wend. 252. Besides, as was decided by the court of errors, in the case last cited, and by the supreme court of the United States, in *Martin v. Hunter's Lessee*, 1 Wheat. 355, a rehearing in such case, cannot, in the absence of statutory authority, be allowed.

Whatever may be the policy of such a rule, in courts whose judgments may be reviewed, the principle that a judgment of a court of last resort, rendered by a tie vote, should determine the rights of parties, while, it is conceded, it does not settle the principles on which those rights depend; nay, while at the very next term, those principles may be differently settled,—strikes us as incompatible with a sound administration of justice. The rule is itself, a technical one, merely. It is, in effect, but saying, that, because on the first hearing, a party fails to obtain a reversal, his rights are to be forever concluded; and its application is universal, whether property, liberty or life be affected by the judgment. No one, it seems to us, can hesitate to admit, that it is wiser to say, in such a case, that the cause should be reheard; so that with the determination of the individual case, the principle which is to govern in future, should be established.

It has been suggested as an objection to this provision, that the concurrence of five judges should not be required, while six may hold the court. This objection is rather theoretical than practical, inasmuch as, with very few exceptions, all the judges have hitherto been present at its sessions. But even were it otherwise, the Commissioners, in view of the doubt as to the right of less than the whole number of judges to hold the court, or, if no such doubt existed, of the propriety of requiring that the decision of the court of last resort which not merely determines the particular controversy, but settles the law of the state as a precedent in similar cases, should be given by a majority of the whole court, deem this provision eminently just and expedient.

§ 35. There are six terms in each year, for the hearing of appeals; to commence on the first Tuesday of January, March, May, July, September and November, and to continue until the fourth Saturday thereafter, inclusive, unless all the causes ready for hearing be sooner heard. They may, however, be continued as much longer as in the opinion of the court the public interests require. Additional terms may also be held, by order of the court.

This section is substantially the same as in the *code of* 1848, *sec.* 13. It was, however, amended in the *amended code, sec.*

13, by providing that "there shall be at least five terms of the court of appeals in each year, to be held at such time, and place as the court shall appoint, and continued for as long a period as the public interests may require."

The reason of this change is not very apparent. The original provision was reported by the Commissioners, not because they supposed the judges of the court of appeals would hold fewer sessions, or for a less period than the public interests required, but because, in view of the pressure of business in that court, they deemed at least six terms in each year necessary, and that they should be held for the time prescribed. The result has proved that they were right in this supposition. They deemed it proper also, to fix the times at which the sessions of the court should be held, to obviate the embarrassment which was formerly occasioned, and which has continued ever since the change, from the court at each session fixing the time when the next session shall be held. For these reasons, therefore, they recommend that this section be re-adopted.

§ 36. The places of holding the terms must be appointed by the court, by an order entered upon the minutes, which may be made annually, before the first day of December. When made, it shall remain in force during the succeeding year, and until changed by another appointment.

The remark made in the note to the last section, as to the embarrassment resulting from the court, at each session, appointing the *time* when the next session shall be held, is equally applicable to the *place*. The Commissioners do not propose to regulate this by positive provision, but to leave it to the court to make an annual appointment in this respect.

§ 37. The court may, however, be held in any other building than a court-house, and at a different place in the same city or town from that appointed; and may be adjourned from the city or town where it is appointed to be held, to any other city or town.

Taken from *amended code, sec.* 16, and from a special act to the same effect, *Laws of* 1849, *p.* 484, *ch.* 333, *sec.* 2, 3.

§ 38. The clerk must cause a copy of the order mentioned in section 36, to be published in the state paper at least once in each week, for three weeks before the holding of a term, in pursuance thereof. The expense of the publication is payable out of the treasury of the state.

CHAPTER IV.

THE SUPREME COURT, INCLUDING THE CIRCUITS.

§ 39. All rules of the common law and all statutes now in force, conferring or defining the jurisdiction of the supreme court, are abrogated and repealed, and it has no other jurisdiction than that prescribed in the next five sections. But the repeal contained in this section does not affect its jurisdiction of actions or proceedings now pending, or heretofore had therein, nor does it any judgment or order already made, or proceeding already taken.

§ 40. The jurisdiction of this court is of two kinds:

1. Original: and

2. Appellate.

§ 41. Its original jurisdiction extends to all civil actions and special proceedings, of which exclusive jurisdiction is not conferred upon another court or officer, by the constitution or by this code.

§ 42. Its appellate jurisdiction extends to reviewing, upon appeal, every actual determination, in the following cases:

1. In a final judgment at a general term of a county or city court, in a civil action commenced therein, or brought there from another court; and upon the appeal from that judgment, to review any intermediate order involving the merits and necessarily affecting the judgment:

2. In an intermediate order affecting a substantial right made in such action, involving the construction of the constitution or of a provision of this code:

3. In a final order, affecting a substantial right, made by a county or city court, in a special proceeding or

upon a summary application in an action, after judgment:

4. In a judgment of a court of oyer and terminer, a court of sessions, or a city court, in a criminal action:

5. In a final order made by either of the courts mentioned in the last subdivision, affecting a substantial right, made in a special proceeding of a criminal nature:

6. In an order or judgment of a surrogate's court, in the cases prescribed by statute:

7. In a final order or decision of a judicial officer, or of an officer or body invested with powers of a judicial nature, in the cases prescribed in this code.

The last four sections are designed to repeal the statutory provisions, now in force, professing to define the jurisdiction of the supreme court, and to substitute in their place an approach, at least, to an intelligible definition on this subject. All that we know respecting the jurisdiction of the supreme court, is contained in a single section of the constitution, and in two sections of the judiciary act. The constitution provides, that "there shall be a supreme court, having general jurisdiction in law and equity." *Const. Art.* 6, *sec.* 3. The judiciary act declares, that "the supreme court organized by this act, shall possess the same powers and exercise the same jurisdiction, as is now possessed and exercised by the present supreme court and court of chancery;" and that "all laws relating to the present supreme court and court of chancery, or any court held by any vice-chancellor, and the jurisdiction, powers and duties of said courts, the proceedings therein and the officers thereof, their powers and duties, shall be applicable to the supreme court organized by this act, the powers and duties thereof, the proceedings therein, and the officers thereof, their powers and duties, so far as the same can be so applied, and are consistent with the constitution, and the provisions of this act." *Laws of* 1847, *p.* 323, *sec.* 16. By reference to the Revised Statutes, it will be seen, that, "the supreme court shall possess the powers and exercise the jurisdiction which belonged to the supreme court of the colony of New-York, with the exceptions, limitations and additions created and imposed by the constitution and laws of this state"; 2 *R. S.*, 3*d ed.*, 259, *sec.* 1; and that "the powers and jurisdiction of the court of chancery are co-extensive with the powers and jurisdiction of the court of chancery in England, with the exceptions, additions and limitations created and imposed by the constitution and laws of this state." 2 *R. S.*, 3*d ed.*, 234, *sec.* 60.

To ascertain what the precise jurisdiction is, it is necessary to recur to the jurisdiction of the courts of Queens' Bench, Common Pleas and Exchequer, in England, on the common law side, and to that of the court of chancery in that country, on the equity side, and to collate with them the various modifications which the constitution and statutes of this state have introduced. The difficulty of this task can only be appreciated by those who have undertaken it; but the necessity of something like a definition respecting it, must be apparent to every one. That which is given in the sections under consideration, is believed by the Commissioners to be both convenient and accurate.

§ 43. In addition to the jurisdiction conferred by the last two sections, this court has the jurisdiction heretofore transferred to it,

1. Of all suits and proceedings now undetermined, and which were pending on the first Monday of July, 1847, in the late supreme court and court of chancery, and in the late courts of common pleas, except in suits originally commenced in justices' courts;

2. To enforce the orders, judgments and decrees of those courts, rendered before that day, or to exercise

such other powers in respect thereto, as it might exercise, if they had been made or rendered by this court.

Conformable to the constitution, *art.* 14, *sec.* 5.

§ 44. This court has also jurisdiction of all civil actions now undetermined, and which were pending in the late mayor's court of the city of Rochester on the thirtieth day of April, 1849, and of all proceedings incident to judgments rendered in that court, in those actions, on or before that day.

Conformable to *Laws of* 1849, *p.* 435, *ch.* 303, *sec.* 5.

§ 45. The state is divided into eight judicial districts, of which the city of New-York is the first, the others being created by special statutes; in each of which there are four judges of this court, and as many more in the first district as may be from time to time authorised by law, but not to exceed in the whole, such number in proportion to its population, as shall be in conformity with the number of such judges in the residue of the state, in proportion to its population.

Conformable to the constitution, *art.* 6, *sec.* 4, and to *Laws of* 1847, *p.* 268, *ch.* 241.

§ 46. This court is distributed into general and special terms and circuit courts; the latter of which are in this code denominated circuits.

The distribution prescribed in this section, is in conformity with the existing practice. It is proposed to designate the circuit courts by the name of circuits, as being not only more convenient, but more in consonance with their powers, which are those of a trial term of the supreme court.

§ 47. The general terms are devoted to the hearing and determination,

1. Of cases now pending in this court for review, in actions or special proceedings commenced therein or brought there from another court, or transferred from the late supreme court or court of chancery, as provided in section 43:

2. Of cases hereafter brought into this court for review, and of appeals from a single judge of this court, as provided in this code:

3. Of controversies submitted without action, as provided in this code:

4. Of questions incidental to the hearing and determination of the cases mentioned in this section:

5. Of such other questions as are prescribed by other provisions of this code.

§ 48. The special terms are devoted,

1. To the hearing and determination of applications, upon failure to answer, and upon complaint and answer:

2. To the hearing and determination of all actions or proceedings now pending in this court, except npon an issue of fact or for review:

3. To the trial of issues of law now pending, or hereafter joined, in actions or proceedings in this court:

4. To the hearing and determination of motions in those actions or proceedings:

5. To the hearing and determination of applications for judgment, upon special verdicts:

6. To the hearing and determination of cases reserved for argument or further consideration:

7. To the hearing and determination of all other questions, not assigned to the general terms or circuits, exclusively.

§ 49. The circuits are devoted to the trial,

1. Of issues of fact, now pending or hereafter joined, in actions or proceedings in this court:

2. Of all other questions of fact, ordered by the court to be tried by a jury.

§ 50. A general term must be held by at least three of the judges: and a special term or circuit may be held by one or more of them.

This section is in conformity with the constitution, *art.* 6, *sec.* 6.

It will be observed, that in mentioning the members of the supreme court, they are designated as judges, instead of justices, the more common designation in the statutes. We do this, because a uniform mode of designating judicial officers, is convenient. The constitution uses both judge and justice, as applicable to a member of the supreme court. "The state shall be divided into eight judicial districts, of which the city of New-York, shall be one; the others to be bounded by county lines, and to be compact, and equal in population, as nearly as may be. There shall be four *justices* of the supreme court in each district, and as many more in the district composed of the city of New-York, as may from time to time be authorized by law, but not to exceed in the whole, such number in proportion to its population, as shall be in conformity with the number of such *judges*, in the residue of the state, in proportion to its population."

§ 51. The general and special terms and circuits may be held by the judges elected in any of the judicial districts.

The judges of this court, though elected in districts, possess co-ordinate powers throughout the state. *Const. art.* 6, *sec.* 6.

§ 52. One of the judges of the first class elected in each district, unless he be a judge of the court of appeals, or elected or appointed to fill a vacancy, or in either of those events, one of the judges of the second class, must preside at a general term.

By the constitution, *art.* 6, *sec.* 6, "provision may be made by law, for designating from time to time, one or more of the justices of the supreme court, who is not a judge of the court of appeals, to preside at the general terms of the said court, to be held in the several districts. Any three or more of the said justices, of whom one of the said justices so designated, shall always be one, may hold such general terms." In pursuance of this requirement, the provision contained in this section, was introduced into the judiciary act, *Laws of* 1847, *p.* 323, *sec.* 15.

§ 53. If a presiding judge do not attend, any three of the judges present may, by an order entered upon the minutes, designate one of their number, to preside during the absence of a presiding judge.

Conformable to *Laws of* 1847, *p.* 282, *ch.* 170, *sec.* 1.

§ 54. The concurrence of a majority of the judges holding a general term, is necessary to pronounce a judgment. If a majority do not concur, the case must be reheard.

Taken from *Amended Code, sec.* 19.

It will be seen in the provisions respecting appeals, that the business of the general terms is to review the judgments given at the special terms and circuits, and the reports of referees. The general terms, therefore, are in the nature of courts of appeal. It may, and not unfrequently will happen, that the judge who rendered the judgment at the special term or circuit, will sit at the general term; and if he do, he will, of course, have a voice in the decision of the cause. If four judges hold the general term, a tie vote will decide the cause, of which the vote of the judge whose judgment is reviewed, may be one. This should not be allowed. The inconvenience of a rehearing is far less than the injustice of a judgment depending upon the mere technical rule, that if the party holding the affirmative fail in obtaining a majority, his case is determined, while his rights remain undecided. This the Commissioners think objectionable, for the reasons stated in the note to section 34, (p. 23, 24,) in respect to the judgment of the court of appeals.

§ 55. The general terms and circuits must be held as loug as, in the opinion of the judge or judges holding them, the public interests require.

§ 56. The judge holding a circuit must at the same time hold a special term, and continue it until the adjournment of the circuit, or longer, if the public interests require; or he may adjourn it to another time and place in the county.

It was provided in the *code of* 1848, *sec.* 19, that "special terms, circuit courts, and courts of oyer and terminer, shall be held at the same places, and commenced on the same day." In the *amended code, sec.* 21, special terms were stricken out. The Commissioners can conceive no good reason why they should not be held at the time of holding a circuit. In the parts of the state where circuits and special terms are of rare occurrence, it is very convenient to suitors, and adds but little to the labor of the judges, to have a special term when a circuit is held.

§ 57. In addition to these special terms, the court is always open, before each of the judges, for the hearing of motions, applications for judgment upon failure to answer, and upon complaint and answer, and for the trial of issues of law. But a judge who appoints for that purpose a certain day in each week when not sitting at a general term or circuit, is not required to hear a contested motion or trial at any other time.

This section is introduced, to afford greater facilities for the hearing and determination of matters which may be disposed of by a single judge. The distinction between the powers of a judge at special term and at chambers, is rather nominal than real, and the interests of suitors will be greatly promoted by the provision in question.

§ 58. The judges must also at all reasonable times, when not engaged in holding court, transact such other business as may be done out of court. One of the judges elected in the first judicial district, to be designated from time to time, among themselves, must attend for that purpose at the city hall in the city of New-York, on every judicial day, from ten o'clock in the forenoon until three o'clock in the afternoon, and longer, if the business require it; and every proceeding commenced before one of those judges, may be continued before another, with the same effect as if commenced before him.

Taken from *original code, sec.* 30, and omitted in the *amended code.* There appears to us a necessity for its restoration.

§ 59. The times and places of holding the general and special terms and circuits, shall continue as at present prescribed, until the thirty-first day of December, 1850, inclusive, and no longer.

§ 60. There must be as many general terms annually, not less than four in each judicial district, and as many special terms and circuits annually, in each county, as are sufficient for the transaction of the business.

In their first report, *p.* 29, 30, *sec.* 16, 18, the Commissioners provided for six general terms in each district, and for a fixed number of special terms and circuits in each county. Their suggestions in this respect, were adopted by the legislature, in the code of 1848, but were omitted in the amended code, probably for the reason that no fixed rule could be adopted on the subject. There can be no just objection, however, to fixing the criterion proposed by this section, for the guidance of the judges in making the appointments.

§ 61. There must be a general session of the judges of the supreme court at the capitol in the city of Albany, on the first Monday of August, 1851, and on the first Monday of August in every second year thereafter, at which session the judges shall make such general rules as may be necessary, pursuant to section 186, and shall also appoint the times and places of holding the general and special terms and circuits for the succeeding two years, commencing on the first of January thereafter, and designating the judges to hold the same. The appointment so made, must be such, that for each general term there shall be designated at least one judge, not elected in the district where the court is held.

§ 62. The governor, whenever in his opinion the public interests require, may appoint extraordinary general and special terms and circuits, and designate the judges by whom they are to be held, who shall hold them accordingly.

The same as *amended code, sec.* 24, except that it authorises the governor to designate the judges by whom the courts are to be held, and makes it the duty of the judges thus designated, to hold them accordingly. This is necessary, in order to prevent a failure in holding the court.

§ 63. The place appointed in each of the counties, for holding the general and special terms and circuits, must be the court house therein.

Taken from *amended code, sec.* 25.

§ 64. In case of the inability, for any cause, of a judge assigned for that purpose, to hold a special term or circuit, or sit at a general term, any other judge may do so; and the governor may, if necessary, assign the judge for that purpose, who must do so accordingly.

The same as *amended code, sec.* 28, except as to the power conferred upon the governor, of assigning the judge to hold the court. This is necessary, for the reason stated in the note to *sec.* 62.

§ 65. Every appointment made as provided in sections 61 and 62, must be immediately transmitted to the secretary of state, who must cause it to be published in the state paper, at least once in each week, for three weeks, before the holding of a court in pursuance thereof. The expense of the publication is payable out of the treasury of the state.

The same as *Amended Code*, *sec.* 26.

CHAPTER V.

THE SUPERIOR COURT OF THE CITY OF NEW-YORK.

§ 66. The court known as the superior court of the city of New-York, is continued, with the jurisdiction conferred by the next five sections, and no other. But nothing contained in this section affects its jurisdiction of actions or proceedings, now pending therein, nor does it affect any judgment or order already made, nor any proceeding already taken.

§ 67. This court has jurisdiction of the following actions and proceedings, when the cause thereof arises or the subject thereof is situated in the city of New-York:

1. For the recovery of real property, or of an estate or interest therein, or for the determination in any form, of such right or interest, and for injuries to real property:

2. For the partition of real property:

3. For the foreclosure of a mortgage of real property:

4. For the recovery of personal property, distrained for any cause:

5. For the recovery of a penalty or forfeiture imposed by statute:

6. Against a public officer or person specially appointed to execute his duties, for an act done by him in virtue of his office, or against a person who by his command or in his aid, does anything touching the duties of the office:

7. For the admeasurement of dower in real property:

8. For the sale of the real property of an infant:

9. To compel a specific performance, by an infant heir or other person, of a contract respecting real property, made by a person who has died before the performance thereof:

10. For the mortgage or sale, on the application of a religious corporation, of its real property, and the appropriation of the proceeds thereof.

The first six subdivisions embrace the jurisdiction conferred upon this court, by the *Amended Code*, sec. 33, subd. 1, comprehending what were formerly known as local actions.

The remaining subdivisions confer the same jurisdiction in respect to special actions and proceedings, as is vested in the county courts by the *Amended Code sec.* 30, *subd.* 4, 5, 6, 8, and retained in the corresponding section of this code, *sec.* 110.

§ 68. This court has jurisdiction, also, in all other civil actions, whether the cause of action arise, or the subject of the action be situated in the city of New-York, or not,

1. In an action arising on contract, when one or more of several defendants reside in that city, or occupy a tenement therein for the transaction of their ordinary business:

2. In an action for any other cause, when all the defendants reside in that city, or occupy a tenement therein for the transaction of their ordinary business, or are personally served with the summons in that city:

3. In an action arising on contract, when one or more of several defendants jointly liable thereon reside in, or are personally served with the summons, or occupy a tenement for the transaction of their ordinary business in that city:

4. In an action arising on contract, when all the defendants reside out of the state, but one or more of them has property in that city:

5. When the defendant is a corporation created under the laws of this state, and transacts its general business, or keeps an office, or has an agency established for the transaction of business in the city of New-York, or is established by law therein: or

6. When the defendant is a corporation, created by or under the laws of another state, government or country, and has property in the city of New-York, or an agency established therein, and the action is for the recovery of money upon a cause of action arising in that city.

The jurisdiction conferred by the first two subdivisions of this section, differs from that contained in the *Amended Code, sec.* 33, *subd.* 2, by which it is extended only to cases "where all the defendants shall reside or be personally served with the summons" in the city of New-York. There can be no injustice in giving the jurisdiction to this court, proposed in the subdivisions under consideration. It is in fact but restoring a jurisdiction which it always had, until the adoption of the Code of 1848. Where persons transact their ordinary business in a particular place, there seems to be no very sufficient reason for exempting them from the jurisdiction of its local courts, because they happen to reside a short distance beyond its limits. In the city of New-York, the existing rule has been found very inconvenient, in compelling the commencement of actions in the supreme court, which can as well be disposed of by the local courts, and without the slightest possible prejudice to the rights of either party.

The fifth and sixth subdivisions are the same as *Amended Code, sec.* 33, *subd.* 3, except that in addition to the cases there mentioned, it allows the action to be brought in the superior court, when the corporation has an agency established in that city, as well as when the corporation is established or has an office therein.

§ 69. The jurisdiction of this court also extends to such civil suits in the supreme court, commenced before the first day of July, 1848, and at issue on or before the first day of July, 1849, as are now transferred to this court pursuant to statute, and to such other civil suits in the supreme court, as may be transferred thereto, as provided in the next section.

Amended Code, sec. 47.

§ 70. Any such suit, (except those brought to the supreme court, for the review of a judgment of the superior court or court of common pleas of the city of New-York,) which may be upon the calendar of the supreme court, at a general or special term in the city of New-York, may, by the order of the court upon whose calendar it is, be transferred to the superior court of the city of New-York, at any time before the first day of January, 1851.

Amended Code, sec. 47.

§ 71. On filing with the clerk of this court a certified copy of the order made pursuant to the last section, this court becomes, vested with as full jurisdiction of the action or proceeding transferred, and may exercise the same powers in relation to any proceeding therein, as the supreme court might have exercised, if the suit transferred had remained in that court.

§ 72. There are six judges of this court, elected by the electors of the city and county of New-York, who are respectively known as the chief justice and associate judges of the superior court of the city of New-York.

Amended Code, sec. 40,

§ 73. The present chief justice shall continue to act as such, until his office shall expire or become vacant. In either of these events, the judges then in office shall, by an order entered upon the minutes, designate one of their number as chief justice, who shall act as such until his office shall expire or become vacant; and so on, from time to time, as often as the office of the judge designated as chief justice shall expire or become vacant.

Laws of 1847, *p.* 281, *sec.* 6.

§ 74. This court is distributed into general, special and trial terms.

§ 75. The general terms are devoted to the hearing and determination,

1. Of appeals now pending or hereafter brought in actions in this court, as provided in this code:

2. Of cases brought to the supreme court for review, and transferred from a general term thereof, as provided in sections 69 and 70:

3. Of cases now pending, for the review of judgments of the marine court of the city of New-York, or of the justices' courts in that city:

4. Of controversies submitted without action, as provided in this code:

5. Of questions incidental to the hearing and determination of the cases mentioned in this section:

6. Of issues of law, and motions for new trials, in suits pending in this court, on the first day of July, 1848.

7. Of such other questions as are prescribed by the provisions of this code.

§ 76. The special terms are devoted,

1. To the hearing and determination of applications for judgment upon failure to answer; and upon complaint and answer:

2. To the hearing and determination of cases transferred by the supreme court at a general term, as provided in sections 69 and 70, except those pending upon an issue of fact or for review:

3. To the hearing and determination of cases transferred by the supreme court at a special term, as provided in sections 69 and 70:

4. To the trial of issues of law, now pending or hereafter joined, in actions commenced in this court:

5. To the hearing and determination of applications for judgment upon special verdicts:

6. To the hearing and determination of cases reserved for argument or further consideration:

7. To the hearing and determination of motions, in actions or proceedings in this court:

8. To the hearing and determination of all other questions not assigned to the general or trial terms, exclusively.

§ 77. The trial terms are devoted to the trial,

1. Of issues of fact now pending or hereafter joined in actions in this court:

2. Of questions of fact in those actions, or in any other proceeding, which are ordered by this court to be tried by a jury.

§ 78. The general terms must be held by at least two, and the special and trial terms by one only, of the judges

§ 79. The chief justice, if he be present, must preside at a general term. If he be not present, the judges holding the term may designate one of their number to preside, and he shall preside accordingly during the absence of the chief justice.

§ 80. The concurrence of a majority of the judges holding a general term is necessary to pronounce a judgment. If a majority do not concur, the case must be reheard.

§ 81. As many general, special and trial terms as the court may appoint, may be held in each year, concurrently or otherwise. They must be held as long as the public interests require.

§ 82. The general, special and trial terms must be held at the city-hall in the city of New-York.

§ 83. The times of holding the general, special and trial terms, shall continue as at present prescribed, until the thirty-first day of December, 1850, inclusive, and no longer.

§ 84. At least thirty days before the first day of January, 1851, the court shall appoint the time of holding the general, special and trial terms for the succeeding year, and until changed by another appointment. A similar appointment may be made annually.

CHAPTER VI.

THE COURT OF COMMON PLEAS OF THE CITY OF NEW-YORK.

§ 85. The court known as the court of common pleas for the city and county of New-York, is continued, with the jurisdiction conferred by the next three sections, and no other; and is denominated the court of common pleas of the city of New-York. But nothing contained in this section affects its jurisdiction of actions or proceedings now pending therein, nor does it affect any judgment or order already made, or proceeding already taken.

§ 86. This court has jurisdiction, concurrently with the superior court of the city of New-York, of the actions and proceedings mentioned in sections 67 and 68.

§ 87. This court has jurisdiction also, of the following proceedings:

1. To remit fines and forfeited recognizances, in the cases and manner provided in this code; and to continue and discharge the docket of judgments entered upon recognizances:

2. To exercise the powers conferred upon it by statutes, in respect to liens filed in the office of the county clerk, and to control, amend or discharge the same:

3. Of all other special proceedings, in the city and county of New-York, of which the county courts have jurisdiction in their counties:

4. To exercise the powers conferred upon it, by other provisions of this code.

This section embraces subjects which have always been a part of the jurisdiction of this court, as the county court in New-York.

§ 88. This court has also the exclusive power to review, in the first instance, a judgment rendered by the marine court of the city of New-York, or by a justice's court in that city.

§ 89. The three judges of this court, elected as such, by the electors of the city and county of New-York, and now in office, and their successors, are the only judges of this court. They shall be known as the chief justice and associate judges of the court of common pleas of the city of New-York.

§ 90. The present first judge shall be the chief justice, until his office shall expire or become vacant. In either of these events, the judges then in office shall, by an order entered upon the minutes, designate one of their number as chief justice, who shall act as such until his office shall expire or become vacant; and so on, from time to time, as often as the office of the judge designated as chief justice shall expire or become vacant.

§ 91. This court is distributed into general, special and trial terms.

§ 92. The general terms are devoted to the hearing and determination,

1. Of appeals now pending or hereafter brought in actions in this court, as provided in this code:

2. Of appeals now pending therein or hereafter brought for the review of judgments of the marine court of the city of New-York, or of the justices' courts in that city:

3. Of controversies submitted without action, as provided in this code.

4. Of questions incidental to the hearing and determination of the cases mentioned in this section:

5. Of issues of law and motions for new trials in suits pending in this court, on the first day of July, 1848:

§ 93. The special terms are devoted,

1. To the hearing and determination of applications for judgment upon failure to answer, and upon complaint and answer:

2. To the trial of issues of law, now pending or hereafter joined, in actions or proceedings commenced in this court:

3. To the hearing and determination of motions in those actions or proceedings:

4. To the hearing and determination of applications for judgment upon special verdicts:

5. To the hearing and determination of cases reserved for argument or further consideration.

6. To all other questions not assigned to the general or trial terms exclusively.

§ 94. The trial terms are devoted to the trial,

1. Of issues of fact now pending or hereafter joined, in actions in this court:

2. Of questions of fact in those actions, or in any other proceeding, ordered by this court to be tried by a jury.

§ 95. The general terms must be held by at least two, and the special and trial terms by one only, of the judges.

§ 96. The chief justice, if he be present, must preside at a general term. If he be not present, the judges holding the term may designate one of their number to preside, and he shall preside accordingly, during the absence of the chief justice.

§ 97. The concurrence of a majority of the judges holding a general term is necessary to pronounce a judgment. If a majority do not concur, the case must be reheard.

§ 98. As many general, special and trial terms as the court may appoint, may be held in each year, concurrently, or otherwise. They must be held as long as the public interests require.

§ 99. The general, special and trial terms must be held at the city hall in the city of New-York.

§ 100. The times of holding the general, special and trial terms, shall continue as at present prescribed, until the thirty-first day of December, 1850, inclusive, and no longer.

§ 101. At least thirty days before the first day of January, 1851, the court must appoint the time of holding the general, special and trial terms, for the succeeding year, and until changed by another appointment. A similar appointment may be made annually.

CHAPTER VII.

THE COURTS OF OYER AND TERMINER.

The provisions of this chapter, are explained in the Code of Criminal Procedure, *p.* 14—19.

§ 102. There is in each of the counties of this state, (except, that for this purpose, Fulton and Hamilton are deemed one county,) a court, denominated the court of oyer and terminer, with the jurisdiction conferred by the next three sections, and no other. But nothing contained in this section, affects its jurisdiction in actions or proceedings now pending therein: nor does it affect any judgment or order already made, or proceeding already taken.

§ 103. The court of oyer and terminer has jurisdiction,

1. To inquire, by the intervention of a grand jury, of all public offences committed or triable in the county:

2. To try and determine any indictment found therein, or which may have been found at the court of sessions of the county, or at a city court within the county, for an offence punishable with death:

3. To try and determine any indictment which may have been found at any of the courts mentioned in the second subdivision of this section, for an offence not punishable with death, and which may be sent or removed to the court of oyer and terminer, if in the opinion of that court, it be proper to be tried therein.

4. To send any indictment found therein, for an offence not punishable with death, or to send back any indictment which may have been sent or removed to that court, to the court of sessions of the county, or a city court therein, when in the opinion of the court of oyer and terminer, the same should not be tried in that court.

5. To inquire into the cause of the detention of persons imprisoned in the jail of the county, and make an order for their re-commitment or discharge, or otherwise, according to law:

6. To exercise the powers conferred upon it, by the code of criminal procedure.

§ 104. In addition to the jurisdiction conferred by the last section, jurisdiction was transferred to the courts of oyer and terminer in their respective counties, on the first Monday of July, 1847, of all indictments and proceedings then pending in the late courts of oyer and terminer; and also of all indictments and proceedings then pending in the late courts of general sessions of the peace, except in the city of New-York, and except in cases of which the courts of sessions may take cognizance as provided in section 125.

Const., art 14, *sec.* 5.

§ 105. Jurisdiction was likewise transferred to this court, in the county of Monroe, on the thirtieth day of April, 1849, of all criminal actions and proceedings then pending in the late mayor's court of the city of Rochester, and of all proceedings incident to judgments rendered in that court in those actions and proceedings, on or before that day.

§ 106. This court, (except in the city and county of New-York,) must be held by a judge of the supreme court, as the presiding judge, together with the county judge, and two justices of the sessions designated, as prescribed by other statutes, or by any two of those officers. If the justices of the sessions, or either of them, be absent at a term of the court of oyer and terminer, or the office of those justices or either of them be vacant, the county jndge may supply the vacancy or deficiency for the term, by designating the requisite number to form the court, from the justices of the peace of the county.

§ 107. In the city and county of New-York, the court of oyer and terminer must be held by a judge of the supreme court, as the presiding judge, together with two of the aldermen of the city of New York, designated as the common council may by ordinance prescribe.

§ 108. The court of oyer and terminer must be held at the same place and commenced on the same day with the circuit in the county, and must be continued as long as the public interests require, whether the circuit remain in session or not.

CHAPTER VIII.

THE COUNTY COURTS.

§ 109. There is in each of the counties of this state, except the city and county of New-York, a county court, with the jurisdiction conferred by the next two sections, and no other. But nothing contained in this section affects its jurisdiction in actions or proceedings now pending therein; nor does it affect any judgment or order already made, or proceeding already taken.

Const., art. 6, *sec.*, 14.

§ 110. The county court has jurisdiction in the following actions and proceedings:

1. The exclusive power to review, in the first instance, a judgment rendered in a civil action, by a justice's court in the county:

2. For the foreclosure or satisfaction of a mortgage, and the sale of mortgaged premises situated in the county:

3. For the partition of real property situated in the county:

4. For the admeasurement of dower in real property situated in the county:

5. For the sale of the real property of an infant, when the property is situated in the county:

6. To compel a specific performance by an infant heir, or other person, of a contract respecting real property situated in the county, made by a party who has died before the performance thereof:

7. For the mortgage or sale, on the application of a religious corporation, of its real property situated in the county, and the appropriation of the proceeds thereof:

8. To enforce the judgments of the late court of common pleas of the county, in suits originally commenced in justices' courts, or to exercise such other powers in respect thereto as it might exercise, if they had been rendered by this court:

9. To exercise the powers vested in it by this code, over judgments rendered by justices' courts, of which transcripts shall have been filed with the county clerk:

10. To exercise the powers conferred by statute upon the late court of common pleas of the county, or the judges thereof, respecting ferries, fisheries, wrecks, physicians, the removal of occupants from state lands, the laying out of railroads through Indian lands, and upon appeal from the determination of commissioners of highways; and to prescribe the manner of exercising such jurisdiction when the provisions of those statutes are inconsistent with the organization of the county court:

11. To remit fines and forfeited recognizances, in the cases and manner provided in this code:

12. To exercise the powers conferred upon it by other provisions of this code.

§ 111. In addition to the jurisdiction mentioned in the last section, jurisdiction was transferred to the county court on the first Monday of July, 1847:

1. Of proceedings then pending in the late court of common pleas of the county, in suits originally commenced in justices' courts:

2. To enforce the orders and judgments of the late court of common pleas of the county, rendered before that day, or to exercise such other powers in respect thereto, as it might exercise if they had been made or rendered by this court.

§ 112. The county court is held by the county judge elected in the county, or in case of his inability or a vacancy in his office, by the surrogate, or in a county where there is a special county judge, by that officer.

§ 113. The terms of this court in each county, shall continue as at present prescribed, until the thirty-first day of December, 1850, inclusive, and no longer.

§ 114. After that time, a term of the county court, for the trial of issues, must be held in each county, on the first Tuesday of January, March, May, July, September and November, in each year, and must be continued as long as the public interests require. The court is always open for the transaction of any other business.

§ 115. The terms of the county court must be held at the court house of the county, or if there be more than one, at either or both, as the supervisors may from time to time appoint. The appointment must be made at least thirty days before the holding of a term in pursuance thereof, and published as the supervisors may direct. It shall continue in force until another appointment be made.

CHAPTER IX.

THE SURROGATES' COURTS.

§ 116. There is in each county a surrogate's court, with the jurisdiction conferred by the next three sections, and no other. But nothing contained in this section affects its jurisdiction of proceedings now pending therein; nor does it affect any judgment or order already made, or proceeding already taken.

§ 117. The surrogate's court has exclusive jurisdiction, in the first instance, in the county, to take proof of wills,

1. When the testator, at or immediately before his death, was an inhabitant of the county, in whatever place he may have died:

2. When the testator, not being an inhabitant of this state, shall have died in the county leaving assets therein:

3. When the testator, not being an inhabitant of this state, shall have died out of the state, leaving assets in the county:

4. When the testator, not being an inhabitant of this state, shall have died out of the state, not leaving assets therein, but where assets thereafter come into the county:

5. When real property, devised by the testator, is situated in the county, and no other surrogate's court has gained jurisdiction, under either of the preceding subdivisions of this section.

Taken from 2 *R. S.*, 3*d ed.*, 126, *sec* 46.

§ 118. The surrogate's court has jurisdiction also,

1. To take proof of a will relating to real property situated in the county, when the testator shall have died out of this state, not being an inhabitant thereof, and not leaving assets therein:

2. To grant and revoke letters testamentary and of administration:

3. To direct and control the conduct, and settle the accounts of executors and administrators:

4. To enforce the payment of debts and legacies, and the distribution of the estates of intestates:

5. To order the sale and disposal of the real property of deceased persons:

6. To appoint and remove guardians, to direct and control their conduct and to settle their accounts:

7. To take the care and custody of the person and estate of a lunatic or habitual drunkard residing in the county, and to appoint and remove committees, to direct and control their conduct, and to settle their accounts:

8. To direct the admeasurement of dower:

9. To exercise the powers conferred upon it by other provisions of this code.

> Taken from 2 *R. S.*, *3d ed.*, 318, *sec.* 1, except sub-division 7, which is new, but deemed a necessary and proper provison. This jurisdiction now rests with the county courts.

§ 119. The jurisdiction acquired by a surrogate's court over a matter or proceeding, is exclusive of that of another surrogate's court, except when otherwise provided by this code. And when a guardian is appointed or any other proceeding is commenced, in the surrogate's court of a particular county, all further proceedings in respect to the same must be continued in that court.

Taken from 2 *R. S.*, *3d ed.*, 322, *sec.* 26.

§ 120. The surrogate's court must be held by the surrogate, in each county having a population exceeding forty thousand, in which the legislature have provided or may provide, for the election of a separate officer to perform the duties of the office of surrogate. In every other county, it must be held by the county judge.

Const., *art.* 6, *sec.* 14.

§ 121. In case of the inability of the surrogate, or of a vacancy in his office, the court must be held by the county judge, or if he be unable to act, or his office be vacant, by the special county judge, in a county where there is such an officer. If there be no county judge or special county judge, or he be unable to act, it must be held by the district attorney.

§ 122. The officer by whom a surrogate's court is held, as authorised by the last two sections, is in this code denominated the surrogate.

§ 123. The surrogate's court is at all times open for the transaction of business within its jurisdiction; but it is the especial duty of the surrogate, to attend at his office on Monday of each week, and there hold a surrogate's court.

CHAPTER X.

THE COURTS OF SESSIONS.

This chapter is sufficiently explained in the code of criminal procedure, *p.* 19–28.

ARTICLE I.

THE COURTS OF SESSIONS, IN GENERAL.

§ 124. There is, in each of the counties of this state, a court, denominated a court of sessions, with the jurisdiction conferred by the next two articles, and no other; but nothing contained in this section affects its jurisdiction in actions or proceedings now pending therein; nor does it affect any judgment or order already made or proceeding already taken.

ARTICLE II.

THE COURTS OF SESSIONS, OTHER THAN IN THE CITY AND COUNTY OF NEW YORK.

§ 125. The courts of sessions embraced in this article have jurisdiction,

1. To inquire, by the intervention of a grand jury, of all public offences committed or triable in the county:

2. To try and determine indictments found therein, or sent thereto by the court of oyer and terminer of the county, for public offences not punishable with death:

3. To remove justices of the peace, police justices, and justices of justices' courts of cities in their respective counties, and their clerks, after due notice and an opportunity of being heard in their defence, for causes to be stated in the order of removal:

4. To hear and determine appeals from orders of justices of the peace, under the provisions of the code of criminal procedure respecting the support of bastards:

5. To examine into the circumstances of persons committed to prison as parents of bastards, and to discharge them in the cases provided by the code of criminal procedure.

6. To hear and determine complaints under the provisions of the code of criminal procedure, respecting masters, apprentices and servants:

7. To review the convictions of disorderly persons actually imprisoned, and to execute the powers conferred and duties imposed by the code of criminal procedure in relation to those persons:

8. To continue or discharge the recognizances, undertakings and bonds of persons bound to keep the peace or to be of good behavior, or both; and to inquire into and determine the complaints on which they were founded, as provided in the code of criminal procedure:

9. To compel relatives of poor persons and committees of the estates of lunatics, to support such persons and lunatics, in the cases and in the manner prescribed by the code of criminal procedure:

10. To exercise the powers conferred by the code of criminal procedure, in relation to the estates of persons absconding and leaving their families chargeable to the public:

11. To exercise the powers conferred upon them by other provisions of this code, or of the code of criminal procedure.

§ 126. In addition to the jurisdiction conferred by the last section, jurisdiction was transferred to and vested in these courts, in their respective counties, on the first

Monday of July, 1847, of all indictments and proceedings similar to those mentioned in the last section, which were then pending in the late courts of general sessions of the peace.

§ 127. When an indictment is found in one of these courts, for an offence punishable with death, the court must send it to the court of oyer and terminer of the county.

§ 128. These courts may also send an indictment, found therein and remaining undetermined, for an offence not punishable with death, to the next court of oyer and terminer of the same county, to be determined according to law; but that court, if in its opinion the same is not proper to be tried therein, may remit it back to the court by which it was sent, which must proceed thereon as if it had remained there.

§ 129. These courts must be held by the county judge, together with two justices of the sessions, designated as provided by other statutes. If the justices of the sessions, or either of them, be absent at a term of a court of sessions, or the office of those justices, or either of them, be vacant, the county judge may supply the vacancy or deficiency for the term by designating the requisite number to form the court, from the justices of the peace of the county.

§ 130. These courts must be held at the same place, and commence on the same day, as the terms of the county courts in their respective counties, and must be continued as long as the public interests require.

ATICLE III.

THE COURT OF SESSIONS OF THE CITY OF NEW-YORK.

§ 131. The court known as the court of general sessions in and for the city and county of New-York, is continued, with the jurisdiction conferred by the next two sections, and no other, and is denominated the court of sessions of the city of New-York. But nothing contained in this section affects its jurisdiction of actions or proceedings now pending therein; nor does it affect any judgment or order already made or proceeding already taken.

§ 132. This court has jurisdiction,

1. To inquire, by the intervention of a grand jury, of all public offences committed or triable in the city and county of New-York:

2. To try and determine any indictment found therein, or sent thereto by the court of oyer and terminer of the city and county of New-York, for a public offence not punishable with death:

3. To remove police justices and justices of the justices' courts of the city of New-York, and their clerks, after due notice and an opportunity of being heard in their defence, for causes to be stated in the order of removal:

4. In cases arising in the city and county of New-York, such as are enumerated in subdivisions 4 to 11, both inclusive, of section 125.

§ 133. When an indictment is found in this court, for an offence punishable with death, it must be sent to the next court of oyer and terminer of the city and county of New-York.

§ 134. This court must be held, except as provided in the next section, by the recorder or city judge of the city of New-York, or by one of the judges of the court of common pleas of that city, as the presiding judge, together with two of the aldermen of the city, designated, as the common council may by ordinance prescribe. But it is the especial duty of the recorder or city judge to hold the court and preside therein.

§ 135. When the court is convened for the purpose of exercising the jurisdiction conferred by the third subdivision of section 125, it must be held by the recorder or city judge of the city of New-York, and at least one of the judges of the court of common pleas of that city, together with the mayor and aldermen thereof, or a majority of those officers then in office.

§ 136. The court must be held on the first Monday of each month, and may be continued until the fourth Saturday thereafter, inclusive. Concurrent terms may also be held as often as the recorder and city judge may from time to time prescribe, by an order filed with the clerk.

§ 137. If the trial of a cause be commenced before the expiration of the term, the court may be continued beyond the term, till the completion of the trial, and the rendering of judgment on the verdict.

§ 138. This court must be held at such place in the city of New-York, as now is or hereafter may be prescribed, by ordinance, by the common council of that city.

CHAPTER XI.

THE CITY COURTS.

§ 139. The courts known as the mayors' courts of the cities of Albany, Hudson and Troy, the recorders' courts of the cities of Buffalo, Utica and Oswego, and the city court of Brooklyn, are continued, with the jurisdiction conferred upon them by the next seven sections and no other: and shall be hereafter known as the city courts of those cities respectively. But nothing contained in this section affects their jurisdiction of actions or proceedings now pending therein, nor does it affect any judgment or order already made or proceeding already taken.

§ 140. The jurisdiction of these courts is of two kinds:

1. Civil: and

2. Criminal.

§ 141. Their civil jurisdiction extends to the following actions and proceedings, where the cause thereof arises or the subject thereof is situated in the city in which the court is established:

1. For the recovery of real property or of an estate or interest therein, or for the determination in any form of such right or interest, and for injuries to real property:

2. For the partition of real property:

3. For the foreclosure of the mortgage of real property:

4. For the recovery of personal property distrained for any cause:

5. For the recovery of a penalty or forfeiture imposed by statute:

6. Against a public officer or person specially appointed to execute his duties, for an act done by him in virtue of his office, or against a person who, by his command or in his aid, does anything touching the duties of the office:

7. For the sale of the real property of an infant:

8. For the mortgage or sale, on the application of a religious corporation, of its real property situated in those cities respectively, and the appropriation of the proceeds thereof:

9. To exercise the powers conferred upon it, by other provisions of this code.

This is substantially the same jurisdiction within the city as is conferred upon the county court within the county.

§ 142. These courts have civil jurisdiction, also whether the cause of action arises, or the subject of the action is situated in the city in which the court is established or not, in the same cases in which jurisdiction is conferred by section 68, upon the superior court of the city of New-York, applying that provision to the city in which the court is established.

§ 143. When organized as provided in section 148, for the purpose of exercising criminal jurisdiction, these courts have jurisdiction:

1. To inquire by the intervention of a grand jury, of all public offences committed in the city in which the court is established:

2. To try and determine an indictment found there in, or sent thereto by the court of oyer and terminer of the county, for a public offence not punishable with death, committed in that city.

§ 144. When an indictment is found at a city court, for an offence punishable with death, the court must send the indictment to the next court of oyer and terminer of the county.

§ 145. These courts may also send an indictment found therein and remaining undetermined, for an offence not punishable with death, to the next court of oyer and terminer of the same county, to be determined according to law; but that court, if in its opinion the same is not proper to be tried therein, may remit it back to the court by which it was sent, which must proceed thereon, as if it had remained there.

§ 146. When an indictment is found at a court of oyer and terminer or of sessions, in a county embracing any of the cities in which a city court is established, for an offence not punishable with death, committed in that city, the court in which it was found may send it to the next city court in which it is triable, which must proceed to try and determine the indictment, as if it had been found therein.

§ 147. These courts must be held, for the exercise of their civil jurisdiction, by the following judges:

1. The city courts of the cities of Albany, Buffalo, Hudson, Oswego; Troy and Utica, by the recorders of those cities:

2. The city court of the city of Brooklyn, by the city judge of that city.

§ 148. They must be held, for the exercise of their criminal jurisdiction, by the respective officers mentioned in the last section, as presiding judge, together with two of the aldermen of the city, designated as the common council may by ordinance prescribe.

§ 149. If the judge authorised to hold or preside at a city court for the exercise of either its civil or criminal jurisdiction, be disqualified from holding the court, as provided in section 188, he must, upon the request of either party, file with the county clerk a certificate, stating the fact constituting the disqualification and directing that the action or proceeding, if civil, be transferred to the supreme court, or if criminal, to the court of oyer and terminer of the county, and it must be transferred accordingly. If he refuse to do so, the supreme court, at a special term in the district, or a judge thereof, may, upon motion after due notice, order the transfer to be made.

§ 150. The times and places of holding the city courts, shall continue as at present prescribed, until the thirty-first day of December, 1850, inclusive, and no longer.

§ 151. After that time, a term of each of these courts, for the trial of issues and for the hearing and determination of all matters appertaining to its civil or criminal jurisdiction, must be held, at such times and places in their respective cities as the common council thereof may by ordinance prescribe, and must be continued as long as the public interests require. The court is always open for the transaction of any other business.

CHAPTER XII.

THE JUSTICES' COURTS.

This chapter embraces a new arrangement of the justices' courts, assimilating their names as well as their jurisdiction. The jurisdiction of these courts is rendered uniform, and with the exception of taking from them the power to try actions upon promises to marry, it is substantially the same as in the existing code. Their organization, which is scattered through various statutes, and is very anomalous in its character, while preserved to the extent rendered necessary, is made as uniform as possible.

ARTICLE I.

THE JUSTICES' COURTS, IN GENERAL.

§ 152. The courts known as the courts of justices of the peace, the justices' courts of the cities of Albany, Hudson and Troy, and the justices' courts of the several justices' districts in the city of New-York, are continued, with the jurisdiction conferred by the next three sections, and no other, and are in this code denominated justices' courts. But nothing contained in this section affects their jurisdiction in actions or proceedings now pending therein, nor does it affect any judgment or order already made, or proceeding already taken.

§ 153. These courts have jurisdiction of the following actions and proceedings:

1. Of an action arising on contract, for the recovery of money only, if the sum claimed do not exceed one hundred dollars:

2. Of an action for damages for an injury to the person, or to real property, or for taking, detaining, or injuring personal property, if the damages claimed do not exceed one hundred dollars:

3. Of an action for a penalty, not exceeding one hundred dollars, given by statute:

4. Of an action upon a bond, conditioned for the payment of money, not exceeding one hundred dollars, though the penalty exceed that sum: the judgment to

be given for the sum actually due. When the payments are to be made by instalments, an action may be brought for each instalment as it becomes due:

5. Of an action upon a surety bond or undertaking taken by them, though the penalty or amount claimed exceed one hundred dollars:

6. To take and enter judgment on the confession of a defendant, when the amount confessed does not exceed two hundred and fifty dollars:

7. In the cities of Albany, Hudson, New-York and Troy, of an action, upon the charter or upon a by-law of the corporation of those cities respectively, when the penalty or forfeiture does not exceed one hundred dollars.

§ 154. The jurisdiction conferred by the last section does not extend, however, to a civil action,

1. In which the title to real property shall come in question:

2. Nor for an assault, battery, false imprisonment, libel, slander, malicious prosecution, criminal conversation or seduction, or upon a promise to marry.

3. Nor involving a matter of account, when the sum total of the accounts of both parties, proved to the satisfaction of the court, exceeds four hundred dollars:

4. Nor of an action against an executor or administrator, as such.

§ 155. The following actions can, however, be brought in these courts, only when the cause of action, or some part of it, arose in the town, city or district in which they are established, or when the defendant resides, or having absconded from his residence, is found therein,

1. For the recovery of a forfeiture or penalty given by statute:

2. Against a public officer or person specially appointed to execute his duties, for an act done by him in virtue of his office, or against a person who, by his command or in his aid, does any thing touching the duties of such officer.

ARTICLE II.

THE JUSTICES' COURTS HELD BY JUSTICES OF THE PEACE.

§ 156. Every justice of the peace must hold a justice's court in the town or city in which he is elected, denominated a justice's court of that town or city, except as provided in the next two sections.

§ 157. If the justice be an inn-holder or tavern-keeper, he is disqualified from holding a court as provided in the last section; but if a judgment have been actually rendered by him, before his becoming so disqualified, he may issue execution thereon as in other cases.

§ 158. If he be a member of the legislature, or a county judge, he is not obliged to hold a justice's court, as provided in section 156, but may do so or not, at his option.

§ 159. An action of which these courts have jurisdiction, as provided in sections 153 to 155, both inclusive, must be brought,

1. In a court held in the town or city in which either the plaintiff or defendant, or one of several plaintiffs or defendants resides, or in another town in the same county, next adjoining the residence of the plaintiff or defendant.

2. If the defendant have absconded from his residence, in a court held in the town or city in which he or his property may be:

3. If the plaintiff or defendant do not reside in the county, it may be brought in a court held in the town or city in which either the plaintiff or defendant may be:

4. If the defendant be a corporation, created under the laws of this state, in a court held in the town or city in which it transacts its general business or keeps an office or has an agency established for the transaction of business, or is established by law.

§ 160. These courts may be held at any place designated by the justice holding the same, in the town or city for which he is elected; and they are always open for the transaction of business.

ARTICLE III.

THE JUSTICES' COURTS OF THE CITIES OF ALBANY, HUDSON AND TROY.

§ 161. There are three justices of each of these courts, elected by the electors of the cities in which they are established.

§ 162. Either of the justices of these courts may hold the court in the city in which he is elected.

§ 163. These courts must be held at the places appointed pursuant to law, or if there be none, at such places as may be from time to time appointed by the common council of their cities, at ten o'clock on every judicial day, and must continue in session as long as the public interests require.

ARTICLE IV.

THE JUSTICES' COURTS IN THE CITY OF NEW-YORK.

§ 164. The city of New-York is divided into six justices' districts, in which there shall continue courts denominated the justices' courts of the first, second, third, fourth, fifth and sixth districts of that city, respectively.

§ 165. The districts mentioned in the last section are as follows:

1. The first district embraces the first, second, third and fifth wards:

2. The second district embraces the fourth, sixth and fourteenth wards:

3. The third district embraces the eighth and ninth wards:

4. The fourth district embraces the tenth, fifteenth and seventeenth wards:

5. The fifth district embraces the seventh, eleventh and thirteenth wards:

6. The sixth district embraces the twelfth, sixteenth and eighteenth wards.

§ 166. An action of which these courts have jurisdiction, as provided in sections 153 to 155, both inclusive, must be brought,

1. In a court held in the district in which either the plaintiff or defendant, or one of several plaintiffs or defendants, resides:

2. If none of the parties reside in the city of New-York, in any of these courts, at the election of the plaintiff:

3. If the defendant be a corporation created under the laws of this state, in a court held in the district in which it transacts its general business or keeps an office or has an agency established for the transaction of business, or is established by law.

§ 167. There is a justice of each of these courts, elected by the electors of the district in which it is established.

§ 168. The justice elected in each district must hold the court therein; or if his office be vacant, it may be held by a justice elected in another district, to be designated by the common council.

§ 169. If a justice be disqualified from holding the court as provided in section 188, he must, upon the request of either party, file with the county clerk, a certificate, stating the fact constituting the disqualification, and directing that the action be transferred to the justice's court of another district designated by him; and it shall be transferred accordingly. If he refuse to do so, the supreme court at a special term in the same judicial district, or a judge thereof, may, upon motion, after due notice, order the transfer to be made.

§ 170. These courts must be held at the places in their districts, now or hereafter appointed by the common council of the city of New-York, at such hours on every judicial day, as the respective justices may direct, and must continue in session as long the public interests require.

CHAPTER XIII.

THE MARINE COURT OF THE CITY OF NEW-YORK.

§ 171. The court, known as the marine court of the city of New-York, is continued, with the jurisdiction conferred by the next section, and no other. But nothing contained in this section affects its jurisdiction of actions or proceedings now pending therein; nor does it affect any judgment or order already made, or proceeding already taken.

§ 172. The marine court of the city of New-York has jurisdiction of the following actions and proceedings:

1. Of the actions and proceedings enumerated in sections 153 to 155, both inclusive:

2. Of an action between a person belonging to a vessel in the merchant service, and the owner, master or commander thereof, demanding compensation for the performance, or damages for the violation of a contract for services on board the vessel, during a voyage performed, in whole or in part, or intended to be performed by the vessel, though the sum demanded exceed one hundred dollars.

3. Of an action by or against a person belonging to or on board of a vessel in the merchant service, for an assault and battery or false imprisonment, committed on board the vessel, upon the high seas, or in a place without the United States, of which the ordinary courts of this state have jurisdiction, though the damages ges demanded exceed one hundred dollars. But nothing in this or the last subdivision of this section, gives this court power to proceed, in any of the cases therein referred to, as a court of admiralty or maritime jurisdiction.

§ 173. There are two judges of this court, elected by the electors of the city and county of New-York. Either of them may hold the court.

§ 174. The court must be held at the city hall in the city of New-York at ten o'clock on every judicial day, and must continue in session as long as the public interests require.

CHAPTER XIV.

THE POLICE COURTS.

§ 175. The courts of special sessions now existing, or which may be organized in pursuance of any statutory provision now in force, are abolished; and courts to be known as the police courts, as organized by this code, are substituted in their stead.

§ 176. The police courts have jurisdiction in the cases prescribed in the next section, of the following public offences committed in their respective counties:

1. Petit larceny, not charged as a second offence:

2. Assault and battery, not charged to have been committed riotously, or upon a public officer in the execution of his duties:

3. Poisoning, killing, maiming, wounding or cruelly beating an animal:

4. Racing animals within one mile of the place where a court is held:

5. Committing a wilful trespass, or severing any produce or article from the freehold, not amounting to grand larceny:

6. Selling poisonons substances, not labelled, as required by statute:

7. Maliciously removing, altering, defacing or cutting down monuments or marked trees:

8. Maliciously breaking, destroying or removing mile-stones, mile-boards or guide-boards, or altering an incription thereon.

§ 177. The jurisdiction conferred upon the police courts, by the last section, can, however, be exercised only in the following cases:

1. When the party charged, upon his being brought before a magistrate, requests to be tried by a police court: or,

2. When, not having made such request, and after having been required by the magistrate to give bail for his appearance at the next court of sessions in the county, he omits to do so for twenty-four hours.

§ 178. In the city and county of New-York, these courts must be held at each of the police offices now or hereafter designated by the common council, on Tuesday and Friday of each week, by two of the police justices of that city, and by no other officer.

§ 179. In the other counties, the police court must be held by the magistrate issuing the warrant of arrest, or before whom the defendant is brought to answer the charge.

CHAPTER XV.

THE COURTS OE CONCILIATION.

§ 180. Tribunals are hereby established in the several counties of this state, to be known as the courts of conciliation.

§ 181. The jurisdiction of these courts, and the manner of its exercise, is prescribed in subsequent parts of this code.

CHAPTER XVI.

GENERAL PROVISIONS RESPECTING THE COURTS OF JUSTICE.

ARTICLE I.

PUBLICITY OF THE PROCEEDINGS OF THE COURTS OF JUSTICE.

§ 182. The sittings of every court of justice, other than a court of conciliation, are public, except as provided in the next section.

§ 183. Upon the agreement of the parties to a civil action, or a proceeding of a civil nature, filed with the clerk, or entered upon the minutes, the court may direct the trial of an issue of law or of fact, or any other proceeding therein, to be private; and upon such direction, all persons shall be excluded, except the officers of the court, the parties, their witnesses and counsel.

ARTICLE II.

INCIDENTAL POWERS AND DUTIES OF THE COURTS OF JUSTICE.

§ 184. Every court, except a court of conciliation, has power,

1. To preserve and enforce order in its immediate presence:

2. To enforce order in the proceedings before it, or before a person or body empowered to conduct a judicial investigation, under its authority:

3. To provide for the orderly conduct of proceedings before it or its officers:

4. To compel obedience to its judgments, orders and process, and to the orders of a judge out of court, in an action or proceeding pending therein:

5. To control, in furtherance of justice, the conduct of its ministerial officers, and of all other persons in any manner connected with a judicial proceeding before it, in every matter appertaining thereto:

6. To compel the attendance of persons, to testify, in an action or proceeding pending therein, in the cases and manner provided in this code:

7. To administer oaths in an action or proceeding pending therein, and in all other cases where it may be necessary in the exercise of its powers and duties.

3. To amend and control its process and orders, so as to make them conformable to law and justice:

§ 185. For the effectual exercise of the powers conferred by the last section, the court may punish for contempt, in the cases provided in this code.

§ 186. In furtherance of the objects embraced in section 3, the court of appeals and the supreme court in general session, may from time to time, make such rules, and such only, for the practice in those courts, as are necessary to carry this code into effect, according to its spirit.

§ 187. The rules so made by the supreme court shall, when applicable, govern the practice in the other courts, except the court of appeals, surrogates' and justices' courts, and courts of conciliation; and no rules made by the supreme court, except at such general session of all the judges or a majority of them, are valid.

ARTICLE III.

PARTICULAR DISQUALIFICATIONS OF JUDGES.

§ 188. A judge cannot act as such, in a court of which he is a member, in any of the following cases:

1. In an action or proceeding to which he is a party, or in which he is interested:

2. When he is related to either party, by consanguinity or affinity within the third degree;

3. When he has been attorney, solicitor or counsel for either party, in the action or proceeding:

4. When the action or proceeding is prosecuted or defended, by a person related to him, by consanguinity or affinity within the third degree, or by a partner of a person so related, as attorney or counsel for either party:

5. When he was not present and sitting as a member of the court, at the hearing of a matter submitted for its decision.

But this section does not apply to the arrangement of the calendar, or the regulation of the order of business.

§ 189. A judge cannot act as attorney or counsel in a court of which he is a judge, or in an action or proceeding removed therefrom to another court for review. But this section does not extend to a person who acts as a judge, in virtue of his office as an alderman of a city, except in cases in which he may have acted as a member of the court.

See 2 *R. S.*, *3d ed.*, 373; *Laws of* 1847, *p.* 647, *sec.* 48.

§ 190. A judge of the court of appeals or supreme court, or of the superior court or court of common pleas of the city of New-York, cannot act as attorney or counsel in any court.

Laws of 1847, *p.* 647, *sec.* 49.

§ 191. A judge cannot have a partner, acting as attorney or counsel in the court of which he is a judge; nor can a judge be interested in the costs of an action or proceeding in that court, except where he is a party.

Laws of 1847, *p.* 648, *sec.* 52.

ARTICLE IV.

JUDICIAL DAYS.

SECTION 192. Courts of justice, to be open every day, except as in next section.
193. Courts not to be open on certain days, except for special purposes.
194. If court appointed for or adjourned to those days, to be deemed for next day.
195. Certain persons, not compellable to act as jurors on seventh day of the week.
196. Penalty for serving process on such persons, for or on that day.

§ 192. The courts of justice may be held, and judicial business may be transacted, on any day, except as provided in the next section.

§ 193. No court can be opened, nor can any judicial business be transacted, on Sunday, on the first day of January, on the fourth day of July, on Christmas day, on a day on which a general election is held, or on a day appointed by the governor of this state as a day of fast or thanksgiving, except for the following purposes:

1. To give, upon their request, instructions to a jury then deliberating on their verdict:

2. To receive a verdict, or discharge a jury:

3. For the exercise of the powers of a single magistrate, in a criminal action, or in a proceeding of a criminal nature.

§ 194. If any of the days mentioned in the last section happen to be a day appointed for the holding of a court, or to which it is adjourned, it is deemed appointed for, or adjourned to the next day.

§ 195. A person, whose religious faith and practice are to keep the seventh day of the week, as a day set apart by divine command, as the Sabbath of rest from labor and dedicated to the worship of God, cannot be compelled on that day to attend as a juror.

§ 196. A person, who shall, on that day, knowingly and maliciously serve, or cause to be served, upon one who is exempted as provided in the last section, process issued from a justice's court, returnable on that or any other day, or who shall, before that day, knowingly and maliciously serve upon him such process returnable thereon, is guilty of a misdemeanor, and may be punished by a fine not exceeding one hundred dollars, or by imprisonment not exceeding thirty days, or both.

As to the last two sections, see *Laws of* 1847, *p.* 451, *ch.* 349.

ARTICLE V.

PARTICULAR PROVISIONS RESPECTING THE PLACES OF HOLDING THE COURTS OF JUSTICE.

§ 197. Every court of justice must sit at the places designated for that purpose in this code, except as provided in the next five sections.

§ 198. Upon the agreement of the parties to a civil action or a proceeding of a civil nature, filed with the clerk or entered upon the minutes, the court may direct that the trial of an issue of law or of fact, or any other proceeding therein, be had elsewhere than at the court-house.

§ 199. The supervisors of a county in which a term of the court of appeals, or a term or circuit of the supreme court, or a term of a court of oyer and terminer or sessions, or county court, is appointed to be held, must provide the court with rooms, furniture, attendants, fuel, lights and stationery, suitable and sufficient for the transaction of its business, and for the jury attending upon it. The common council of the city in which a term of a city court, and in the city of New-York, a term of the superior court or court of common pleas of that city, is appointed to be held, must make for those courts the same provision.

§ 200. If a board of supervisors or common council neglect to make the provision required by the last section, the court may order the sheriff to do so; and the expense incurred by him in carrying the order into effect, when certified by the court, is a county or city charge.

§ 201. The governor may, by proclamation filed with the secretary of state and published as he may prescribe, direct that a session of the court for the trial of impeachments, a term of the court of appeals, a term or circuit of the supreme court, or a term of a court of oyer and terminer or sessions, be held at a place other than that appointed, when war, pestilence or other public calamity, or the danger thereof, may render it necessary; and may in the same manner revoke the proclamation, and in his discretion appoint another place for holding the court.

§ 202. A judge authorised to hold or preside at a court appointed to be held in a city or town, may, by an order filed with the county clerk, and published as he may prescribe, direct that the court be held or continued at any other place in the city or county than that appointed, when war, pestilence or other public calamity, or the danger thereof, or the destruction of the building appointed for holding the court, may render it necessary; and may, in the same manner revoke the order, and in his discretion appoint another place in the same city or county, for holding the court.

§ 203. When a court is held at a place appointed, as provided in the last two sections, every person held to appear at the court must, appear at the place so appointed.

§ 204. Intoxicating liquors must not, on any pretence, be sold in the court-house of a county. A violation of this section is punishable as a contempt and as a misdemeanor.

ARTICLE VI.

PROCEEDINGS, WHEN JUDGES DO NOT ATTEND, TO HOLD A COURT.

SECTION 205, 206. Adjournment of court, for want of attendance of judges.

§ 205. If no judge attend on the day appointed for holding a court, before four o'clock in the afternoon, the court shall stand adjourned until the next day at nine o'clock; and if no judge attend on that day, before four o'clock in the afternoon, it shall then stand adjourned for the term.

§ 206. If less than a sufficient number of judges attend, on the day appointed for holding a court, or on the day to which it stands adjourned, as provided in the last section, the judge or judges attending must adjourn the court until the next day at ten o'clock; and may in the same manner adjourn it from day to day, not beyond the same week, until a sufficient number of judges attend.

ARTICLE VII.

SEALS OF THE COURTS OF JUSTICE.

§ 207. Each of the following courts, and no other, has a seal:

1. The court of appeals:

2. The supreme court:

3. The superior court of the city of New-York:

4. The court of common pleas of the city of New-York:

5. The courts of oyer and terminer:

6. The county courts:

7. The surrogates' courts:

8. The courts of sessions:

9. The city courts:

10. The marine court of the city of New-York.

§ 208. The seals now used by these courts shall continue to be so used, until and including the thirty-first day of December, 1850. After that day, the seals devised as provided in the next section, shall be the seals thereof.

§ 209. At least thirty days before the first day of January, 1851, the secretary of state must procure and transmit, at the expense of the state, to the clerks of the several courts and to the surrogates mentioned in section 207, seals, with the arms of the state engraved in the centre thereof, and with the following inscriptions surrounding the same:

1. For the court of appeals, "Court of Appeals—State of New-York."

2. For the supreme court, "New-York Supreme Court. —— County," inserting the name of each county.

3. For the superior court of the city of New-York, "Superior Court of the City of New-York."

4. For the court of common pleas of the city of New-York, "Court of Common Pleas of the City of New-York."

5. For the courts of oyer and terminer, "Oyer and Terminer, —— County, N. Y." inserting the name of each county; and in the city and county of New-York, "Oyer and Terminer—City and County of New-York."

6. For the county courts, "County Court, —— County, N. Y.," inserting the name of the county.

7. For the surrogates' courts, "Surrogate's court; —— County, N. Y.," inserting the name of the county.

8. For the courts of sessions, "Court of sessions, —— County, N. Y." or in the city and county of New-York, "Court of sessions—City and county of New-York."

9. For the city courts, "City court of the city of ——, N. Y., inserting the name of the city.

10. For the marine court of the city of New-York, "Marine court of the City of New-York."

§ 210. The secretary of state must, at the same time and in the same manner, transmit to each county clerk, a seal for his county, with the device mentioned in the last section, and the following inscription surrounding the same, "—— County,—State of New-York," inserting the name of the county; or, in the city and county of New-York, "City and County of New-York.—State of New-York."

§ 211. The clerk of each court mentioned in section 207, except the surrogate's court, must keep the seal thereof. The seal of the surrogate's court must be kept by the surrogate.

§ 212. The seal of a court need not be affixed to any proceedings therein, except,

1. To a writ specially ordered by the court:

2. To the proof of a will or the appointment of an executor, administrator or general guardian: or,

3. To the authentication of a copy of a record or other proceeding of the court or an officer thereof, for the purpose of evidence in another court.

§ 213. The seal may be affixed by impressing it on the paper, or on a substance attached to it and capable of receiving the impression.

TITLE II.

OF JUDICIAL OFFICERS.

CHAPTER I.

JUDICIAL OFFICERS IN GENERAL.

214. A judicial officer is a person authorised to act as a judge, in a court of justice.

CHAPTER II.

ELECTION, TENURE OF OFFICE, CLASSIFICATION AND COMPENSATION OF JUDICIAL OFFICERS.

§ 215. Judicial officers are elected by the electors of the state at large, or of a county, city, town or district thereof; or, when their offices become vacant, are appointed in the manner prescribed by the constitution and by special statutes. The tenure of their offices, and their classification, are provided for in the same manner.

§ 216. All judicial officers, except justices of the peace, receive, at stated times, for their services, a compensation established by special statutes, which cannot be increased or diminished during their continuance in office; and are prohibited from receiving, to their own use, any fees or perquisites of office.

CHAPTER III.

PARTICULAR DISQUALIFICATIONS OF JUDICIAL OFFICERS.

§ 217. The judges of the court of appeals and of the supreme court, cannot hold another office or public trust; and all votes for any of them, for an elective office, except that of a judge of those or other courts, given by the legislature or the people, are void. They are also prohibited from exercising any power of appointment to public office.

CHAPTER IV.

REMOVAL OF JUDICIAL OFFICERS FROM OFFICE.

§ 218. The judges of the court of appeals and supreme court may be removed by concurrent resolution of both houses of the legislature, if two-thirds of all the members elected to the assembly, and a majority of all the members elected to the senate, concur therein.

§ 219. All other judicial officers, except justices of the peace, police justices, and the justices of justices' courts in cities, may be removed from office,

1. By the court for the trial of impeachments, upon an impeachment by the assembly, for wilful and corrupt misconduct in office:

2. By the senate, on the recommendation of the governor.

§ 220. No removal can be made by the concurrent resolution of both houses of the legislature, or by the senate on the recommendation of the governor, as provided in the last two sections, unless the cause thereof be entered on the journals, nor unless the party complained of shall have been served with a copy of the complaint against him, and shall have had an opportunity of being heard in his defence. On the question of removal, the ayes and noes must be entered on the journal.

§ 221. Justices of the peace, police justices, and the justices of justices' courts in cities, may be removed by the courts of sessions in their respective counties, after due notice and an opportunity of being heard in their defence, for causes to be stated in the order of removal

CHAPTER V.

INCIDENTAL POWERS AND DUTIES OF JUDICIAL OFFICERS.

§ 222. A judge may exercise, out of court, all the powers expressly conferred upon a judge as contradistinguished from the court. But when an order has been made in court, it cannot be suspended or affected by the order of a judge out of court.

§ 223. A judge, upon an affidavit showing cause therefor, may enlarge the time within which any act in an action or special proceeding before him or in his court, must be done, after its commencement and before judgment, except the time within which an appeal must be taken, or may stay proceedings therein, for the purpose of a motion to the court. But the time cannot be enlarged or the proceedings stayed for more than twenty days, except upon previous notice to the adverse party; and a copy of the affidavit must be served with the order, or the order may be disregarded; and no judge, except the one who tried the cause, unless he be absent from the county or unable to act, can, after a trial by the court or jury, extend the time for preparing a case, exceptions or special verdict, or stay proceedings thereon.

224. If the action or proceeding be in the supreme court, the powers conferred upon a judge of that court by the last two sections, may be exercised by a county judge, in his county, where one of the parties or attorneys reside therein except as provided in this chapter.

§ 225. If an application for an order, made to a judge of the court in which the action or proceeding is pending, be refused in whole or in part, or be granted conditionally, no subsequent application for the same order can be made to any other judge.

226. A violation of the last section is punishable as a contempt; and an order made contrary thereto may be revoked by the judge who made it, or vacated by a judge of the court in which the action or proceeding is pending.

§ 227. When the time to answer or reply, in an action in the supreme court, has been extended by a county judge, neither he nor any other county judge can grant a further extension; and if an application be made to any judge for a further extension, the applicant must show by affidavit the time of service of the pleading to be answered, the time previously granted him to answer, and when the next circuit will be held in the county. If a further extension be made by a county judge, it may be disregarded.

§ 228. Every judicial officer has power,

1. To preserve and enforce order in his immediate presence, and in the proceedings before him, when he is engaged in the performance of a duty imposed upon him by this code:

2. To compel obedience to his lawful orders, as provided in this code:

3. To compel the attendance of persons to testify in a proceeding pending before him, in the cases and manner provided in this code:

4. To administer oaths to persons, in a proceeding pending before him, and in all other cases where it may be necessary, in the exercise of his powers and duties.

§ 229. For the effectual exercise of the powers conferred by the last section, a judicial officer may punish for contempt, in the cases provided in this code.

§ 230. The judges of the court of appeals, and of the supreme court, have power, in any part of the state, to take and certify,

1. The proof and acknowledgment of a conveyance of real property, or of any other written instrument:

2. The acknowledgment of satisfaction of a judgment in any court, including a judgment of a justice's court,

or of the marine court of the city of New-York, when a transcript thereof has been filed with a county clerk:

3. An affidavit to be used in any court of justice of this state:

4. To exercise any other power, and perform any other duty conferred or imposed upon them by this code, or by other statutes.

§ 231. Every other judicial officer may, within the county, city, village, town, district or ward, in which he is elected or appointed,

1. Exercise the powers mentioned in the first three subdivisions of the last section:

2. Exercise any other power, and perform any other duty, conferred or imposed upon him by this code or by other statutes.

CHAPTER VI.

VACANCIES IN OFFICE, AND THE POWERS OF CERTAIN SPECIAL JUDGES.

§ 232. The local officer, for whose election in certain cases provision is made by section fifteen of the sixth artiticle of the constitution, is in this code known as a special county judge.

§ 233. In case of the inability of a county judge or surrogate, or of a vacancy in his office, the special county judge is invested with his powers and charged with his duties during the inability or vacancy.

§ 234. In a county in which there is no special county judge,in case of inability of the surrogate, or of a vacancy in his office, his powers and duties devolve on the county judge, or if the office of judge and surrogate are united in the same person, then on the district attorney, during the vacancy or in the particular case. In the city of New-York, if the surrogate be unable to act, or there be a vacancy in his office, one of the judges of the court of common pleas, to be designated by the mayor of that city, must act as surrogate during the disability or vacancy.

§ 235. A special county judge has also the powers, in his county, which by law are conferred on the county judge, in actions and proceedings in the supreme court.

§ 236. A vacancy in the office, or the disability of a judge or surrogate, whether existing in reference to a particular action or proceeding under the provisions of section 188, or from any other cause, must be determined by an order of the supreme court, entered with the clerk of the proper county. The order may be made upon affidavit, without notice, or upon notice, or upon an order to show cause, in the discretion of the court.

§ 237. In the city of New-York, there is a judicial officer, known as the city judge of the city of New-York. His election, term of office, and compensation, are provided for by special statutes. His duties are prescribed by particular provisions of this code.

CHAPTER VII.

MISCELLANEOUS PROVISIONS, RESPECTING COURTS AND JUDICIAL OFFICERS.

§ 238. No proceeding in a court of justice in an action or special proceeding pending therein, is affected by a vacancy in the office of all or any of the judges, or by the failure of a term thereof.

§ 239. An application or other proceeding addressed to a court, must be addressed to it by its style, as given in this code; and when the name of a judge is mentioned in an order or other proceeding in court, it must be mentioned without any other title than his style of office. An application or other proceeding addressed to a judicial officer, must be addressed to him by his name, without any other title than his style of office.

§ 240. Every written proceeding in a court of justice of this state, or before a judicial officer, must be in the

English language: but such abbreviations as are now commonly used in that language, may be used, and numbers may be expressed by figures or numerals, in the customary manner.

§ 241. A judicial officer is guilty of a misdemeanor, and is also liable to a civil action, at the suit of a party aggrieved, when he performs an official act corruptly, or wilfully neglects or violates an official duty.

It is held, that, by the common law, a judge of a court of record is not accountable in a civil action for misconduct as such judge, though he act corruptly. *Cunningham vs. Bucklin*, 8 Cow., 178; *Yates vs. Lansing*, 5 John., 282, 9 John., 395. It is easy to perceive that this is a law, made by judges and not by the legislature, or, to use the more expressive phrase of Bentham, judge-made law. The principle does not obtain, it is believed, in the jurisprudence of countries, where there is a written code. There are many cases, in which, by the law of continental Europe, a judge is held to be guilty of a denial of justice, (*deni de justice*,) and responsible to the party.

§ 242. A court or judicial officer has power to create or fill a vacancy in any office held by appointment thereof, or to adjourn any proceeding from time to time, as may be necessary, unless otherwise expressly provided, by a particular provision of this code; and a special proceeding, or a proceeding in an action, out of court, commenced before a judicial officer, may be continued before any other judicial officer, before whom it might have been commenced.

§ 243. When jurisdiction is, by this code, or by any other statute, conferred on a court or judicial officer, all the means to carry it into effect are also given; and in the exercise of the jurisdiction, if the course of proceeding be not specifically pointed out by this code, any suitable process or mode of proceeding may be adopted, which may appear most conformable to the spirit of this code.

In these few provisions respecting the duties of courts and judicial officers, we trust we have not lost sight of what is due both to the public and the judges. The office of judge is one of the greatest with which a human being can be clothed. To him who exercises it with the knowledge, the integrity, the firmness and the dignity, which befit a judicial station, there is no name of respect too great. And in the same degree should he, who yields himself to prejudice or caprice, or by neglect, levity or rudeness, dishonors his office, receive, as he deserves, the severest condemnation.

The bench is best protected by a vigilant and unsparing public opinion. Immunity is its danger. Impressed with such views, we have framed these and other provisions of this code, for the purpose as well of supporting the judiciary in the discharge of its duty, as of turning upon it the eye of the whole community. That community will certainly sustain a judge in the performance of his whole duty, while it will as certainly punish a departure from it.

TITLE III.

OF PERSONS SPECIALLY INVESTED WITH POWERS OF A JUDICIAL NATURE.

CHAPTER I.

ARTICLE I.

JURORS, IN GENERAL.

§ 244. A jury is a body of men temporarily selected from the citizens of a particular district, and invested with the power to present or indict a person for a public offence, or to try a question of fact.

245. A jury is of three kinds:

1. A grand jury:

2. A trial jury: and,

3. A jury of inquest.

§ 246. A grand jury is a body of men, not less than sixteen nor more than twenty-three in number, returned at stated periods from the citizens of the county, before a court of competent jurisdiction, and chosen by lot and sworn to inquire of public offences committed or triable within the county.

§ 247. A trial jury is a body of men, returned from the citizens of a particular district, before a court or officer of competent jurisdiction, and chosen by lot and sworn to try and determine, by an unanimous verdict, a question of fact.

§ 248. A jury of inquest is a body of men, summoned from the citizens of a particular district, before the sheriff, coroner, or other ministerial officer, to inquire of particular facts.

§ 249. A trial jury consists of twelve men, except as otherwise provided in this code in respect to a justice's or police court, or a special proceeding.

§ 250. Foreign juries, juries *de medietate linguæ*, and trials by a jury at the bar of the court, are abolished; and no question of fact triable by a jury, can be tried except by a jury returned, chosen and sworn as provided in this code.

ARTICLE II.

THE QUALIFICATIONS AND EXEMPTIONS OF JURORS.

§ 251. A person is not competent to act as a juror, unless he be,

1. A citizen of the United States:

2. A white male inhabitant of the town or ward from which he is returned:

3. Over twenty-one and under sixty years of age:

4. In the possession of his natural faculties, and not decrepid.

5. Of good moral character, of sound judgment, and well informed: and,

6. Subject to assessment, for personal property belonging to him, or for land in his possession, which he holds under contract for the purchase thereof, upon which improvements have been made of the value of one hundred and fifty dollars; or having a freehold estate in the county, in his own right or in right of his wife, of the value of one hundred and fifty dollars.

§ 252. A person is exempt from liability to act as a juror, if he be,

1. A judicial officer, as defined in section 214:

2. Any other civil officer of this state or of the United

states, whose duties are at the time inconsistent with his attendance as a juror:

3. An attorney and counsellor:

4. A minister of the gospel, or a priest of any denomination:

5. A teacher in a college, academy or school:

6. A practising physician:

7. An acting non-commissioned officer, musician or private, of an uniformed company or troop, duly equipped and organized according to law; the evidence of which is the certificate of the commanding officer, verified by oath, and dated within three months of the time when the exemption is claimed:

8. An acting member of a company of firemen, duly organized according to law; the evidence of which is the certificate of the foreman or other chief officer of the company:

9. A person who, on the first day of May, 1849, had served, or who thereafter may serve, as an acting member of a company of firemen in a city or village of this state, for five years; the evidence of which is the certificate of the chief engineer or head of the fire department of the city or village:

10. A superintendent, engineer, collector or conductor of a canal or railroad, constructed by the authority of this state, and in actual use:

11. An officer, keeper, or attendant of an alms-house, poor-house, hospital, asylum, or other charitable institution, created by or under the laws of this state:

12. A person in the actual employment of an incorporated manufacturing company, by the year, month or season: or

13. A person specially exempted by any other statute, from serving on a jury.

§ 253. A person may be excused from acting as a juror, when, for any reason, his interests or those of the public will be materially injured by his attendance: or when his own health, or the death or sickness of a member of his family, requires his absence.

ARTICLE III.

MANNER OF RETURNING THE GRAND JURY LIST, AND DRAWING AND SUMMONING THE GRAND JURY.

§ 254. The board of supervisors of each county must annually make a list, denominated the grand jury list, containing the names of persons to serve as grand jurors at the courts of oyer and terminer and sessions and city courts in the county, until a new list be returned, in the following manner:

1. In the city and county of New-York, it must be made annually on the first Monday of July, and must contain the names of twelve hundred persons:

2. In the other counties, it must be made at the annual meeting of the board of supervisors, and must contain the names of three hundred persons, apportioned among the different towns and wards, according to the number of persons assessed on the last preceding assessment roll.

§ 255. In preparing the grand jury list, the names of those persons only must be selected, who are known or believed to be possessed of the qualifications prescribed in section 251, and not entitled to exemption, as provided in section 252.

§ 256. The grand jury list must contain the christian and surname at length, and the place of residence and occupation of each person named therein, and must be certified by the clerk of the board of supervisors, and filed in the office of the clerk of the county, within ten days after the day on which it is required to be prepared.

§ 257. The county clerk must keep in his office, two sufficient boxes, carefully secured, the one of which is denominated the grand jury box, and the other the box of drawn grand jurors.

§ 258. On receiving the grand jury list, he must destroy all ballots remaining in both boxes, and must prepare and deposit in the grand jury box, separate ballots, containing the name, place of residence and occupation of each person embraced in the list, and folded as nearly alike as possible, and so that the name cannot be seen.

§ 259. The grand jury for every court in the county, must be drawn from the names deposited in the grand jury box. But if it be drawn for a city court, the clerk must return to the box, every ballot containing the name of a person not stated thereon to reside in the city in which the court is established.

§ 260. A grand jury must be drawn for every term of the following courts:

1. The court of oyer and terminer, except in the city and county of New-York:

2. The court of sessions of the city of New-York, and the city courts.

§ 261. A grand jury may also be drawn,

1. For every other court of sessions, when specially ordered by the court, or by the board of supervisors:

2. For the court of oyer and terminer in the city and county of New-York, upon the order of a judge of the supreme court elected in the first judicial district.

§ 262. If made by the court, the order must be entered upon its minutes, and a copy thereof filed with the county clerk, at least thirty days before the term for which the jury is ordered. If made by the board of supervisors, a copy thereof, certified by the clerk of the board, must be filed with the county clerk, at least thirty days before the term; and when so filed, is conclusive evidence of the authority for drawing the jury.

§ 263. A misdescription, however, of the title of the court, does not affect the validity of the order, if it can be plainly understood therefrom, what court is intended.

§ 264. To constitute a grand jury, thirty-six ballots must be drawn from the grand jury box, for the court of sessions in the city of New-York, and twenty-four for the courts in every other city and county.

§ 265. The drawing must take place at the office of the county clerk, not less than fourteen, nor more than twenty days before the holding of the court.

§ 266. At least six days notice of the time and place of the drawing must be given, by publication in a newspaper of the county, or if there be none, by affixing the notice on the outer door of the court house. A copy of the notice must also be served on the sheriff of the county, and on one of the persons anthorised to act as a judge of the court, at least three days before the time appointed for the drawing.

§ 267. At the time appointed, the sheriff or under sheriff, and the judge upon whom notice has been served, as prescribed in the last section, must attend at the office of the county clerk, to superintend the drawing. If either of those officers do not appear, the clerk must adjourn the drawing to the next day; and must, by written notice, require the delinquent sheriff or judge, or any two justices of the peace or police justices, to attend the drawing at that time. If the officers receiving notice, then appear, but not otherwise, the clerk must proceed in their presence to draw the grand ju r.

§ 268. The drawing must be conducted, as follows:

1. The clerk must shake the box containing the ballots, so as to mingle them as much as possible:

2. He must then publicly draw out of the box, as many of the ballots as there are grand jurors required:

3. A minute of the drawing must be kept, in which the name contained on each ballot drawn must be entered, before another ballot can be drawn:

4. If, when the whole number of ballots required is drawn, it appear that a person, whose name is drawn, is dead or insane, or resides out of the county, that fact must be entered in the minute of the drawing, and the ballot containing the name, destroyed:

5. Another ballot must then be drawn in place of that destroyed, and the name contained thereon must in the same manner be entered in the minute of the drawing:

6. The same proceedings must be had, as often as necessary, until the requisite number of ballots is drawn:

7. The minute of the drawing must then be signed by the clerk and the attending officers, and immediately filed in the clerk's office.

§ 269. A panel of the names of the persons drawn as grand jurors, with their places of residence and occupations, and stating for what court they were drawn, must then be made and certified by the clerk and the attending officers, and delivered without delay to the sheriff of the county.

§ 270. If the grand jury be drawn for a city court, the fact of the return to the grand jury box, of a ballot containing the name of a person not stated thereon, to reside in the city in which the court is established, as provided in section 259, must be entered in the minute of the drawing, and the grand jury must be completed from the names of persons residing in that city.

§ 271. At least six days before the court, the sheriff must summon the persons named in the panel delivered to him, to attend the court, by giving written notice to each of them personally, or by leaving it at his place of residence, with some person of suitable age and discretion.

§ 272. The sheriff must also return the panel to the court, at its opening, specifying the persons summoned, and the manner in which each was notified.

§ 273. The court to which the panel of grand jurors is returned by the sheriff, may impose a fine not exceeding twenty-five dollars, for each day a grand juror, without reasonable cause, neglects to attend. If, however, the notice to attend were not personally served, the fine cannot be imposed, until, upon an order to show cause, an opportunity is afforded him to be heard.

§ 274. At any time after the drawing of the grand jury, the county clerk or sheriff must, without charge, furnish any person applying therefor, a copy of the panel thereof.

§ 275. The county clerk must preserve the ballots drawn, as provided in section 268, until after the adjournment of the court, and must then, if he be also the clerk of that court, or if not, upon receiving the certificate mentioned in the next section,

1. Destroy the ballots containing the names of those who were discharged, for want of a qualification mentioned in section 251, or by reason of an exemption mentioned in section 252:

2. Deposit in the grand jury box, the ballots containing the names of those who did not appear, or were discharged, for any other reason than those mentioned in the last subdivision:

3. Deposit in the box of drawn grand jurors, the ballots containing the names of those who attended and served.

§ 276. The clerk of the court, when he is not also the county clerk, must, within one week after its adjournment, deliver to the county clerk a certified list of all the grand jurors returned to the court, specifying,

1. Those who were discharged for want of qualification, or by reason of exemption:

2. Those who did not appear, or were discharged for any other reason:

3. Those who attended and served.

§ 277. When a person drawn as a grand juror has attended and performed his duty, during the year for which his name was returned, he cannot again be required to serve as a grand juror during that year, except as provided in the next section.

§ 278. If a new grand jury list be not returned to the county clerk, before the list for the year is exhausted, he must draw the grand jurors from the box of drawn grand jurors; and persons so drawn must be summoned, and must serve, and are subject to the same penalties for neglect, as if the year had not expired.

§ 279. When a person is drawn both as a grand and trial juror for the same court, his name must be omitted from the panel of trial jurors, and another name drawn in its place; but after the completion of the drawing of trial jurors, his name must be returned to the trial jury box.

ARTICLE IV.

MANNER OF RETURNING THE TRIAL JURY LIST, EXCEPT IN THE CITY OF NEW-YORK.

§ 280. The assessors of the several towns or wards in each county, except the city and county of New-York, at their annual meeting for the purpose of completing the assessment roll, must make two lists, the one denominated the county trial jury list, the other the justices' jury list, containing the names of persons to serve as trial jurors, until a new list is returned.

§ 281. In preparing the trial jury lists, the assessors must select for the county jury list, the names of not more than one-fourth, nor less than one-fifth of those persons assessed who are known or believed to be possessed of the qualifications prescribed in section 251, and not entitled to exemption, as provided in section 252. The lists must contain the christian and surname at length, and the place of residence and occupation, of each person named therein.

§ 282. The assessors must divide the justice's jury list into parts, corresponding, in a town, with the number of justices therein; and in a city, with the number of justice's districts therein, and must deliver to each justice in a town and justice's clerk in a city, his jury list, duly certified by them. They must also, without delay, transmit to the county clerk's office, the county jury list, certified by them On the justice's jury list in cities, there must be placed those jurors only who reside in the city; and in all cases the jurors who reside nearest the justice's office, must, as far as practicable, be placed on his list. The number of jurors on the lists may be unequal, reference being had to the location and estimated amount of business of each justice.

§ 283. Each clerk and justice mentioned in the last section, must keep in his office two sufficient boxes, carefully secured, the one of which is denominated the undrawn jury box, and the other the drawn jury box.

§ 284. On receiving the justice's jury list, the clerk or justice must destroy all ballots remaining in both boxes, and must prepare, and deposite in the undrawn jury box, separate ballots containing the name of each person embraced in the list, and folded as nearly alike as possible, and so that the name cannot be seen.

ARTICLE V.

MANNER OF RETURNING THE TRIAL JURY LIST, IN THE CITY OF NEW-YORK.

§ 285. There is, in the city of New-York, an officer known as the commissioner of jurors, who is appointed by the supervisors of the city and county of New-York, and the judges of the superior court and court of common pleas of that city, and who holds his office during their pleasure.

§ 286. His office must be kept at the place designated from time to time by the board of supervisors, who must also regulate his compensation, and the number and compensation of his clerks and assistants.

§ 287. The commissioner of jurors must annually, between the first days of May and June, make and enter in a book known as the jury register, a list denominated the trial jury list of the city of New-York, containing the names of persons to serve as trial jurors in that city and county, until a new list be returned.

§ 288. Every person must, upon the application of the commissioner of jurors, or any of his assistants, give correct information of his knowledge or belief of the liability of a person to serve as a juror. For his refusal to do so, or his wilfully giving incorrect information in respect thereto, he is liable to a penalty of fifty dollars, recoverable in a civil action by the corporation of the city of New-York

§ 289. In preparing the trial jury list, the commissioner of jurors must select the name of every person who is known or believed to be possessed of the qualifications prescribed in section 251, and not entitled to exemption, as provided in section 252.

§ 290. As soon after the first day of June in each year, as the trial jury list is completed, the commissioner of jurors must publish, for at least ten days, in the manner prescribed by the board of supervisors, a notice that the trial jury list will be open at his office daily, between nine o'clock in the forenoon and five o'clock in the afternoon, for examination and correction, until a specified day, at least thirty days from the last publication of the notice.

§ 291 The commissioner of jurors must attend at his office, at the times mentioned in the notice, for the purpose of determining the right to exemption, of a person, whose name is on the trial jury list, and may take proof and administer oaths in respect thereto.

§ 292. Upon proof that a person, whose name is on the trial jury list, is exempt for any of the causes mentioned in section 252, and not otherwise, the commissioner of jurors must strike his name from the list, and enter in a book known as the exemption register,

1. The name of the person exempt:

2. The ground of exemption:

3. The name of the person by whose certificate or oath the exemption was proved: and

4. The day when the name was stricken from the list.

§ 293. Within ten days after the time appointed for the examination and correction of the trial jury list, as provided in section 290, the commissioner of jurors must file with the county clerk, a certified copy of the list as corrected.

§ 294. He must also, within the same time, make and deliver to the clerk of the justice's court of each justice's district in the city of New-York, a certified list denominated the justice's jury list, containing the name, place of residence, and occupation of each person embraced in the corrected trial jury list, who resides in the district.

§ 295. Each clerk mentioned in the last two sections must keep in his office two sufficient boxes, carefully secured, the one of whieh is denominated the undrawn jury box, and the other the drawn jury box.

§ 296. On receiving the trial or justice's jury list, as provided in sections 293 and 294, both inclusive, the clerk must destroy all ballots remaining in both boxes, and must prepare and deposit in the undrawn jury box, separate ballots, containing the name, place of residence and occupation of each person embraced in the list, and folded as nearly alike as possible, and so that the name cannot be seen.

§ 297. If, after the return of a trial jury list, the commisioner of jurors discover that the name of a person, qualified to act as a juror and not exempt, has been omitted, he must give written notice to the person so omitted, to appear at his office at a specified time, at least five days after the service, to show cause why his name should not be placed on the trial jury list. The notice must be served on the person to whom it is directed, personally, or by delivering it to a person of suitable age and discretion, at his place of residence.

§ 298. If the person so served, fail to appear or to show by proof, as prescribed in section 291, that he is exempt, his name must be immediately returned to the county clerk, and to the clerk of the justice's court, in the district in which he resides, in the manner provided in sections 293 and 294, in respect to the original trial or justice's jury list; and a ballot containing the name, must be prepared and deposited in the undrawn jury box, in the manner provided in section 296.

ARTICLE VI.

DRAWING AND SUMMONING THE TRIAL JURY FOR THE CIRCUITS AND COURTS OF OYER AND TERMINER, THE SUPERIOR COURT AND COURT OF COMMON PLEAS OF THE CITY OF NEW-YORK, THE COURTS OF SESSIONS, AND THE COUNTY, SURROGATES' AND CITY COURTS.

§ 299. A trial jury, when required for either of the courts embraced in this article, must be drawn from the undrawn jury box of the county in which the court is held. But if it be drawn for a city court, the clerk must return to the box, every ballot containing the name of a person not stated thereon to reside in the city in which the court is established.

§ 300. A trial jury must be drawn.

1. For every circuit:

2. For every trial term of the superior court or court of common pleas of the city of New-York:

3. For every term of the court of sessions of the city cf New-York, and

4. For every term of a city court.

§ 301. A trial jury may also be drawn,

1. For a term of a county court or of a court of sessions, except in the city and county of New-York, when specially ordered by the county judge or by the board of supervisors:

2. For a surrogate's court, when specially ordered by the court, in the cases and manner prescribed in this code.

§ 302. The order when made for a county court or court of sessions, may require that the trial jury be drawn for a particular term; when made by a surrogate's court, that it be drawn for a time and place specified in the order. In either of the cases mentioned in this section, the order must specify the number of jurors to be drawn, not exceeding thirty-six, and the name of the court for which they are to be drawn.

§ 303. If made by the court, the order must be entered upon its minutes, and a copy thereof filed with the county clerk, at least thirty days before the day for which the jury is ordered. If made by the board of supervisors, a copy thereof, certified by the clerk of the board, must be filed with the county clerk at least thirty days before the day for which the jury is ordered; and when so filed, is conclusive evidence of the authority for drawing the jury.

§ 304. A misdescription, however, of the title of the court, does not affect the validity of the order, if it can be plainly understood therefrom what court is intended.

§ 305. The number of jurors drawn for the courts mentioned in section 300, must be as follows:

1. For a circuit, in the city and county of New-York, seventy-two, and in every other county, thirty-six:

2. For the superior court, or court of common pleas, of the city of New-York, seventy-two:

3. For the court of sessions of the city of New-York, seventy-two:

4. For a city court, thirty-six.

§ 306. The trial jurors duly drawn and summoned for a circuit, are the trial jurors for the court of oyer and terminer held at the same time; and those drawn and summoned for a city court, are in like manner the trial jurors in criminal actions therein.

§ 307. The provisions of sections 265 to 278, both inclusive, in respect to grand jurors, (substituting the word trial, in place of the word grand,) apply to trial jurors in all the courts embraced in this article.

ARTICLE VII.

DRAWING AND SUMMONING THE TRIAL JURY FOR THE MARINE COURT OF THE CITY OF NEW-YORK.

§ 308. A trial jury, when required for the marine court of the city of New-York, must be drawn from the undrawn jury box of that city,

§ 309. A trial jury of twenty persons must be drawn for this court, for every alternate Monday, commencing with the first Monday of January, 1851, to serve until the second Saturday, inclusive, after the day for which they were drawn.

§ 310. The drawing must take place publicly, at the office of the county clerk, on the Wednesday preceding the day for which the jury is drawn; and must be conducted by him in the manner prescribed in section 268, in respect to grand jurors, except that no other officer need be present. He must also immediately deliver to the clerk of this court a certified list of the persons drawn as jurors, with their places of residence and occupations, and stating that they were drawn for this court, and the day for which they were drawn.

§ 311. The clerk of this court must immediately deliver the list to a constable, or to a policeman detailed by the mayor to attend the court, with a written notice directed to each person named in the list, requiring him to attend as a trial juror at this court on the day for which the jury was drawn.

§ 312. The officer must thereupon, at least three days before the court, summon each of the persons named in the list, by giving him the notice mentioned in the last section personally, or by leaving it at his place of residence with some person of suitable age and discretion; and must return the list to the court, at its opening on the day for which the jury was drawn, specifying the persons summoned and the manner in which each was notified. If the officer be a policeman, he is not entitled to any fee for summoning the jury.

§ 313. When the list is returned, the court may impose a fine, not exceeding ten dollars, for each day a juror without reasonable cause neglects to attend. But if the notice were not personally served, the fine cannot be imposed, until, upon an order to show cause, an opportunity is afforded him to be heard.

§ 314. The county clerk must preserve the ballots drawn, as provided in section 275, until after the expiration of the period of service for which the jury was drawn. The clerk of this court must then deliver to him a certified list of the persons returned, in the manner prescribed in section 276; and the county clerk must thereupon dispose of the ballots retained, as provided in section 275.

§ 315. The provisions of sections 277 and 278, in respect to grand jurors, (substituting the word trial in place of the word grand,) apply to trial jurors in this court.

ARTICLE VIII.

DRAWING AND SUMMONING THE TRIAL JURY, FOR THE JUSTICES' AND POLICE COURTS.

§ 316. A trial jury, when required for a justice's or police court, must be drawn from the undrawn jury box of the justice or justices' district.

§ 317. A trial jury of twelve persons must be publicly drawn,

1. For a justice's court, when demanded by either party, at the time when an issue of fact is joined:

2. For a police court, when demanded by the defendant, at the time of pleading, unless he plead guilty.

§ 318. The justice or clerk of the court for which the jury is drawn, must immediately deliver the list to a constable or marshal of the city or town, with a written notice directed to each person named in the list, requiring him to attend as a juror at a time and place specified therein.

§ 319. The officer must thereupon immediately summon each of the persons named in the list, by giving him the notice mentioned in the last section personally, or by leaving it at his place of residence with some person of suitable age and discretion, and must return the list to the court, at its opening on the day for which the jury was drawn, specifying the persons summoned, and the manner in which each was notified.

§ 320. The court to which the list is returned, may impose a fine, not exceeding five dollars, for the neglect of a juror, without reasonable cause, to attend. But if the notice were not personally served, the fine cannot be imposed, until, upon an order to show cause, an opportunity is afforded him to be heard.

§ 321. The provisions of sections 277 and 278, in respect to grand jurors, (substituting the word justices' in place of the word grand,) apply to justices' jurors.

ARTICLE IX.

DRAWING AND SUMMONING THE TRIAL JURY, IN SPECIAL PROCEEDINGS.

§ 322. The trial jury in a special proceeding in a court, is the same which is drawn and summoned for the trial of questions of fact therein.

§ 323. A trial jury, when required in a special proceeding before a judicial officer, as provided in this code, must be drawn as follows:

1. If before a justice of the peace or of a justice's court, from the justice's undrawn jury box:

2. If before any other judicial officer, from the undrawn jury box of the county in which the trial is to be had. But if it be before a judge elected in a city, the clerk must return to the box, every ballot containing the name of a person not stated therein to reside in the city in which the trial is to be had.

§ 324. The order for a jury must specify the number of jurors to be drawn; and when made by a judicial officer other than a justice of the peace or of a justice's court in a city, must specify the time and place for which it is to be drawn.

§ 325. The jury, in a special proceeding before a justice, must be drawn and summoned as provided in sections 316, 318 and 319, and the provisions of sections 277 and 278, (substituting the word trial in place of the word grand,) and of section 320, (substituting the word justice in place of the word court,) are applicable thereto.

§ 326. When drawn in a proceeding before any other judicial officer, it must be drawn by the county clerk, in the manner provided in section 268: and the provisions of sections 277 and 278, (substituting the word trial in place of the word grand,) and of section 320, (substituting the word judge in place of the word court,) are applicable thereto.

ARTICLE X.

MANNER OF RETURNING A SPECIAL TRIAL JURY.

§ 327. A special jury may be ordered, on motion, by the supreme court, the superior court or court of common pleas of the city of New-York, or a county, city or surrogate's court, for the trial of a question of fact in a civil action or in a special proceeding of a civil nature, when the importance or intricacy of the case requires it, or a fair and impartial trial cannot otherwise be had.

§ 328. The party obtaining the order must give notice of at least five days, of the time when he will attend before the county clerk, for the purpose of selecting the names of persons to form the jury.

§ 329. At the time appointed, the county clerk must attend at his office, with the list of trial jurors of the county, and publicly select the persons to form the jury in the following manner:

1. He must select from the trial jury list, the names of forty-eight persons, indifferent between the parties, and in his judgment best qualified to try the question:

2. The parties or their attorneys, must then, alter-

nately, commencing with the party who obtained the order, strike out one of the names of the persons selected, until each party shall have stricken out twelve names:

3. If either party fail to attend, or neglect to strike out twelve names, as provided in the last subdivision, the clerk must do so for him:

4. The clerk must thereupon deliver to the sheriff, a panel of the twenty-four persons not stricken out, and must certify that they are the persons selected to form the special jury.

§ 330. If, upon the motion for a special jury, it appear that the clerk is a party to, or interested in the action or proceeding, or is related to either of the parties thereto, by consanguinity or affinity within the third degree, or for any other cause is not impartial between the parties, the court must appoint two impartial persons to select the jury, who must perform the duties imposed upon the clerk by the last section.

§ 331. The sheriff must summon the persons whose names are contained on the panel delivered to him, as provided in section 271, and make return thereof as provided in section 272.

§ 332. The jury must be formed from the persons summoned and appearing, in the manner prescribed by this code in respect to other jurors; and the court has the same power to fine, excuse or discharge any of them, as in other cases.

CHAPTER II.

REFEREES.

§ 333. A referee is a person appointed by the court, or a judicial officer,

1. To try an issue of law or of fact in a civil action, and report a judgment thereon:

2. To ascertain any other fact in a civil action or in a special proceeding of a civil nature, when necessary for the information of the court, and report the fact either with or without his opinion thereon:

3. To execute an order or judgment.

See the code, as amended at the last session, sec. 270, 271, 272, 273, and the act to facilitate the determination of existing suits, sec. 3, 4, 5, 6.

§ 334. The appointment of a referee, is denominated a reference.

§ 335. Upon the agreement of the parties to a civil action or a proceeding of a civil nature, filed with the clerk or entered upon the minutes, a reference may be ordered,

1. To try any or all of the issues in a civil action, whether of fact or of law, (except an issue of fact when the action is for a divorce dissolving the marriage contract,) and to report a judgment thereon:

2. To hear and determine a suit pending in the supreme court, before the first day of July, 1848, on what was then known as the equity side of that court, or any issue therein, whether of fact or of law, or both, (except an issue of fact when the suit is for a divorce dissolving the marriage contract,) or to report facts therein: or,

3. To execute a judgment or order, in an action or suit embraced in this section, except when an execution is the appropriate remedy, as provided in this code.

4. To try an issue or ascertain a fact, in a special proceeding of a civil nature.

§ 336. When the parties do not consent, the court may, upon the application of either, or of its own motion, direct a reference in the following cases:

1. When the trial of an issue of fact requires the examination of a long account on either side; in which case, the referees may be directed to hear and decide the whole issue, or to report upon any specific question of fact involved therein;

2. When the taking of an account is necessary for the information of the court, before judgment, or for carrying a judgment or order into effect:

3. When a question of fact, other than upon the pleadings, arises upon motion or otherwise, in any stage of the action: or

4. When it is necessary for the information of the court, in a special proceeding of a civil nature.

§ 337. A reference may be ordered, in a civil action or in a special proceeding of a civil nature, in any court except a justice's court or the marine court of the city of New-York. It may be so ordered at a special or trial term or circuit, or by a judge of the cout, but by no other officer.

§ 338. A reference may be ordered to any person or persons, not exceeding three, agreed upon by the parties. If the parties do not agree, the court or judge, must appoint one or more referees, not exceeding three, who reside in the county in which the action or proceeding is triable.

§ 339. When the appointment of referees is made by the court or a judge, the referee must be,

1. Qualified as a juror, as provided in section 251:

2. Competent as a juror between the parties: or

3. Not related, by consanguinity or affinity within the third degree, to the judge by whom the court is held, or the order made, or to one who is interested or connected as a partner with a person so related.

CHAPTER III.

COMMISSIONERS OF DEEDS.

§ 340. Commissioners of deeds are appointed in counties or cities, in pursuance of special statutes, and the tenure of their offices is provided for in the same manner.

§ 341. A commissioner of deeds has power, in the county or city in which he is appointed, and in no other place, to take and certify,

1. The proof or acknowledgment of a conveyance of real property, or of any other written instrument:

2. The acknowledgment of satisfaction of a judgment in any court, including a judgment of a justice's court, or of the marine court of the city of New-York, when a transcript thereof has been filed with a county clerk:

3. An affidavit to be used in any court of justice of this state: and

4. To exercise any other power, and perform any other duty conferred or imposed upon him by this code, or by other statutes.

CHAPTER IV.

COMMISSIONERS TO TAKE AFFIDAVITS, AND THE PROOF AND ACKNOWLEDGMENT OF DEEDS, OUT OF THIS STATE.

§ 342. The governor may appoint as many commissioners, in each of the other states, or in a territory of the United States, or in the District of Columbia, as he may deem expedient, who shall hold their offices for three years, and may in the state, territory or district for which they are appointed, and in no other place, take and certify,

1. The proof or acknowledgment of a conveyance of real property, or of any other written instrument:

2. The acknowledgment of satisfaction of a judgment in any court, including a judgment of a justice's court, or of the marine court of the city of New-York, when a transcript thereof has been filed with a county clerk:

3. An affidavit to be used in any court of justice of this state: and

4. To exercise any other power, and perform any other duty conferred or imposed upon them by this code, or by other statutes.

§ 343. A commissioner appointed under the last section must, before he can exercise the powers therein conferred, take and subscribe an oath before a judicial officer in the county or city where he resides, faithfully to perform the duties of the office of a commissioner to take affidavits and the proof and acknowledgment of deeds out of this state, according to the laws thereof; and must file the oath in the office of the secretary of this state.

TITLE IV.

OF THE MINISTERIAL OFFICERS OF THE COURTS OF JUSTICE

CHAPTER I.

THE ATTORNEY GENERAL.

§ 344. The attorney general is elected by the electors of the state, for two years, or, when his office becomes vacant, is appointed, in the manner prescribed by the constitution and by special statutes.

§ 345. He receives for his services, a compensation established by special statutes, which cannot be increased or diminished during his continuance in office, and is prohibited from receiving to his own use, any fees or perquisites of office or other compensation.

§ 346. He may be removed from office by the court for the trial of impeachments, upon an impeachment by the assembly, for wilful and corrupt misconduct in office.

§ 347. The attorney general has power and it is his duty,

1. To prosecute and defend all civil actions or special proceedings of a civil nature, to which the people of this state are a party, or in which they are interested:

2. To collect, if possible, costs adjudged to the people of this state, in an action prosecuted by him, to which they are a party or in which they are interested, and when collected, to pay them into the state treasury, deducting his legal disbursements in the prosecution or defence of the action:

3. Upon the requisition of the comptroller, or the state engineer and surveyor, to prepare the draft of a contract, obligation or other instrument required for the use of the state:

4. Upon the requisition of the governor, to attend a court of oyer and terminer or sessions, for the purpose

of conducting a criminal action prosecuted by the people of this state:

5. Upon the requisition of the governor, the secretary of state, the comptroller, the treasurer, or the state engineer and surveyor, to prosecute a person charged with the commission of a public offence, in violation of statutes which either of those officers is specially required to execute, or in relation to matters connected with the department of either of them:

6. To cause a person indicted for corrupting, or attempting to corrupt a member, or a member elect of the legislature, or a commissioner of the land office, or for an offence against the statutes for the prevention of duelling, to be brought to trial without delay; and to attend in person to the discharge of this duty:

7. When he ascertains that real property, mortgaged to the people of this state is encumbered by prior mortgages or judgments, to discharge those liens and take an assignment thereof to the people, with the consent of the comptroller; and to receive the necessary moneys for this purpose, out of the state treasury:

8. With the consent of the comptroller, to redeem, in the manner provided in this code, real property mortgaged to the people of this state, or purchased for them on the foreclosure of a mortgage, when sold upon a prior judgment:

9. To acknowledge satisfaction of a judgment in favor of the people of this state, when it is satisfied by payment, or when he is directed by the legislature:

10. To attend the legislature during its session, and to report on all matters referred to him by the legislature, or by the senate or assembly:

11. To administer oaths, in all matters relating to his office, in respect to which he may legally require proof:

12. To exercise any other power conferred upon him by the constitution, or by this code or by special statutes.

§ 348. When money is due to the people of this state, by several mortgages or contracts of the same nature, and executed by the same person, one action only can be commenced by the attorney general, for the recovery thereof.

§ 349. When separate actions are instituted by the attorney general, in behalf of the people of this state, against several persons on the same mortgage or contract, or who claim under the same title, he must, upon the request of the defendants, consent to a consolidation of the actions into one.

§ 350. All moneys received by the attorney general, for debts due or penalties forfeited to the people of this state, must be paid by him, immediately after the receipt thereof, into the treasury.

§ 351. The attorney general cannot act as attorney, in a civil action or in a special proceeding of a civil nature, unless the people of this state are a party or interested therein; nor can he act as counsel in such action or proceeding, for a private party against whom a criminal action for a felony is pending, or who is the prosecutor therein.

§ 352. He must keep, in suitable books provided at the expense of the state, a register of all civil actions and special proceedings of a civil nature, prosecuted or defended by him in behalf of the people, and of the proceedings in relation thereto; and must deliver the same to his successor in office.

§ 353. There must be kept in the office of the attorney general a record of the statistics of litigation in the state, comprehending in tabular form;

1. The number of general terms held, with the time when the term commenced and the place where it was held:

In the court of appeals:

In the supreme court:

In the superior court of the city of New-York:

In the court of common pleas of the city of New-York:

And showing in respect to each term,

The number of judges present:

The number of days actual session of the court:

The whole number of hours of actual session of the court:

The number ot cases on the calender:

The number of cases contested, argued or submitted:

The number not reached on the calandar for want of time:

The number decided by the court during the term which were submitted or argued at the same term:

The number decided by the court which were argued or submitted at a preceding term.

2. The number of circuits and courts of oyer and terminer in each county:

The number of trial terms in the superior court and court of common pleas of the city of New-York:

The number of days' actual session of the court:

The average number of hours' session of the court daily:

The number of civil cases on the calendar for trial at each term:

The number actually tried and contested, excluding judgments upon failure to answer:

The number not reached on the calendar for want of time:

3. The number of criminal actions tried, including convictions by confession in each county:

The whole number of convictions:

The number of convictions under each of the following heads: Murder, manslaughter, arson, robbery, burglary, rape, thefts over fifty dollars, other felonies, all other offences.

§ 354. The attorney general must prepare and cause to be printed blank tabular forms for the proper returns from the clerks of the several courts, embracing the particulars specified in the last section, and to transmit annually in the first week in July a sufficient number of such blanks for one year's returns to the clerks of the several courts mentioned in section .

4. The several reports when received from the clerks must be filed and preserved with the records of the attorney general's office, and he must annually on or before the first Monday of December in each year, compile the statistical record of litigation in the state, required in section 353, which shall be duly recorded and certified by him in a book to be kept for that purpose in his office.

The purpose of these provisions is to bring annually before the legislature and the people, the state of the judicial department of the government. We can hardly urge too strongly the importance of providing the means of obtaining complete and accurate information, concerning the operations of that department. The operations of the legislative and executive departments are accessible and well known. But in the judicial, adequate information is nearly inaccessible. There are, it is true, immensefiles of papers, the judgment book, and the judgment rolls. To collect, from these scattered sources, all that is necessary to make known the working of the system, and the effect of changes, is next to impossible. This information is most desirable. Without it, legislation upon the subject must be made upon a view of a few particulars without a view of the rest. There can be no safe comprehensive plan, unless the whole subject is presented together. The worst of all legislation, is that which makes a general law to suit a particular case; for it thus commonly happens, that while in that particular there is an amendment, the change affects another part for the worse. Without a view of the whole subject, neither the magnitude of an existing evil, nor the benefit of an existing provision is seen.

There is no reason for publicity in respect to any branch of the public service, that does not apply with increased force to this. No better view of the progress of public morals, in either direction can be obtained than from the records of the courts. Nor is there, within the whole circle of influences, preventive or penal, that operate upon the administration of justice, any one more efficacious, than that complete publicity which would follow from a periodical collection and condensation carefully made, of the proceedings in all the courts of the state; in short, an annual report of the *statistics of litigation.*

Nowhere in this country, nor in England, have such reports yet been made. But in France, annual reports have been published, as to the civil tribunals, since 1826, and as to the criminal tribunals, since 1831. The work there, is thoroughly systematized. The minister of justice watches over the operation of all the tribunals from the highest to the lowest; minute reports are made to him of their proceedings; and he annually presents a general report, made up from these, and consisting of a series of statistical tables, showing the number of cases brought in each of the courts of France, the nature of each case, its duration, the judgment pronounced, whether by default or after litigation, the number of cases settled, the number referred, the number arbitrated, the number settled by the tribunals of conciliation, the number of appeals and their result; the whole preceded by a summary from the minister, giving the most important conclusions deducible from the tables.

The report for the criminal department in 1846 consists of 34 folio pages in the general summary, and 298 pages of tables. (Compte General de l'administration de la justice criminelle en France, pendant l'annee, 1846.) The report for the civil department in 1845, consists of 48 folio pages in the general summary, and 389 pages of tables. (Compte General de l'administration de la justice civile et commerciale en France, pendant l'annee 1845.) The following are some of the facts stated in this report:

In 1846 there were placed on the calendars of the 361 civil tribunals 121,644 new causes. In 1845, 118,913 were placed on the calendars, and in 1844 119,928. The number of causes has increased since 1841. In this last year, (1841) there were 111,109. The increase for six years has been 10,535, about 10 per cent. Besides the 121,644 new causes commenced in 1846, the civil tribunals had 46,767 remaining on hand undisposed of on the 31st of December, 1845, and 8,584 were restored to the calendars during the year, after having been previously stricken from them as terminated———making in all 176,995 causes, new and old.—In 1846 the civil tribunals disposed of 130,397 causes on their calendars; in 1845 of 126,699; in 1844, of 128,529. The average number of suits terminated from 1841 to 1845, was 123,768; of the suits terminated in 1846, the number of 63,083 were disposed of by final judgment after litigation; 32,397 by judgment of default, and 34,917 were stricken from the calendars in consequence of abandonment or settlement. Of this last number, 11,759 were not settled until after preparatory or interlocutory judgment had been rendered, which led to the amicable solution.—As to the duration of the cases, 130,397 civil suits were terminated in 1846; and are classed as follows: 47,857 were not on the calendar three months; 23,606 were on the calendar from three to sixmonths; 33,454 from six to twelve months; 18,133 from one to two years, and 7,347 more than two years. In 1846 these civil tribunals pronounced 48,824 definitive judgments in the cases brought directly before them without being first inscribed on the general calendars. Of these, 38,854 were decided in open court, and 9,970 at chambers.

In 1846, 207,279 new suits were brought before the 390 commercial tribunals of France. —— On the 31st of December, 1845, there remained undisposed of 7,932 causes, and 3,864 which had been considered as terminated by settlement or abandonment, were again brought before the court in 1846. These two classes of old suits united, added to the 207,279 new suits, form a total of 219,033 causes to be tried. Of these 219,033 suits, 69,323 were disposed of by litigation; 115,308 by default; 4,019 were sent by the court before arbitrators, and 32,705 were stricken from the calendar as terminated by abandonment or settlement. Only 7,678 remained undisposed of on the 31st of December, 1846.

Of 986,123 cases brought for conciliation in 1846, by a simple notice to appear, (billet d'avertissement,) 726,556, or 74-100, were immediately settled by the care of the conciliating magistrate.

It will be long, we fear, before the people of this state have so complete a body of statistics presented to them respecting their tribunals; but a beginning may now be made, and a system established, which will lead to constant improvement.

The attorney-general seems to be the proper officer to take charge of such a work. He is a high law officer of the state, and stands in an intimate relation with the whole judicial establishment. From him the people may expect carefully prepared statements. and useful suggestions for the despatch of business in the various tribunals.

CHAPTER II.

DISTRICT ATTORNEYS.

§ 355. There is a district attorney in each county in this state, who is elected by the electors of the county, or, when his office becomes vacant, is appointed, in the manner prescribed by the constitution and by special statutes.

§ 356. The district attorney may be removed from office, by the court for the trial of impeachments, upon an impeachment by the assembly, for wilful and corrupt misconduct in office.

§ 357. The district attorney in each county, is the public prosecutor therein.

§ 358. He must attend the courts of oyer and terminer and sessions in his county, and the city court, if any, having criminal jurisdiction therein, and conduct, on behalf of the people, all prosecutions for public offences.

§ 359. If he fail to attend any of those courts, the court must designate another person to perform the duties of the district attorney during his absence from the court, who shall receive a reasonable compensation, to be certified by the court, and paid from the county treasury.

§ 360. The district attorney must also institute proceedings before magistrates, for the arrest of persons charged with or reasonably suspected of public offences, when he has information that any such offence has been committed; and for that purpose must attend upon the magistrate, in cases of arrest, when required by him, and must advise the grand jury, when asked to do so, as provided in the Code of Criminal Procedure.

§ 361. The district attorney must prosecute for all penalties and forfeitures to the people of this state, exceeding fifty dollars, which may be incurred in his county, and for which no other manner of collection is provided by statute.

§ 362. When he receives money or property in his official capacity, he must deliver a receipt therefor to the person from whom he receives it, and file a duplicate thereof with the county treasurer.

§ 363. He must, on or before the first Tuesday of October in each year, file in the office of the county treasurer an account in writing, verified by oath, of all money received by him in his official capacity during the preceding year; and must at the same time pay it over to the county treasurer.

§ 364. If he refuse or neglect to account for and pay over money so received by him, as required by the last section, the county treasurer must bring an action against him for the recovery thereof, in the name of the county.

§ 365. The district attorney of each county shall receive an annual salary, to be fixed by the board of supervisors of the county, and paid out of the county treasury.

§ 366. His salary must, at each annual meeting of the board of supervisors in November, be fixed for the ensuing year, and must be paid quarterly out of the county treasury; but at the end of the year, the board may make such additional allowances as are reasonable, for extraordinary services performed during the year; and no district attorney can receive any other compensation, costs or fees, for a service rendered in his official capacity.

§ 367. The district attorney cannot act as counsel, in a civil action or in a special proceeding of a civil nature, for a private party against whom a criminal action for a felony is pending, or who is the prosecutor therein.

§ 368. The district attorney must keep a register of his official business, in which must be entered a note of every indictment, the time when it was found, and the proceedings thereon. The register must, at the expiration of his term of office, be delivered by him to his successor in office.

CHAPTER III.

THE STATE REPORTER.

§ 369. The state reporter is appointed by the governor, lieutenant governor and attorney general, and holds his office for three years, but may be sooner removed by the legislature, a majority of the members elected to each house voting for his removal. His compensation is fixed by special statutes.

§ 370. The state reporter must report and publish, within thirty days after the adjournment of each term, of the court of appeals, a concise outline of the facts and decision in every case determined at that term, with any opinion of the court delivered to him for that purpose; omitting, however, every opinion dissenting from the decision, except in a case involving the construction of the constitution of this state or of the United States.

§ 371. The state reporter can have no pecuniary interest in the publication of the reports, nor can a copyright for them be secured by him or any other person: but they are free for publication by all.

§ 372. The reports must be published in pamphlet form, under the supervision of the state reporter, by contract, as prescribed by special statutes, and designated "The New-York Reports." Each volume must contain at least six hundred pages, with a suitable table of the names of the cases reported, head notes to each case, and an index of the principal matters contained in each volume. Their sale and distribution is provided for special statutes.

CHAPTER IV.

THE CLERKS OF THE COURTS OF JUSTICE.

ARTICLE I.

THE CLERKS OF TEE COURTS OF JUSTICE, IN GENERAL.

§ 373. The following courts and no other, have clerks:

1. The court for the trial of impeachments:

2. The court of appeals:

3. The supreme court:

4. The superior court of the city of New-York:

5. The court of common pleas of the city of New-York:

6. The courts of oyer and terminer:

7. The county courts.

8. The courts of sessions:

9. The city courts:

10. The justices' courts of the cities of Albany, Hudson, New-York and Troy:

11. The marine court of the city of New-York:

12. The police courts in the city of New-York.

§ 374. Except where their compensation is fixed by special statutes, the clerks are entitled, for their services, to receive to their own use the fees provided in this code. When their compensation is fixed by special statutes, they must receive those fees, and account for and pay them over in the manner therein provided.

§ 375. The clerks are elected or appointed in the manner prescribed by the constitution and by special statutes, except as provided in this article. Their qualifications for and tenure of office, and the manner of their removal therefrom and of filling a vacancy therein, are provided for in the same manner.

§ 376. The clerk of the senate is, by virtue of his office, the clerk of the court for the trial of impeachments.

§ 377. The clerk of the court of appeals is, by virtue of his office, clerk of the supreme court.

§ 378. The county clerk of each county is. by virtue of his office, the clerk, in his county, of each of the following courts:

1. The supreme court:

2. The courts of oyer and terminer and sessions, except in the city and county of New-York:

3. The county court.

§ 379. There are six police clerks in the city of New-York, who are appointed by the common council of that city, and hold their offices for four years. They are assigned to police districts, in the manner prescribed by the common council, under the authority of special statutes, and are, by virtue of their offices, clerks of the police courts in the districts to which they are thus assigned.

§ 380. The court of common pleas of the city of New-York shall have a clerk, to be appointed by the court, until the legislature otherwise provide, and to hold his office during the pleasure of the court.

§ 381. The common council of the city of New-York must, by ordinance, assign the clerk so appointed, a suitable office in the city hall in that city. The board of supervisors must, regulate his compensation and the number and compensation of his clerks, which compensation must be paid out of the fees received by the clerk, in the manner provided by special statutes, in respect to the clerk of the superior court.

§ 382. The county clerk of the city and county of New-York must also, on demand, deliver all property, books, records, and papers appertaining to the court of common pleas, to the clerk of that court.

ARTICLE II.

POWERS AND DUTIES OF THE CLERKS OF THE COURTS OF JUSTICE.

§ 383. It is the duty of the clerk of each of the courts mentioned in section 373, except the police clerks in the city of New-York,

1. To keep the seal of the court, and affix it in cases mentioned in section 212, and to any other writ, when required to do so:

2. To record the proceedings of the court:

3. To keep the records, and other books and papers appertaining to the court:

4. To file all papers delivered to him for that purpose, in an action or special proceeding in the court:

5. To attend the terms and circuits of the court of which he is clerk; to administer oaths in an action or special proceeding, in the presence of the court, and under its direction; and to receive the verdict of a jury:

6. To keep the minutes of the proceedings of the court, at its terms or circuits, and under the direction of the court, to enter its orders and judgments:

7. To authenticate, by certificate or exemplification, as may be required, the records or proceedings of the

court, or any other paper appertaining thereto, and filed with him:

8. To deposit all monies paid, or brought into court, and delivered to him, with the county treasurer, as provided in this code:

9. To exercise the powers and perform the duties conferred and imposed upon him by other provisions of this code, or by other statutes:

10. In the performance of his duties, to conform to the directions of the court.

§ 384. It is the duty of each of the police clerks in the city of New-York,

1. To prepare, under the direction of the magistrate, all papers appertaining to any matter pending before him, when acting as a magistrate or holding a police court:

2. To keep the records and other papers appertaining to the police office or police court:

3. To attend at the police office to which he is assigned, at such times as are or may be prescribed by ordinance, by the common council of that city:

4. To attend the police court in the district to which he is assigned; to keep the minutes of its proceedings: under its direction, to enter its orders and judgments; and to authenticate its proceedings by his certificate:

5. To exercise the powers and perform the duties conferred and imposed upon him by the code of criminal procedure.

§ 385. The clerk of each of the courts mentioned in section 373, has power to take affidavits to be read or used in a court or before a judicial officer: but when the clerk is elected or appointed in a county, city, town or district, his power in this respect is co-extensive therewith only.

§ 386. When money is paid or brought into court for any purpose, in an action or special proceeding, the clerk must within five days thereafter deliver the same to the treasurer of the county, by whom it must be kept subject to the order of the court.

ARTICLE III.

THE PLACES OF KEEPING THE CLERKS' OFFICES, AND THEIR OFFICE HOURS.

§ 387. The office of the clerk of the court of appeals must be kept in the state hall in the city of Albany; that of the clerk of every other court, in the building provided for that purpose, by the supervisors of the county or the common council of the city in which the court is held.

§ 388. Each of the clerks must keep his office open for the transaction of business, on every day, except those mentioned in section 193, as follows:

1. In the city of New-York, from nine in the forenoon to four o'clock in the afternoon:

2. In every other part of the state, from eight to twelve in the forenoon, and from one to five o'clock in the afternoon.

ARTICLE IV.

DEPUTY CLERKS.

§ 389. The clerk of the court of appeals, the county clerks, and the clerks of the city courts and of the superior court and courts of common pleas and sessions of the city of New-York, must each have a deputy, appointed by him in writing, and to continue during his pleasure. The appointment must be filed in the office of the clerk by whom it is made.

§ 390. The deputy clerk must attend at the office of the clerk during the office hours prescribed in section 388, and must perform such services relating to the duties of the clerk, as may be required by that officer.

§ 391. When the office of the clerk is vacant, or, by reason of his absence from the office or other disability, he is unable to perform his duties, they may be performed by the deputy.

ARTICLE V.

REMOVAL OF PAPERS FROM ONE CLERK'S OFFICE OF THE SUPREME COURT TO ANOTHER.

§ 392. The supreme court may, for good cause, on motion, direct the removal from one clerk's office to another, of records or other papers relating to an action or proceeding therein.

ARTICLE VI.

MISCELLANEOUS PROVISIONS, RESPECTING THE CLERKS AND DEPUTY CLERKS OF THE COURTS OF JUSTICE.

§ 393. The clerk of each of the courts mentioned in section 389, must within one week after the close of a term or circuit, prepare duplicate reports of the business in his court, by filing the blanks transmitted to him by the attorney general, pursuant to notice, one of which duplicates must be filed and preserved in his office, and the other he must immediately transmit to the attorney general. For his services under this section, the clerk is entitled to the same fees as for certified copies of papers; and the expense thereof is a county charge.

§ 394. The clerk of each of the courts mentioned in section 389, and his deputy, are prohibited during their continuance in office,

1. From acting, or having a partner who acts, as an attorney or counsellor therein:

2. From being interested in the costs or fees in an action or proceeding therein, except when they are parties to the action or proceeding, or interested in the subject thereof.

CHAPTER V.

SHERIFFS.

ARTICLE I.

SHERIFFS, AND THEIR DUTIES, IN GENERAL.

§ 395. There is a sheriff in each of the counties of this state, who is elected by the electors of the county, at a general election, once in every three years, and as often as there is a vacancy. The manner of his election and removal, of giving and renewing his official bonds, and of supplying a vacancy in his office, is prescribed by the constitution and by special statutes. His compensation is prescribed by this code, and by the code of criminal procedure.

§ 396. The sheriff is the chief executive officer, and conservator of the peace of his county.

§ 397. In the execution of his office, it is his duty,

1. To arrest and commit to prison, all persons who break the peace or attempt to break it, and all persons guilty of public offences:

2. To defend his county against the public enemies, and against those who, by riot or otherwise, endanger the public peace or safety:

3. To execute the process and orders of the courts of justice or of judicial officers, when delivered to him for that purpose, according to the provisions of this code, or of the code of criminal procedure:

4. To execute all warrants delivered to him for that purpose, by other public officers, according to the provisions of special statutes:

5. To attend the term of a court within his county, (except a justice's court or the marine court of the city of New-York,) when required by the court, and to obey its lawful orders and directions:

6. To exercise the powers and perform the duties conferred and imposed upon him by the constitution, and by other statutes:

7. In the execution of these powers and duties, to command the aid of as many male inhabitants of his county, as he may think proper, and any military company or companies, armed and equipped.

398. A sheriff can hold no other office, and is ineligible for the next three years after the termination of his office.

§ 399. The county is not responsible for the acts of the sheriff.

ARTICLE II.

SHERIFFS' OFFICES, AND OFFICE HOURS.

§ 400. The sheriff must keep an office in the place in which the county court house is situated, of which he must file a notice in the office of the county clerk. If there be more than one such place, the notice must state in which of them the office is kept, or it may be kept in each.

§ 401. The sheriff's office must be kept open on the days, and during the hours, mentioned in section 388.

§ 402. Service of a paper upon the sheriff may be made by delivering it to a person belonging to and in the office during office hours, or if no such person be there, by leaving it in the office. If, however, no notice of the place of keeping his office be filed, the service may be made at the county clerk's office, upon the county clerk or his deputy. The service, in the cases provided in this section, is equivalent to a personal service on the sheriff.

ARTICLE III.

UNDER AND DEPUTY SHERIFFS.

§ 403. The sheriff, immediately after entering upon his office, must appoint an under sheriff, to hold during his pleasure: and must make a similar appointment, as often as a vacancy occurs in the office of under sheriff. He may also appoint as many deputies as he thinks proper; and may grant a special written authority to any other person to do a particular act.

§ 404. The appointment of an under sheriff and of a deputy sheriff, must be in writing, and filed in the office of the county clerk. The person appointed must also, before entering upon his office, take and file with the county clerk, the constitutional oath of office.

§ 405, The under sheriff must perform such services relating to the duties of the sheriff, as may be required by that officer. A deputy sheriff must execute all orders or process of a court or judicial officer, delivered to him for that purpose, and may perform every act incidental thereto.

§ 406. During a vacancy in the office of sheriff, the under sheriff must act as sheriff: and his neglect or misconduct in office, is a breach of the official bond of the sheriff by whom he was appointed as well as of the security given by him to the sheriff.

ARTICLE IV.

DUTIES OF OFFICERS, IN THE EXECUTION AND RETURN OF PROCESS.

§ 407. When process of any description is delivered to an officer, to be executed, he must deliver to the person delivering it, if required, on payment of his fee, a written memorandum, signed by him, specifying the names of the parties in the process, the general nature thereof, and the day on which it was received. He must also, upon the request of the party served, without fee, deliver to him a copy thereof.

§ 408. An officer to whom process is delivered, must execute it according to its command, or as required by this code or by special statutes: and must make a written return of the execution thereof. For a failure to do so, he is liable to an action, at the suit of the party aggrieved, for the damages sustained by him, in addition to any other fine or punishment.

ARTICLE V.

PROCEEDINGS, IN CASE OF RESISTANCE TO THE EXECUTION OF PROCESS.

§ 409. When an officer finds or has reason to apprehend, that resistance will be made to the execution of process, delivered to him for service, he may command as many male inhabitants of his county as he may think proper, and any military company or companies in the county, armed and equipped, to assist him in overcoming the resistance, and if necessary in seizing, arresting and confining the resisters and their aiders and abettors, to be punished according to law.

§ 410. Every person commanded by an officer to assist him in the execution of process, as provided in section 409, who without lawful cause, refuses or neglects to obey the command, is guilty of a misdemeanor.

ARTICLE VI.

CONDUCT OF THE SHERIFF, TO PERSONS ARRESTED ON CIVIL PROCESS.

§ 411. Neither the sheriff, nor any other officer, can charge or receive from a person arrested on civil process, compensation for necessaries or lodging furnished to him while he is in custody, or for his commitment or discharge, except as specially authorised by this code; nor can he demand or receive a gratuity for keeping a prisoner out of jail, or for waiting for him to find bail, or agree with the adverse party, or for any other purpose.

§ 412. If a person arrested be kept in a house other than the county jail, neither the officer arresting him, nor the person in whose custody he is, can receive from him a greater sum for lodging or necessaries, than is prescribed by the county judge. If no such rate have been prescribed, the officer or person in whose custody the prisoner is, cannot receive a greater sum than may be allowed by a justice of the peace, of the town, on proof that the lodging or necessaries were furnished at the request of the prisoner. And no compensation can in any case be received, for intoxicating liquors, sold or delivered to the prisoner.

§ 413. A person arrested and kept in a house, other than a county jail, may procure such necessaries as he may think fit, without the detention thereof, or payment therefor, to the officer arresting him, or the person in whose custody he is.

§ 414. A sheriff or other officer who has arrested a person in one county, may pass through such parts of another county or counties, as are in the usual route of travel, from the place where the prisoner was arrested, to that to which he is to be conveyed and delivered. And neither the prisoner nor the officer having him in custody, can be arrested on civil process, while passing through any other county than that in which the arrest was made.

ARTICLE.

COUNTY JAILS ; THE KEEPING OF PRISONERS THEREIN ; AND THE PROTECTION THEREOF.

§ 415. There is in each of the counties of this state, a prison known as the county jail.

§ 416. The county jail is kept by the sheriff, and is, (except in the city and county of New-York,) used as a prison,

1. For the detention of persons committed in default of security to appear as witnesses in a criminal action, as provided in the code of criminal procedure :

2. For the detention of persons committed for trial for a public offence:

3. For the confinement of persons committed for a contempt, or upon civil process: and

4. For the confinement of persons sentenced to imprisonment therein, upon conviction for a public offence.

§ 417. In the city and county of New-York, the sheriff has the custody of the county jail for the confinement of persons committed for contempt or upon civil process. The prison in that city and county, for the detention of persons committed in default of security to appear as witnesses in a criminal action, or charged with crime and committed for trial, or sentenced to imprisonment therein upon conviction of a public offence, is known as the city prison; and that for the imprisonment therein upon conviction of a public offence, is known as the penitentiary. Both these prisons are under the charge of the governors of the alms-house of the city of New-York, whose powers in this respect are regulated by special statutes.

§ 418. The sheriff may appoint a keeper of the county jail, for whose acts as such he is responsible.

§ 419. The county jail must be provided by the supervisors of the county, and must contain a sufficient number of rooms,

1. For the confinement of persons committed for trial in criminal actions, separate and distinct from prisoners under sentence:

2. For the confinement of prisoners under sentence:

3. For the confinement of persons committed on civil process for contempt, or as witnesses, separate from those mentioned in the last two subdivisions.

§ 420. Persons committed on criminal process and detained for trial, and those committed for contempt or upon civil process, must be kept in separate rooms from those in which persons convicted and under sentence are confined; and on no pretence whatever, can persons detained for trial or committed for contempt or on civil process, be kept or put in the same room with those convicted and under sentence.

§ 421. Male and female prisoners, (except husband and wife,) must not be kept or put in the same room. The supervisors of each county must as soon as can conveniently be done, so construct or alter the jail or other prison of the county, as to enable the sheriff to confine all persons committed for trial or upon conviction for public offences, in separate rooms. And after such provision is made, each person must be confined in a separate room, and not be permitted to associate with another prisoner.

§ 422. The buildings now used as county jails are continued as such, until other buildings are designated for that purpose by the supervisors of the county.

§ 423. Except as provided in this article, the regulations of the county jails and prisons, in respect to prisoners committed thereto for trial or sentence upon conviction for a public offence, are prescribed by special statutes.

§ 424. When there is no jail in the county, or when the jail becomes unfit or unsafe for the confinement of prisoners, the county judge must, by a written appointment, filed with the county clerk, designate the jail of a contiguous county for the confinement of the prisoners of his county, or of any of them, and may at any time modify or annul the appointment.

§ 425. A copy of the appointment, certified by the county clerk, must be served on the sheriff and keeper of the jail designated; who must receive into his jail, and safely keep, all prisoners authorised to be confined therein pursuant to the last section; and who is responsible for the safe keeping of the persons so committed, in the same manner and to the same extent, as if he were sheriff of the county for whose use his jail is designated; and with respect to the persons so committed, he is deemed the sheriff of the county from which they were removed.

§ 426. If a person confined on civil process, have been previously admitted to the jail liberties of the county for which the designation is made, he may remain within those liberties, or may be removed to the jail designated, by the sheriff to whom he has given an undertaking for the liberties, in the same cases and in the same manner as the sheriff might legally confine him in the jail of his own county.

§ 427. If a person in the custody of the sheriff of the county for which the designation has been made, be entitled to the jail liberties, he must be confined within the jail liberties, of the original county, as if no such designation had been made, but may be removed by the sheriff to the jail so designated, and confined therein, in the same cases and in the same manner, as he might legally confine him in the jail of his own county.

§ 428. If a person confined in the jail so designated, on civil process, or removed there, as provided in section 425, be entitled to the jail liberties, the sheriff of the county in which the jail so designated is, must admit him to the jail liberties, as if he had been originally arrested by him.

§ 429. When a jail is erected in the county for whose use the designation was made, or its jail is rendered fit and safe for the confinement of prisoners, the county judge of that county must, by a written revocation, filed with the county clerk thereof, declare that the necessity for the designation has ceased and that it is revoked.

§ 430 The county clerk must immediately serve a copy of the revocation upon the sheriff of his county, who must thereupon remove his prisoners to his own jail; and if a prisoner have been admitted to the jail liberties of the other county, he must also be removed, and is entitled to the jail liberties of the county to which he is removed, as if he had been originally arrested therein.

§ 431. The sheriff of a county in which there is more than one jail, may confine his prisoners in either of them, and may remove them from one jail to another in the county, when he deems it necessary for their safe keeping or for their appearance at court.

§ 432. When a county jail or a building contiguous to it is on fire, and there is reason to apprehend that the prisoners may be injured or endangered, the sheriff or jailer may remove them to a safe and convenient place, and there confine them, so long as is necessary to avoid the danger.

§ 433 When a pestilence or contagious disease breaks out in or near to a jail, and the physician thereof certifies that it is likely to endanger the health of the prisoners, the county judge of the county, or the mayor or recorder of a city in which it is situated, may, by a written appointment, designate a safe and convenient place in the county, or the jail of a contiguous county, as the place of their confinement. The appointment must be filed in the office of the county clerk, and must authorise the sheriff to remove the prisoners to the place or jail designated, and there confine them, until they can be safely returned to the jail from which they were taken.

§ 434. The board of supervisors of each county must, from time to time, appoint a physician to the jail of the county; and if there be more than one jail in the county, a physician to each jail.

§ 435. Intoxicating liquors must not, on any pretence, be sold in a county jail; nor can they be brought into a jail for the use of a person confined therein, without a written permit by the physician.

§ 436. A person who sells or brings into jail intoxicating liquors, contrary to the last section, and a sheriff or other officer employed about a jail, who knowingly suffers them to be sold or used contrary thereto, is guilty of a misdemeanor, and on conviction, is punishable by imprisonment not exceeding one year, or by a fine not exceeding two hundred and fifty dollars, or both; and a sheriff so convicted, shall forfeit his office.

§ 437. A sheriff or jailer, upon whom a paper in a judicial proceeding, directed to a prisoner in his custody, is served, must forthwith deliver it to the prisoner, with a note thereon of the time of its service. For a neglect to do so, he is liable to the prisoner for all damages occasioned thereby; and by a wilful omission in this respect, is guilty of a misdemeanor.

§ 438. On the written application of the sheriff, with the assent of the county judge, or in the city of New-York, of the recorder or city judge, the governor may authorise the sheriff to organise a guard, not exceeding a specified number, for the protection of the county jail or any other prison in the county, or to arrest or detain a prisoner, or to enforce the process, order or judgment of a court. He may also authorise the sheriff to contract with one or more uniform companies to form the guard, and may at any time revoke or modify the authority.

§ 439. The guard must be under the command of the officers designated by the governor, or if he make no designation, under that of the sheriff, and of such civil and military officers as he may assign; and is subject to the regulations and penalties prescribed by the governor, before or after its organization. The governor may also direct the delivery to the guard, of such ammunition as he may deem necessary.

§ 440. The guard is entitled to the allowance agreed upon before or after their employment, not exceeding one dollar a day for a private, or two dollars a day for an officer.

§ 441. The comptroller may require vouchers and proofs of the agreement, services and expenses, relating to the guard, and may allow such sum therefor as he deems just. He may draw therefor upon the state treasury, and must charge it to the county for whose benefit it was paid, and certify the amount thereof, to the treasurer of the county, by whom it must be laid before the supervisors at their next annual meeting.

§ 442. The supervisors must thereupon direct the amount to be levied and collected, as a county charge; but if they think it would be unreasonably burdensome to raise it all in one year, they may divide it into not exceeding three equal parts, and order it to be levied in an equal proportion in three successive years.

§ 443. When collected in whole or in part, the money must be paid to the county treasurer, by whom it must be paid to the state treasurer, to the credit of the county, on or before the first day of May, after its collection.

§ 444. The sheriff, when he deems it necessary, may, with the assent of the county judge, or, in the city and county of New-York, of the recorder or city judge, employ a temporary guard for the protection of the county jail, or of any other prison in his county, or for the safe keeping of prisoners, until a guard can be organized, as provided in section 438; the expenses of which are a county charge.

§ 445. The expenses of the sheriff, or any other county officer, incurred pursuant to the last seven sections, are also a county charge.

ARTICLE VIII.

JAIL LIBERTIES; AND THE ADMISSION OF PRISONERS THERETO.

§ 446. The jail liberties in each county, are continued as now established, subject to alteration as provided in section 448.

§ 447. When the jail liberties have not been established, and in counties hereafter erected, the supervisors of the county must appoint a reasonable space of ground, adjacent to the jail of the county, to be denominated the jail liberties, as follows:

1. The liberties must be laid out as nearly as may be, in a square; except that a stream of water, canal, or highway, may be adopted as an exterior line, though not in a straight line, or at right angles with the other exterior lines:

2. They must not exceed five hundred acres in extent, and must include the court house, and the office of the county clerk:

3. A minute description of their boundaries and extent, must be filed with the county clerk:

4. The boundaries and limits of the liberties must be designated, by visible and permanent objects.

§ 448. The jail liberties may be altered by the supervisors, not oftener than once in three years, and must be designated in the same manner and subject to the same restrictions, as are prescribed in the last section. But when they have been fixed by statute, no alteration can be made excluding a part of the existing jail liberties.

§ 449. A copy of the order establishing or altering the jail liberties, must be filed with the county clerk, by whom a certified copy must be immediately delivered to the sheriff, which must be conspicuously posted in the county jail.

§ 450. A person in the custody of the sheriff, in a civil action, by virtue of an order of arrest or an execution, or upon a surrender in exoneration of bail, or upon a commitment, for not paying money, may go at large within the jail liberties, with the consent of the sheriff He must, however, be admitted to the jail liberties, upon giving security therefor, as provided in the next section.

§ 451. The security for the jail liberties must be by a written undertaking, executed by two or more sufficient sureties, stating their places of residence and occupations, to the effect that the prisoner shall not go beyond the jail liberties, until legally discharged, or that the sureties will pay to the person at whose suit the prisoner is in custody, a sum mentioned in the undertaking, and which must be as follows:

1. If upon an order of arrest, or a surrender in exoneration of bail, in a civil action, before judgment, the sum recovered by the judgment, not exceeding that mentioned in the warrant of arrest, with interest and the sheriff's fees.

2. If upon an execution in a civil action, or a commitment for not paying money, a sum not exceeding that mentioned therein, with interest and the sheriff's fees.

§ 452. If the sheriff at any time discover that either of the sureties for the jail liberties is insufficient, he may re-commit the prisoner to jail, until other sufficient security be given.

§ 453. The sureties, at any time before judgment against them upon their undertaking, may surrender the prisoner, or he may surrender himself to the sheriff or jailer, in exoneration of his sureties from a future liability, but not from a liability incurred before the surrender. The sheriff or jailer must thereupon, on the written requirement of the sureties, receive the prisoner into custody, and must endorse the surrender upon the undertaking, and if required, give to the sureties a certificate thereof.

§ 454. If a prisoner, allowed by the sheriff to go at large within the jail liberties, go beyond them without the consent, connivance or procurement of the adverse party, the sheriff in whose custody he is, may pursue and re-take him, as if he had escaped from the jail.

ARTICLE IX.

ESCAPES, AND THE LIABILITIES OF SHERIFFS THEREFOR.

§ 455. A prisoner committed to the county jail for a contempt, or for trial or upon conviction for a public offence, or in default of security to appear as a witness in a criminal action, must be actually confined in the jail, until he is legally discharged; and if he be permitted to go at large out of the jail, except by virtue of a legal order or process, it is an escape, and the sheriff or jailer permitting it is punishable for a misdemeanor; and when the prisoner escaping is also held until he pay a sum of money to a private party, that party may recover, in a civil action against the sheriff, his damages sustained by reason of the escape.

§ 456. A sheriff who suffers the escape of a prisoner, arrested or in jail, without the consent or connivance of the party in whose behalf the arrest or imprisonment was made, is liable to an action by such party therefor as follows:

1. When the arrest is upon an order of arrest in a civil action, when the presence of the defendant at the return of the summons is necessary to enable the plaintiff to proceed in the action, and the defendant does not

appear at the time and place specified for the return of the summons:

2. When the arrest or imprisonment is upon an order of arrest in any other civil action, or upon a surrender in exoneration of the sheriff or of bail, and the defendant is not found upon an execution against his person, issued to the proper county on a judgment in such action:

3. When the arrest is on an execution or commitment to enforce the payment of money, and the party arrested is not recaptured or surrendered into custody, at the expiration of the time limited for the service thereof, or legally discharged therefrom:

4. When a person is imprisoned on an execution or commitment to enforce the payment of money, and he escapes after the time limited for the service and is not recaptured or surrendered before an action brought for the escape.

§ 457. The measure of damages, in an action for an escape, as provided in the last section is as follows:

1. For the escape mentioned in subdivision 1 of the last section:

2. In any other case, the amount expressed in the execution or commitment:

3. The actual damages sustained

§ 458. An action for the escape of a prisoner confined in a jail for either of the causes mentioned in section

450, or admitted to the jail liberties, may be brought, by the adverse party against either the sheriff or the sureties for the jail liberties; but the election to sue the sureties discharges the sheriff.

§ 459. The action cannot however be maintained, if, after his escape and before the commencement of the action, the prisoner return to the jail or the liberties thereof, or be retaken by the sheriff.

§ 460. If the action be brought against the sheriff, and he give written notice thereof to the prisoner or to his sureties, a judgment against the sheriff is conclusive evidence of his right to recover against the prisoner or his sureties, as to any matter which was or might have been controverted in the action against the sheriff. In an action by the sheriff against the prisoner or his sureties, the judgment against the sheriff for the escape of the prisoner, is evidence of the damages sustained by him, in the same manner as if it had been collected; and he is also entitled to recover his costs and reasonable expenses in defending the action against him, as part of his damages.

§ 461. If the action be brought against the sheriff, when security for the jail liberties has been taken, the court must, unless the escape was with the assent of the sheriff, stay all proceedings upon a judgment thereon against him, until the expiration of a reasonable time to enable him to prosecute the sureties. and collect from them the amount of the judgment he may recover.

§ 462. A sheriff, jailer or other officer, who demands or receives a reward or gratuity, to aid, assist or connive at the escape of a prisoner in his custody, is punishable for a misdemeanor; and if he be a sheriff, forfeits his office. If a sheriff be convicted, as provided in this section, the court must immediately report the fact of his conviction to the governor.

ARTICLE X.

ASSIGNMENT OF THE JAIL AND OF PRISONERS AND PROCESS, TO A NEW SHERIFF.

§ 463. When a new sheriff is elected or appointed, and has qualified and given the security required by special statutes, the county clerk must give a certificate of that fact, under his seal of office; upon the service of which on the former sheriff, his powers cease, except when otherwise specially provided.

§ 464. Within three days after the service of the certificate upon the former sheriff, he must deliver to his successor,

1. The jail or jails of the county, with their appurtenances and the property of the county therein:

2. The prisoners then confined in the county jail:

3. The process, or other papers in his custody, authorising or relating to the confinement of the prisoners, or if they have been returned, a written statement of their contents and the time of their return:

4. All process for the arrest of a party, and all papers relating to the summoning of a grand or trial jury, which have not been fully executed:

5. All executions, attachments and final process, except those which he has executed or has begun to execute, by the collection of money or a levy on property.

§ 465. He must also, at the same time, deliver to the new sheriff, a written assignment of the property, process, papers, and prisoners delivered, specifying the authority by which each prisoner was committed and is detained, and whether or not it be returned or delivered to the new sheriff. The new sheriff must thereupon acknowledge, in writing, upon a duplicate of the assignment, the receipt of the property, process, papers and prisoners therein specified.

§ 466. Notwithstanding the election or appointment of a new sheriff, the former sheriff must return all process before or after judgment, which he has fully executed, and must complete the execution of all final process which he has begun to execute.

§ 467. If the former sheriff neglect or refuse to deliver to his successor the jail, process, papers and prisoners in his charge, as required by section 464, the new sheriff may, notwithstanding, take possession of the jail, and of the prisoners confined therein, and may compel the delivery of the process and papers, in the manner prescribed in this code.

ARTICLE XI.

PROVISIONS RESPECTING PERSONS COMMITTED UNDER THE AUTHORITY OF COURTS OF THE UNITED STATES, TO A COUNTY JAIL.

§ 468. The sheriff must receive and keep in the county jail, every prisoner who is committed thereto, under civil process issued by a court of the United States, until he be discharged according to the laws thereof, as if he had been committed under civil process issued under the authority of this state. He may also receive, to his own use, the sum payable by the United States for the use of the jail.

§ 469. A sheriff or jailer, to whose custody a prisoner is committed, as provided in the last section, is answerable for his safe keeping, in the courts of the United States, according to the laws thereof.

ARTICLE XII.

MISCELLANEOUS PROVISIONS RESPECTING SHERIFFS AND THEIR OFFICERS.

§ 470. No direction or authority, by a party or his attorney, to a sheriff, or to an under or deputy sheriff or jailer, in respect to the execution of process or the return thereof, or to any act or omission relating thereto, is available to discharge or excuse the sheriff from a liability for neglect or misconduct, unless it be contained in a writing signed by the party to be charged or affected thereby, or his attorney.

§ 471. When the sheriff is committed to the custody of another sheriff or of a coroner, under an execution or commitment for not paying over money received by him by virtue of his office, and remains committed for thirty days, the fact must be reported by the officer in whose custody he is, to the governor.

§ 472. When the sheriff or other officer is legally required to perform a service in behalf of the people of this state, which is not chargeable to his county, or to some other person, his account therefor must be audited by the comptroller, and paid out of the state treasury.

§ 473. When a sheriff is authorised to summon a jury of inquest, or when, in any special proceeding, a jury is authorised, and express provision for drawing it is not made by a particular provision of this code, the jury may be drawn from any justice's jury-box, in the presence of the justice, by drawing the names of eighteen jurors, summoning them, and at the time of appearance, drawing or selecting from those who appear, the number sufficient to complete the jury.

§ 474. A sheriff, or other ministerial officer, is justified in the execution of process, regular on its face, and appearing to have been issued by competent authority, whatever may be the defect in the proceedings upon which it was issued.

§ 475. The officer executing a warrant, order or process of any kind, is then, and at all times subsequent, so long as he retains it, bound to show the same, with all papers attached, to any person interested therein.

§ 476. A sheriff, under or deputy sheriff or jailer, is prohibited during his continuance in office,

1. From acting, or having a partner who acts, as an attorney or counsellor:

2. From being interested in the costs or fees in an action or special proceeding, except where he is a party thereto or interested in the subject thereof.

CHAPTER VI.

CORONERS.

ARTICLE I.

CORONERS AND THEIR DUTIES, IN GENERAL.

§ 477. There is one coroner in the city and county of New-York, and four in every other county of this state, who are elected by the electors of the county, at a general election, once in every three years, and as often as there is a vacancy. The manner of their election and removal, of giving and renewing their official bonds, and of supplying a vacancy in their office, is prescribed by the constitution and by special statutes. Their compensation is prescribed by this code.

§ 478. A coroner has power, and it is his duty,

1. When he is informed that a person has been killed or dangerously wounded by another, or has suddenly died, under such circumstances as to afford a reasonable ground to suspect that his death has been occasioned by criminal means, or has committed sui-

cide, to inquire by the intervention of a jury, into the cause of the death or wound, and to perform the other duties incidental thereto, in the manner prescribed by the code of criminal procedure:

2. To execute civil process in an action or special proceeding, when the sheriff is a party, as prescribed in sections 482 to 485, both inclusive:

3. To exercise the powers and perform the duties conferred and imposed upon him, by the constitution and by other statutes.

§ 479. When an act is directed by statute to be performed by a sheriff, or process is issued to him, the duty, in case of the inability of the sheriff, from any cause, to perform it, devolves on the coroner, in the same manner, and with the same powers, duties and responsibilities, as if the process or order had required its performance by that officer.

§ 480. In the city and county of New-York, if the coroner be absent or unable to attend to the duties prescribed by the first subdivision of section 478, they may be performed by a police justice, but by no other officer, with the like authority and subject to the same obligations and penalties as are attached to the office of coroner.

§ 481. Each coroner is entitled to receive for his services, in holding an inquest and performing any other duty incidental thereto, such compensation as may be fixed by the board of supervisors of his county; and can receive for those services no other compensation or fees whatever. In the city and county of New-York, the compensation so fixed, must be an annual salary.

ARTICLE II.

DUTIES OF CORONERS, WHEN THE SHERIFF IS A PARTY.

§ 482. When the sheriff is a party to an action or special proceeding, the process therein, which it would otherwise be the duty of the sheriff to execute, must, except when otherwise provided by this code, be executed by the coroner of the county to whom it is delivered.

§ 483. When process is directed to the coroners of a county generally, it may be executed and returned by either of them, whose acts in respect thereto can in no degree prejudice the others. He must execute it in the same manner as the sheriff must have done, if it might have been executed by him.

§ 484. If the sheriff, on being arrested by a coroner, on an order of arrest in a civil action, neglect to give bail or make a deposite of money instead thereof, or if he be arrested on an execution against his body, or on a commitment, he must be confined by the coroner in a house within the jail liberties, other than the house of the sheriff or the county jail, in the same manner as the sheriff is required to confine a prisoner in the county jail. The house in which he is thus confined, thereupon becomes, for that purpose, the county jail. If a person be arrested by a coroner, on process in an action in which the sheriff is plaintiff, he must, when his commitment is required by this code, be committed to the county jail; but the coroner is not liable for his escape from the jail, after he is committed thereto.

§ 485. A coroner who executes process in an action or special proceeding to which the sheriff is a party, as provided in the last three sections, is invested with the powers, duties and responsibilities of the sheriff, in the execution of the process, and in every matter incidental thereto.

CHAPTER VII.

COUNTY TREASURERS.

§ 486. There is, in each of the counties of this state except the city and county of New-York, a county treasurer. In the city and county of New-York, the chamberlain of that city is the county treasurer. The manner of their election and removal, of giving and renewing their official bonds, and of supplying a vacancy in their office, is prescribed by special statutes. Their compensation for the services required of them by this chapter, is prescribed by this code.

§ 487. When a bond, mortgage or other security upon real property is ordered by the court to be taken, it must, unless otherwise directed by the court, be taken by the county treasurer of the county where the real property is situated, or by any other county treasurer designated by the court, by his name of office.

§ 488. All other securities, and all certificates and transfers of stocks ordered by the court, must, unless otherwise directed, be taken by a county treasurer designated by the court, by his name of office.

§ 489. The county treasurer, by whom a bond, mortgage or other security upon real estate, or any other security, certificate or transfer is taken, as provided in the last two sections, is thereupon vested in trust for the owners of the fund with full title thereto, and may sue for and collect the same, in his name of office.

§ 490. When money is brought or paid into court, (except a justice's court,) in an action or special proceeding, the clerk must, within five days thereafter, pay it to the county treasurer of the county, unless it be ordered by the court to be paid to another county treasurer, or to be invested or disposed of as provided in section 493. The county treasurer must thereupon make an entry, stating the amount thereof, the time when, and by or for whom, and in what action or proceeding it was so deposited, and the time from which the interest thereon, if any, is to commence.

§ 491. An order upon a county treasurer, for the payment of money deposited with him, as provided in this chapter, must be payable to the order of the person entitled thereto or his attorney, and must specify in what particular action or proceeding, or on what account it is to be paid out, and the time when the order authorising the payment was made.

§ 492. No money brought or paid into court, and deposited with the county treasurer, can be paid out by him, without the production of the order of the court for that purpose, authenticated by the signature of the judge by whom the court was held.

§ 493. The court into which money is brought, may direct it to be invested in a public stock, or to be placed at interest with a corporation, or on approved landed security, and from time to time, to be transferred or disposed of, as it thinks proper.

§ 494. At the first general term of the supreme court, held in each year, in the district embracing his county, the county treasurer must present a statement of all moneys remaining in court, containing,

1. The title of the action or proceeding, in or on account of which the money was paid:

2. The party by whom it was paid, and generally for what purpose:

3. The time of payment, and the amount paid; and,

4. The investment or other disposition thereof.

He must also present a similar statement to every other court in his county, at its first general term, or if there be none, at its first term, of all monies remaining in his hands and paid to him in actions or proceedings therein.

§ 495. The county treasurer must keep books of entry for money received, invested, or paid out, in legal proceedings, separate from those in which entries are made of county funds, and these books must be delivered to his successor in office. He must also, at each annual meeting of the board of supervisors, report a statement of the bonds, mortgages and other securities in his hands, and of monies paid to and deposited or invested by him, as provided in this chapter or by special statutes.

§ 496. The board of supervisors must thereupon examine into the situation of the securities or moneys in the hands of the treasurer, and must ascertain and report to the supreme court, at its next general term in the district, whether the moneys are safely and securely deposited or invested, and whether the securities are sufficient.

CHAPTER VIII.

CRIERS.

§ 497. A crier may be appointed by the board of supervisors of each county, for all or either of the courts in the county, except as provided in the next section.

§ 498. The crier of each of the following courts in the city and county of New-York, is appointed by the court, and holds his office during its pleasure:

1. The superior court:

2. The court of common pleas:

3. The court of sessions.

§ 499. The compensation of the crier must be fixed by the board of supervisors of the county in which he is appointed.

§ 500. It is the duty of the crier,

1. To attend the sessions of the courts for which he is appointed:

2. To call parties and witnesses, and all other persons bound to appear at the court:

3. To make proclamation of the opening or adjournment of the court, or of any other matter, under its direction.

TITLE V.

OF PERSONS SPECIALLY INVESTED WITH MINISTERIAL POWERS, RELATING TO THE COURTS OF JUSTICE.

CHAPTER I.

ATTORNEYS AND COUNSELLORS

ARTICLE I.

ATTORNEYS AND COUNSELLORS, IN GENERAL.

§ 501. An attorney is a person authorised to appear for and represent a party, in the written proceedings in an action or special proceeding, in any stage thereof.

§ 502. A counsellor is a person authorised to appear for and represent a party, in an action or special proceeding, in court only.

§ 503. A person authorised to act as attorney, may also act as counsel.

§ 504. An attorney or counsellor is not a public officer, but any person may act in that capacity, who is declared to be, or admitted as such, according to sections 506 to 510, both inclusive.

In reporting this section and the next, we beg to be understood as not expressing an opinion of our own, respecting the policy or justice of the law, which limits the legal profession, to those who are admitted by the courts. The provision of the judiciary act, allowing any person to appear as special attorney, is not reported in the code, because it has been adjudged to be unconstitutional. Whether it be really so, upon a just construction of the constitution, or whether in that view the constitution should be changed, so as to throw open the profession to all the world, as other professions are opened, it is not for us to determine.

§ 505. A civil action may be prosecuted or defended, by a party in person or by attorney, except that a corporation appears by attorney in all cases; and where a party appears by attorney, the written proceedings must be in the name of the attorney, who is the sole representative of his client, as between him and the adverse party.

ARTICLE II.

ADMISSION OF ATTORNEYS AND COUNSELLORS.

§ 506. The following persons are entitled to practice as attorneys and counsellors, in all the courts of this state:

1. Those who were duly admitted as attorneys or counsellors of the supreme court, before the first Mon-

day of July, 1847, and whose names are still on the rolls of attorneys or counsellors of that court:

2. Those in respect to whom an order has been entered by the supreme court, at any time since the first Monday of July, 1847, stating that they have been examined, and found to possess the qualifications required by the constitution, to entitle them to practice as attorneys and counsellors in the courts of this state.

§ 507. Any male citizen of the age of twenty-one years, of good moral character, and who possesses the requisite qualifications of learning and ability, is entitled to admission to practice in all the courts of this state.

§ 508. For the purpose of admission, he must apply to the supreme court in the district where he resides, on the first day of a general term, and must shew,

1. That he is a citizen of the United States, of the age of twenty-one years; which proof may be made by his own affidavit: and,

2. That he is a person of good moral character; which may be proved by certificate, or other evidence satisfactory to the court.

§ 509. The applicant must also be examined, in open court, as to his qualifications of learning and ability, by the judges, or under their direction, at the term at which application for admission is made.

§ 510. If, upon the examination, he be found duly qualified, the court must direct an order to be entered, to the effect that the applicant is a citizen of the United States, of the age of twenty-one years, of good moral character, and possesses the requisite qualifications of learning and ability, to practice as an attorney and counsellor in all the courts of this state; and upon the entry of the order, he is entitled to practice as such attorney and counsellor.

ARTICLE III.

DUTIES OF ATTORNEYS AND COUNSELLORS.

SECTION 511. Their general duties.
512. Punishment for deceit or collusion.
513. Not to permit other persons to use his name.

§ 511. It is the duty of an attorney and counsellor,

1. To support the constitution and laws of the United States, and of this state:

2. To maintain the respect due to the courts of justice and judicial officers:

3. To counsel or maintain such actions, proceedings or defences, only, as appear to him legal and just, except the defence of a person charged with a public offence:

4. To employ, for the purpose of maintaining the causes confided to him, such means only as are consistent with truth, and never to seek to mislead the judges by any artifice or false statement of fact or law:

5. To maintain inviolate the confidence, and at every peril to himself, to preserve the secrets, of his clients:

6. To abstain from all offensive personality, and to advance no fact prejudical to the honor or reputation of

a party or witness, unless required by the justice of the cause with which he is charged:

7. Not to encourge either the commencement or the continuance of an action or proceeding, from any motive of passion or interest: and

8. Never to reject, for any consideration personal to himself, the cause of the defenceless or the oppressed.

The provisions of this section are taken substantially from the oath, prescribed to advocates by the laws of Geneva. That oath is as follows:

"I swear before God,

To be faithful to the Republic and the canton of Geneva;

Never to depart from the respect due to the tribunals and authorities;

Never to counsel or maintain a cause, which does not appear to be just or equitable, unless it be the defence of an accused person;

Never to employ knowingly, for the purpose of maintaining the causes confided to me, any means contrary to truth, and never to seek to mislead the judges by any artifice or false statement of fact or law;

To abstain from all offensive personality, and to advance no fact contrary to the honor or reputation of the parties, if it be not indispensable to the cause, with which I may be charged;

Not to encourage either the commencement or the continuance of a suit from any motive of passion or interest;

Not to reject, for any considerations personal to myself, the cause of the weak, the stranger, or the oppressed."

This appears to us to express so justly the general duties of lawyers, that we cannot do better than take almost the very terms of it, in prescribing their duties.

The profession of a lawyer is essential to society. Its character and honor are public interests. Not only is the advice of lawyers necessary in the more difficult transactions of private life, but their intervention is necessary to represent the suitor, and advocate his rights before the courts. In this position everything is confided to their integrity. The magnitude of the interests placed in their hands, property, character, liberty, life, the responsibility which they assume, the confidence which they receive, all demand and presuppose the highest qualities and character. No dishonest or dishonorable man can retain the confidence of honest and honorable men. The most intimate connection, in reality, subsists between the character of the community, and the character of the bar. An unscrupulous bar could not exist in a highminded community; and if anywhere a corrupt legal profession is to be found, it is found in the midst of a corrupt and corrupting people.

The judicial department is recruited from the legal profession. Judges must be lawyers. This circumstance alone, the mere fact that one of the great departments of government, co-ordinate in power, equal in dignity, and the one, upon which, especially the safety of the citizen depends, is, by the law of its condition, eligible only out of the ranks of one profession, is enough to give it a pre-eminence. The integrity of the judiciary, more than that of any other class of magistrates, is evidence of the soundness of the public mind, The character of the judges however is the character of the lawyers. Made at the bar; their moral characters there take their complexion. To degrade the bar therefore leads directly and inevitably to the degradation of the bench.

There are certain grave errors, somewhat current respecting the duties of lawyers, which deserve serious consideration. We refer particularly to their alleged indifference to the moral aspects of the causes they advocate—not that there is any thing like the indifference, which is supposed to exist. On the contrary, persons, more scrupulously exact never to take part with wrong, or seem to do so, cannot be found in any profession. But there is nevertheless an impression widely diffused, not only in the profession, but out of it, that a lawyer may properly advocate a bad cause. This view of the case, we here venture briefly to consider.

When a lawyer is asked for his opinion upon a purely legal question, his duty ends with stating the law as it is. In many instances, however, more than this is asked. His client seeks his advice respecting his future conduct. In such cases his duty as a moral being requires him to advise justice. His position as a legal adviser does not exempt him from the moral duties which bind other men. He has no more right than another friend to advise what is unjust or oppressive. Undoubtedly the client must judge for himself of the moral quality of his own actions, and if he desires no more than to know what course the law requires under particular circumstances, the adviser's duty ends with explaining that. But in practice the client generally expects and asks more. He asks advice from a friend who knows what his legal rights are, and who probably has more of his confidence than an other person. In such circumstances, he is bound by moral and should be bound by human laws, to throw his influence upon the side of integrity. To assent to the bad scheme of an unjust client, is to become equally guilty with him, and the two are as much conspirators to effect a wrong, as if they had originally concocted a plan of iniquity with the view of sharing in the plunder. And when, in addition to advice, the client wants an advocate, and asks for active co-operation, the same laws bind him just as strongly to refrain from pursuing an unjust object.

It is sometimes said, that a lawyer is not at liberty to refuse his services to any person, and that when once engaged he is at liberty to employ every means in his power for his client. Indeed so eminent a person as Lord Brougham, is reported to have said, in a speech in the British House of Lords, that the advocate is bound to forget that there is any other person in the world besides his client, and to lose sight of every other consideration than of success.

Is it possible that this can be just? Should the advocate forget that there is a society, whose welfare he is bound by the highest sanctions to promote; that there are other parties, whose rights are at stake; that there are duties to society, to every member of it, as well as to the one who retained him?

The doctrine appears to us unsound in theory, and most pernicious in practice. It assumes that a man has a right to whatever the law can give him, that the law is so plain that it cannot be mistaken or perverted, and that one may rightfully avail himself of every defect in an adversary's proof which the rules of evidence, or accident, or time, may have created; three propositions, every one of which is without foundation. Suppose that a client makes claim to land, in the possession and apparent ownership of another, whose evidence of title, however, has been destroyed by accident. The advocate knows from confidential communications, made to him as counsel, that his client has not a just claim to the land; but from defect of proof on the part of the possessor, it is easy for him to recover it. If the client asks it, is he bound to assist him? Few persons will maintain that. But if the doctrine is a sound one, does it not embrace this case? There is, as it strikes us, no middle ground. If the advocate is to overlook the moral aspects of the claim, he must recover this property for his client. Putting so extreme a case tests the principle, and shows it to be unsound, by showing that it leads to a consequence so revolting.

The law, moreover, is not so clear and precise, but that it may be mistaken or perverted. A strong mind at the bar, and a weak one on the bench, lead often to erroneous judgments. The argument we oppose, takes for granted the infallibility of judges, and the certainty of law. Who, conversant with the proceedings of courts, does not know that neither can be counted on? Before ordinary tribunals, more depends on the advocate than is generally imagined.

Is it lawful to use the power of reason and eloquence, to sustain a bad cause, to support the guilty, or what is more revolting, to persecute innocence? May the faculties be abused, and learning perverted, to make false reasons seem true, to cover up weak points, to give undue prominence to some facts, to conceal others, to magnify one's own cause, to vilify an adversary's? To hold this proceeds upon the fallacy that truth and right cannot be misrepresented or concealed. Who does not know the contrary?

If it be said, that it is the duty of an advocate to go no farther than to present the cause of his client truly, leaving the results to the courts and juries, it may be answered, that truth is absolute, not relative. To present a case truly requires the whole truth on both sides, as well that which makes against, as that which makes for, a client. If he present the favorable circumstances, and suppress the unfavorable, does he present the case truly? Does he not rather impose a false impression on those who have to judge?

We by no means assert, that an advocate may not take upon himself the defence of a man whom he believes to be guilty. He may. The section we propose permits him to do so. If he have derived his belief from the confession of the accused, he should pause in assuming his defence. The law gives to every man charged with crime, the benefit of the rule that his innocence is to be presumed by his judges, until the prosecution have established his guilt, by proof beyond a reasonable doubt. Of this rule the advocate is the intermediate minister. Notwithstanding his own conjectures, surmises, or even belief as to the guilt of his client; he may not become his judge, but is justified if not bound to enforce its application to the inconclusiveness of the evidence of guilt. He may do this, the more readily, because even the jury themselves are bound to secure to the accused the benefit of its application. He may also undertake to show the circumstances of his case; to present the palliating circumstances of temptation, or of provocation, or anything else, that may affect the moral quality of the action, or determine the degree of punishment. He may also in civil cases present defences recognised and provided by law, although he may himself disapprove of the principle and policy of the law.

But here the advocate should stop. The law and all its machinery are means, not ends; the purpose of their creation is justice; and he, who, in his zeal for the means, forgets the ends, betrays not only an unsound heart, but an unsound understanding.

§ 512. An attorney and counsellor who is guilty of deceit or collusion or consents thereto, with intent to deceive a court or judge, or a party to an action or judicial proceeding, is punishable for a misdemeanor, and shall also forfeit to the party injured, treble damages, recoverable in a civil action.

§ 513. If an attorney and counsellor knowingly permit a person not his general law partner, to sue out process, or to prosecute or defend an action or proceedin his name, he and every person who so uses his name, shall severally forfeit to the party against whom the process was issued, or the action or proceeding prosecuted or defended, the sum of fifty dollars, recoverable in a civil action.

ARTICLE IV.

AUTHORITY OF AN ATTORNEY AND ITS DURATION.

§ 514. An attorney and counsellor has authority,

1. To bind his client, in any of the proceedings in an action or special proceeding, by his agreement filed with the clerk, or entered upon the minutes of the court, and not otherwise:

2. To receive money claimed by his client in an action or special proceeding, during the pendency thereof, or within one year after judgment; and upon the payment thereof, and not otherwise, to discharge the claim, or acknowledge satisfaction of the judgment.

But this section does not prevent a party from employing a new attorney, to issue an execution upon a judgment, or to take the other proceedings, prescribed by this code, for its enforcement; and when he does so, the authority of the former attorney ceases.

§ 515. If it be alleged by a party for whom an attorney appears, that he does so without authority, the court may, at any stage of the proceedings, relieve the party for whom the attorney has assumed to appear, from the consequences of his acts. It may also summarily, upon motion, compel the attorney to repair the injury to either party, consequent upon his assumption of authority.

§ 516. The court, or a judge, may, on motion of either party, and on showing reasonable ground therefor, require the attorney for the adverse party, or for any one of several adverse parties, to produce or prove the authority under which he appears, and until he does so, may stay all proceedings by him on behalf of the party for whom he assumes to appear.

ARTICLE V.

CHANGE OF ATTORNEY.

§ 517. The attorney in an action or special proceeding, may be changed at any time before judgment or final determination, as follows:

1. Upon his own consent filed with the clerk or entered upon the minutes: or,

2. Upon the order of the court or a judge thereof, on the application of the client or for other sufficient cause.

§ 518. When an attorney is changed, as provided in the last section, written notice of the change and of the substitution of a new attorney, or of the appearance of the party in person, must be given to the adverse party. Until then, he is bound to recognise the former attorney.

§ 519. When an attorney dies, or is removed or suspended, or ceases to act as such, a party to an action for whom he was acting as attorney, must at least thirty days before any further proceeding against him, be required by the adverse party, by written notice, to appoint another attorney, or to appear in person.

ARTICLE VI.

LIEN OF ATTORNEYS.

SECTION 520. The lien of an attorney, and its effect.

§ 520. An attorney has a lien for his compensation, whether specially agreed upon, or implied, as provided in this code,

1. Upon the papers of his client, which have come into his possession in the course of his professional employment:

2. Upon money in his hands belonging to his client:

3. Upon money in the hands of the adverse party, in an action or proceeding in which the attorney was employed, from the time of giving notice of the lien to that party:

4. Upon a judgment, to the extent of the costs included therein, or if there be a special agreement, to the extent of the compensation specialy l agreed on, from the time of giving notice to the party against whom the judgment is recovered.

This lien is, however, subordinate to the rights existing between the parties to the action or proceeding.

ARTICLE VII.

SUMMARY POWER OF THE COURT, OVER ATTORNEYS.

SECTION 521. Proceedings to compel attorney to deliver over money or papers.
522. Court, how to proceed, if attorney claim lien.

§ 521. When an attorney refuses to deliver over money or papers, to a person from or for whom he has received them in the course of professional employment, whether in an action or not, he may be required by an order of the court in which an action, if any, was prosecuted, or if no action were prosecuted, then by an order of the supreme court, to do so within a specified time, or show cause why he should not be punished for a contempt.

§ 522. If however, the attorney claim a lien upon the money or papers, under the first two subdivisions of section 520, the court may,

1. Impose as a condition of making the order, that the client give security, in a form and amount to be

directed, to satisfy the lien, when determined in an action; or,

2. Summarily inquire into the facts on which the claim of a lien is founded, and determine the same: or

3. Direct the trial of the controversy by a jury, or refer it, and upon the verdict or report, determine the same as in other cases.

ATICLE VIII.

RESIGNATION OF ATTORNEYS AND COUNSELLORS, AND THE EFFECT THEREOF.

§ 523. An attorney and counsellor may, at any time, file in the office of the clerk of the county in which he resides, a written resignation; and after the filing thereof, he is not entitled to the rights, nor is he subject to the disabilities or prohibitions, incident to that relation; except that he is still subject to the power of the court, as provided in the last three sections, in respect to matters arising while he was an attorney and counsellor.

§ 524. An attorney and counsellor who shall have resigned as provided in the last section, may at any time thereafter be re-admitted to practice as such, in the same manner, as if he had never been so admitted.

ARTICLE IX.

REMOVAL OR SUSPENSION OF ATTORNEYS AND COUNSELLORS.

§ 525. An attorney and counsellor may be removed or suspended by the supreme court, at a general term in the district in which he resides, or keeps his office, for either of the following causes, arising after his admission to practice:

1. Upon his being convicted of a felony, or of a misdemeanor involving moral turpitude; in either of which cases, the record of his conviction is conclusive evidence:

2. Upon its being shown to the satisfaction of the court, that he has knowingly signed a frivolous pleading, or has been guilty of any other deceit, or wilful misconduct in his profession:

3. For a wilful disobedience or violation of the order of a court, requiring him to do or forbear an act connected with, or in the course of his profession:

4. For a wilful violation of any of the provisions of section 511.

§ 526. The proceedings to remove or suspend an attorney and counsellor, as provided in the last section, must be taken by the court, of its own motion, for matters within its knowledge, or may be taken upon the information of another.

§ 527. If the proceeding be upon the information of another, the accusation must be in writing, and must be presented to the court.

§ 528. The accusation must state the matters charged, and must be verified by the oath of the person making it, or of some other person, to the effect that the charges therein contained are true.

§ 529. After receiving the accusation, the court must, if, in its opinion, the case require it, make an order requiring the accused to appear and answer the accusation, at a specified time in the same or a subsequent term: and must cause a copy of the order and of the accusation to be served upon the accused, within a prescribed time, before the day appointed in the order.

§ 530. The accused must appear at the time appointed in the order, and answer the accusation, unless, for sufficient cause, the court assign another day for that purpose. If he do not appear, the court may proceed and determine the accusation in his absence.

§ 531. The accused may answer the accusation, either by objecting to its sufficiency, or by denying its truth.

§ 532. If he object to the sufficiency of the accusation, the objection must be in writing, but need not be in any specific form; it being sufficient, if it present intelligibly the grounds of the objection. If he deny the truth of the accusation, the denial may be oral and without oath, and must be entered upon the minutes.

§ 533. If an objection to the sufficiency of the accusation be not sustained, the accused must answer it forthwith.

§ 534. If the accused plead guilty, or refuse to answer the accusation, the court must proceed to judgment of removal or suspension. If he deny the matters charged, the court must immediately, or at such time as it may appoint, proceed to try the accusation.

§ 535. In case of a judgment of suspension or removal, the accused may, within ten days after it is pronounced, make a case, setting forth the evidence and other proceedings in the matter upon the hearing thereof; which must be settled by the court in the same manner as a case in a civil action. When settled, it must be filed with the clerk of the court by which the judgment was given.

§ 536. The following papers must be annexed together and filed by the clerk, within ten days after the filing of the case, or within such further time as the court or a judge thereof may prescribe;

1. The accusation:

2. The objections or answer thereto:

3. The case mentioned in the last section:

4. A copy of the entries upon the minutes of the court, relating to the accusation, and the proceedings thereon, including the order of suspension or removal.

§ 537. A judgment of acquittal is final, and without appeal. But from a judgment of suspension or removal, the accused may appeal to the court of appeals, in the same manner as from a judgment of the supreme court in a criminal action.

§ 538. The powers and jurisdiction of the court of appeals, upon the appeal, and its proceedings and judgment thereon, are the same as upon an appeal from a judgment of the supreme court in a criminal action, except that the court may reverse or modify the judgment, as well upon the facts appearing in the judgment roll, as upon the law.

§ 539. Any court, except a justice's court or a court of conciliation, may suspend an attorney and counsellor from practicing therein, for any of the causes mentioned in section 525, for a period not beyond the adjournment of the next general term of the supreme court in the district. The order of suspension must state the cause thereof, and must be entered upon the minutes; and a certified copy thereof, transmitted by the court by which it is made, to the next general term of the supreme court in the district, which may proceed thereon against the person suspended, in the manner provided in this article.

CHAPTER II.

PERSONS SPECIALLY AUTHORIZED TO EXECUTE THE DUTIES OF THE SHERIFF IN PARTICULAR CASES.

§ 540. Process in an action or special proceeding may be executed by two persons residing in the county, designated by the court, and denominated elisors, in either of the following cases:

1. When the sheriff and coroner are parties:

2. When either of those officers is a party, and the process is against one of them, for a disobedience of an order or process against the other.

They may be required by the court to give security, in such manner as it may direct.

§ 541. When process of arrest is delivered to elisors, they must execute it in the same manner as the sheriff must have done, if it might have been executed by him.

§ 542. If the sheriff or coroner, on being arrested by a person specially appointed to execute the office of sheriff, or by elisors, on an order of arrest in a civil action, neglect to give bail or make a deposite of money instead thereof, or if he be arrested on execution against his body, or on attachment, he must be confined in a house within the jail liberties, other than the house of the sheriff or the county jail, in the same manner as the sheriff is required to confine a prisoner in the county jail. The house in which he is thus confined, thereupon becomes, for that purpose, the county jail.

§ 543. If the coroner be arrested on process in an action in which the sheriff is plaintiff, or if another person be so arrested in an action in which both the coroner and sheriff are plaintiffs, he must be committed to the county jail, when his commitment is required by this code: but the persons making the arrest are not liable for his escape from the jail, after he is committed thereto.

§ 544. Elisors appointed to execute process in the cases mentioned in section 540, are invested with the powers, duties and responsibilities of the sheriff, in the execution of the process and in every matter incidental thereto.

CHAPTER III.

RECEIVERS.

§ 545. A receiver is a person appointed by a court or judicial officer, to take charge of property during the pendency of a civil action or a special proceeding of a civil nature, or upon a judgment or order therein, and to dispose of it as the court or officer may direct.

§ 546. A receiver may be appointed,

1. In a civil action, before judgment, provisionally, on the application of either party, when his right to property, the subject of the action, and which is in the possession of an adverse party, is probable, and the property, or its rents and profits, are in danger of being lost or materially injured or impaired:

2. In a civil action, after judgment, to carry the judgment into effect:

3. In a civil action after judgment, to dispose of the property, according to the judgment, or to preserve it during the pendency of an appeal, or when an execution has been returned unsatisfied, and the judgment debtor refuses to apply his property in satisfaction of the judgment:

4. In the cases provided in this code, and by special statutes, when a corporation has been dissolved, or is insolvent or in imminent danger of insolvency, or has forfeited its corporate rights:

5. In the cases provided in this code, when a debtor has been declared insolvent.

§ 547. A receiver, before entering upon his duties, must be sworn faithfully to discharge his trust, to the best of his ability, and must also file with the clerk of the court, an undertaking in writing, of one or more sufficient sureties, in a specified sum, fixed by the court or officer, to the effect that he will faithfully discharge the duties of receiver, and will obey the orders of the court or officer in respect thereto. The sureties must justify in the same manner as bail upon an arrest.

CHAPTER IV.

GUARDIANS.

§ 548. A guardian is a person appointed to take the charge of the person or estate of an infant, or both, or to appear for him in the prosecution or defence of a civil action.

§ 549. A guardian may be appointed,

1. By the father, whether of full age or not, of a child likely to be born, or of a living child under the age of twenty-one years and unmarried, or by a surrogate's court, to take the custody and tuition of the infant, to maintain actions for wrongfully taking or detaining him, and to manage his personal property, and the profits of his real property:

2. By the court in which a civil action by or against an infant is brought, or by a judge thereof, and in the supreme court by a county judge, to appear for the infant in the prosecution or defence of the action, as provided in this code.

§ 550. No guardian appointed for an infant, can be permitted to receive property of the infant, until he has given sufficient security, approved by a judge of the court, or in the supreme court, by a county judge, to account for and apply the same, under the direction of the court.

§ 551. The manner of the appointment of a guardian, his powers and duties, and the incidents of his trust, are prescribed by other provisions of this code.

CHAPTER V.

COMMITTEES OF LUNATICS AND HABITUAL DRUNKARDS.

§ 552. A committee is a person appointed by a court, to take the care and custody of an insane person, or of one who is incapable of conducting his own affairs in consequence of habitual drunkenness, and of his property.

§ 553. The manner of the appointment of a committee, his security, powers and duties, and the incidents of his trust, are prescribed by other provisions of this code.

PART II.

OF CIVIL ACTIONS.

TITLE I.

OF THE FORM OF CIVIL ACTIONS.

§ 554. The distinction between actions at law and suits in equity, and the forms of all such actions and suits, heretofore existing, are abolished; and, there shall be in this state, hereafter, but one form of action, for the enforcement or protection of private rights and the redress or prevention of private wrongs, which shall be denominated a civil action.

See *Amended Code*, § 69. The references do not always indicate that the provision referred to and that reported are precisely the same, though we have intended to note the substantial differences.

§ 555. In such action, the party complaining is known as the plaintiff, and the adverse party as the defendant.

Amended Code, § 70.

§ 556. There can be no feigned action or issue, but a question of fact, not put in issue by the pleadings, may be tried by a jury, upon an order for the trial, stating, distinctly and plainly, the question of fact to be tried, and such order is the only authority necessary for a trial.

Amended Code, § 72.

TITLE II.

OF THE TIME OF COMMENCING CIVIL ACTIONS.

CHAPTER I.

THE TIME OF COMMENCING ACTIONS IN GENERAL.

§ 557. Civil actions can only be commenced within the periods prescribed in this title, after the cause of action shall have accrued, except where in special cases, a different limitation is prescribed by statute.

Amended Code, § 74.

CHAPTER II.

THE TIME OF COMMENCING ACTIONS FOR THE RECOVERY OF REAL PROPERTY.

§ 558. The people of this state will not sue any person for or in respect to any real property, or the issues or profits thereof, by reason of the right or title of the people to the same, unless,

1. Such right or title shall have accrued within forty years before any action, or other proceeding, for the same is commenced; or unless,

2. The people, or those from whom they claim, shall have received the rents and profits of such real property, or of some part thereof, within the space of forty years.

Amended Code, § 75.

§ 559. No action can be brought for, or in respect to, real property, by any person claiming under letters patent, or grants from the people of this state, unless the same might have been commenced by the people, as herein specified, in case such patent had not been issued or grant made.

Amended Code, § 76.

§ 560. When letters patent, or grants of real property, issued or made by the people of this state, are declared void by the determination of a competent court, rendered upon an allegation of a fraudulent suggestion, concealment, forfeiture, or mistake, or ignorance of a material fact, or wrongful detaining, or defective title, in such case, an action for the recovery of the property so conveyed, may be brought either by the people of this state, or by any subsequent patentee or grantee of the same property, his heirs or assigns, within twenty years after such determination; but not after that period.

Amended Code, § 77.

§ 561. No action for the recovery of real property, or for the recovery of the possession thereof, can be maintained, unless it appear that the plaintiff, his ancestor, predecessor, or grantor, was seised or possessed of the property in question, within twenty years before the commencement of the action.

Amended Code, § 78.

§ 562. No cause of action or defence to an action arising out of the title to real property, or to rents or services out of the same, can be effectual, unless it appear that the person prosecuting the action, or making the defence, or under whose title the action is prosecuted or the defence is made, or the ancestor, predecessor or grantor of such person, was seised or possessed of the property in question, within twenty years before the commission of the act in respect to which such action is prosecuted or defence made.

Amended Code, § 79.

§ 563. No entry upon real estate is deemed sufficient or valid as a claim, unless an action be commenced thereupon within one year after the making of the entry, and within twenty years from the time when the right to make it descended or accrued.

Amended Code, § 80.

§ 564. In every action for the recovery of real property, or the possession thereof, the person establishing a legal title to the property is presumed to have been possessed thereof within the time required by law; and the occupation of the property by any other person, is deemed to have been under and in subordination to the legal title, unless it appear that the property has been held and possessed adversely to such legal title, for twenty years before the cemmencement of the action.

Amended Code, § 81.

§ 565. When it appears that the occupant, or those under whom he claims, entered into the possession of land under claim of title, exclusive of other right, making such claim upon a written instrument, as being a conveyance of the land in question, or upon the judgment of a competent court; and that there has been a continued occupation and possession of the land included in such instrument, or judgment, or of some part of the land, under such claim, for twenty years, the land so included is deemed to have been held adversely, except that when it consists of a tract divided into lots, the possession of one lot is not deemed a possession of any other lot of the same tract.

Amended Code, § 82.

§ 566. For the purpose of constituting an adverse possession, by any person claiming a title founded upon a written instrument or a judgment, land is deemed to have been possessed and occupied in the following cases:

1. Where it has been usually cultivated or improved:

2. Where it has been protected by a substantial inclosure:

3. Where, although not inclosed, it has been used for the supply of fuel or of fencing timber, for the purposes of husbandry, or the ordinary use of the occupant:

4. Where a known farm or a single lot has been partly improved, the portion of such farm or lot that

may have been left not cleared, or not inclosed according to the custom of the adjoining country, is deemed to have been occupied for the same length of time as the part improved.

Amended Code, § 83.

§ 567. Where it appears that there has been an actual continued occupation of land, under a claim of title, exclusive of any other right, but not founded upon a written instrument, or judgment, the land so actually occupied and no other, is deemed to have been held adversely.

Amended Code, § 84.

§ 568. For the purpose of constituting an adverse possession, by a person claiming title not founded upon a written instrument, or a judgment, land is deemed to have been possessed and occupied in the following cases only, viz:

1. Where it has been protected by a permanent enclosure:

2. Where it has been usually cultivated or improved.

Amended Code, § 85.

§ 569. When the relation of landlord and tenant has existed between any persons, the possession of the tenant is deemed the possession of the landlord, until the expiration of twenty years from the termination of the tenancy; or where there has been no written lease, until the expiration of twenty years from the time of the last payment of rent; notwithstanding that such tenant may have acquired another title, or may have claimed to hold adversely to his landlord. But such presumption can not be made after the periods herein limited.

Amended Code, § 86.

570. The right of a person to the possession of real property, is not impaired or affected by a descent cast, in consequence of the death of a person in possession of such property.

Amended Code, § 87.

§ 571. If a person entitled to commence an action for the recovery of real property, or to make an entry or defence founded on the title to real property, or to rents or services out of the same, be at the time such title first descends or accrues, either,

1. Within the age of twenty-one years, or

2. Insane, or

3. Imprisoned on a criminal charge; or in execution upon conviction of a criminal offence, for a term less than for life, or

4. A married woman;

The time, during which such disability continues, is not deemed any portion of the time in this chapter limited for the commencement of such action, or the making of such entry or defence; except that the disabiliities cannot extend the period of limitation, so as to allow such action to be commenced, or entry or defence made, more than thirty years after the right accrued.

Amended Code, § 88.

The qualification at the end of this section is new. There seems no reason at the present day, for extending the limitation further than is here proposed. Actions can be brought by persons under disability, and the rights of persons in possession require that they should be brought or abandoned. It will be remembered, that the operation of this provision is prospective, and affects no rights already accrued.

CHAPTER III.

THE TIME OF COMMENCING ACTIONS OTHER THAN FOR THE RECOVERY OF REAL PROPERTY.

§ 572. The periods prescribed in section 557, for the commencement of actions other than for the recovery of real property, are as follows:

Amended Code, § 89.

§ 573. Within twenty years:

1. An action upon a judgment or decree of a court of the United States, or of any state or territory within the United States:

2. An action upon a sealed instrument:

Amended Code, § 90.

§ 574. Within six years:

1. An action upon a contract, or other obligation, express or implied; excepting those mentioned in the last section:

2. An action upon a liability created by statute, other than a penalty or forfeiture:

3. An action for trespass upon real property:

4. An action for taking, detaining or injuring personal property, including actions for the specific recovery thereof:

5. An action for criminal conversation, or for any other injury to the person or rights of another, not arising on obligation, and not hereinafter enumerated:

6. An action for relief, on the ground of fraud; the cause of action in such case not to be deemed to have accrued, until the discovery by the aggrieved party, of the facts constituting the fraud.

Amended Code, § 91.

§ 575. Within three years:

1. An action against a sheriff, coroner or constable upon a liability incurred by the doing of an act in his official capacity, and in virtue of his office, or by the omission of an official duty; including the failure to pay money collected upon an execution; but this section does not apply to an action for an escape:

2. An action upon a statute, for a penalty or forfeiture, where the action is given to the party aggrieved, or to such party and the people of this state, except where the statute imposing it prescribes a different limitation.

Amended Code, § 92.

§ 576. Within two years:

1. An action for libel, slander, assault, battery, or false imprisonment:

2. An action upon a statute, for a forfeiture or penalty to the people of this state.

Amended Code, § 93.

§ 577. Within one year:

1. An action against a sheriff or other officer, for the escape of a prisoner arrested or imprisoned on civil process.

Amended Code, § 94.

§ 978. In an action brought to recover a balance due upon a mutual, open and current account, where there have been reciprocal demands between the parties, the cause of action is deemed to have accrued, from the time of the last item proved in the account, claimed, or proved to be chargeable, on the adverse side.

Amended Code, § 95, modified as it seems to us it ought to be.

§ 579. An action upon a statute, for a penalty or forfeiture, given in whole or in part to the person who prosecutes for the same, must be commenced within one year after the commission of the offence; and if the action be not commenced within the year by a private party, it may be commenced within two years thereafter, in behalf of the people of this state, by the attorney-general or the district attorney of the county where the offence was committed.

Amended Code, § 96.

§ 580. An action for relief, not hereinbefore provided for, must be commenced within ten years after the cause of action shall have accrued.

Amended Code, § 97.

§ 581. The limitations prescribed in this chapter apply to actions brought in the name of the people of this state, or for their benefit, in the same manner as to actions by private parties.

Amended Code, § 98.

CHAPTER IV.

GENERAL PROVISIONS AS TO THE TIME OF COMMENCING ACTIONS.

§ 582. An action is commenced as to each defendant when the summons is served on him, or on a co-defendant, who is a joint contractor, or otherwise united in interest, with him.

Amended Code, § 99. This section and the next are changed in phraseology, so as to avoid the incongruity of the former provision, which allowed two modes of commencing an action inconsistent with each other.

§ 583. An attempt to commence an action, is deemed equivalent to the commencement thereof, within the meaning of this title, when the summons is delivered, with the intent that it shall be actually served, to the sheriff or other officer of the county, in which the defendants, or one of them, usually or last resided; or if a corporation be defendant, to the sheriff, or other officer, of the county, in which such corporation was established by law, or where its general business was transacted, or where it kept an office for the transaction of business. But such an attempt must be followed by the first publication of the summons, or the service thereof within sixty days.

§ 584. If, when the cause of action accrue against a person, he be out of the state, the action may be commenced within the term herein limited, after his return to the state; and if, after the cause of action accrues, he depart from the state, the time of his absence is not part of the time limited for the commencement of the action.

Amended Code, § 100.

§ 585. If a person, entitled to bring an action mentioned in the last chapter, except for a penalty or forfeiture, or against a sheriff or other officer for an escape, be at the time the cause of action accrued, either:

1. Within the age of twenty-one years; or

2. Insane; or

3. Imprisoned on a criminal charge, or in execution under the sentence of a criminal court, for a term less than his natural life; or

4. A married woman;

The time of such disability is not a part of the time limited for the commencement of the action, except that the period, within which the action must be brought, cannot be extended more than five years, by any such disability, except infancy, nor can it be so extended in any case longer than one year after the disability ceases.

Amended Code, § 101. Modified, so as to limit the time, according to the views expressed in the note to section 571.

§ 586. If a person, entitled to bring an action, die before the expiration of the time limited for the commencement thereof, and the cause of action survive, an action may be commenced by his representatives, after the expiration of that time, and within one year from his death. If a person, against whom an action may be brought, die before the expiration of the time limited for the commencement thereof, and the cause of action survive, an action may be commenced against his representatives after the expiration of that time, and within one year after the issuing of letters testamentary, or of administration.

Amended Code, § 102.

§ 587. When a person is an alien subject, or citizen of a country at war with the United States, the time of the continuance of the war is not part of the period limited for the commencement of the action.

Amended Code, § 103.

§ 588. If an action be commenced within the time prescribed therefor, and a judgment therein for the plaintiff be reversed, on appeal, the plaintiff, or if he die and the cause of action survive, his representatives may commence a new action, within one year after the reversal.

Amended Code, § 104.

§ 589. When the commencement of an action is stayed by injunction, or statutory prohibition, the time of the continuance of the injunction, or prohibition, is not part of the time limited for the commencement of the action.

Amended Code, § 105.

§ 590. No person can avail himself of a disability, unless it existed when his right of action accrued.

Amended Code, § 106.

§ 591. When two or more disabilities co-exist, at the time the right of action accrues, the limitation does not attach, until they are all removed.

Amended Code, § 107.

§ 592. This title does not affect actions to enforce the payment of bills, notes, or other evidences of debt, issued by monied corporations, or issued or put in circulation as money.

Amended Code, § 108.

§ 593. Actions against directors or stockholders of a monied corporation, or to recover a penalty or forfeiture imposed, or to enforce a liability created by law, must be brought within six years after the discovery, by the aggrieved party, of the facts upon which the penalty or forfeiture attached, or the liability was created.

Amended Code, § 109.

§ 594. No acknowledgment or promise is sufficient evidence of a new or continuing contract, by which to take the case out of the operation of this title, unless the same is contained in some writing signed by the party to be charged thereby; but this section does not alter the effect of any payment of principal or interest.

Amended Code, § 110.

§ 595. This title does not extend to actions already commenced, nor does any part of it, except section 583, extend to cases where the right of action has already accrued: but the statutes now in force are applicable to such cases, according to the subject of the action, and without regard to the form.

Amended Code, § 73.

TITLE III.

OF THE PARTIES TO CIVIL ACTIONS.

§ 596. The people of this state, in their political or corporate capacity, the United States of America, every sister state of the United States, every organized territory of the United States, every foreign state or sovereign prince in amity with the United States, all other corporations, foreign or domestic, and all natural persons, not alien enemies, or adjudged civilly dead, may be parties, plaintiffs, in the courts of this state ; every state, sovereign, and body politic mention in this section, and every other corporation and natural person may be a party, defendant.

New, for the purpose of defining who may be parties to actions in our courts.

§ 597. Every action must be prosecuted in the name of the real party in interest, except as otherwise provided in section 599.

Amended Code, § 111.

§ 598. In the case of an assignment of a thing in action, the action by the assignee is without prejudice to any set-off or other defence existing at the time of, or before notice of, the assignment; but this section does not apply to a negotiable promissory note or bill of exchange, transferred in good faith, and upon good consideration, before due.

Amended Code, § 112.

§ 599. An executor or administrator, a trustee of an express trust, or a person expressly authorised by statute, may sue without joining with him the persons for whose benefit the action is prosecuted. A person with whom, or in whose name, a contract is made, for the benefit of another, is a trustee of an express trust within the meaning of this section.

Amended Code, § 113. The last sentence is added to remove a doubt which has been expressed.

§ 600. When a married woman is a party, her husband must be joined with her, except that,

1. When the action concerns her separate property, she may sue alone:

2. When the action is between herself and her husband, she may sue or be sued alone.

Amended Code, § 114.

§ 601. If a husband and wife be sued together, the wife may defend for her own right, and if the husband neglect to defend, she may defend for his right also.

See 2 *R. S.*, 340, *sections* 4 & 5. There is no reason why the provision should not be extended to all actions as well as those concerning real property.

§ 602. When an infant is a party, he must appear by guardian, who may be appointed by the court in which the action is prosecuted, or by a judge thereof.

Amended Code, § 115.

§ 603. The guardian must be appointed as follows:

1. When the infant is plaintiff, upon the application of the infant, if he be of the age of fourteen years, or if under that age, upon the application of some other party to the action, or of a relative or friend of the infant:

2. When the infant is defendant, upon the application of the infant, if he be of the age of fourteen years, and apply within twenty days after the service of the summons. If he be under the age of fourteen, or neglect so to apply, then upon the application of any other party to the action, or of a relative or friend of the infant.

Amended Code, § 116.

§ 604. An unmarried female may prosecute, as plaintiff, an action for her own seduction, and may recover therein such damages as shall be assessed in her favor.

The purpose of this section and the next is to wipe away from our law a reproach, to which it has long been subject, that of giving no adequate remedy for one of the greatest offences against society, which a man can commit, that of seduction. At present the law gives only an action to the parent, or to one who stands in his relation, founded upon the notion, that he has suffered a pecuniary injury by the loss of service of the person seduced. Now the seduction of a woman, by which is meant inducing her, by persuasion, threats, or fraud, to consent to the sacrifice of her virtue, is an injury to herself and to her relations, of the gravest character. For this injury the law should provide a remedy, not by means of a fiction, but open and direct, in favor of the person injured.

The objection, that will be made to an action by the woman, is that she has consented to the act. That however does not seem to us an answer, for two reasons. First, there are many other cases, where the law does now give an action for an injury to a party consenting; or for example, in the case of property obtained by false representation or other fraud, money lost upon stocks, at play, or borrowed upon usury. Secondly, the woman and her seducer do not stand upon equal grounds; she is the weaker party, and the victim of his arts.

With this short statement of our own views, and the following passage from Paley, we submit these sections to the judgment of the legislature.

"The seducer practices the same stratagems to draw a woman's person into his power, that a swindler does to get possession of your goods or money; yet the law of honor, which abhors deceit, applauds the address of a successful intrigue; so much is this capricious rule guided by names, and with such facility does it accommodate itself to the pleasures and conveniency of higher life.

Seduction is seldom accomplished without fraud; and the fraud is by so much more criminal than other frauds, as the injury effected by it is greater, continues longer, and less admits reparation.

This injury is threefold; to the woman; to her family; and to the public.

1. The injury to the woman is made up of the pain she suffers from shame, or the loss she sustains in her reputation and prospects of marriage, and of the depravation of her moral principle.

1. This pain must be extreme, if we may judge of it from those barbarous endeavors to conceal their disgrace, to which women, under such circumstances, sometimes have recourse; comparing also their barbarity with their passionate fondness for their offspring in other cases. Nothing but an agony of mind the most insupportable can induce a woman to forget her nature, and the pity which even a stranger would show to a helpless and imploring infant. It is true, that all are not urged to this extremity; but if any are, it affords an indication of how much all suffer from the same cause. What shall we say to the authors of such mischief?

2. The loss which a woman sustains by the ruin of her reputation, almost exceeds computation. Every person's happiness depends in part upon the respect and reception which they meet with in the world; and it is no inconsiderable mortification, even to the firmest temper, to be rejected from the society of their equals, or received by them with neglect and disdain. But this is not all, nor the worst. By a rule of life, which it is not easy to blame, and which it is impossible to alter, a woman loses with her chastity the chance of marrying at all, or in any manner equal to the hopes she had been accustomed to entertain. Now marriage, whatever it be to a man, is that from which every woman expects her chief happiness. And this is still more true in low life, of which condition the women are, who are most exposed to solicitations of this sort. Add to this, that when a woman's maintenance depends upon her character, (as it does in a great measure, with those who are to support themselves by service,) little

sometimes is left to the forsaken sufferer, but to starve for want of employment, or to have recourse to prostitution for food and raiment.

3. As a woman collects her virtue into this point, the loss of her chastity is generally the destruction of her moral principles; and this consequence is to be apprehended, whether the criminal intercourse be discontinued or not.

II. The injury to the family may be understood, by the application of that infallible rule, "of doing to others, what we would that others should do unto us." Let a father or brother say, for what consideration they would suffer this injury to a daughter or sister; and whether any, even a total loss of fortune, could create equal affliction or distress. And when they reflect upon this, let them distinguish, if they can, between a robbery, committed upon their property by fraud or forgery, and the ruin of their happiness by the treachery of a seducer.

III. The public at large lose the benefit of the woman's service in her proper place and destination, as a wife and parent. This to the whole community may be little; but it is often more than all the good, which the seducer does to the community, can recompense. Moreover prostitution is supplied by seduction; and in proportion to the danger there is of the woman, betaking herself, after her first sacrifice, to a life of public lewdness, the seducer is answerable for the multiplied evils to which his crime gives birth.

Upon the whole, if we pursue the effects of seduction through the complicated misery which it occasions, and if it be right to estimate crimes by the mischief they knowingly produce, it will appear something more than mere invective to assert, that not one half of the crimes, for which men suffer death, by the laws of England, are so flagitious as this.

Yet the law has provided no punishment for this offence, beyond a pecuniary satisfaction to the injured family; and this can only be come at, by one of the quaintest fictions in the world; by the father's bringing his action against the seducer, for the loss of his daughter's service, during her pregnancy and nurturing." Paley's Moral Philosophy, p. 199.

§ 605. A father, or in case of his death or desertion of his family, the mother, may prosecute as plaintiff for the seduction of the daughter, and the guardian for the seduction of the ward, though the daughter or ward be not living with, or in the service of, the plaintiff, at the time of the seduction or afterwards, and there be no loss of service.

§ 606. A father, or in case of his death or desertion of his family, the mother, may maintain an action for the injury or death of a child, and a guardian for the injury or death of his ward.

To settle a question of some doubt.

§ 607. When a husband and father has deserted his family, the wife and mother may prosecute or defend, in his name, any action which he might have prosecuted or defended, and shall have the same powers and rights therein as he might have had.

To provide for cases of great hardship, that sometimes happen.

§ 608. All persons having an interest in the subject of the action, and in obtaining the relief demanded, may be joined as plaintiffs, except when otherwise provided in this title.

Amended Code, § 117.

§ 609. Any person may be made a defendant, who has or claims an interest in the controversy, adverse to the plaintiff, or who is a necessary party to a complete determination or settlement of the question involved therein.

Amended Code, § 118.

§ 610. Of the parties to the action, those who are united in interest must be joined as plaintiffs or defendants; but if the consent of any one, who should have been joined as plaintiff, cannot be obtained, he may be made a defendant, the reason thereof being stated in the complaint: and when the question is one of a common or general interest of many persons, or when the parties are numerous and it is impracticable to bring them all before the court, one or more may sue or defend for the benefit of all.

Amended Code, § 119.

§ 611. Persons severally liable upon the same obligation or instrument, including the parties to bills of exchange and promissory notes, and sureties on the same or separate instruments, may, all or any of them, be included in the same action, at the option of the plaintiff.

Amended Code. § 120, *amended.*

§ 612. An action does not abate by the death, marriage or other disability of a party, or by the transfer of any interest therein, if the cause of action survive or continue. In case of the death, marriage, or other disability of a party, the court on motion, may allow the action to be continued by or against his representative or successor in interest. In case of any other transfer of interest, the action may be continued in the name of the original party; or the court may allow the person to whom the transfer is made to be substituted in the action.

Amended Code, § 121.

§ 613. The court may determine any controversy between parties before it, when it can be done without prejudice to the rights of others, or by saving their rights; but when a complete determination of the controversy cannot be had without the presence of other parties, the court must order them to be brought in. And when, in an action for the recovery of real or personal property, a person, not a party to the action, but having an interest in the subject thereof, makes application to the court to be made a party, it may order him to be brought in by the proper amendment.

Amended Code, § 122.

§ 614. A defendant, against whom an action is pending, upon a contract, or for specific, real, or personal property, may, at any time before answer, upon affidavit, that a person, not a party to the action, and without collusion with him, makes against him a demand for the same debt or property, apply to the court for an order to substitute such person in his place, and discharge him from liability to either party, on his depositing in court the amount of the debt, or delivering the property or its value to such person as the court may direct. And the court, after notice to the plaintiff and such person, may, in its discretion, make the order;

and thereupon the substituted defendant shall stand in the place of the original defendant, and the latter be discharged from liability to either party.

The object of this section is to save the necessity, in most cases, of an action to compel two parties, claiming the same thing, to settle the controversy between them by interpleading. The interpleader act in England was passed for the same purpose.

§ 615. When two or more persons, associated in any business, transact such business under a common name, whether it comprise the names of such persons or not, the associates may be sued by such common name, the summons in such case being served on one or more of the associates; and the judgment in the action shall bind the joint property of all the associates in the same manner as if all had been named defendants, and had been sued upon their joint liability. Any one of the associates may also be sued for the obligation of all.

See Laws of 1836, *chap.* 385.

TITLE IV.

OF THE PLACE OF TRIAL OF CIVIL ACTIONS.

§ 616. Actions for the following causes, must be tried in the county in which the subject of the action or some part thereof is situated, subject to the power of the court to change the place of trial, as provided in section 620:

1. For the recovery of real property or of an estate or interest therein, or for the determination, in any form, of such right or interest, and for injuries to real property:

2. For the partition of real property:

3. For the foreclosure of a mortgage of real property:

4. For the recovery of personal property, distrained for any cause.

Amended Code, § 123.

§ 617. Actions for the following causes, must be tried in the county where the cause or some part thereof arose, subject to the like power of the court, to change the place of trial, as,

1. For the recovery of a penalty or forfeiture imposed by statute; except, that when it is imposed for an offence committed on a lake, river, or other stream of water, situated in two or more counties, the action may be brought in any county bordering on such lake, river or stream, and opposite to the place where the offence was committed:

2. Against a public officer or person specially appointed to execute his duties, for an act done by him in virtue of his office, or against a person, who by his command or in his aid, does anything touching the duties of such officer.

Amended Code, § 124.

§ 618. In all other cases, the action must be tried in the county in which the parties or some of them reside at the commencement of the action; or if none of the parties reside in the state, the same may be tried in any county which the plaintiff may designate in his complaint; subject, however to the power of the court to change the place of trial, as provided in section 620.

Amended Code, § 125.

§ 619. If the county designated for that purpose in the complaint, be not the proper county, the action may, notwithstanding, be tried therein, unless the defendant before the time for answering expire, demand in writing that the trial be had in the proper county, and the place of trial be thereupon changed by consent of parties, or by the order of the court, as provided in the next section.

Amended Code, § 126.

§ 620. The court may change the place of trial on the application of all the defendants, who answer in the following cases:

1. When the county designated for that purpose in the complaint is not the proper county:

2. When there is reason to believe that an impartial trial cannot be had therein:

3. When the convenience of witnesses and the ends of justice would be promoted by the change.

New, for the purpose of declaring the cases in which the place of trial may be changed by order of the court.

TITLE V.

OF THE MANNER OF COMMENCING CIVIL ACTIONS.

§ 621. Civil actions in the courts of this state must be commenced by the service of a summons.

Amended Code, § 127.

§ 622. The summons must be subscribed by the plaintiff, or his attorney, and directed to the defendant, requiring him to answer the complaint, and serve a copy of his answer on the person whose name is subscribed to the summons, at a place within the state, therein specified, in which there is a post office, within twenty days after the service of the summons, exclusive of the day of service.

Amended Code, § 128.

§ 623. The plaintiff must also insert in the summons a notice, in substance as follows:

1. In an action, arising on obligation for the recovery of money only, that he will take judgment for a

sum specified therein, if the defendant fail to answer the complaint:

2. In other actions, that if the defendant fail to answer the complaint, the plaintiff will apply to the court for the relief demanded therein.

Amended Code, § 129.

§ 624. A copy of the complaint must be served with the summons, unless the complaint itself be already on the files of the court. In the latter case, the service of a copy with the summons may be omitted, but then the summons must state where the complaint is filed; and if the defendant, within ten days thereafter, in person or by attorney, demand in writing, a copy of the complaint, specifying a place within the state where it may be served, a copy thereof must be served accordingly, and after such service the defendant has twenty days to answer; but only one copy need be served on the same attorney.

Amended Code, § 130.

It will be seen, that this section differs from the code as amended in this important respect, that while the latter permits a plaintiff to commence an action without filing or serving his complaint, the former requires it to be either filed or served.

The reason for the change is this. If a defendant be served with a summons, requiring him merely to answer a complaint, which will be filed, he must, almost as a matter of necessity, employ a lawyer, to see that no advantage is taken of him. But if the summons inform the defendant that the complaint against him is on file, and where he may find it, or, what is better, if it be accompanied by a copy, he can determine for himself in most cases, whether there be any occasion for him to make a defence. If it be desirable to relieve defendants, as far as possible, from the necessity of employing a lawyer, then the section, as we have it, ought to stand.

If it be objected, that there are cases of great urgency, not admitting of the delay incident to the preparation of a complaint, it is to be answered, that such cases are very rare, that an arrest or other provisional remedy cannot in any case be had, without an affidavit, which requires as much time as a complaint, and that formerly no serious embarrassment resulted from requiring a bill to be filed before an injunction was issued.

§ 625. In the case of a defendant against whom no personal claim is made, the plaintiff may deliver to him with the summons, a notice subscribed by the plaintiff or his attorney, setting forth the general object of the action, a brief description of the property affected by it, if it affect specific real or personal property, and that no personal claim is made against such defendant. If a defendant, on whom such notice is served, unreasonably defend the action he must pay costs to the plaintiff.

Amended Code, § 130. Changed, so as to embrace every action instead of confining it, as before, to actions for partition of real property or foreclosure of mortgages.

§ 626. In an action affecting the title to real property, the plaintiff, at the time of filing the complaint, or at any time afterwards, may file with the clerk of each county in which the property is situated, a notice of the pendency of the action, containing the names of the parties, the object of the action, and a description of the property in that county affected thereby. If the action be for the foreclosure of a mortgage, such notice must be filed twenty days before judgment, and must contain the date of the mortgage, the names of the parties thereto, and the time and place of recording the same. From the time of filing, and for two years thereafter only, the pendency of the action is constructive notice to a purchaser or incumbrancer of the property affected thereby, but the notice may be refiled from time to time with the same effect.

Amended Code, § 132.

§ 627. The summons may be served, by the sheriff of the county where the defendant is found, or by any other person not a party to the action. The service must be made, and the summons returned, with proof of the service, to the person whose name is subscribed thereto, with all reasonable diligence. The person subscribing the summons, may, at his option, by an endorsement on the summons, fix a time for the service thereof, and the service must then be made accordingly.

Amended Code, § 133.

§ 628. The summons must be served by delivering a copy thereof, as follows:

1. If the suit be against a corporation, to the president or other head of the corporation, secretary, cashier, or managing agent thereof:

2. If against a minor under the age of fourteen years, to such minor personally, and also to his father, mother,

or guardian, or if there be none within the state, then to any person having the care and control of such minor, or with whom he resides or in whose service he is employed:

3. If against a person judicially declared to be of unsound mind, or incapable of conducting his own affairs in consequence of habitual drunkenness, and for whom a committee has been appointed, to such committee, and to the defendant personally:

4. In all other cases to the defendant personally.

Amended Code, § 134.

§ 629. Where the person on whom the service of the summons is to be made, cannot, after due diligence, be found within the state, and that fact appears by affidavit to the satisfaction of the court or a judge thereof, and it in like manner appears, that a cause of action exists against the defendant, in respect to whom the service is to be made, or that he is a necessary or proper party to an action, relating to real property in this state, such court or judge may grant an order that the service be made, by the publication of a summons, in either of the following cases:

1. Where the defendant is a foreign corporation:

2. Where the defendant being a resident of this state, has departed therefrom, with intent to defraud his creditors, or avoid the service of a summons, or keeps himself concealed therein, with the like intent, and the action arises on obligation:

3. Where he is not a resident of this state, but has property therein, and the action arises on obligation, and the court has jurisdiction of the subject of the action:

4. Where the subject of the action is real or personal property in this state, and the defendant has, or claims, a lien or interest, actual or contingent, therein, or the relief demanded consists, wholly or partly, in excluding the defendant from any interest therein:

5. Where the action arises upon a mortgage on property in this state, and the defendant is personally chargeable with the debt for which the mortgage is security:

6. Where the action is for divorce, in the cases prescribed by law.

Amended Code, § 135.

§ 630. The order must direct the publication to be made in two newspapers to be designated, as most likely to give notice to the person to be served, and for such length of time as may be deemed reasonable, not less than once a week, for six weeks. In case of publication, the court or judge must also direct a copy of the summons and complaint, to be forthwith deposited in the post office, directed to the person to be served, at his place of residence, unless it appear that such esidence is neither known to the party making the application, nor can with reasonable diligence be ascertained by him. When publication is ordered, personal service of a copy of the summons and complaint, out of the state, is equivalent to publication, and deposite in the post office. In either case the service of the summons is to be deemed complete, at the expiration of the time prescribed by the order for publication.

Amended Code, § 135.

§ 631. If the summons be not personally served on a defendant, nor received by him through the post office, in the cases provided for in the last two sections, he or his representatives, on application and sufficient cause shown, at any time before judgment, must be allowed to defend the action; and, except in an action for divorce, the defendant or his representatives, may in like manner, be allowed to defend after judgment, or at any time within one year after notice thereof, and within seven years after its rendition, on such terms as may be just; and if the defence be successful, and the judgment, or any part thereof, have been collected or otherwise enforced, such restitution may thereupon be compelled as the court directs.

Amended Code, § 135.

§ 632. Where the action is against two or more defendants, and the summons is served on one or more, but not on all of them, the plaintiff may proceed as follows:

1. If the action be against the defendants jointly indebted upon an obligation, he may proceed against the defendants served, unless the court otherwise direct,

and if he recover judgment, it may be entered against all the defendants thus jointly indebted, so far only as that it may be enforced against the joint property of all, and the separate property of the defendants served, and, if they are subject to arrest, against their persons: or,

2. If the action be against defendants severally liable, he may proceed against the defendants served, in the same manner as if they were the only defendants.

Amended Code, §136. Modified, so as to explain the mode of proceeding without reference to the former law.

§ 633. Proof of the service of the summons, and of the complaint or notice, if any, accompanying the same must be as follows:

1. If served by the sheriff, his certificate thereof; or

2. If by any other person, his affidavit thereof; or

3. In case of publication, the affidavit of the printer, or his foreman, or principal clerk, showing the same; and an affidavit of a deposit of a copy of the summons in the post office, if the same shall have been deposited: or

4. The written admission of the defendant:

In case of service, otherwise than by publication, the certificate, affidavit or admission must state the time and place of the service.

Amended Code, § 138.

§ 634. From the time of the service of the summons in a civil action, or the allowance of a provisional remedy, the court is deemed to have acquired jurisdiction, and to have control of all the subsequent proceedings. A voluntary appearance of a defendant is equivalent to personal service of the summons upon him.

Amended Code, § 139. Enlarged, so as to include a voluntary appearance without service of process.

TITLE VI.

OF THE PLEADINGS IN CIVIL ACTIONS.

CHAPTER I.

THE PLEADINGS IN GENERAL.

§ 635. The pleadings are the formal allegations by the parties of their respective claims and defences, for the judgment of the court.

§ 636. All the forms of pleading heretofore existing, are abolished; and hereafter, the forms of pleading in civil actions, and the rules by which the sufficiency of the pleadings is to be determined, are those prescribed in this code.

Original Code, § 118.

§ 637. The only pleadings allowed on the part of the plaintiff are

1. The complaint,

2. The reply; and on the part of the defendant,

1. The demurrer, or

2. The answer.

Amended Code, § 141--143 *and* 156.

CHAPTER II.

THE COMPLAINT.

§ 638. The first pleading on the part of the plaintiff, is the complaint.

Amended Code, § 141.

§ 639. The complaint must contain:

1. The title of the cause, specifying the name of the court in which the action is brought, the name of the county in which the plaintiff desires the trial to be had, and the names of the parties to the action, plaintiff and defendant:

2. A statement of the facts constituting the cause of action, in ordinary and concise language, without repetition, and in such a manner as to enable a person of common understanding to know what is intended:

3. A demand of the relief, to which the plaintiff supposes himself entitled. If the recovery of money be demanded, the amount thereof must be stated.

Amended Code, § 142.

CHAPTER III.

THE DEMURRER.

§ 640. The defendant may demur to the complaint, within twenty days after the service of a copy thereof, when it appears upon the face thereof, either,

1. That the court has no jurisdiction of the person of the defendant, or the subject of the action: or,

2. That the plaintiff has not legal capacity to sue: or,

3. That there is another action pending between the same parties, for the same cause: or,

4. That there is a defect of parties, plaintiff or defendant: or,

5. That several causes of action have been improperly united: or,

6. That the complaint does not state facts sufficient to constitute a cause of action.

Amended Code, § 144.

In the Code, as originally reported, a demurrer was only allowed to a complaint. Demurrers to answers and replies are allowed by an amendment made at the last session. The Commissioners adhere to their former system, and recommend that there should not be a demurrer to an answer or reply. The question is important as a question of time. Demurrers are considerable hindrances to the progress of a cause. Now, the defendant puts in his answer at his peril; but the risk of mischance is small. If he have a defence, it is scarcely possible he should lose it. But if demurrers be allowed, they will become fruitful sources of expense and delay. A demurrer to an answer was not allowed in chancery, and no harm ever came from its exclusion. If the restoration we propose be not made, not only will demurrers often be interposed to answers, as a means of harrassing defendants and subjecting them to expense, but demurrers to replies will be resorted to by defendants who desire delay.

§ 641. The demurrer must distinctly specify the grounds upon which any of the objections to the complaint are taken. Unless it do so, it may be disregarded. It may be taken to the whole complaint, or to any of the causes of action alleged therein.

Amended Code, § 145.

§ 642. If the complaint be amended, a copy thereof must be served on the defendant, who must answer it within twenty days, or the plaintiff, upon filing with the clerk proof of the service, and of the defendant's omission, may proceed to obtain judgment, as in other cases of failure to answer, but where an application to the court for judgment is necessary, eight days' notice thereof must be givento the defendant.

Amended Code, § 146.

§ 643. When any of the matters enumerated in section 640 do not appear upon the face of the complaint, the objection may be taken by answer.

Amended Code, § 147.

§ 644. If no such objection be taken, either by demurrer or answer, the defendant must be deemed to have waived the same, excepting only the objection to the jurisdiction of the court, and the objection that the complaint does not state facts sufficient to constitute a cause of action.

Amended Code, § 148.

CHAPTER IV.

THE ANSWER.

§ 645. The answer of the defendant must contain:

1. A denial of each allegation of the complaint controverted by the defendant, or of any knowledge or information thereof, sufficient to form a belief:

2. A statement of any new matter, constituting a defence or counterclaim, in ordinary and concise language, without repetition, and in such a manner as to enable a person of common understanding to know what is intended.

Amended Code, § 149.

§ 646. The counterclaim mentioned in the last section, must be one existing in favor of a defendant, and against a plaintiff, between whom a several judgment might be had in the action, and arising out of one of the following causes of action:

1. A cause of action, arising out of the contract or transaction set forth in the complaint, as the foundation of the plaintiff's claim, or connected with the subject of the action:

2. In an action arising on obligation, any other cause of action arising also on obligation, and existing at the commencement of the action.

In what cases a cross-demand should be litigated in the same action with the original claim, is a question of some importance. On one side it is said, that there is great inconvenience in having several distinct controversies thrown together into one trial; while on the other it is answered, that there is a greater inconvenience in having several law-suits, where one would answer the purpose.

The statute of set-off was the first innovation upon the common law. That, however, was quite limited in its operation. Of late years, the courts have let in a new set of cross-demands, under the name of recoupement. We propose in this section to open the door still wider, and to admit many cross-demands, now excluded. Further experience may show, that the door should be opened wider still.

The first subdivision of this section is intended to remove a doubt which has been sometimes expressed, whether affirmative relief can be given, upon an answer setting up a defence which heretofore would have been accounted equitable only. For example, in the case of an action to dispossess an occupant of land; the defendant claims to occupy under a contract to purchase, and asks on his part for a judgment that the plaintiff give him a conveyance. It is the intention of the code, that the whole controversy between the parties should be settled in one action, and that either plaintiff or defendant should have such relief, as the nature of the case requires. It is as easy to do this, as it is to decide upon what was considered a mere equitable defence to a legal demand, and there is no difficulty in either.

Suppose an action upon a written agreement to recover damages for not performing it. The defendant answers that the writing does not express the intention of the parties, and that he did perform it according to the real agreement between them. Is such a defence admissable under the code? That question involves another, which is this; is the agreement by the law of the land binding upon the defendant as it stands, or is it not?

Now if it be not binding upon him, that is, if before the code he could by any form of action get rid of it, he can do so now in the action prosecuted under the code. The effect of the code is to open the door to remedies without disturbing rights. It has not changed the rights of the parties. It has simplified and shortened their remedies.

It should be borne in mind, that the rules of courts of equity are already in numberless instances administered by courts of law, even in those states where courts of equity exist, and universally in those states where there are no courts of equity, so far as the strict forms of common law courts will allow. Take the case of Pennsylvania. The common law courts have from time immemorial administered equity law. The only embarrassment that has attended it, has arisen from the imperfect machinery of the courts of law. If they had enlarged their forms, as our code has enlarged them, their system would have been excellent. Their courts of law have always held that the defendant may set up an equitable defence. In the case of Jordan & Cooper 3, S. & R. 578, Chief Justice Tighlman said, "That equity is a part of the law of Pennsylvania, has never been disputed, and that a defendant may put in a plea founded upon equity only, is equally clear."

A jurist of Pennsylvania, in an edition of an English work on Equity, uses the following remarkable language :

"The rules of equity being consolidated with those of law, it is evident that our only deficiency is in the special *machinery* of chancery, where that machinery is better adapted than the forms of law to the due attainment of justice. Whether it is not more consistent with judicial perfection, that there should be a single rule of action for every subject matter, serving all courts alike, and whether the better mode of improving the jurisprudence of the state, would not be to foster the growth of a mixed system, that may in time combine the advantages of law and equity with amendments of their known imperfections, are great problems that have occupied the most distinguished jurists of all ages, and are not likely soon to receive an acknowledged solution." (1 Fonblanque's Equity, 4th Am. edition, p. 20.)

Indeed it may now be considered an inevitable tendency of the times, to obliterate the distinction between legal and equitable forms, and to administer law and equity, in one tribunal and one action. Even in England, the country where the resistance to innovation is strongest, there appear to be indications of a movement in that direction. In a late number of the Law Magazine, a journal of authority in that country, there is an article on English and Scottish judicature, in which the following language is used—"The system," that is, the administration of law and equity separately, "is not one, that can, in any absolute and conclusive sense, try, hear, and determine the merits of any cause. It does not begin at the beginning and go on to the end. It moves here and it moves there, with ever and anon some by-battle on extrinsic questions, by such edifying enlighteners of *the merits of a cause* (*!*) as demurers on the ground of duplicity, demurrers for want of equity, demurrers to the jurisdiction, and the like, for which of course the litigants have to pay—but it does not by its direct and immediate operation ascertain the truth of the controversy. It does not profess to do so. The several courts *minister to* but do not *administer justice.* They may exhaust all their judicial powers, but something will be left behind. The law courts will not deal with "the equities," the courts of equity will not interfere where law has jurisdiction, and thus the suitor is tossed about from court to court—it is a sort of battledore and shuttlecock litigation—and the un fortunate litigant has to incur the costs of both courts, and that, be it observed, for one single remedy, demandable wit reference to one particular state of facts!"

And again p. 67, " In this country however, equity decides equity, and law decides law. But is there, we ask, for it comes to this, is there in all England a single tribunal which ADMINISTERS JUSTICE? Would it be presumptuous in us, would it be untrue to say there is NOT?

§ 647. If the defendant omit to set up a counter-claim in the cases mentioned in the first sub-division of the last section, he cannot afterwards maintain an action against the plaintiff therefor.

§ 648. When cross demands have existed between persons, under such circumstances, that if one had brought an action against the other, a counter-claim could have been set up, neither can be deprived of the benefit thereof, by the assignment or death of the other, but the two demands must be deemed compensated, so far as they equal each other.

§ 649. The defendant may set forth by answer, as many defences and counter-claims as he may have. They must each be separately stated, and the several defences must refer to the causes of action which they are intended to answer, in a manner by which they may be intelligibly distinguished. The defendant may also answer one or more of the several causes of action alleged in the complaint and demur to the residue.

Amended Code, § 150.

§ 650. If the answer set up new matter, which is not replied to as provided in the next section, and the issue be tried on complaint and answer alone, and judgment be given thereon for the plaintiff, the court may permit the defendant to withdraw or amend the answer, unpon such terms as may be just.

See § 130 of original code.

CHAPTER V.

THE REPLY.

SECTION 651. When the answer contains a counter-claim, a reply may be put in, and what it may contain.

§ 651. When the answer contains new matter constituting a counter-claim, the plaintiff may within twenty days, reply to such new matter, denying each allegation controverted by him, or any knowledge or information thereof sufficient to form a belief; and he may allege, in ordinary and concise language, without repetition, and in such a manner as to enable a person of common understanding to know what is intended, any new matter, not inconsistent with the complaint, constituting a defence to the counter-claim.

Amended Code, § 153.

In respect to the reply, we propose this modification; that it shall only be required, when the answer sets up a counter-claim. When the answer is drawn by a very wary or a very unskilful hand, the sentences become sometimes so involved, and the admissions or denials so clogged with qualifications, that it is not easy to separate the new matter from that which is strictly responsive to the complaint. If the pleader would confine himself to facts strictly pertinent to the case, and would state these in distinct allegations separately numbered, there would be no difficulty. When this is not done, and the answer is loosely drawn, the reply under the existing rule may occasion some embarrassment. To obviate this, we propose, that the reply be confined to the case of a counter-claim; in which case it seems indispensible, for the cross demand is of the nature of a new action by the defendant against the plaintiff, to which the latter ought to make answer.

CHAPTER VI.

GENERAL RULES OF PLEADING.

§ 652. Every pleading must be subscribed by the party, or his attorney, and the complaint, answer and reply, must be verified by the party, his agent or attorney, to the effect that he believes it to be true. The verification must be made, by the affidavit of the party, or, if there be several parties united in interest and pleading together, by one at least of such parties, if such party be within the state and capable of making the affidavit; otherwise the affidavit may be made by the agent or attorney of the party. The affidavit may also be made by the agent or attorney, if the action or defence be founded upon a written instrument for the payment of money only, and such instrument be in the possession of the agent or attorney, or if all the material allegations of the pleading be within the personal knowledge of the agent or attorney. When the affidavit is made by the agent or attorney, it must set forth the reason of his making it.

The verification may be omitted, when an admission of the truth of the complaint might subject the party to prosecution for felony. And no pleading, verified as herein required, can be used in a criminal prosecution against the party, as proof of a fact admitted or alleged in such pleading.

Amended Code, § 157.

This section, it will be perceived, is changed from the form which it bears, in the amended code, to that substantially which the Commissioners recommended in their second report. The original code required the pleadings to be verified in all cases, except when the party would be privileged from testifying as a witness to the same matters; the amended code requires it only in those cases where the previous pleading has been verified. So that the plaintiff may in all cases verify his complaint or not, as he pleases; if, however, he do verify it, then the answer must be verified, otherwise it need not. Still the defendant may, if he choose, verify his answer, and in that case the reply must be verified. The difference between the two schemes is this, that the one does not permit a party to make an allegation, when he is not willing to make oath of his belief in it; the other permits him to make what allegations he pleases, whether he believes them or not.

Ought these solemn allegations of the parties, which are called pleadings, and which set forth the cause of action and defence, to be verified or not? The solution of this question depends upon two others: first, whether a party should be allowed to aver what he does not believe; and second, whether there be any better test of his belief, than his own affidavit. Both questions admit of easy answers.

There are several reasons, why a party should not be permitted to aver, in a court of justice, what he does not believe:

First. The courts are, or should be, schools of morals. It becomes them to set virtuous examples. Of all the institutions of society, they should be most sacred to truth. Whenever, therefore, they sanction, connive at, or open the door to untruths, they falsify their own professions, and become the corrupters, rather than the teachers of mankind.

Second. Men should be protected, as far as possible, against false charges. It is signally unjust, that any person should vex another with a claim, founded upon statements which he does not believe. Nay more, it is the highest duty of society, to protect every member of it in the enjoyment of his rights. What sort of protection does it afford, if it allows their rights to be assailed by every adventurer, even though he furnishes, not only no security against his misconduct, and no proofs of his charge, but no test of his sincerity, not so much even as his affidavit of belief in it.

Third. Lawsuits are a disadvantage to society at large. They require a large array of public officers. They require the attendance of citizens, either as jurors or as witnesses, to the detriment of their own affairs. It seems consequently most fit, that a check, at least as great as this, should be interposed to the prosecution of frivolous or fictitious lawsuits.

Fourth. If the party be not confined in his pleading to what he believes, no adequate reform in pleading can ever be affected. Should the rule adopted by the last legislature be retained, plaintiffs may put in the old form of declarations as complaints under the code; defendants then must answer every allegation specifically, or it will be taken as true. Will this be tolerated any considerable length of time? It will not; and then either the oath will be required; or this rule of pleading will be abrogated, and the general issue, as formerly brought into use.

If then it be clear, that no party should be allowed to aver in a court of justice what he does not believe, the remaining inquiry is, whether there be any better test of one's belief than his affidavit. Here there seems no room for question. The oath is the universal test applied to the consciences of witnesses. If it be good for the witnesses, it is equally good for the litigants.

What reason is there, that the affidavit should not be required? The multiplication of oaths, says one. Then abolish oaths altogether. Let witnesses be no more sworn. But so long as you administer the oath to the witness, require it also of the party. Requiring it of him, so far from multiplying oaths, diminishes them. For every oath required of a party more than two witnesses are dispensed with. Who that is at all conversant with the courts, but knows, that every day in court sees numerous witnesses brought, at great inconvenience to themselves, to swear to facts, which the parties would not dare deny, if they were put to their oaths. Can there be a doubt which is better, to harrass the witnesses, or to purge the consciences of the parties?

§ 653. It is not necessary for a party to set forth in a pleading the items of an account therein alleged, where they exceed twenty in number, but he must deliver to the adverse party, within ten days, after a demand thereof in writing, a copy of the account verified by his own oath, or that of his agent or attorney, to the effect that he believes it to be true, or be precluded from giving evidence thereof. The court, or a judge thereof, or a county judge, may order a further account, when the one delivered is defective.

Amended Code, § 158.

§ 654. In the construction of a pleading, for the purpose of determining its effect, its allegations must be liberally constued, with a view to substantial justice between the parties.

Amended Code, § 159.

§ 655. If irrelevant or redundant matter be inserted in a pleading, it may be stricken out, on motion of any person aggrieved thereby. And when the allegations of a pleading are so indefinite or uncertain, that the precise nature of the charge or defence is not apparent, the court may require the pleading to be made definite and certain, by amendment.

Amended Code, § 160.

§ 656. In an action for the recovery of real property, it must be described in the complaint with such convenient certainty, as to enable an officer upon execution to identify it.

2 *R. S.*, 304, *s.* 8.

§ 657. In pleading a judgment, or other determination, of a court or officer of special jurisdiction, it is not necessary to state the facts conferring jurisdiction, but such judgment or determination may be stated to have been duly given or made. If such allegation be controverted, the party pleading must establish on the trial, the facts conferring jurisdiction.

Amended Code, § 161.

§ 658. In pleading the performance of conditions precedent in a contract, it is not necessary to state the facts, showing such performance; but it may be stated generally, that the party duly performed all the conditions on his part; and if such allegation be controverted, the party pleading must establish on the trial the facts showing such performance.

Amended Code, § 162.

§ 659. In pleading a private statute, or a right derived therefrom, it is sufficient to refer to such statute, by its title and the day of its passage, and the court must thereupon take judicial notice thereof.

Amended Code, § 163.

§ 660. In an action for libel or slander, it is not necessary to state in the complaint, any extrinsic facts, for the purpose of showing the application to the plaintiff, of the defamatory matter out of which the cause of action arose; but it is sufficient to state generally, that the same was published or spoken concerning the plaintiff, and if such allegation be controverted, the plaintiff must establish, on the trial, that it was so published or spoken.

Amended Code, § 164.

§ 661. In the actions mentioned in the last section, the defendant may in his answer, allege both the truth of the matter charged as defamatory, and any mitigating circumstances, to reduce the amount of damages; and whether he prove the justification or not, he may give in evidence the mitigating circumstances.

Amended Code, § 165.

§ 662. In an action to recover the possession of property distrained for doing damage, an answer that the defendant, or person by whose command he acted, was lawfully possessed of the real property upon which the distress was made, and that the property distrained was at the time doing damage thereon, is sufficien without setting forth the title to such real property.

Amended Code, § 166.

§ 663. The plaintiff may unite several causes of ac tion in the same complaint, where they all arise out of

1. Contract, express or implied: or,

2. Claims to recover specific real property, with o without damages, for the withholding thereof, and th rents and profits of the same: or,

3. Claims to recover specific personal property, witl or without damages, for the withholding thereof: or,

4. Claims against a trustee, by virtue of a contract, o by operation of law: or,

5. Injuries to character: or,

6. Other injuries to person and property, or either:

But the causes of action, so united, must all belon to one only of these classes, and must affect all th parties to the action, and not require different places o trial, and must be separately stated.

Amended Code, § 167, altered, so as to allow some cause of action to be united, which can not be united under th section.

§ 664. Every material allegation of the complaint no specifically controverted by the answer, as prescribe in section 645; and every material allegation of ne matter in the answer constituting a counter slaim, not specifically controverted by the reply, as prescrtbed in section 651, must for the purposes of the action, be taken as true. But the allegation of new matter in the answer not relating to a counter claim, or of new matter in a reply, is to be deemed controverted by the adverse party, as upon a direct denial, or avoidance, as the case may require.

Amended Code, § 168.

§ 665. A material allegation in a pleading, is one essential to the claim or defence, and which could not be stricken from the pleading, without leaving it insufficient.

New.

CHAPTER VI.

MISTAKES IN PLEADING, AND AMENDMENTS.

§ 666. No variance between the allegation in a pleading and the proof, is to be deemed material, unless it have actually misled the adverse party, to his prejudice in maintaining his action or defence, upon the merits. Whenever it is alleged, that a party has been so misled that fact must be proved to the satisfaction of the court and it must be shown in what respect he has been misled; and thereupon the court may order the pleading to be amended, upon such terms as may be just.

Amended Code, § 169.

§ 667. Where the variance is not material, as provided in the last section, the court may direct the fact to be found according to the evidence, or may order an immediate amendment, without costs.

Amended Code, § 170.

§ 668. Where, however, the allegation of the claim or defence to which the proof is directed is unproved, not in some particular or particulars only, but in its general scope and meaning, it is not to be deemed a case of variance, within the last two sections, but a failure of proof.

Amended Code, § 171.

§ 669. Any pleading may be once amended by the party of course, without costs, and without prejudice to the proceedings already had, at any time before the period for answering it expires, or, if it do not delay the trial, it can be so amended at any time within twenty days after service of the answer to such pleading. In such case a copy of the amended pleading must be served on the adverse party. After the decision of a demurrer, either at a general or special term, the court may, in its discretion, if it appear that the demurrer was interposed in good faith, allow the defendant to answer, upon such terms as to trial by the court or referees, or as to costs, or otherwise, as may be just.

Amended Code, § 172.

§ 670. The court may, at any time, in furtherance of justice, and on such terms as may be proper, amend any pleading or proceeding, by adding or striking out the name of any party, or by correcting a mistake in the name of a party or a mistake in any other respect, or by inserting other allegations material to the case, or, when the amendment does not change substantially the claim or defence, by conforming the pleading or proceeding to the facts proved. The court may likewise, in its discretion, allow an answer or reply to be made, after the time limited by this act, or by an order enlarging such time, and may also, at any time within one year after notice thereof, relieve a party from a judgment, order, or other proceeding, taken against him through his mistake, inadvertence, surprise, or excusable neglect; and may supply an omission, in any proceeding. And whenever any proceeding taken by a party fails to conform in any respect to the provisions of this code, the court may permit an amendment of such proceeding, so as to make it comformable thereto.

Amended Cod, § 173, modified in the latter part of the first sentence.

§ 671. When the plaintiff is ignorant of the name of a defendant, such defendant may be designated in any pleading or proceeding, by any name; and when his true name is discovered, the pleading or proceeding may be amended accordingly.

Amended Code, § 175.

§ 672. The court must, in every stage of an action, disregard any error, or defect, in the pleadings or proceedings, which does not affect the substantial rights of the adverse party; and no judgment can be reversed or affected by reason of such error or defect.

Amended Code, § 176.

§ 673. The plaintiff and defendant respectively, may be allowed, on motion, to make a supplemental complaint, answer or reply, alleging facts material to the case, occurring after the former complaint, answer or reply.

Amended Code, § 177, omitting an addition made at the last session, which relates rather to an amendment of a pleading, than to a supplemental pleading.

TITLE VII.

OF THE PROVISIONAL REMEDIES IN CIVIL ACTIONS.

CHAPTER I.

ARREST AND BAIL.

674. No person can be arrested in a civil action, except as prescribed by this chapter; but this provision does not apply to proceedings for contempt.

Amended Code, § 178. It has been sometimes doubted whether this section abolishes the writ of ne exeat. Why it should be doubted we cannot understand. The language appears to us as explicit as it can be made. Nothing certainly was farther from our intention than to leave any mode of arrest not provided for in this chapter, except upon proceedings for contempt, and under the act to abolish imprisonment for debt. As it is now proposed to repeal the latter, this section is intended to embrace every case of arrest in a civil action, except for contempt.

§ 675. The defendant may be arrested, as hereinafter prescribed, in the following cases:

1. In an action for the recovery of damages, on a cause of action arising on obligation, where the defendant is not a resident of the state, or is about to remove therefrom, or where the action is for a wilful injury to person, or to property knowing the property to belong to another:

2. In an action for a fine, or penalty, or on a promise to marry, or for money or property embezzled, or fraudulently missapplied, or converted to his own use, by a public officer, or an officer of a corporation, or an attorney, factor, broker, agent or clerk, in the course of his employment as such, or by any other person in a fiduciary capacity, or for misconduct or neglect in office or in a professional employment:

3. In an action to recover the possession of personal property unjustly detained, where the property or any part thereof has been concealed, removed or disposed of, so that it cannot be found or taken by the sheriff:

4. When the defendant has been guilty of a fraud, in contracting the debt, or incurring the obligation, for which the action is brought, or in concealing or disposing of the property, for the taking, detention, or conversion of which the action is brought:

5. When the defendant has removed, concealed or disposed of, his property, or is about to do so, with intent to defraud his creditors.

6. When the arrest of the defendant is expressly authorized by special statutes, in an action for a fine or penalty, or for a wilful violation of duty. But no female can be arrested, in any action, except for a wilful injury to person, character or property:

Amended Code, § 179. Varied in expression and enlarged, so as to include the cases mentioned in subdivision 6.

§ 676. An order for the arrest of the defendant, must be obtained from a judge of the court in which the action is brought, or if the action be in the supreme court, from a county judge.

Amended Code, § 180.

§ 677. The order may be made, whenever it appears to the judge by the affidavit of the plaintiff, or of any other person, that a sufficient cause of action exists, and that the case is one of those mentioned in section 675.

Amended Code, § 181.

§ 678. Before making the order, the judge must require a written undertaking on the part of the plaintiff, with or without sureties, to the effect, that if the defendant recover judgment, the plaintiff will pay all costs and charges that may be awarded to the defendant, and all damages which he may sustain by reason of the arrest, not exceeding the sum specified in the undertaking, which must be at least one hundred dollars. If the undertaking be executed by the plaintiff, without sureties, he must annex thereto an affidavit, that he is a resident and householder or freeholder within the state, and worth double the sum specified in the undertaking, over all his debts and liabilities.

Amended Code, § 182.

§ 679. The order may be made, to accompany the summons, or at any time afterwards, before judgment. It must require the sheriff of the county, where the defendant may be found, forthwith to arrest him and hold him to bail in a specified sum, and to return the order at a time and place therein mentioned, to the plaintiff or attorney by whom it is subscribed or endorsed.

Amended Code, § 183.

§ 680. The affidavit and order of arrest must be delivered to the sheriff, who, upon arresting the defendant, must deliver to him a copy thereof.

Amended Code, § 184.

681. The sheriff must execute the order, by arresting the defendant and keeping him in custody, until discharged by law.

Amended Code, § 185.

§ 682. The defendant, at any time before execution, may be discharged from the arrest, either upon giving bail, or upon depositing the amount mentioned in the order of arrest, as provided in this chapter.

Amended Code, § 186

§ 683. The defendant may give bail, by causing a written undertaking to be executed by two or more sufficient bail, stating their places of residence and occupations, to the effect, that the defendant shall at all times render himself amenable to the process of the court, during the pendency of the action, and to such as may be issued to enforce the judgment therein, or if he be arrested for the cause mentioned in the third subdivision of section 675, an undertaking to the same effect as that provided by section 707.

Amended Code, § 187.

§ 684. At any time before a failure to comply with their undertaking, the bail may surrender the defendant in their exoneration, or he may surrender himself to the sheriff of the county where he was arrested, in the following manner:

1. A certified copy of the undertaking of the bail must be delivered to the sheriff, who shall detain the defendant in his custody thereon, as upon an order of arrest, and by a certificate in writing acknowledge the surrender:

2. Upon the production of a copy of the undertaking and sheriff's certificate, a judge of the court or, if the action be in the supreme court, a county judge may, upon a notice to the plaintiff, of eight days with a copy of the certificate, order that the bail be exonerated; and on filing the order and the papers used on such application, they shall be exonerated accordingly.

But this section does not apply to an arrest for the cause mentioned in the third subdivision of section 675.

Amended Code, § 188.

§ 685. For the purpose of surrendering the defendant, the bail, at any time or place, before they are finally charged, may themselves arrest him, or by a written authority, endorsed on a certified copy of the undertaking, may empower any person of suitable age and discretion to do so,

Amended Code, § 189.

§ 686. In case of failure to comply with the undertaking, the bail can be proceeded against by action only.

Amended Code, § 190.

§ 687. The bail may be exonerated, either by the death of the defendant, or his imprisonment in a state prison, or by his legal discharge from the obligation to render himself amenable to the process, or by his surrender to the sheriff of the county where he was arrested, in execution thereof, within twenty days after the commencement of the action against the bail, or within such further time as may be granted by the court.

Amended Code, § 191.

§ 688. Within the time limited for that purpose, the sheriff must deliver the order of arrest to the plaintiff or attorney by whom it is subscribed, with his return endorsed, and the undertaking of the bail or a copy thereof. The plaintiff, within ten days thereof, may serve upon the sheriff, a notice that he does not accept the bail, or he must be deemed to have accepted it, and the sheriff shall be exonerated from liability.

Amended Code, § 192.

§ 689. On the receipt of the undertaking or copy and notice, the sheriff or defendant may, within ten days thereafter, give to the plaintiff or attorney by whom the order of arrest is subscribed, notice of the justification of the same or other bail, (specifying the places of residence and occupations of the latter,) before a judge of the court, or county judge, or justice of the peace, at a specified time and place; the time to be not less than five, nor more than ten days thereafter. In case other bail be given, there must be a new undertaking, in the form prescribed in section 683.

Amended Code, § 193.

§ 690. The qualifications of bail must be as follows:

1. Each of them must be a resident, and householder or freeholder, within the state:

2. They must each be worth the amount specified in the order of arrest, exclusive of property exempt from execution, but the judge, or a justice of the peace, on justification, may allow more that two bail to justify severally in amounts less than that expressed in the order, if the whole justification be equivalent to that of two sufficient bail.

Amended Code, § 194.

§ 691. For the purpose of justification, each of the bail must attend before the judge, or a justice of the peace, at the time and place mentioned in the notice, and may be examined on oath, on the part of the plaintiff, touching his sufficiency, in such manner as the judge or justice of the peace, in his discretion, may think proper. The examination must be be reduced to writing and subscribed by the bail, if required by the plaintiff.

Amended Code, § 195.

§ 692. If the judge or justice find the bail sufficient, he must annex the examination to the undertaking, endorse his allowance thereon, and cause them to be filed with the clerk; and the sheriff shall thereupon be exonerated from liability.

Amended Code, § 196.

§ 693. The defendant may, at the time of his arrest, instead of giving bail, deposit with the sheriff the amount mentioned in the order. The sheriff must thereupon give the defendant a certificate of the deposit, and the defendant shall be discharged out of custody.

Amended Code, § 197.

§ 694. The sheriff must, within four days after the deposit, pay the same into court; and take from the officer receiving the same, two certificates of such payment, the one of which he must deliver to the plaintiff, and the other to the defendant. For any default in making such payment, the same proceedings may be had on the official bond of the sheriff to collect the sum deposited, as in other cases of delinquincy.

Amended Code, § 198.

§ 695. If money be deposited, as provided in the last two sections, bail may be given and justified upon notice, as prescribed in section 689, at any time before judgment; and thereupon the judge before whom the justification is had, must direct, in the order of allowance, that the money deposited be refunded by the sheriff to the defendant, and it must be refunded accordingly.

Amended Code, § 199.

§ 696. Where money shall have been so deposited, if it remain on deposit at the time of an order or judgment for the payment of money to the plaintiff, the clerk must, under the direction of the court, apply the same in satisfaction thereof, and after satisfying the judgment, refund the surplus, if any, to the defendant. If the judgment be in favor of the defendant, the clerk must refund to him the whole sum deposited and remaining unapplied.

Amended Code, § 200.

§ 697. If, after being arrested, the defendant escape or be rescued, or bail be not given or justified, or a deposite be not made instead thereof, the sheriff shall himself be liable as bail. But he may discharge himself from such liability, by the giving and justification of bail as provided in sections 689, 690, 691, and 692, at any time before process against the person of the defendant, to enforce an order or judgment in the action.

Amended Code, § 201.

§ 698. If a judgment be recovered against the sheriff, upon his liability as bail, and an execution thereon be returned unsatisfied, in whole or in part, the same proceedings may be had on the official bond of the sheriff, to collect the deficiency, as in other cases of delinquency.

Amended Code, § 202.

§ 699. The bail taken upon the arrest, shall, unless they justify, or other bail be given or justified, be liable to the sheriff, by action, for the damages which he may sustain by reason of such omission.

Amended Code, § 203.

§ 700. A defendant arrested may, at any time before the justification of bail, apply, on motion, to vacate the order of arrest, or to reduce the amount of bail.

Amended Code, § 204.

701. If the motion be made upon affidavits on the part of the defendant, but not otherwise, the plaintiff may oppose the same by affidavits or other proofs, in addition to those on which the order of arrest was made.

Amended Code, § 205.

CHAPTER II.

CLAIM AND DELIVERY OF PERSONAL PROPERTY.

§ 702. The plaintiff, in an action to recover the possession of personal property, may at the time of issuing the summons, or at any time before answer, claim the immediate delivery of such property as provided in this chapter.

§ 703. Where a delivery is claimed, an affidavit must be made by the plaintiff, or by some one in his behalf, showing,

1. That the plaintiff is the owner of the property claimed, (particularly describing it,) or is lawfully entitled to the possession thereof, by virtue of a special property therein, the facts in respect to which must be set forth:

2. That the property is wrongfully detained by the defendant:

3. The alleged cause of the detention thereof, according to his best knowledge, information and belief.

4. That the same has not been taken for a tax, assessment or fine, pursuant to a statute; or seized under an execution or attachment against the property of the plaintiff; or if so seized, that it is, by statute exempt from such seizure; and,

5. The actual value of the property.

Amended Code, § 207.

§ 704. The plaintiff may, thereupon, by an endorsement in writing upon the affidavit, require the sheriff of the county where the property claimed may be, to take the same from the defendant, and deliver it to the plaintiff.

Amended Code, § 208.

§ 705. Upon the receipt of the affidavit and notice, with a written undertaking, executed by one or more sufficient sureties, approved by the sheriff to the effect that they are bound, in double the value of the property as stated in the affidavit, for the prosecution of the action, for the return of the property to the defendant, if return thereof be adjudged, and for the payment to him of such sum as may, for any cause, be recovered against the plaintiff, the sheriff must forthwith take the property described in the affidavit, if it be in the possession of the defendant or his agent, and retain it in his custody. He must also, without delay, serve on the defendant a copy of the affidavit, notice and undertaking, by delivering the same to him personally, if he can be found, or to his agent, from whose possession the property is taken; or if neither can be found, by leaving them at the usual place of abode of either, with some person of suitable age and discretion.

Amended Code, § 209.

§ 706. The defendant may within three days after the service of a copy of the affidavit and undertaking, give notice to the sheriff that he excepts to the sufficiency of the sureties. If he fail to do so, he must be deemed to have waived all objection to them. When the defendant excepts, the sureties must justify on notice in like manner, as upon bail on arrest. And the sheriff shall be responsible for the sufficiency of the sureties until the objection to them is either waived as above provided, or until they justify. If the defendant except to the sureties, he cannot reclaim the property as provided in the next section.

Amended Code, § 210.

§ 707. At any time before the delivery of the property to the plaintiff, the defendant may, if he do not except to the sureties of the plaintiff, require the return thereof, upon giving to the sheriff a written undertaking, executed by two or more sufficient sureties, to the effect that they are bound, in double the value of the property, as stated in the affidavit of the plaintiff, for the delivery thereof to the plaintiff, if such delivery be adjudged, and for the payment to him of such sum as may, for any cause, be recovered against the defendant. If a return of the property be not so required within three days after the taking and service of notice to the defendant, it must be delivered to the plaintiff, except as provided in section 712.

Amended Code §211.

§ 708. The defendant's sureties, upon notice to the plaintiff of not less than two nor more than six days, must justify before a judge or justice of the peace, in the same manner as upon bail on arrest; and upon such justification, the sheriff must deliver the property to the defendant. The sheriff shall be responsible for the defendant's sureties, until they justify, or until the justification is completed or expressly waived, and may retain the property until that time, but if they or others in their place, fail to justify, at the time and place appointed, he must deliver the property to the plaintiff.

Amended Code, § 212.

§ 709. The qualification of sureties and their justification, must be such as are prescribed by sections 690 and 691, in respect to bail upon an order of arrest.

Amended Code, § 213.

§ 710. If the property or any part thereof be concealed in a building or enclosure, the sheriff must publicly demand its delivery. If it be not delivered, he must cause the building or enclosure to be broken open, and take the property into his possession, and if necessary, he may call to his aid the power of his county.

Amended Code, § 214.

§ 711. When the sheriff shall have taken property, as in this chapter provided, he must keep it in a secure place, and deliver it to the party entitled thereto, upon receiving his lawful fees for taking, and his necessary expenses for keeping, the same.

Amended Code, § 215.

§ 712. If the property taken be claimed by any other person than the defendant or his agent, and such person make affidavit of his title thereto or right to the possession thereof, stating the grounds of such title or right and serve the same upon the sheriff, the sheriff shall not be bound to keep the property, or deliver it to the plaintiff, unless the plaintiff, on demand of him or his agent, indemnify the sheriff against such claim, by an undertaking, executed by two sufficient sureties, accompanied by their affidavits, that they are each worth double the value of the property as specified in the affidavit of the plaintiff, and freeholders and householders of the county. And no claim to such property by any other person than the defendant or his agent, shall be valid against the sheriff unless so made and notwithstanding such claim, when so made, he may retain the property a reasonable time to demand such indemnity.

Amended Code, § 216.

§ 713. The sheriff must file the notice and affidavit with his proceedings thereon, with the clerk of the court in which the action is pending, within twenty days after taking the property mentioned therein.

Amended Code, § 217.

CHAPTER III.

INJUNCTION.

§ 714. An injunction is a writ or order, requiring a person to refrain from a particular act. When granted as a provisional remedy, it is by order. The order may be made by the court in which the action is brought, or by a judge thereof, in the cases prescribed in the next section; and when made bya judge, may be enforced as the order of the court.

Amended Code, § 218.

§ 715. Where it appears by the complaint, that the plaintiff is entitled to the relief demanded, and such relief, or any part thereof, consists in restraining the commission or continuance of some act, the commission or continuance of which, during the litigation, would produce great or irreparable injury to the plaintiff, or when during the litigation, it appears that the defendant is doing, or threatens, or is about to do, or is procuring or suffering to be done, some act in violation of the plaintiff's rights, respecting the subject of the action, and tending to render the judgment ineffectual, a temporary injunction may be granted, to restrain such act. And where, during the pendency of an action, the defendant threatens, or is about, to remove, or dispose of, his property, with intent to defraud his creditors, a temporary injunction may be granted to restrain such removal or disposition.

Amended Code, § 219. Inserting before "injury," the words "great or irreparable," which were omitted at the last session.

§ 716. The injunction may be granted at the time of issuing the summons, or at any time afterwards, before judgment, upon its appearing satisfactorily to the court or judge, by the affidavit of the plaintiff, or of any other person, that sufficient grounds exist therefor. A copy of the affidavit must be served with the injunction.

Amended Code, § 220.

§ 717. An injunction can not be allowed, after the defendant has answered, unless upon notice, or upon an order to show cause; but in such case, the defendant may be restrained, until the decision of the court or judge, granting or refusing the injunction.

Amended Code, § 221.

§ 718. Where no provision is made by special statute, as to security upon an injunction, the court or judge must require a written undertaking, on the part of the plaintiff, with or without sureties, to the effect that the plaintiff will pay to the party enjoined, such damages, not exceeding an amount to be specified, as he may sustain by reason of the injunction, if the court, finally decide that the plaintiff was not entitled thereto. The damages may be ascertained by a reference, or otherwise, as the court may direct.

Amended Code, § 222.

§ 719. If the court or judge deem it proper that the defendant, or any of, several defendants, should be heard before granting the injunction, an order may be made requiring cause to be shown, at a specified time and place, why the injunction should not be granted; and the defendant may in the mean time be restrained.

Amended Code, § 223.

§ 720. An injunction to suspend the general and ordinary business of a corporation must not be granted except by the court. Nor must it be granted, without due notice of the application therefor, to the proper officers of the corporation, except where the people of this state are a party to the proceeding, and except in proceedings to enforce the liability of stockholders in corporations and associations for banking purposes, after the first day of January, one thousand eight hundred and fifty, as such proceedings are or shall be provided by law, unless the plaintiff give a written undertaking, executed by two sufficient sureties, to be approved by the court, to the effect that the plaintiff will pay all damages not exceeding the sum to be mentioned in the undertaking, which such corporation may sustain, by reason of the injunction, if the court finally decide that the plaintiff was not entitled thereto. The damages may be ascertained by a reference, or otherwise, as the court directs.

Amended Code, § 224.

§ 721. If the injunction be granted by a judge without notice, the defendant, at any time before the trial, may apply, upon notice, to any judge of the court in which the action is brought, to vacate or modify the same. The application may be made upon the complaint and the affidavits on which the injunction was granted, or upon affidavits on the part of the defendant, with or without the answer.

Amended Code, § 225.

§ 722. If the application be made upon affidavits on the part of the defendant, but not otherwise, the plaintifi may oppose the same by affidavits or other evidence, in addition to those on which the injunction was granted.

Amended Code, § 226.

CHAPTER IV.

ATTACHMENT.

§ 723. In an action for the recovery of money against a corporation, created by or under the laws of any other state gevernment or country, or against a defendant who is not a resident of this state, or against a defendant who has absconded or concealed himself as hereinafter mentioned, the plaintiff, at the time of issuing the summons, or at any time afterwards, may have the property of such defendant attached, in the manner hereinafter prescribed, as a security for the satisfaction of such judgment as the plaintiff may recover.

Amended Code, § 227.

§ 724. An order for the attachment must be obtained from a judge of the court in which the action is brought, or if the action be in the supreme court, from a county judge.

Amended Code, § 228, substituting an order for a warrant of attachment, as more in conformity with the three previous chapters.

§ 725. The order may be made whenever it appears by affidavit, that a cause of action exists against such defendant, specifying the amount of the claim, and the grounds thereof, and that the defendant is either a foreign corporation, or not a resident of this state, or has departed therefrom with intent to defraud his creditors or to avoid the service of a summons, or keeps himself concealed therein with the like intent.

Amended Code, § 229.

§ 726. Before making the order, the judge must require a written undertaking on the part of the plaintiff, with sufficient surety, to the effect, that if the defendant recover judgment, the plaintiff will pay all costs and charges that may be awarded to the defendant, and all damages which he may sustain, by reason of the attachment, not exceeding the sum specified in the undertaking, which must be at least two hundred and fifty dollars.

Amended Code, § 230.

§ 727. The order must be directed to the sheriff of any county in which property of such defendant may be, and require him to attach and safely keep all the property of such defendant within his county not exempt from execution, or so much thereof as may be sufficient to satisfy the plaintiff's demand, the amount of which must be stated, in conformity with the complaint. Several orders may be issued at the same time to the sheriffs of different counties.

Amended Code, § 231.

§ 728. The rights or shares which the defendant may have in the stock of any corporation, together with the interest and profits thereon, and all other property in this state of such defendant, may be attached and sold to satisfy the judgment and execution.

Amended Code, § 234.

§ 729. The sheriff, to whom the order is directed and delivered, must execute the same without delay, as follows:

1. Real property must be attached, by leaving with the occupant thereof, or if there be no occupant, in a conspicuous place thereon, a copy of the order certified by the sheriff:

2. Personal property, capable of manual delivery to the sheriff must be attached by taking it into his custody:

3. Other personal property must be attached by leaving a certified copy of the order, and a notice specifying the property attached, with a person holding the same, or as to a debt with the debtor, or as to stock or interest in stock of a corporation, with the president or other head of the same, or the secretary, cashier, or managing agent thereof. The sheriff must make a full inventory of the property attached, and return the same with the order of attachment.

Amended Code, § 232 and 235, altered, so as to prescribe the sheriff's mode of proceeding without referring to existing statutes.

§ 730. Whenever the sheriff, with an order of attachment, or with an execution against the defendant, applies to any person mentioned in the third subdivision of the last section, for the purpose of attaching or levying upon the property mentioned therein, such person must furnish him with a certificate, designating the number of rights or shares of the defendant in the stock of the corporation, with any dividend or incumbrance thereon, or the amount and description of the property held by such corporation or person, for the benefit of the defendant, or the debt owing to the defendant. If such person refuse to do so, he may be required by the court or judge to attend before him, and be examined on oath concerning the same, and disobedience to the order may be punished as a contempt.

Amended Code, § 236.

§ 731. If any of the property attached be perishable, the sheriff must sell the same in the manner in which property is sold on execution, and immediately deposit the proceeds with the clerk of the court. He must also collect, and if necessary, in his name of office, sue for the debts and credits attached, and deposit the amount collected with the clerk. Other property attached by him, must be retained by him to answer any judgment that may be recovered in the action, unless sooner subjected to execution upon another judgment.

Amended Code, § 233, altered, so as to dispense with a reference to existing statutes.

§ 732. The sheriff may deliver any of the property attached to the defendant, to or any other person claiming it, upon his giving a written undertaking therefor, executed by one or more sufficient sureties, engaging to re-deliver it or pay the value thereof to the sheriff, to whom execution, upon a judgment obtained by the plaintiff in that action, may be issued.

See 2 *R.* S., 5, §§ 13, 14, 15, 16, 17, 18, 19, 20, 21 *and* 231. §§ 33 *and* 34.

§ 733. If an action be brought upon such undertaking against the principal or his sureties, it shall be a defence, that the property for which the undertaking was given, did not, at the execution of the order of attachment, belong to the defendant against whom it was issued.

See 2 *R. S.*, 5, § 17 *and* 231. § 36.

§ 734. If the property attached, be claimed by a third person as his property, the sheriff may summon a jury to try the validity of such claim, and such proceedings must be had thereon, with the like effect, as in case of seizure upon execution.

See 2 *R S.*, 4, §§ 10 *and* 11.

§ 735. The defendant or claimant may be required to attend before the court or judge, for the purpose of giving any necessary information respecting the property attached, and may be thereupon examined on oath concerning the same.

Amended Code, § 236.

§ 736. If judgment be recovered by the plaintiff in such action, the sheriff must satisfy the same out of the property attached by him, if it be sufficient for that purpose;

1. By paying to the plaintiff the proceeds of all sales of perishable property, and of any vessel, or share or interest therein, sold by him, or of any debts or credits collected by him, or so much as shall be necessary to satisfy the judgment:

2. If any balance remain due, and an execution shall have been issued on the judgment, he must sell under the execution so much of the attached property, real or personal, except as provided in subdivision four of this section, as may be necessary to satisfy the balance, if enough for that purpose remain in his hands; and in case of the sale of any rights or shares in the stock of of a corporation, the sheriff must execute to the purchaser a certificate of the sale, and the purchaser shall thereupon have all the rights and privileges in respect thereto which were had by the defendant.

3. If any of the attached property belonging to the defendant, shall have passed out of the hands of the sheriff, without having been sold or converted into money, the sheriff must re-possess himself of the same, and for that purpose shall have all the authority, which he had to seize the same under the attachment, and any person who shall wilfully conceal or withhold such property from the sheriff, shall be liable to double damages at the suit of the party injured.

4. Until the judgment against the defendant be paid, the sheriff may collect the notes, other evidences of

debt, and debts that may have been attached, and may prosecute any bond he may have taken in the course of such proceedings, and apply the proceeds thereof to the payment of the judgment; or, upon the order of the court, he may sell such notes, evidences and debts, and apply the proceeds in like manner.

When the judgment and costs shall have been paid, the sheriff upon reasonable demand, must deliver over to the defendant the residue of the attached property or the proceeds thereof.

Amended Code, § 237.

§ 737. The actions authorised by sections 731 and 736, to be brought by the sheriff, may be prosecuted by the plaintiff, or under his direction, upon the delivery by him to the sheriff of an undertaking executed by two sufficient sureties, to the effect, that the plaintiff will indemnify the sheriff from all damages, costs and charges on account thereof, not exceeding two hundred and fifty dollars in any one action. Such sureties shall in all cases, when required by the sheriff, justify, by making an affidavit that each is a householder, and worth double the amount of the penalty of the bond, over and above all debts and liabilities.

Amended Code, § 238.

§ 738. If the foreign corporation, or absent, absconding or concealed defendant, recover judgment against the plaintiff, in such action, any undertaking received by the sheriff, except such as is mentioned in the last section, all the proceeds of sales and money collected by him, and all the property attached remaining in his hands, must be delivered by him to the defendant or his agent on request; the order of attachment must be discharged, and the property released therefrom.

Amended Code, § 239.

§ 739. Whenever the defendant shall have appeared in the action, he may apply to the judge who issued the attachment, or to the court, for an order to discharge the same, upon the execution of the undertaking mentioned in the next section; and if the application be granted, all the proceeds of sales and moneys collected by the sheriff, and all the property attached remaining in his hands, must be released from the attachment, and delivered to the defendant.

Amended Code, § 240.

§ 740. Upon such application, the defendant must deliver to the court or judge an undertaking executed by at least two sureties, resident and freeholders in this state, approved by such court or judge, to the effect, that the sureties will on demand pay to the plaintiff, the amount of the judgment that may be recovered against the defendant in the action, not exceeding the sum specified in the undertaking, which must be at least double the amount claimed by the plaintiff in his complaint.

Amended Code, § 241.

§ 741. The defendant may also, any time before the time for answering expires, apply on motion to vacate the order of attachment.

Conformable to the provision, in similar cases made in previous chapter.

§ 742. If the motion be made upon affidavits on the part of the defendant, but not otherwise, the plaintiff may oppose the same by affidavits or other evidence, in addition to those on which the order of attachment was made.

Conformable to the provision, in similar cases in previous chapters.

§ 743. When the order of attachment is fully executed or discharged, the sheriff must return the same with his proceedings thereon, to the court in which the action was brought.

Amended Code, § 242.

CHAPTER V.

RECEIVERS.

§ 744. In the cases mentioned in the first subdivision of section 546, the court may provisionally appoint a receiver of property; and may protect and support him in the proper discharge of his duties.

This chapter and the next, with sections 545, 546 and 547, are designed to fill up the space left in our first report, and there indicated by section 200. The chapters explain themselves, and will be found, we think to answer the purposes designed.

§ 745. A receiver subject always to the control of the court, has power to bring and defend actions; to take and keep possession of property; collect debts; receive the rents and profits of real property; and generally to do such acts in respect to the property committed to him, as the court may authorize.

CHAPTER VI.

DEPOSIT IN COURT.

§ 746. When it is admitted by the pleading, or examination, of a party, that he has in his possession, or under his control, any money or other thing, capable of delivery, which, being the subject of the litigation, is held by him as trustee for another party, or which belongs, or is due, to another party, the court may order the same to be deposited in court, or delivered to such party, with or without security, subject to the further direction of the court.

§ 747. Whenever, in the exercise of its authority, a court shall have ordered the deposit, or delivery, of money or other thing, and the order is disobeyed, the court, besides punishing the disobedience, may make an order requiring the sheriff to take the money or thing, and deposit or deliver it, in conformity with the direction of the court.

TITLE VIII.

OF THE TRIAL AND JUDGMENT IN CIVIL ACTIONS.

CHAPTER I.

JUDGMENT IN GENERAL.

§ 748. A judgment is the final determination of the rights of the parties in the action.

Amended Code, § 245.

§ 749. Judgment may be given, for or against one or more of several plaintiffs, and for or against one or more of several defendants, and it may, when the justice of the case require it, determine the ultimate rights of the parties on each side, as between themselves.

Amended Code, § 274.

§ 750. In an action against several defendants, the court may, in its discretion, render judgment against one or more of them, leaving the action to proceed against the others, whenever a several judgment is proper.

Amended Code, § 274

§ 751. The relief granted to the plaintiff, if there be no answer, cannot exceed that which he shall have demanded in his complaint; but in any other case, the court may grant him any relief consistent with the case made by the complaint, and embraced within the issue.

Amended Code, § 275.

§ 752. The action may be dismissed without a final determination of its merits, in the following cases:

1. By the plaintiff himself, at any time before trial, if a provisional remedy has not been allowed, or counter claim made:

2. By either party, with the written consent of the other:

3. By the court, when, upon the trial and before the final submission of the case, the plaintiff abandons it;

4. By the court, when the plaintiff fails to appear on the trial, and the defendant appears and asks for the dismissal;

5. By the court, on the application of some of the defendants, when there are others whom the plaintiff fails to prosecute with diligence. All other modes of dismissing an action by non-suit, or otherwise, are abolished.

The dismissal mentioned in the first two subdivisions is made by an entry in the clerk's register, and a notice served on the adverse party. Judgment may thereupon be entered accordingly.

§ 753. In every case, other than those mentioned in the last section, the judgment must be rendered on the merits.

The three last sections are new, and designed as a substitute for a portion of the old practice, not supplanted by the existing code.

§ 754. Though all the defendants have been served with the summons, judgment may be taken against any of them severally, when the plaintiff would be entitled to judgment against such defendants, if the action had been against them alone.

Amended Code, § 136, *sub.* 3.

CHAPTER II.

JUDGMENT UPON FAILURE TO ANSWER.

§ 755. Judgment may be had, if the defendant fail to answer the complaint, as follows:

1. In an action arising on obligation, for the recovery of money only, the plaintiff may file with the clerk, proof of personal service of the summons, and that no

answer has been received. The clerk must thereupon enter judgment for the amount mentioned in the summons, against the defendant, or against one or more of several defendants, in the cases provided for in section 632;

2. In other actions, the plaintiff may, upon the like proof, apply to the court, after the expiration of the time for answering, for the relief demanded in the complaint. If the taking of an account or the proof of any fact be necessary, to enable the court to give judgment, or to carry the judgment into effect, the court, may take the account or hear the proof, or may, in its discretion, order a reference for that purpose. And where the action is for the recovery of money only, or of specific, real or personal property, with damages for the withholding thereof, the court may order the damages to be assessed by a jury, or if the examination of a long account be involved, by a reference as above provided;

3. In actions, where the service of the summons was by publication, the plaintiff may in like manner apply for judgment, and the court must thereupon require proof to be made of the demand mentioned in the complaint, aud if the defendant be not a resident of the state, must require the plaintiff or his agent to be examined on oath, respecting any payments that have been made to the plaintiff, or to any one for his use, on account of such demand, and may render judgment for the amount which he is entitled to recover. Before

judgment the plaintiff must give satisfactory security, to abide the order of the court, touching the restitution of any property collected or received under the judgment, in case the defendant or his representatives are admitted to defend the action, and succeed in the defence.

Amended Code, § 246, changed in some respects.

CHAPTER III.

ISSUES, AND THE MODE OF TRIAL.

§ 756. Issues arise upon the pleadings, when a fact or conclusion of law is maintained by the one party and controverted by the other. They are of two kinds:

1. Of law: and,

2. Of fact.

Amended Code, § 248.

§ 757. An issue of law arises,

1. Upon a demurrer to the complaint, or to some part thereof.

Amended Code, § 249.

§ 758. An issue of fact arises,

1. Upon a material allegation in the complaint, controverted by the answer: or,

2. Upon new matter in the answer constituting a counter-claim, controverted by the reply; or, upon other new matter in the answer: or,

3. Upon new matter in the reply: Issues both of law and of fact may arise upon different parts of the pleadings in the same action.

Amended Code, § 250, 251.

§ 759. A trial is the judicial examination of the issues between the parties, whether they be issues of law or of fact.

Amended Code, § 252.

§ 760. An issue of law must be tried by the court, unless it be referred, as provided in sections 335 and 336.

Amended Code, §§ 253 and 254.

§ 761. An issue of fact, in an action for the recovery of money only, or of specific real or personal property, or for a divorce from the marriage contract on the ground of adultery, must be tried by a jury, unless a jury trial be waived, as provided in section 796, or a reference be ordered, as provided in sections 335 and 336.

Amended Code, § 253.

§ 762. Every other issue of fact must be tried by the court, subject, however, to the right of the parties to consent, or of the court to order, that the whole issue, or any specific question of fact involved therein, be tried by a jury, or be refered, as provided in sections 335 and 336.

Amended Code, § 254.

§ 763. All issues, whether of law or fact, triable by a jury or by the court, must be tried before a single judge. Issues of fact in the supreme court, must be tried at the circuits, issues of law in the first instance at a circuit, or special term, or before a single judge, as provided in section 49.

Amended Code, § 255.

The provision allowing an issue of law to be tried before a single judge, at any time, is designed to prevent the delay which now sometimes arises from a demurrer, put in for that purpose alone.

§ 764. At any time after issue, and at least ten days before the court, either party may give notice of trial. The party giving the notice must furnish the clerk, at least four days before the court, with a note of the issue, containing the title of the action, the names of the attorneys, and the time when the last pleading was served; and the clerk must thereupon enter the cause upon the calendar, according to the date of the issue. The issues, once placed upon the calendar of a circuit or special term, if not tried at the circuit or term for which the notice was given, need not be noticed for a subsequent circuit or term, but must remain upon the calendar, from court to court, until finally disposed of. But when an issue of law is to be tried before a judge out of court, no calendar need be made or note of issue furnished.

Amended Code, § 256.

An important change is proposed by the alteration of this section. It is to save the necessity of repeated notices of trial. If a cause be not tried, as it ought to be, at the first term, it must remain upon the calendar at subsequent terms, until reached. A similar practice exists in many of the states, where no inconvenience results from it.

§ 765. The issues on the calendar must be disposed of in the following order; unless, for the convenience of parties, or the despatch of business, the court otherwise direct;

1. Issues of fact to be tried by a jury:
2. Issues of fact to be tried by the court:
3. Issues of law.

Amended Code, § 257.

§ 766. Either party, after the notice of trial, whether given by himself, or by the adverse party, may bring the issue to trial, and in the absence of the adverse party, unless the court, for good cause, otherwise direct, may proceed with his case, and take a dismissal of the action, or a verdict, or judgment, as the case may require.

Amended Code, § 258.

§ 767. A separate trial, between the plaintiff and any of several defendants, may be allowed by the court, whenever, in its opinion, justice will be thereby promoted.

New. It may sometimes be highly just to parties, between whom an issue is joined, and who are ready for trial, to have their controversy determined, without waiting for the movements of other parties, over whom they have no control.

§ 768. A motion to postpone a trial for the absence of evidence, can only be made upon affidavit, showing the materiality of the evidence expected to be obtained, and that due diligence has been used to procure it. The court may also require the moving party to state the evidence which he expects to obtain, and if the adverse party thereupon admit, that such evidence would be given, and that it be considered as actually given on the trial, or offered and overruled as improper, the trial must not be postponed.

New; to prevent parties from obtaining delay by the unfounded pretence of absent witnesses.

§ 769. The plaintiff must furnish the court before the trial begins with a copy of the summons and pleadings, and the offer of the defendant, if any shall have been made.

Amended Code, § 259.

CHAPTER III.

TRIAL BY JURY.

ARTICLE I.

FORMATION OF THE JURY.

§ 770. When the action is called for trial by jury, the clerk must draw from the trial jury box of the court, the ballots containing the names of jurors, until the jury is completed or the ballots are exhausted. If the ballots become exhausted before the jury is complete, the sheriff, under the direction of the court, must summon from the bystanders or the body of the county, so many qualified persons as to complete the jury.

The provisions of this chapter, for the most part, explain themselves. Those relating to challenges depend upon the same principles as in criminal actions. In the Code of Criminal Procedure, we have given all the explanations which appear to be necessary.

§ 771. As soon as the drawing of the jury is completed, an oath must be administered to each juror, that he will well and truly try the matter in issue between ——— the plaintiff and ——— the defendant, and a true verdict give, according to the evidence.

§ 772. When the jury is completed and sworn, the ballots containing the names of the jurors sworn must be laid aside, till the jury so sworn is discharged, and then they must be returned to the box; and every ballot drawn containing the name of a juror not so sworn must be returned to the box as soon as the jury is completed.

§ 773. Either party may challenge the jurors, but when there are several parties on either side, they must join in a challenge before it can be made. The challenges are to the panel and to individual jurors, as in criminal actions, except that there can be but two peremptory challenges on each side. And the provisions of the Code of Criminal Procedure, on the subject of challenges, and the disposition thereof, omitting section 415, are to apply, so far as in their nature applicable and consistent with the provisions of this code, to challenges in civil actions and the disposition thereof, substituting "plaintiff" for "people" and for "person alleged to be injured by the offence charged or on whose complaint the prosecution was instituted."

ARTICLE I.

CONDUCT OF THE TRIAF.

§ 774. When the jury has been completed and sworn, the trial must proceed in the following order, unless the court, for special reasons, otherwise directs:

1. The plaintiff after stating the issue, must open the case and produce the evidence on his part:

2. The defendant may then open his defence, and offer his evidence in support thereof:

3. The parties may then respectively offer rebutting evidence only, unless the court for good reason, in furtherance of justice, permit them to offer evidence upon their original case:

4. When the evidence is concluded, unless the case is submitted to the jury on either side, or on both sides, without argument, the defendant must commence, and the plaintiff conclude the argument to the jury:

5. If several defendants, having separate defences, appear by different counsel, the court must determine their relative order in the evidence and argument:

6. The court may then charge the jury.

The length to which trials are now protracted is a matter of great and just complaint. The remedy lies chiefly with the courts. If they would adhere inflexibly to the rule, that a question once decided shall not be debated anew; and would stop the examination of a witness when he has been already sufficiently examined, a vast deal of time might be saved. It is a rule in the English courts, and in the courts of some of our states, that a counsel shall stand while he is examining a witness. The same rule would be useful here. As trials are now sometimes conducted, the counsel sits leisurely in his seat, writing down at length all the questions and answers, and the court meeting at ten and adjourning at three, a single witness remains under examination from day to day, and the trial lasts for weeks, when it should be ended in as many days.

By a provision in another place, we propose that counsel shall be limited in their arguments to a fixed time. With resolution on the part of the courts, and a few rules, such as they should adopt, we are persuaded that more than half the time now spent in trials might be saved.

§ 775. Whenever, in the opinion of the court, it is proper that the jury should have a view of real property which is the subject of the litigation, or of the place in which any material fact occurred, it may order the jury to be conducted in a body, in the custody of proper officers, to the place, which will be shown to them by the judge, or by a person appointed by the court for that purpose. While the jury are thus absent, no person, other than the judge or person so appointed, must speak to them on any subject connected with the trial.

§ 776. The jurors may be kept together in charge of proper officers, or may, in the discretion of the court, at any time before the submission of the cause to the jury, be permitted to separate. In either case, they may be admonished by the court, that it is their duty not to converse with any other person or among tthemselves, on any subject connected with the trial, or to form or express any opinion thereon, until the cause is finally submitted to them.

§ 777. If, after the impaneling of the jury, and before verdict, a juror become sick, so as to be unable to perform his duty, the court may order him to be discharged. In that cese a new juroı may be sworn, and the trial begin anew, or the jury may be discharged, and a new jury then or afterwards impanelled.

§ 778. In charging the jury, the court must state to them all matters of law which it thinks necessary for their information in giving their verdict; and if it present the facts of the case, it must also inform the jury that they are the exclnsive judges of all questions of fact.

§ 779. After hearıng the charge, the jury may either decide in court, or retire for deliberation. If they retire, they must be kept together in a room provided for them, or some other convenient place, under the charge of one or more officers, until they agree upon their verdict, or are discharged by the court. The officer must, to the utmost of his ability, keep the jury thus together, separate from other persons, without drink except water, and without food, except ordered by the court; he must not suffer any communication to be made to them, nor make any himself, unless by order of the court, except to ask them if they have agreed upon their verdict, and he must not, before the verdict is rendered, communicate to any person the state of their deliberations or the verdict agreed on.

§ 780. If, while the jury are kept together, either during the progress of the trial or after their retirement for deliberation, the court order them to be provided with suitable and sufficient food and lodging, they must be so provided by the sheriff, at the expense of the county, or if the trial be in a city court, at the expense of the city.

§ 781. Upon retiring for deliberation, the jury may take with them all papers, (except depositions,) which have been received as evidence in the cause, or copies of such parts of public records or private documents, given in evidence, as ought not, in the opinion of the court, to be taken from the person having them in possession; and they may also take with them notes of the testimony or other proceedings on the trial, taken by themselves or any of them, but none taken by any other person.

§ 782. After the jury have retired for deliberation, if there be a disagreement between them as to any part of the testimony, or if they desire to be informed of any point of law arising in the cause, they may require the officer to conduct them into court. Upon their being brought into court, the information required must be given, in the presence of, or after notice to the parties or counsel.

§ 783. Except as provided in sections 777 and 786, or in case of some accident or calamity, requiring their discharge, the jury cannot be discharged after the cause is submitted to them, until they have agreed upon their verdict, and rendered it in open court, unless by the consent of both parties entered upon the minutes, or unless at the expiration of such time as the court deem proper, it satisfactorily appear, that there is no probability of an agreement.

§ 784. In all cases where a jury are discharged, or prevented from giving a verdict, by reason of accident or other cause, during the progress of the trial, or after the cause is submitted to them, the action may be again tried, immediately, or at a future time, as the court directs.

§ 785. While the jury are absent, the court may adjourn from time to time, in respect to other business; but it is nevertheless to be deemed open, for every purpose connected with the cause submitted to the jury, until a verdict is rendered or the jury discharged. A final adjournment of the court discharges the jury.

§ 786. When the jury have agreed upon their verdict, they must be conducted into court by the officer having them in charge. Their names must then be called; and if all do not appear, the rest must be discharged without giving a verdict.

§ 787. If the jury appear, they must be asked by the court or the clerk, whether they have agreed upon their verdict; and if the foreman answer in the affirmative, they must, on being required, declare the same.

§ 788. When a verdict is rendered, and before it is recorded, the jury may be polled on the request of either party; for which purpose each juror must be asked whether it be his verdict; if any one answer in the negative, the jury must be sent out for further deliberation. If the verdict be informal or insufficient, it may be corrected by the jury under the advice of the court, or the jury may be again sent out.

§ 789. When the verdict is given, and is such as the court may receive, the clerk must immediately record it in full in the minutes, and must read it to the jury and inquire of them whether it be their verdict. If any juror disagree, the fact must be entered in the minutes, and the jury again sent out; but if no disagreement be expressed, the verdict is complete, and the jury must be discharged from the case.

ARTICLE III.

THE VERDICT.

§ 790. The verdict of a jury is either general or special. A general verdict, is that by which they pronounce generally upon all or any of the issues either in favor of the plaintiff or defendant. A special verdict is that by which the jury find the facts only, leaving the judgment to the court. It must present the conclusions of fact as established by the evidence, and not the evidence to prove them, and those conclusions of fact must be so presented, as that nothing remains to the court but to draw from them conclusions of law.

Amended Code, § 260. Changed so as to be more conformable to the original code.

§ 791. In every action for the recovery of money only, or specific real property, the jury in their discretion, may render a general or special verdict. In all other cases, the court may direct the jury to find a special verdict in writing, upon all or any of the issues; and in all cases may instruct them if they render a general verdict, to find upon particular questions of fact, to be stated in writing, and may direct a written finding thereon. The special verdict or finding must be filed with the clerk and entered upon the minutes.

Amended Code, § 261.

§ 792. Where a special finding of facts is inconsistent with the general verdict, the former controls the latter, and the court must give judgment accordingly.

Amended Code, § 262.

§ 793. When a verdict is found for the plaintiff, in an action for the recovery of money, or for the defendant, when a counter claim for the recovery of money is established, beyond the amount of the plaintiff's claim as established, the jury must also assess the amount of the recovery.

Amended Code, § 263.

§ 794. In an action for the recovery of specific personal property, if the property have not been delivered to the plaintiff, or the defendant by his answer claim a return thereof, the jury must, if their verdict be in favor of the plaintiff, or if being in favor of the defendant, they also find that he is entitled to a return thereof, must assess the value of the property, and may at the same time assess the damages, if any are claimed in the complaint or answer, which the prevailing party has sustained by reason of the taking or detention of such property.

Amended Code, § 264.

§ 795. Upon receiving a verdict, an entry must be made, in the minutes of the court, specifying the time and place of the trial, the names of the jurors and witnesses, the verdict, and either the judgment to be rendered thereon, or where the court is in doubt what judgment ought to be given, it may order that the case be reserved for argument or further consideration.

Amended Code, sec. 267.

CHAPTER IV.

TRIAL BY THE COURT.

§ 796. Trial by jury may be waived by the several parties, to an issue of fact, in actions arising on obligations, and with the assent of the court, in other actions, in the manner following:

1. By failing to appear at the trial:

2. By written consent, in person or by attorney, filed with the clerk:

3. By oral consent in open court, entered in the minutes.

Amended Code, § 266.

§ 797. Upon the trial of a question of fact by the court, its decision must be given in writing, and filed with the clerk, within twenty days after the circuit or term at which the trial took place. In giving the decision, the facts found, and the conclusions of law, must be separately stated. Judgment upon the decision must be entered accordingly.

Amended Code, § 267. Changed so as to be more conformable to the original code.

§ 798. On a judgment for the plaintiff upon an issue of law, the plaintiff may proceed in the manner prescribed by the first two sub-divisions of section 755, upon the failure of the defendant to answer, where the summons was personally served. If judgment be for the defendant, upon an issue of law, and the taking of an account or the proof of any fact be necessary to enable the court to complete the judgment, a reference may be ordered, as in that section provided.

Amended Code, § 269.

CHAPTER VI.

TRIAL BY REFEREES.

§ 799. A trial by referees is conducted in the same manner as a trial by the court.

The sections referred to are conformable to the existing code.

§ 800. The report of the referees upon the whole issue stands as the decision of the court, and judgment may be entered thereon in the same manner, as if the action had been tried by the court; and their decision may be excepted to and reviewed in like manner.

When the reference is to report the facts, the report has the effect of a special verdict.

Amended Code, § 272.

CHAPTER VII.

PROVISIONS RELATING TO TRIALS IN GENERAL.

ARTICLE I.

EXCEPTIONS.

§ 801. An exception is an objection taken at the trial to a decision upon a matter of law, whether such trial be by the jury, court, or referees, and whether the decision be made during the formation of a jury, the production of evidence, the charge to a jury, or at any other time from the calling of the action for trial to the rendering of the verdict or decision. But no exception is to be regarded on a motion for a new trial, or on an appeal, unless the exception be material, and affect substantial rights of the party.

This chapter and the next are new, and fill up a space left in the former code. The provisions explain themselves.

§ 802. The point of the exception must be particularly stated, and either delivered in writing to the judge, or entered in his minutes, and immediately corrected or added to, until made conformable to the truth, or it may afterwards be settled, in a statement of the case, as provided in section 807.

§ 803. No particular form of exception is required. The objection must be stated, with so much of the evidence as is necessary to explain it, but no more, and the whole as briefly as possible. If the decision excepted to be verbally made, it must, upon the exception being taken, be reduced to writing, and entered either in the judge's minutes, or the minutes of the court, or in the statement.

It has been too often the practice to encumber exceptions with details of the evidence, to an unreasonable length. In most cases, with a little care, all the evidence necessary to explain the exception can be given in a narrow compass. The following is a bill of exceptions, taken in Massachusetts, which, for its shortness, is worthy of imitation:

Berkshire ss.—Common Pleas, June Term, 1849.

Commonwealth,
vs.
Robert Walden.

The defendant was indicted for malicious mischief, under that branch of § 39, ch. 126, of rev. statutes, which prohibits the wilfully and maliciously destroying or injuring the personal property of another, in any manner, or by any means not particularly described or mentioned in said chapter.

The indictment is made a part of the case. The court defined the word maliciously, in said part of said section, to mean the wilfully doing of any act prohibited by law, and for which defendant had no lawful excuse—that moral turpitude of mind was not necessary to be shewn, and so instructed the jury.

To this instruction the defendant excepts, and prays that his exceptions may be allowed.

By H. W. B.,
His Attorney.

The foregoing exceptions being found conformable to the truth, are allowed.

H. B.,
Just. C. C. Pleas.

ARTICLE II.

NEW TRIALS.

§ 804. A new trial is a re-examination of an issue of fact, in the same court, after a trial and decision by a jury, court, or referees.

§ 805. The former verdict or other decision may be vacated and a new trial granted, on the application of the party aggrieved, for any of the following causes, materially affecting the substantial rights of such party:

1. Irregularity in the proceedings of the court, jury, or prevailing party, or any order of the court, or abuse of discretion, by which either party was prevented from having a fair trial:

2. Misconduct of the jury, or of the prevailing party:

3. Accident or surprise, which ordinary prudence could not have guarded against:

4. Excessive damages, appearing to have been given under the influence of passion or prejudice:

5. Insufficiency of the evidence to justify the verdict or other decision: or that it is against law:

6. Newly discovered evidence, material for the party making the application, which he could not with reasonable diligence have discovered and produced at the trial:

7. Error in law, occurring at the trial, and excepted to by the party making the application.

§ 806. When the application is made for a cause, mentioned in the fourth, fifth, and seventh subdivisions of the last section, it is made either upon the judge's minutes, or a statement of the case, prepared as prescribed in the next section; for any other cause it is madeupon affidavit.

§ 807. The party preparing a statement is to propose a draft of it, and, within five days after the trial, serve it upon the adverse party, who may within five days thereafter, propose amendments to it. If no amendment be proposed, the draft is adopted; if proposed, the statement and amendments may be submitted for settlement to the judge, or referee, before whom the trial was had, upon a notice of five days; if such notice be not served within five days after the amendments are proposed, they are adopted.

It is our wish to substitute for the present cases and bills of exceptions, a simple statement of the exception or other part of the case sufficient to present the question.

§ 808. The application for a new trial must, in the first instance, be made at a special term, except when made upon an appeal.

§ 809. The application for a cause mentioned in the 4th and 5th subdivisions of section 805 can only be made, when notice thereof, oral or written, was given in open court, immediately after the verdict or other decision rendered; and thereupon if the adverse party consent, the court must appoint a day in the same term for hearing the application upon the judge's minutes. If however the application be not heard at the same term, or if an appeal be taken, a statement of the case must be made.

ARTICLE III.

GENERAL PROVISIONS,

§ 810. Whenever damages are recoverable, the plaintiff may claim and recover any rate of damages, to which he may be entitled, for the cause of action established.

Amended Code, § 276.

§ 811. Any party may, and if required by the court, must when the evidence is closed, submit in distinct and concise propositions, the conclusions of fact which he claims to be established, or the conclusions of law, which he desires to have adjudged, or both; they may be written and handed to the court, or at the option of the court, oral and entered in the judge's minutes; but in either case they must be entered with any exceptions that may be taken, if either party require it.

The design of this section is to enable the court referee or jury to have before them in a definite form the result which the party seeks to establish. It will be found especially convenient in those cases, where the court or referee is required to find separately on the conclusions of fact and of law, with a view to their separation, when necessary upon an appeal.

The practice here proposed is but applying to trials on questions of fact, what the courts have long since required on appeals, whether they include questions of fact, or those of law only. The points which each party produces, before argument, are the same thing as here intended to be made applicable to the first trial. Although no provision for the practice exists in any rule of the court, as applicable to the original trial, yet in point of fact it has long been used in the oral summary, which counsel usually present to the court or jury on the conclusion of a trial.

In some other states, it has become a part of the recognized system of procedure, and with results very beneficial. The object of this section is to give to the practice a legal sanction, and to introduce it in definite form, with a view to facilitate a more logical analysis of the results of a legal controversy than has sometimes been had.

When the conclusions of fact are distinctly pointed out by counsel, it will necessarily relieve the court from some labor in preparing a summary of the facts, inasmuch as it will be able either to decide either in the affirmative or negative, upon the several points, or it can easily modify them to its own conclusions.

§ 812. The provisions of this title, respecting trials by jury, apply, so far as they are in their nature applicable, to trials by the court or referees, and, in the same manner, the provisions respecting trials by the court apply to trials by referees.

CHAPTER VIII.

THE MANNER OF GIVING AND ENTERING JUDGMENT.

§ 813. When a trial by jury has been had, judgment must be entered by the clerk, in conformity to the verdict, unless the court order the case to be reserved for argument or further consideration, or grant a stay of proceedings.

Amended Code, § 265.

§ 814. When the case is reserved for argument or further consideration, as mentioned in the last section, on the ground that judgment ought not to be given in conformity to the verdict, or that it is doubtful what judgment should be given, the questions reserved may be decided by the court, and judgment thereupon rendered, without further argument, or if not so decided they may be brought before the court for judgment, at a special term, upon notice; and judgment thereupon rendered.

New.

§ 815. If a counter-claim, established at the trial, exceed the plaintiffs demand so established, judgment for the defendant must be given for the excess, or if it appear that the defendant is entitled to any other affirmative relief, judgment must be given accordingly.

See 2 R. S., 355, § 22.

§ 816. In an action to recover the possession of personal property, judgment for the plaintiff may be for the possession, or the value, thereof, in case a delivery cannot be had, and of damages for the detention. If the property have been delivered to the plaintiff, and the defendant claim a return thereof, judgment for the defendant may be for a return of the property, or the value thereof, in case a return cannot be had, and damages for taking and withholding the same.

Amended Code, § 277.

§ 817. Judgment upon an issue of law, or of fact, or upon confession, or upon failure to answer, (except where the clerk is authorised to enter the same by the first subdivision of section 755,) must, in the first instance, be entered upon the direction of a single judge, or the report of referees upon the whole issue, subject to review at the general term, on the demand of either party, as provided in this code.

Amended Code, § 278

§ 818. The clerk must keep among the records of the court, a book for the entry of judgments, to be called the "judgment book."

Amended Code, § 279.

§ 819. The judgment must be entered in the judgment book, and must specify clearly the relief granted, or other determination of the action.

Amended Code, § 280.

§ 820. If a party die after a verdict or decision upon an issue of fact, and before judgment, the court may nevertheless render judgment thereon. Such judgment is not a lien on the real property of the deceased party, but is payable in the course of administration on his estate.

§ 821. Immediately after entering the judgment, the clerk must attach together and file the following papers, which constitute the judgment roll:

1. In case the complaint be not answered by any defendant, the summons and complaint, or copies thereof, proof of service, and that no answer has been received, the report, if any, and a copy of the judgment.

2. In all other cases, the summons, pleadings, or copies thereof, and a copy of the judgment with any verdict or report, the offer of the defendant, exceptions, and all orders relating to a change of parties, or in any way involving the merits, and necessarily affecting the judgment. If a statement of the case be made, the same may be attached to the judgment roll, on the request of either party, and thenceforth forms a part thereof.

When the defendant is entitled to judgment, if the plaintiff shall not have filed the summons, with proof of service and the pleadings on his part, the copies of summons and pleadings served on the defendant, may be substituted therefor in making the judgment roll, or the plaintiff may, at the instance of the defendant, be ordered by a judge forthwith to file such papers.

Upon an exemplification of a judgment, as evidence only that part of the roll which consists of the summons, pleadings, and judgment need be given.

Amended Code, § 281. Slightly changed in respect to the time of filing the case or exceptions.

§ 822. On filing a judgment roll, upon a judgment requiring the payment of money, the judgment may be docketed with the clerk of the county where it was rendered, and in any other county, upon filing with the clerk thereof a transcript of the original docket; and thereupon the judgment becomes a lien on real property in the county, from the time of docketing it therein.

Amended Code, § 282.

§ 823. The lien, mentioned in the last section, extends to all the real property of the judgment debtor in the county, owned by him at the time of the judgment, or afterwards acquired, and continues till the first day of July, 1860, on all unsatisfied judgments rendered or which may be rendered before that time. But after the first day of January, 1860, there can be no such lien.

See 2 *R. S.*, 355, §§ 3, 4, 5.

This section proposes an important change in respect to the lien of judgments. We believe the multiplication of liens upon real property has come to be a serious evil. They are but embarrassments in the way of the transfer of property. If all the money collected annually out of real property, upon judgments a year old, could be ascertained, we believe it would not equal half the expense paid in the same year upon searching for the liens.

The liens of existing judgments cannot be cut off, and since they are to continue, it seems proper that subsequent judgments should be put upon the same footing, and the liens of all cease at the same period. That it may be seen at a glance, how many of these incumbrances upon real property, every purchaser and every borrower upon mortgage must search for, we present the following list of them, as they exist in the city of New-York:

General Liens:

Judgments, U. S. circuit court.
U. S. district court.
Supreme, to June, 1840.
Superior, "
Com. pleas, to April 1, 1844, Laws, 1844, p. 91.
Transcripts since June, 1840, Laws, 1840, p. 334, § 26.

Surrogate's Decrees, 2, R. S. 46,
Laws of 1837, p. 535.
" 1844, p. 91.

Insolvent Assignments, 1 R. S., ch. 5, arts. 1 to 10.

Insolvent Notices, 2 R. S., p. 8, sections 32, 33.

Collectors' Bonds and their sureties.
Laws, 1838, p. 184.
" 1843, p. 314.

Forfeited Recognizances, Laws, 1844, p. 475.

Bonds of receiver of taxes, and deputy, and sureties, to be filed in comptroller's office. 1843, p. 315.

Notes given to Mutual Insurance Company, 1836, p. 91, which is a pattern act, and including others framed upon it.

Specific Liens:

Conveyances, 1 R. S., 762, § 38.

Mortgage to U. S. loan commissioners, 1837, p. 121.

Mechanics' liens, 1844, p. 339.

Notice of action pending, 2 R. S., 174, § 48.

Certificates of sheriff and U. S. marshal sales. 2 R. S., 370.

Taxes and sales for unpaid taxes.

Assessments and sales for unpaid assessments.

Water rents, 1849, p. 542.

§ 824. The docket mentioned in section 822 is a book, which the clerk must keep in his office, and in which he must enter alphabetically, under the name of each person,

1. The names of the parties to the judgment:

2. The amount of the judgment: and

3. The precise time of his entry.

See 2 *R. S.* 359 § 6, & 361 § 13.

§ 825. Satisfaction of a judgment may be entered in ihe clerk's register and docket, upon an execution returned satisfied, or upon an acknowledgment of satisfaction filed with the clerk, made in the manner of an acknowledgment of a conveyance of real property, by the judgment creditor, or within two years after the judgment, by the attorney, unless a revocation of his authority is previously entered upon the register. Whenever a judgment is satisfied in fact, otherwise than upon an execution, it is the duty of the party or attorney to give such acknowledgment, and upon motion, the court may compel it, or may order the entry of satisfaction to be made without it. And whenever a judgment is satisfied in fact as to any one of several defendants, an entry to that effect may be made in the register and docket.

See 2 *R. S.* 362, §§ 22, 23, 24, 25, 26.

TITLE IX.

OF THE EXECUTION OF THE JUDGMENT IN CIVIL ACTIONS.

CHAPTER I.

THE EXECUTION.

§ 826. The party in whose favor judgment is given, may at any time within five years after the entry thereof, proceed to enforce the same as prescribed in this title.

§ 827. There are three kinds of writs of execution; one against the property of the judgment debtor; another against his person; and the third for the delivery of the possession of real or personal property, or such delivery with damages for withholding the same. They are issued in the name of the people and are deemed the process of the court, but they need not be sealed nor subscribed, except as prescribed in the next section.

Amended Code, § 286.

§ 828. The writ of execution must be directed to the sheriff, subscribed by the party issuing it, or his attorney, and must intelligibly refer to the judgment, stating the court, the county where the judgment roll or transcript is filed, the names of the parties, the amount of the judgment, if it be for money, the amount actually due thereon, and the time of docketing in the county to which the execution is issued, and must require the sheriff substantially as follows:

1. If it be against the property of the judgment debtor, it must require the sheriff to satisfy the judgment, with interest, out of the personal property of such debtor, and if sufficient personal property cannot be found, out of his real property, or if the judgment be a lien on real property, then out of the real property belonging to him on the day when the judgment was docketed in the county, or at any time thereafter, or

if the judgment be entered pursuant to the first subdivision of section 632, the execution must conform to such judgment:

2. If it be against real or personal property, in the hands of personal representatives, heirs, devisees, legatees, tenants of real property, or trustees, it must require the sheriff to satisfy the judgment, with interest, out of such property;

3. If it be against the person of the judgment debtor, it must require the sheriff to arrest such debtor, and commit him to the jail of the county, until he pay the judgment, with interest, or be discharged according to law;

4. If it be for the delivery of the possession of real or personal property, it must require the sheriff to deliver the possession of the same, particularly describing it, to the party entitled thereto, and may at the same time require the sheriff to satisfy any costs, charges, damages, rents, or profits recovered by the same judgment, out of the personal property of the party against whom it was rendered, and the value of the property for which the judgment was recovered to be specified therein, if a delivery thereof cannot be had, and if sufficient personal property cannot be found, then out of real property, as provided in the first subdivision of this section, and in that respect it is to be deemed an execution against property.

Amended Code, § 289.

§ 829. The execution must be made returnable within sixty days after its receipt by the sheriff, to the clerk with whom the judgment roll is filed.

Amended Code, § 290.

§ 830. Where a judgment requires the payment of money or the delivery of real or personal property, the same is enforced in those respects by execution, as provided in the last three sections. Where it requires the performance of any other act, a certified copy of the judgment may be served upon the party against whom it is given, or upon the person or officer who is required thereby, or by law, to obey the same, and his obedience thereto enforced. If he refuse, he may be punished by the court, as for a contempt.

Amended Code, § 285.

§ 831. After the lapse of five years from the entry of judgment, if no execution have been already issued, an execution can be issued only by leave of the court on motion, upon notice to the adverse party. Such leave must not be given unless it be established by the oath of the party, or other proof, that the judgment, or some part thereof, remains unsatisfied and due.

When the judgment has been rendered in a justice's court, and docketed in the office of the clerk of the county, the application for leave to issue execution must be to the county court of the county where the judgment was rendered, or in the city and county of New-York, to the court of common pleas of that city, and such court has jurisdiction over the judgment and execution.

Amended Code, § 284.

§ 832. Notwithstanding the death of a party after judgment, execution thereon against his property may be issued and executed in the same manner and with the same effect, as if he were still living, except that such execution cannot be issued within a year after his death, unless upon permission granted by the surrogate.

See 2 *R. S.*, 368, § 27.

§ 833. Where the execution is against the property of the judgment debtor, it may be issued to the sheriff of any county where the judgment is docketed. Where it requires the delivery of real or personal property, it must be issued to the sheriff of the county where the property, or some part thereof, is situated. Executions may be issued, at the same time, to different counties.

Amended Code, § 287.

§ 834. If the action be one in which the defendant might have been arrested, as provided in the first three subdivisions of section 675, an execution against the person of the judgment debtor may be issued to any county within the jurisdiction of the court, after the return of an execution against his property, unsatisfied in whole or in part. An execution against the person may likewise be issued, after such return, in the cases mentioned in the fourth and fifth subdivisions of that section, where the defendant has been provisionally arrested in the action, and the order for his arrest has not been vacated, or upon an order of arrest obtained in the same manner as for a provisional arrest.

Amended Code, § 288, modified.

§ 835. A person arrested on execution must be imprisoned within the jail, or the liberties thereof, and there kept at his own expense, until satisfaction of the execution, or his legal discharge.

1 *R. S*, 376, § 76.

§ 836. When a defendant has been once imprisoned upon execution, no other execution can issue upon the same judgment, unless he escape or die, while charged in execution, or unless he be discharged without the consent of the judgment creditor.

2 *R. S.*, 36, *and* §§ 7 *and* 8.

§ 837. All property liable to an attachment is liable to execution. It must be levied on, in the same manner as similar property is attached, pursuant to section 729. Until a levy, property is not affected by the execution.

New.

§ 838. If the property levied on be claimed by a third person as his property, the sheriff may summon from his county any twelve persons, qualified as jurors between the parties, to try the validity of the claim. They and the witnesses must be sworn by the sheriff, and if their verdict be in favor of the claimant, the sheriff may relinquish the levy, unless the judgment creditor give him a sufficient indemnity for proceeding thereon. The fees of the jury must be paid by the claimant, if the verdict be against him, otherwise by the plaintiff.

§ 839. The following property owned by a householder, and in actual use, or kept for use by and for his family, or when being removed from one habitation to another upon a change of residence, is exempt from execution, except as herein otherwise specially provided:

1. Books, pictures, and musical instruments, to the value of fifty dollars:

2. Necessary household, table and kitchen furniture, including stoves, stove pipe, and stove furniture, wearing apparel, beds, bedding and bedsteads, provisions actually provided for family use, sufficient for six months, including meat, fish, vegetables, flour and meal, with fuel for sixty days, one cow, ten sheep, two swine, and food for them for three months:

3. The seat or pew occupied by the debtor or his family, in a house of public worship;

4. The tools and implements of a mechanic, necessary to carry on his trade:

5. A horse, harness, and cart or other vehicle, by the use of which a physician, constable, cartman, teamster, or other laborer, habitually earns his living. But the aggregate value of all the property so exempt, cannot exceed two hundred and fifty dollars; nor is any article exempt from an execution issued on a judgment for its price.

2 *R. S.*, 367, § 22, modified and extended. Whether the exemption should be carried still further, so as to save the homestead of a family, is a high question of public policy, which it is for the legislature alone to entertain.

§ 840. The sheriff must execute the writ against the property of the judgment debtor, by levying on the property, collecting the things in action, as prescribed by section 731 and the fourth subdivision of section 736, selling the other property, and paying to the plaintiff the proceeds, or so much thereof as will satisfy the execution.

§ 841. Before the sale of property on execution, notice thereof must be given as follows:

1. In case of personal property, by posting written notice of the time and place of sale, in three public places of the town where the sale is to take place, six days successively:

2. In case of real property, by posting a similar notice describing the property with the certainty pre-

scribed by section 656, for six weeks successively, in three public places of the town where the property is situated, and also where the property is to be sold, and publishing a copy thereof once a week for the same period, in a newspaper of the county, if there be one, or if there be none, and the property is not occupied by the judgment debtor, or by a tenant or purchaser under him, then in the state paper. After the first of July, 1860, such notice shall be a lien upon the property until the sale thereof, and the filing the certificate of the sale with the clerk of the county.

2 *R. S.*, 366, § 21, 368, §§ 34 *and* 35.

§ 842. An officer selling without the notice prescribed by the last section, shall forfeit one hundred dollars to the aggrieved party, in addition to his actual damages, and a person, taking down or defacing the notice posted, if done before the sale or the satisfaction of the execution, and without the consent of the parties, shall forfeit fifty dollars; but the validity of the sale is not affected by either act.

See 2. *R. S.*, 369, § 37 *and* 39, *and* 40.

§ 843. A sale must be made by auction, between nine o'clock in the morning and sunset; after sufficient property has been sold to satisfy the execution, no more must be sold; neither the officer holding the execution nor his deputy can purchase; when the sale is of personal property, capable of manual delivery, it must be within view of those who attend the sale, and be sold in such parcels as are likely to bring the highest price; and when the sale is of real property, and consisting of several known lots, or parcels, they must be sold separately, or when a portion of such real property is claimed by a third person, and he requires it to be sold separately, such portion must be thus sold.

2 *R. S.* 367, § 23, 369, *and* § 36, 38.

§ 844. Upon a sale of real property, where the estate is less than a leasehold of two years unexpired term, the sale is absolute. In all other cases the property sold is subject to redemption as provided in the next five sections; the officer must give to the purchaser a certificate of the sale, proved or acknowledged so that it may be recorded, containing,

1. A particular description of the property sold:

2. The price bid for each distinct lot or parcel:

3. The whole price paid:

4. When subject to redemption, it must be so stated, a duplicate of which certificate must be filed by the officer with the clerk of the county.

2 *R. S.*, 370, §§ 42, 43, 44.

§ 845. Property sold subject to redemption, as provided in the last section, or any part sold separately, may be redeemed, in the manner provided in the next four sections, by the following persons or their successors in interest:

1. The judgment debtor, or his successor in interest, in the whole or any part of the property.

2. A creditor, having a lien by judgment or mortgage on the property sold, or on some share or part thereof, subsequent to that on which the property was sold. The persons mentioned in the last four subdivisions, are in this chapter termed redemptioners.

§ 846. The judgment debtor, or a redemptioner, may redeem the property from the purchaser within sixty days after the sale, on paying him the amount of his purchase, and if he be also a creditor having a lien prior to that of the redemptioner, the amount of such lien, with interest.

§ 847. If, the property be so redeemed, by a redemptioner, either the judgment debtor or another redemptioner, may, within thirty days after the last redemption, again redeem it from the last redemptioner on paying the sum paid on his redemption, with interest, and, unless his lien be prior to that of the preceeding redemptioner, the amount of such lien, with interest. The property may be again, and as often as the debtor or owner, or any redemptioner is so disposed, redeemed from any redemptioner within thirty days after his redemption, and notice thereof filed with the sheriff. If no redemption is made in sixty days after the sale, the purchaser is entitled to a conveyance; or if so redeemed, whenever thirty days have elapsed, and no redemption has been made and notified therein, the time for redemption has expired, and the last redemptioner is entitled to a sheriff's deed. If the debtor or owner redeem at any time before the time for redemption expires, the effects of the sale are terminated, and he is restored to his estate.

§ 848. The payment mentioned in the last two sections, may be made to the purchaser or redemptioner, as the case may be, or for him, to the officer who made the sale; and a tender of the money is equivalent to payment.

§ 849. A redemptioner must produce to the officer or person from whom he seeks to redeem, and file with his notice in the sheriff's office.

1. A copy of the docket of the judgment, under which he claims the right to redeem, certified by the clerk of the court or of the county, where the judgment is docketed, or if he redeem upon a mortgage or other lien, a note of the record thereof, certified by the clerk:

2. A copy of any assignment necessary to establish his claim, verified by the affidavit of himself or of a subscribing witness thereto: and

3. An affidavit by himself or his agent showing the amount then actually due on the lien.

It has been for some years the policy of our laws to allow a redemption of real property upon sales on execution. 2 *R. S.* 370, § 45—62. Whether this policy is founded in sound principles, or even affords any benefit to the debtor, has been seriously questioned by judicious men. The Commissioners do not deem it expedient for them to propose to abolish redemptions, but there are some features in the existing system which are unnecessary, and so clearly indefensible that they have felt it a duty to endeavor, by a change, to make it more conducive to the real policy of the law: favor to an unfortunate debtor, and the appropriation of his property in such manner as to pay the largest possible amount of his debts.

The existing system presents the following, among other results:

It, in effect, delays the collection of a debt out of real property, for fifteen months after the sale;

It suspends the remedy of all junior judgment creditors against the same property for the same period;

If redeemed upon judgment or other lien, the redemption effects no payment on the lien debt, but the creditor takes the debtor's land by redemption, and keeps his debt against him also in full force, and may sell other property upon it in the same manner as if he had not redeemed; even if paid afterwards, the payment does not restore the land.

Although the provisions proposed by the Commissioners do not wholly obviate these objections, they at least have that tendency.

There seems no good reason for the great lapse of time heretofore allowed, nor for preventing the debtor from redeeming his land at any time while it is open for redemption to a creditor. The uncertainty whether the holder of the oldest lien will redeem, and the advantage of waiting until the last hour, in case he fails, has often led to subsequent litigation. The plan the Commissioners offer, partially obviates at least these objections.

§ 850. Until the expiration of the time allowed for redemption, the court may restrain the commission of waste on the property by order granted with or without notice, on the application of the purchaser or the judgment creditor. But it is not waste for the person in possession of the property at the time of sale, or entitled to possession afterwards during the period allowed for redemption, to continue to use it in the same manner in which it was previously used, or to use it in the ordinary course of husbandry, or to make the necessary repairs of buildings thereon, or to use wood or timber on the property therefor, or for the repair of fences, or for fuel in his family, while he occupies the property.

2 *R. S.*, 336, §§ 20, 21, 22, 23, 24, 25, 26, 27, 28 and 29.

§ 851. If the purchaser of real property sold on execution, or his successor in interest, be evicted therefrom in consequence of irregularity in the proceedings concerning the sale, or of the reversal or discharge of the judgment, he may recover the price paid with interest from the judgment creditor. Such judgment creditor, if the recovery was in consequence of the irregularity, shall thereupon be entitled to a new execution on the judgment, for the price paid on the sale with interest; and for that purpose the judgment shall be deemed valid against the judgment debtor, his personal representatives, heirs, or devisees, but not against a purchaser in good faith, or an incumbrancer, whose title or incumbrance shall have accrued before a levy on such new execution.

2 *R. S.*, 375, § 68, 69, 70, 71, 72, 73, 74.

§ 852. When property, liable to an execution against several persons, is sold thereon, and more than a due proportion of the judgment is levied upon the property of one of them, or one of them pays without a sale more than his proportion, he may compel contribution from the others. And when a judgment is against several, and is upon an obligation of one of them, as security for another, and the surety pays the amount or any part thereof, either by sale of his property or before sale, he may compel repayment from the principal. In such cases the person so paying, or contributing, is entitled to the benefit of the judgment to enforce contribution or repayment, if within ten days after his payment he file with the clerk of the court, where the judgment was rendered, notice of his payment and claim to contribution or repayment. Upon the filing of such notice, the clerk must make an entry thereof in the margin of the docket.

2 *R. S.*, 375, § 70, extended.

It will be observed, that the provisions of this chapter extend the execution, so as in all cases to reach the property which can be reached by attachment. In a case where an attachment has been issued, the execution is as extensive in its operation as the attachment, and there seems no good reason for making one execution against property less extensive than another.

CHAPTER II.

PROCEEDINGS SUPPLEMENTARY TO THE EXECUTION.

§ 853. When an execution against property of the judgment debtor, or of any one of several debtors, in the same judgment, issued to the sheriff of the county where he resides, or if he do not reside in this state, to the sheriff of the county where the judgment roll, or a transcript of a justice's judgment, is filed, is returned unsatisfied in whole or in part, the judgment creditor, at any time after such return made, is entitled to an order from a judge of the court, or a county judge of the county to which the execution was issued, requiring such judgment debtor to appear and answer, concerning his property, before such judge, or a referee appointed by a judge of the court, at a time and place specified in the order.

Amended Code, § 292.

§ 854. After the issuing of an execution against property, and upon proof by affidavit, of a party or otherwise, to the satisfaction of the court, or a judge thereof, or county judge, that any judgment debtor has property, which he unjustly refuses to apply towards the satisfaction of the judgment, such court or judge may, by an order, require the judgment debtor to appear at a specified time and place, to answer concerning the same; and such proceedings may thereupon be had, for the application of the property of the judgment debtor towards the satisfaction of the judgment, as are provided, upon the return of an execution.

Amended Code, § 292.

§ 855. Instead of the order requiring the attendance of the judgment debtor, as provided in the last two sections, the judge may, upon proof by affidavit or otherwise, to his satisfaction that there is danger of the debtor's leaving the state, or concealing himself, issue a warrant requiring the sheriff of any county where such debtor may be, to arrest him and bring him before such judge. Upon being brought before the judge, he may be examined on oath, and ordered to enter into an undertaking with one or more sureties, that he will attend from time to time before the judge or referee, as he shall direct, during the pendency of the proceeding, and until the final determination thereof, and will not in the meantime dispose of any portion of his property, not exempt from execution. In default of entering into such undertaking, he may be committed to prison, by warrant of the judge.

Amended Code, § 292.

§ 856. After the issuing of execution against property, any person indebted to the judgment debtor, may pay to the sheriff the amount of his debt, or so much thereof as may be necessary to satisfy the execution, and the sheriff's receipt shall be a sufficient discharge for the amount so paid.

Amended Code, § 293.

§ 857. After the issuing or return of an execution against property of the judgment debtor, or of any one of several debtors in the same judgment, and upon proof by affidavit, or otherwise, to the satisfaction of the judge, that any person or corporation has property of such judgment debtor, or is indebted to him in an amount exceeding ten dollars, the judge may by an order require such person or corporation, or any officer or member thereof, to appear at a specified time and place, and answer concerning the same. The judge may also, in his discretion, require notice of such proceeding to be given to any party to the action, in such manner as may seem to him proper.

Amended Code, § 294.

§ 858. Witnesses may be required to appear and testify upon any proceedings under this chapter, in the same manner as upon the trial of an issue.

Amended Code, § 295.

§ 859. The party or witness may be required to attend before the judge, or before a referee, appointed by the court or judge. If before a referee, the examination must be taken by the referee, and certified to the judge. All examinations and answers before a judge or referee, under this chapter, must be on oath, except that when a corporation answers, the answer must be on the oath of an officer thereof.

Amended Code, § 296.

§ 860. The judge may order any property of the judgment debtor, not exempt from execution, in the hands either of himself or any other person, or due to the judgment debtor, to be applied towards the satisfaction of the judgment, except that the earnings of the debtor for his personal services, at any time within thirty days next preceding the order, cannot be so applied, when it is made to appear by the debtor's affidavit, or otherwise, that such earnings are necessary for the use of a family supported wholly or partly by his labor.

Amended Code, § 297. Modified, so as to preserve the current earnings of a debtor for the use of his family, if necessary for their support.

§ 861. The judge may also, by order, appoint a receiver of the property of the judgment debtor, in the same manner and with the like authority, as if the appointment were made by the court. The judge may also, by order, forbid a transfer or other disposition of the property of the judgment debtor, not exempt from execution, and any interference therewith.

Amended Code, § 298.

§ 862. If it appear that a person or corporation alleged to have property of the judgment debtor, or indebted to him, claims an interest in the property, adverse to him, or denies the debt, such interest or debt is recoverable only in an action against such person or corporation, by the receiver: but the judge may, by order, forbid a transfer or other disposition of such property or interest, till a sufficient opportunity be given to the receiver to commence the action, and prosecute the same to judgment and execution. Such order may be modified or vacated, by the judge granting the same, at any time, on such security as he may direct.

Amended Code, § 299.

§ 863. The judge may, in his discretion, order a reference to a referee agreed upon or appointed by him, to report the evidence or the facts.

Amended Code, § 300.

§ 864. The judge may allow to the judgment creditor, or to any person so examined, whether a party to the action or not, his charges, and a fixed sum in addition, not exceeding ten dollars, as costs.

Amended Code, § 301.

§ 865. If any person, party or witness, disobey an order of the judge or referee, duly served, such person, party or witness, may be punished by the judge, as for a contempt. The proceedings therefor are prescribed in the title of the third part of this code, respecting the punishment of contempts.

Amended Code, § 203.

TITLE X.

OF THE COSTS IN CIVIL ACTIONS.

§ 866. All statutes, establishing or regulating the costs or fees of attorneys and counsel in civil actions, and all existing rules and provisions of law, restricting or controlling the right of a party to agree with an attorney, or counsel, for his compensation, are repealed; and hereafter the measure and mode of such compensation must be left to the agreement, express or implied, of the parties. But there may be allowed to the prevailing party, certain sums by way of indemnity, for his expenses in the action; which allowances are in this code termed costs.

Amended Code, § 303.

§ 867. Costs are allowed of course to the plaintiff, upon a judgment in his favor, in the following cases;

1. In an action for the recovery of real property, or when a claim of title to real property arises on the pleadings, or is certified by the court to have come in question at the trial;

2. In an action to recover the possession of personal property;

3. In the actions of which, according to section 154, a justice's court has not jurisdiction:

4. In an action for the recovery of money, where the plaintiff recovers fifty dollars or more. But in an action for assault, battery, false imprisonment, libel, slander, malicious prosecution, criminal conversation, or seduction, if the plaintiff recover less than fifty dollars damages, he can recover no more costs and charges than damages. And in an action to recover the possession of personal property, if the plaintiff recover less than fifty dollars damages, he can recover no more costs and charges than damages, unless he recover also property, the value of which with the damages amounts to fifty dollars. Such value must be determined by the jury, court, or referee, by whom the action is tried.

Amended Code, § 304.

§ 868. When several actions are brought on one bond, undertaking, promissory note, bill of exchange, or other instrument in writing, or in any other case for the same cause of action, against several parties who might have been joined as defendants in the same action, no costs can be allowed to the plaintiff, in more than one of such actions, which may be at his election, if the parties proceeded against in the other actions were at the commencement of the previous action, openly within this state; but the disbursements of the plaintiff may be allowed to him, as provided in section 874.

Amended Code, § 304.

§ 869. Costs are allowed of course to the defendant upon a judgment in his favor, in an action for the recovery of money, where the plaintiff recovers less than fifty dollars, and also in the other actions mentioned in section 867.

Amended Code, § 305.

§ 870. In other actions, costs may be allowed or not, and if allowed, may be apportioned between the parties, on the same or adverse sides, in the discretion of the court.

When there are several defendants, not united in interest, and making separate defences by separate answers, and the plaintiff fails to recover judgment against all, the court may award costs to such of the defendants as have judgment in their favor, or any of them

And in the following cases the costs of an appeal are in the discretion of the court;

1. Where a new trial is ordered:

2. Where a judgment is modified.

Amended Code, § 304.

§ 871. Costs can not be allowed to the plaintiff, in an action upon a judgment of a court of this state, between the same parties, unles such action was brought with previous leave of the court for cause shown; but this prohibition does not apply to an action upon the judgment of a justice's court, brought in another county, or brought in the same county, in case of the summons not having been served on all the defendants, or the death of a party, or the death, resignation, incapacity to act or removal from the county of the justice, or the loss of his docket.

Amended Code, § 71.

§ 872. When allowed, costs are as follows:

1. To the plaintiff, for all proceedings before notice of trial (including judgment when entered;)

In an action arising on obligation for the recovery of money only, seven dollars; in another action, twelve dollars; for all subsequent proceedings before trial, seven dollars;

2. To the defendant; for all the proceedings before notice of trial, five dollars; for all subsequent proceedings before trial, seven dollars:

3. For the trial of issues of law, if separate from the trial of issues of fact, to the plaintiff, fifteen dollars; to the defendant, twelve dollars:

4. For the trial of the issues of fact, if separate from the trial of the issues of law, to the plaintiff, fifteen dollas; to the defendant, twelve dollars:

5. For the trial of the issues of fact and of law, when tried at the same time, to the plaintiff, twenty dollars; to the defendant, fifteen dollars:

6. To either party on appeal, excepting to the court of appeals, before argument, fifteen dollars: for argument thirty dollars: but this provision does not apply to appeals in the cases mentioned in section .

7. To either party on appeal to the court of appeals; before argument, twenty-five dollars; for argument, fifty dollars:

8. To either party, for every circuit or term not exceeding three, at which the cause necessarily remains on the calendar not reached or postponed, excluding that at which it is tried or heard, ten dollars.

In actions for the foreclosure of mortgages upon real property, or for the partition of real property, the plaintiff is also entitled to the additional allowance of five per cent on the first five hundred dollars, and one per per cent on all over that sum, upon the price of the property sold, or the value of the property partitioned, such value to be determined by the referees making the partition. But such allowance can in no case exceed two hundred dollars.

Amended Code, § 307, 308 and 309, altered so as to reduce the costs in the 8th subdivision, and to limit both the per centage and the cases in which it may be allowed.

§ 873. When the judgment is for the recovery of money, interest from the time of the verdict or report, until judgment be finally entered, must be computed by the clerk, and added thereto.

Amended Code, § 310.

§ 874. The clerk must insert in the entry of judgment, on the application of the prevailing party, upon two days notice to the other, the sum of the allowances for costs, as above provided, and the necessary disbursements, including the fees of officers allowed by law, the fees of witnesses, the necessary expenses of commissions, the compensation of referees, and the expense of printing the papers upon any appeal, which disbursements are in this code also termed charges. The disbursements must be stated in detail, and verified by affidavit, which must be filed. Whenever costs are allowed by this code, the charges also are allowed, and when costs are not allowed, the charges are not allowed, except where express provision is made therefor.

Amended Code, § 311.

§ 875. The clerk may receive,

On every trial, from the party bringing it on, one dollar:

On entering judgment, fifty cents; except in courts where the clerks receive salaries, and in such courts one dollar:

On docketing a judgment rendered by a justice in his county, and filing a transcript thereof, twenty-five cents, including execution when issued.

He can receive no other fee, for any services whatever in a civil action, except for copies of papers, at the rate of five cents for every hundred words.

Amended Code, § 312.

§ 876. The fees of referees are three dollars to each, for every day spent in the business of the reference; but the parties may agree in writing upon any other rate of compensation and thereupon such rate must be allowed.

Amended Code, § 313.

§ 877. When an application is made to a court or referees, to postpone a trial, the payment to the adverse party of a sum not exceeding ten dollars, besides the fees of witnesses, may be imposed, as the condition of granting the postponement.

Amended Code, § 314.

§ 878. Costs may be allowed on an original motion, or on an appeal from an order, in the discretion of the court, not exceeding ten dollars. And when costs are ordered against a party, upon a motion, proceedings on his part may be stayed until payment thereof.

Amended Code, § 315.

§ 879. When costs are adjudged against an infant plaintiff, the guardian, by whom he appeared in the action, is responsible for them, and judgment therefor may be entered, against both the guardian and infant.

Amended Code, § 316.

§ 880. When, in an action for the recovery of money only, the defendant alleges in his answer, that, before the commencement of the action, he tendered to the plaintiff, the full amount to which he was entitled, and thereupon deposits in court for the plaintiff, the amount so tendered, and the allegation be found true, the plaintiff cannot recover costs, but must pay costs to the defendant.

§ 881. In an action prosecuted or defended by an executor, administrator, trustee of an express trust, or a person expressly authorized by statute, costs may be recovered, as in an action by and against a person prosecuting or defending in his own right, but such costs must by the judgment be made chargeable only upon the estate, fund, or party represented, unless the court direct the same to be paid by the plaintiff or defendant, personally, for mismanagement or bad faith in the action or defence. But no costs are recoverable in such action, if brought without leave of the surrogate, against an executor or administrator within one year after the death of the person whom he represents, nor after that time, unles it appear that the demand was first presented to the executor or administrator, verified by oath, and payment demanded.

Amended Code, § 317.

§ 882. When the decision of a court of inferior jurisdiction in a special proceeding, is brought before the supreme court for review, such proceeding is for all purposes of costs, to be deemed an action at issue, on a question of law, from the time the same is brought into the supreme court, and costs thereon may be awarded and collected in such manner as the court may direct, according to the nature of the case.

Amended Code, § 318.

§ 883. In all civil actions prosecuted in the name of the people of this state, by an officer duly authorized for that purpose, the people are liable for costs in the same cases, and to the same extent, as private parties. If a private person be joined with the people as plaintiff, he is liable in the first instance for the defendant's costs; which can not be recovered of the people, till after execution issued therefor against such private party and returned unsatisfied. And when costs are awarded, and recoverable, against the people, payment thereof must be made by the comptroller, upon the production of proper evidence thereof.

Amended Code, § 319.

§ 884. In an action prosecuted in the name of the people of this state for the recovery of money or property, or to establish a right or claim, for the benefit of any county, city, town, village, corporation or person, costs awarded against the plaintiff, must by the judgment be made a charge against the party for whose benefit the action was prosecuted, and not against the people.

Amended Code, § 320.

§ 885. In an action in which the cause of action, after the commencement of the action, by assignment, or in any other manner, becomes the property of a person not a party to the action, and the prosecution or defence is thereafter continued, such person is liable for the costs, in the same manner as if he were a party, and payment thereof may be enforced by order.

Amended Code, § 321.

§ 886. Upon the settlement, before judgment, of any action mentioned in section 867, no greater sum can be demanded from the defendant as costs, than at the rates prescribed by section 872.

Amended Code, § 322.

§ 887. The attorney of a plaintiff, who resides out of the state, or is a foreign corporation, against whom costs are awarded to a defendant, is responsible to such defendant therefor, to an amount not exceeding two hundred dollars. And the attorney, neglecting to pay the same, after due proceedings against him, may be removed by the court. But he may relieve himself from responsibility, at any time before judgment, by filing an undertaking, for the payment to the defendant of the costs, and charges, executed by a sufficient surety.

2 *R. S.*, 620, § 1, 2, 3, 4, 5, 6, 7, *and* 8.

TITLE XI.

ACTIONS IN PARTICULAR CASES.

The form of civil actions under the code, is in its nature adapted to almost every case requiring the interposition of judicial authority. In making provisions for proceedings in special cases, it has been deemed wise to conform as far as practicable, to the system already adopted in civil actions, and to make provision for the points of difference only. By this means the advantage is afforded of following the beaten track already enlightened by the judicial consideration to which the code has been subjected. The length and number of statutory enactments, are by the same means greatly abridged. This remark is applicable not only to most of the provisions under this title, but also to the special proceedings for which rules are prescribed in part 3.

By comparing the provisions with those of the revised statutes on the same subject, it will be found that the volume of matter has been greatly reduced, while it contains, as we believe, a more certain, safe and simple mode of procedure in every case.

CHAPTER I.

ACTIONS TO DETERMINE CONFLICTING CLAIMS TO REAL PROPERTY, AND OTHER PROVISIONS RELATING TO ACTIONS CONCERNING REAL PROPERTY.

§ 888. An action may be brought by any person in possession, by himself, or his tenant, of real property, against any person, who claims an estate or interest therein, adverse to him, for the purpose of determining such adverse claim, estate, or interest.

§ 889. If the defendant, in such action, disclaim in his answer any interest or estate in the property, or suffer judgment to be taken against him without answer, the plaintiff cannot recover costs.

R. S., part 3, chap. 5, title 2.

The salutary provisions of this entire title are secured in the two preceding sections. The form of action under the code being adapted to these cases, it only requires a provision declaring them the subject of an action, and regulating the judgment, when the defendant disclaims, or makes no defence.

§ 890. In an action, for the recovery of dower before admeasurement, or by a tenant in common, or joint tenant of real property, against a co-tenant, the plaintiff must show, in addition to the evidence of his right, that the defendant either denied the plaintiff's right, or did some act amounting to such denial.

The provisions of the Revised Statutes are extended, so as to include actions for the recovery of dower not set off, as coming within the reason of the rule which applies to other tenants in common.

§ 891. In an action for the recovery of specific real or personal property, where the plaintiff shows a right to recover at the time the action was commenced, but it appears that his right has terminated during the pendency of the action, the verdict and judgment must be according to the fact, and the plaintiff may recover damages for withholding the property.

The provisions of the Revised Statutes extended, so as to include actions for specific personal property as well as real.

§ 892. Any person, against whom a judgment for the recovery of specific real property is rendered may, within six months after written notice of the judgment, upon payment of all costs and damages recovered thereby, demand another trial, by notice in writing to the adverse party, or to his attorney in the action, and thereupon the action may be brought to trial by either party.

It appears to have been the policy of our law, at an early period, to regard real property, and all legal proceedings relating to it, with peculiar caution and jealousy of the courts. This arises from the source. whence we have drawn most of our system of judicial policy, and is the legitimate descendant of feudal times in England. But a few years since real property could not be sold on execution. Until the Revised Statutes, a judgment in ejectment, though based exclusively on evidence of title, decided nothing but the right of possession for the time being, and other actions might be brought the next day by the defendant to recover back the same property.

By the Revised States, when the action by writ of right was abolished and ejectment substituted, the judgment was made conclusive upon the title, but the losing party was allowed three years to pay the costs and demand a new trial. If unsuccessful again, he might even then within two years apply to the court for another new trial.

There seems no good reason for allowing so long a period, within which an unsuccessful party may determine whether, to submit to the result of the first trial. After a second trial with a similar result, the judgment ought to be conclusive.

The remaining sections of this title embrace all the remaining provisions of the existing laws relating to actions concerning real property, which the Commissioners deem necessary.

§ 893. If on a second trial, as provided in the last section, judgment be to the same effect, as on the first, no further trial can be had, unless the court, in its discretion, on motion by the party as to whom the judgment last rendered is less favorable than the first, order a third trial.

§ 894. The judgment given on a trial, to be had under the last two sections, must be annexed to the judgment roll of the former trial, and the judgment last given, shall be the final determination of the rights of the parties. If a prior judgment shall have been executed, restitution must be ordered, as the last judgment may determine the rights of the parties, and the same may be enforced by execution.

§ 895. Damages for withholding the property recovered, can in no case exceed the fair value of the property, (exclusive of the use of improvements, made by the defendant,) for a period not exceeding six years; and when permanent improvements have been made by a defendant, or those under whom he claims, holding under color of title, adversely to the claims of the plaintiff, in good faith, the value thereof must be allowed as a set off, against the damages of the plaintiff, for the use of the property.

§ 896. The court, in which an action is pending for the recovery of real property, may on motion, upon notice, by either party, and for cause shown, grant an order, allowing to such party the right to enter upon the property, and make survey and measurement thereof, for the purposes of the action.

§ 897. The order must describe the property, and a copy thereof must be served on the owner, or occupant, and thereupon such party may enter upon the property, with necessary surveyors and assistants, and make such survey and measurements, but if any unnecessary injury be done to the property, he is liable therefor.

§ 898. A mortgage of real property is not to be deemed a conveyance, so as to enable the owner of the mortgage to recover possession of the real property, without a foreclosure.

§ 899. The court may, by injunction, on cause shown, restrain the party in possession, from doing any act to the injury of real property, during the summary foreclosure of a mortgage thereon, or after a sale on execution, before a conveyance.

§ 900. When real property shall have been sold on execution, the purchaser thereof, or any person, who may have succeeded to his interest, may, after his estate becomes absolute, recover damages for injury to the property, by the tenant in possession, after the sale, and before possession is delivered under the conveyance.

§ 901. An action for the recovery of real property against a person in possession, or in the receipt of the rents or profits thereof, can not be prejudiced by any alienation, made by such person, either before or after the commencement of the action; but in such case, if the defendant have no property sufficient to satisfy the damages recovered, for the withholding of possession, such damages may be collected by action against the purchaser.

§ 902. When in case of a lease of real property, and the failure of the tenant to pay rent, the landlord has a subsisting right to re-enter for such failure, he may bring an action to recover possession of the property; and such action is equivalent to a demand of the rent and a re-enty upon the property. But if at any time before the expiration of six months after possession obtained by the plaintiff, on a recovery in the action, the lessee, or his successor in interest as to the whole or part of the property, pay to the plaintiff, or bring into court, the amount of rent then in arrear with interest, and the costs of the action, and perform the other covenants on the part of the lessee, he may be restored to the possession and hold the property according to the terms of the original lease.

CHAPTER II.

ACTIONS FOR THE FORECLOSURE OF MORTGAGES.

This chapter contains all the provisions deemed necessary in actions for foreclosure of mortgages, which are substituted for the provisions formerly in use for that purpose. When mortgages are given for the payment of money only, as most of them are, ample provisions are made in part 3, for their foreclosure in a summary, and as we think safe, manner. In cases other than those, the action of the court, in determining the amount is almost invariably necessary; and these are the only cases in which a mortgage foreclosure will necessarily be by action.

§ 903. In an action for the foreclosure or satisfaction of a mortgage of real property, or the satisfaction of a lien or incumbrance upon property, real or personal, the court has power, by its judgment, to direct a sale of the property, or any part of it; the application of the proceeds to the payment of the amount due on the mortgage, lien, or incumbrance with costs; and execution, for the balance, against any party liable therefor, as principal, surety, or otherwise.

§ 904. Real property adjudged to be sold, must be sold in the county where it lies, by the sheriff of the county, or by a referee, appointed by the court for that purpose, and thereupon the sheriff or referee must execute a conveyance to the purchaser, which conveyance passes the title of the parties to the action. And upon the sale of property, real or personal, pursuant to a judgment, the court may enforce the delivery of possession thereof to the purchaser.

§ 905. When a debt is secured by mortgage of real or personal property, or a lien or incumbrance thereon, separate actions respecting the debt and the security cannot be allowed, but the creditor must include in one action all his claims upon both.

To prevent multiplicity of actions.

§ 906. If there be surplus money, remaining after payment of the amount mentioned in section 903, the court may cause the same to be paid to the person entitled to it, and in the mean time, may direct it to be deposited in court.

§ 907. If the debt, for which the mortgage, lien or incumbrance is held, be not all due, so soon as sufficient of the property has been sold to pay the amount due, with costs the sale must cease; and afterwards as often as more becomes due, for principal or interest, the court may, on motion, order more to be sold. But if the property cannot be sold in portions, without injury to the parties, the whole may be ordered to be sold in the first instance, and the entire debt and costs be paid, there being a rebate of interest, where such rebate is proper.

CHAPTER III.

ACTIONS FOR NUISANCE, WASTE, TRESPASS ON INDIAN LANDS, AND WILFUL TRESPASS ON OTHER REAL PROPERTY.

§ 908. Anything, which is injurious to health, or indecent, or offensive to the senses, or an obstruction to the free use of property, so as to interfere with the comfortable enjoyment of life or property, is a nuisance and the subject of an action. Such action may be brought by any person whose property is injuriously affected, or whose personal enjoyment is lessened by the nuisance;

and by the judgment, the nuisance may be enjoined or abated, as well as damages recovered.

§ 909. If a guardian, tenant by the curtesy, in dower, for life or years, joint tenant or tenant in common of real property, commit waste thereon, any person aggrieved by the waste, may bring an action against him therefor, in which action, there may be judgment for treble damages, forfeiture of the estate of the party offending, and eviction from the property.

§ 910. Judgment of forfeiture and eviction can only be given, in favor of the person entitled to the reversion, against the tenant in possession, when the injury to the estate in reversion is adjudged in the action, to be equal to the value of the tenant's estate or unexpired term, or to have been done in malice.

The injuries known at common law by the expressive terms of waste and nuisance, have been heretofore remediable only by special writs and a peculiar form of proceeding, or by suit in chancery. The injuries themselves are not defined in the revised statutes, but are left to be gleaned from the reports of common law cases, and elementary writers, while the method of proceeding to obtain redress is defined at some length. The system of civil action sin the code is perfectly well adapted to these cases, and it only requires a definition of them sufficiently comprehensive to prevent the loss of a remedy, and to declare them within the cases for which an ordinary action may be brought.

This the commissioners believe they have accomplished by these provisions. The necessity is dispensed with for the special writs and peculiar proceedings for which those parts of the re ised statutes were enacted.

§ 911. Every person who cuts down, or carries off, any wood or underwood, tree or timber, or girdles or otherwise injures any tree timber or shrub on the land of another person, or on the street or highway, in front of any person's house, village or city lot, or cultivated grounds, or on the commons, or public grounds, of any city or town, or on the street or highway, in front thereof, without lawful authority, is liable to the owner of such land, or to such city or town, for treble the amount of damages, which may be assessed therefor, in a civil action, in any court having jurisdiction, except as provided in the next section.

The cases to which a penalty is attached for wilful trespass, extended so as to include ornamental trees in the streets.

§ 912. If, upon the trial of such action, it appear, that the trespass was casual or involuntary, or that the defendant had probable cause to believe, that the land, on which the trespass was committed, was his own, or that of the person in whose service, or by whose direction, the act was done, judgment must be given for only the single damages assessed in the action.

§ 913. Nothing in the last two sections authorises the recovery of more than the just value of the timber, taken from uncultivated wood land, for the repair of a public highway or bridge upon the land or adjoining it.

§ 914. If a person be put out of real property in a forcible manner, without lawful authority, or, being so put out, be afterwards kept out by force, recover damages therefor, judgment may be entered for three times the amount at which the actual damages are assessed.

§ 915. In case of forcible entry or forcible detention, if a person claiming in good faith, under color of title, to be rightfully in possession, so put out or kept out, recover damages therefor, judgment may be entered in his favor, for three times the amount, at which the actual damages are assessed.

§ 916. For trespass, by any person other than an Indian, on lands possessed by Indians, an action may be brought in the name of the people of this state.

§ 917. Such action must be prosecuted by the district attorney of the county where the lands are situated, or by an attorney to be designated for that purpose, by the county judge.

§ 918. The damages recovered in such action, after defraying the expenses of the prosecution, must be distributed among the Indians occupying such lands, according to their respective interests therein, to be determined by the county judge, on summary application before him.

§ 919. Before such action can be commenced, security for costs must be given, satisfactory to the county judge, or to the supervisor of the town where the lands are situated, by an undertaking in writing to pay to the defendant, the costs which may be adjudged against the plaintiff.

The last three sections contain the substance of the provisions for the same purpose, in sec. 8 and 9, of chapter 234, session laws, 1841, with some definite provisions to regulate them, and prevent abuse.

CHAPTER IV.

ACTIONS FOR THE PARTITION OF REAL PROPERTY.

SECTION 920. Action for partition of real property allowed.
921. To whom summons is addressed.
922. Contents of complaint.
923. Creditors having general liens may be parties.
924. Liens on undivided shares.
925. Unknown owners made parties.
926. Rights of parties may be put in issue.
927. Order may allow sale or partition.
928. Manner of making partition.
929. Referees to make report.
930. Effect of confirmation of report.
931. Tenants in dower, &c., not affected.
932. Expenses of referees and surveyor.
933. Sale, when allowed.
934. When part only is sold, life estate.
935. Before sale, creditors having specific liens.
936. Certificate as to general liens.
937, 938. Court may order reference as to liens.
939. Notice to creditors to make proof.
940. Referee to report priority.
941. Creditor may have report corrected.
942. Proceeds of sale, how applied.
943. Sale not to be delayed by reference.
944. Referees may deliver securities to parties.
945. Manner of litigating as to claims.
946. Sales to be at auction.
947. Terms of sale to be ordered.
948. Separate securities allowed.
949. Estate for life, how disposed of.
950. What passes by sale.
951. Sum in gross allowed for dower, &c.
952. Investment, if no consent given.
953. Proportion of proceeds ascertained.
954. Unknown tenants in dower, &c.
955. Investment for inchoate right of dower.
956. Dower, how released.
957. Terms of sale to be published.

This proceeding is one of those which has existed heretofore, separate from the ordinary forms of actions, by special statutory provisions in detail, providing for its prosecution in both courts of law and equity.

The nature of the remedy is so unlike those sought in ordinary actions, as to require many distinct provisions, differing from the general course of procedure.

We have endeavored to unite all that was valuable in the old law and equity modes of practice, and to make the procedure conform as far as the nature of the remedy admits, to the procedure in ordinary actions. There are such a variety of interests and contingencies to be guarded and provided for, that the provisions necessarily occupy a considerable space though condensed into nearly half the volume, they have heretofore occupied in the revised statutes. Among other improvements in the system heretofore in use, is that by which, in case of a sale of property, the proceeds, whether money or securities, may, in certain cases, be paid or delivered directly to the parties interested, without the tedious and expensive ceremony of being first paid into court, and afterwards taken out on a formal application.

See 2 *R. S.*, 316—332.

§ 920. When several persons hold, and are in possession of real property, as joint tenants, or as tenants in common, in which one or more of them have an estate of inheritance, or for life or years, an action may be brought by one or more of such persons, for a partition thereof, according to the respective rights of the persons interested therein, and for a sale of such property, or a part of it, if it appear that a partition cannot be made, without great prejudice to the owners.

§ 921. The summons must be addressed by name to all the joint tenants, and tenants in common, who are known, and generally to all persons unknown, having or claiming an interest in the property.

§ 922. The interests of all persons in the property, whether such persons be known or unknown, must be set forth in the complaint specifically and particularly, as far as known to the plaintiff, and if any one or more of the parties, or the share or quantity of interest of any of the parties, be unknown to the plaintiff, or be uncertain or contingent, or the ownership of the inheritance depend upon executory devise, or the remainder be a contingent remainder, so that such parties can not be named, that fact must be set forth in the complaint.

§ 923. The plaintiff may at his option, make creditors, having a specific or general lien upon the property, or upon any particular portion thereof, parties to the action.

§ 924. When the lien is on an undivided interest or estate of any of the parties, such lien, if a partition be made, is thenceforth a charge only on the share assigned to such party; but such share must be first charged with its just proportion of the costs of the partition, in preference to such lien.

§ 925. If a party having a share or interest be unknown, or either of the known parties reside out of the state or cannot be found therein, and such fact be made to appear by affidavit, the summons may be served on such absent or unknown party, by publication, directed by the court or judge, in the manner prescribed by sections 629 and 630. When publication is made, the summons, as published, must be accompanied by a brief description of the property, which is the subject of the action.

§ 926. The rights of the several parties, plaintiffs as well as defendants, may be put in issue, tried and determined by such action; and where a defendant fails to answer, or where a sale of the premises is necessary, the title must be ascertained by proof to the satisfaction of the court, before the judgment for partition or sale is given.

§ 927. If it be alleged in the complaint, and established by evidence, to the satisfaction of the court, that the property or any part of it, is so situated that partition cannot be made, without great prejudice to the owners, the court may order a sale thereof, and for that purpose may appoint one or more referees. Otherwise, upon the requisite proofs being made, it must order a partition, according to the respective rights of the parties, as ascertained by the court, and appoint three referees therefor; and must designate the portion to remain undivided, for the owners, whose interests remain unknown or not ascertained.

§ 928. In making the partition, referees must divide the the property, and allot the several portions thereof to the respective parties, quality and quantity relatively considered, according to the respective rights of the parties, as determined by the court, designating the several portions by proper landmarks, and may employ a surveyor, with the necessary assistants, to aid them therein.

§ 929. The referees must make report of their proceedings, specifying therein the manner of excuting their trust, describing the property divided, and the shares allotted to each party, with a particular description of each share.

§ 930. The court may confirm or set aside the report, and if necessary, appoint new referees. Upon the report being confirmed, judgment must be rendered, that such partition be effectual forever, which judgment is binding and conclusive:

1. On all the parties named therein, and their legal representatives, who have at the time any interest in the property divided, as owners in fee, or as tenants for years, or as entitled to the reversion, remainder or inheritance of such property, after the termination of a

particular estate therein: or who, by any contingency, may be entitled to a beneficial interest in the property, or who have an interest in an individual share thereof, as tenants for years, for life, by the curtesy, or in dower;

2. On all persons interested in the property, who may be unknown, to whom notice shall have been given of the application for partition by the publication directed by section 925: and,

3. On all other persons claiming from such parties or persons, or either of them.

§ 931. But such judgment and partition cannot affect tenants, or persons having claims as tenants, in dower, by the curtesy or for life, to the whole of the property, which is the subject of the partition; nor can such judgment and partition preclude any person, except such as are specified in the last section, from claiming title to the property in question, or from controverting the title of the parties between whom the partition is made.

§ 932. The expenses of the referees, including those of a surveyor and his assistants, when employed, must be ascertained and allowed by the court; and the amount thereof, together with the fees allowed by law to the referees, must be paid by the plaintiff, and may be allowed as part of the charges.

§ 933. If the referees report to the court, that the property, of which partition shall have been directed, or any distinct portion thereof, is so situated, that a partition thereof cannot be made, without great prejudice to the owners; and the court is satisfied that such report is correct, it may thereupon, by an order, direct the referees to sell the property or portion so situated.

§ 934. When a part of the property only is ordered to be sold, if there be an estate by the curtesy, in dower, or for life, or years, in an undivided share of the property, the whole of such estate may be set off in any part of the property not ordered to be sold.

§ 935. Before the making of an order for sale, where the creditors having specific liens have not been made parties, the court on the motion of either party, must direct the plaintiff to amend his complaint, if necessary, by making every person having a specific lien on the undivided interest or estate of any of the parties, by mortgage, devise, or otherwise, a party to the action.

§ 936. The plaintiff must produce to the court the certificate of the clerk of the county where the property is situated, showing whether there are any general liens by judgment upon the property, or any part thereof.

§ 937. Unless it be made to appear to the court by the certificate of the clerk pursuant to the last section, that there are outstanding no general liens on the property, or on any share or parcel thereof, the court must order a reference to ascertain them.

§ 938. If it appear by the certificate that there are outstanding of record such general liens, the court must appoint a referee to ascertain whether such liens have been paid, or if not paid, what amount remains due or secured by them respectively, and the order of priority in which they are entitled to be paid out of the property.

§ 939. The plaintiff must cause a notice to be served, at least ten days before the time for appearance, on each person having such general lien, to appear before the referee at a specified time and place, to make proof by his own affidavit or otherwise, of the true amount due, or to become due, contingently or absolutely, on his judgment.

§ 940. The referee must receive the evidence, and report the names of the creditors whose liens are established, the amounts thereof, and their priority respectively, and if such liens are contingent he must specify them. He must attach to his report the proof of service of the notices, and the affidavits and copies of other evidence before him.

§ 941. Any creditor having a lien, and being dissatisfied with the report of the referee, may move the court to correct it, at any time before distribution of the proceeds of sale, on ten days' notice to the plaintiff and the other persons in whose favor liens are reported, and thereupon the court may correct the report on the evidence reported, or if necessary, may order a new reference of the whole or of any part of the matter. When confirmed, the report is conclusive of the rights of the several creditors on whom notice was served.

§ 942. The proceeds of the sale of the incumbered property, must be applied under the direction of the court, as follows:

1. To pay its just proportion of the general costs of the action:

2. To pay the costs of the reference:

3. To satisfy and cancel of record the several liens in their order of priority, by payment of the sums due and to become due, the amount remaining due to be verified by affidavit at the time of payment:

4. The residue, among the owners of the property sold, according to their respective shares therein.

§ 943. The proceedings to ascertain the amount of incumbrances, and to determine their priority as above provided, or those herein authorized to determine the rights of parties, to funds paid into court, must not delay the sale, nor affect any other party, whose rights are not involved in such proceedings.

§ 944. The proceeds of sale, and the securities taken by the referees, or any part thereof, may be distributed by them to the persons entitled thereto, whenever the court so directs. But in case no direction be given, all such proceeds and securities must be paid into court, or deposited as required by law, or directed by the court.

§ 945. When the proceeds of sales of any shares or parcels, belonging to persons, who have become parties to the action, and who are known, are paid into court, the action may be continued as between such parties, for the determination of their respective claims thereto, which must be ascertained and adjudged by the court. Further testimony may be taken, in court, or by a referee, at the discretion of the court, and the court may, if necessary, require such parties to present the facts or law in controversy, by pleadings, as in an original action.

§ 946. All sales of real property, made by referees under this chapter, must be made by public auction to the highest bidder, upon notice, published in the manner required for the sale of real property on execution. The notice must state the terms of sale, and if the property or any part of it is to be sold, subject to a prior estate, charge or specific lien, that must be stated in the notice.

§ 947. The court must, in the order for sale, direct the terms of credit which may be allowed, for the purchase money, of any portion of the premises of which it may direct a sale on credit, and for that portion of which the purchase money is required, by the provisions hereinafter contained, to be invested for the benefit of unknown owners, infants, parties out of the state, or tenants in dower, or by the curtesy or for life or years, when the estate of such tenants is ordered to be sold.

§ 948. The referees may take separate mortgages and other securities, for the whole or convenient portions of the purchase money, of such parts of the property as are directed by the court to be sold on credit, in the name of the clerk of the court and his successors in office, and for the shares of any known owner of full age, in the name of such owner.

§ 949. When the estate of a tenant in dower, or by the curtesy, or for life or years, in the whole or any part of the property in question, has been admitted by the parties, or ascertained by the court, to be existing at the time of the order for sale, and the person entitled to such estate, has been made a party to the action, such estate may be first set off out of any part of the property, and a sale made of such parcel, subject to the prior unsold estate of such tenant therein. But if in the judgment of the court, a due regard to the interests of all the parties, require that such estate be also sold, the sale may be so ordered.

§ 950. If a sale of the property, including such estate, be ordered, the estate and interest of every such tenant or person passes thereby; and the purchaser, his heirs and assigns, shall hold the property discharged from all claims, by virtue of such estate or interest, whether the same be to the individual share of a joint tenant, or tenant in common, or to the whole or any part of the property sold.

§ 951. The persons entitled to such estate in dower, tenancy by the curtesy, or tenancy for life or years, whose estate shall have been sold, are entitled to receive such sum in gross, as may be deemed, upon principles of law applicable to annuities, a reasonable satisfaction for such estate, and which the person so entitled may consent to accept instead thereof, by an instrument under seal, duly acknowledged or proved, in the same manner as deeds for the purpose of record.

§ 952. If such consent be not given, at or before the report of sale, the court must ascertain and determine what proportion of the proceeds of the sale, after deducting expenses, will be a just and reasonable sum to be invested, for the benefit of the person entitled to such estate, in dower, by the curtesy, or for life; and must order the same to be deposited in court for that purpose.

§ 953. The proportion of the proceeds of the sale to be invested must be ascertained and determined in the several cases as follows:

1. If an estate in dower be included in the order of sale, its proportion must be one-third of the proceeds of the sale of the property, or of the sale of the individual

share in such property, upon which the claim of dower existed:

2. If an estate by the curtesy, or other estate for life or years, be included in the order of sale, its proportion must be the whole proceeds of the sale of the property, or of the sale of the undivided share thereof, in which such estate may be:

And in all cases, the proportion of the expenses of proceedings must be deducted from the proceedsof the the sale.

§ 954. If the persons entitled to such estate in dower, by the curtesy, or for life or years, be unknown, the court must provide for the protection of their rights in the same manner, as far as may be, as if they were known and had appeared.

§ 955. In all cases of sales in partition, when it appears that a married woman has an inchoate right of dower in any of the property divided or sold, or that any person has a vested or contingent future right or estate therein, the court must ascertain and settle the proportional value of such inchoate, contingent, or vested right or estate, according to the principles of law applicable to annuities and survivorships, and must direct such proportion of the proceeds of the sale to be invested, secured, or paid over, in such manner, as to protect the rights and interests of the parties.

§ 956. A married woman may release such right, interest or estate, to her husband, and acknowledge the same in the manner required by law, in respect to the acknowledgment of deeds by married women, before any officer authorized to take acknowledgment of deeds, or if executed out of this state, before any officer residing in the state, district or county, where the acknowledgment is made, who is authorized to take the acknowledgment of deeds, to be recorded in this state. Upon the release, the share of the proceeds of the sale, arising from her contingent interest, must be paid to her husband, and the release, or the payment, investment, or otherwise securing of, a share of the proceeds of a sale, shall be a bar against such right, estate, or claim.

§ 957. The terms of the sale must be made known at the time; and if the premises consist of distinct farms, or lots, they must be sold separately.

§ 958. Neither of the referees, nor any person for the benefit of either of them, can be interested in the purchase; nor can a guardian of an infant party be interested in the purchase of any real property, being the subject of the action, except for the benefit of the infant. All sales contrary to the provisions of this section are void.

§ 959. After completing the sale, the referees must report the same to the court, with a description of the different parcels of land sold to each purchaser, the name of the purchaser, the price paid or secured, the terms and conditions of the sale, and the securities if any taken. The report must be filed in the office of the clerk of the county, where the property is situated.

§ 960. If the sale be confirmed by the court, an order must be entered, directing the referees to execute conveyances and take securities pursuant to such sale; which they are hereby authorized to do. Such order may also give directions to them respecting the disposition of the proceeds of the sale.

§ 961. When a party entitled to a share of the property, or an incumbrancer entitled to have his lien paid out of the sale, becomes a purchaser, the referees may take his receipt for so much of the proceeds of the sale as belongs to him, and must also pay over to the plaintiff or his attorney, and take his receipt for, the costs and charges of the action.

§ 962. The conveyances must be recorded in the county, where the premises are situated, and shall be a bar against all persons interested in the property in any way, who shall have been named as parties in the action, and against all such parties and persons as were unknown, if the summons have been served as is directed by section 925, and against all persons claiming from them or either of them.

§ 963. The conveyances shall also be a bar against all persons having specific or general liens or incumbrances by judgment, on any undivided share or interest in the premises sold, who shall have been served with notice as prescribed by section 939; and also against all persons having specific liens on any undivided share or interest therein, who shall have been made parties to the action. But no creditor having such specific lien can be affected by the sale or conveyance unless he has been made party.

§ 964. When there are proceeds of sale, belonging to an unknown owner, or to a person without the state, who has no legal representative within it, or when there are proceeds arising from the sale of an estate, subject to the prior estate of a tenant in dower, or by the curtesy, or tenant for life, or years, which are paid into court, or deposited with an officer by order of the court, the same must be invested in securities on interest, for the benefit of the persons entitled thereto.

§ 965. When security for the proceeds of sale is taken, or when an investment of any such proceeds is made, it must be done, except as herein otherwise provided, in the name of the clerk of the county, where the papers are filed, and his successors in office, who shall hold the same for the use and benefit of the parties interested, subject to the order of the court.

§ 966. When security is taken by the referees on a sale, and the parties interested in such security, by an instrument in writing under their hands, delivered to the referees, agree upon the shares and proportions to which they are respectively entitled, or when such shares and proportions have been previously adjudged by the court, such securities must be taken in the names of, and payable to, the parties respectively entitled thereto, and must be delivered to such parties upon their receipt therefor. Such agreement and receipt must be returned and filed with the clerk.

§ 967. The clerk, in whose name a security is taken, or by whom an investment is made, and his successors in office, must receive the interest and principal, as it becomes due, and apply and invest the same, as the court may direct, and must file in his office all securities taken, and keep an account, in a book provided and kept for that purpose in the clerk's office, free for inspection by all persons, of investments, and moneys received by him thereon, and the disposition thereof.

§ 968. When it appears that partition cannot be made equal between the parties, according to their respective rights, without prejudice to the rights and interests of some of them, the court may adjudge compensation to be made, by one party to another for equality of partition. But such compensation cannot be required to be made to others, by owners unknown, nor by infants, unless, in the case of an infant, it appear that he has personal property sufficient for that purpose, and that his interest will be promoted thereby.

§ 969. When the share of an infant is sold, the proceeds of the sale may be paid by the referees making the sale, to his general guardian, or to the special guardian appointed for him in the action, if such general or special guardian, before the payment of such share into court, shall have given the security required by section 550.

§ 970. The committee who may be entitled to the custody and management of the estate of an insane person, or other person adjudged incapable of conducting his own affairs, whose interest in real property shall have been sold, may receive, in behalf of such person, his share of the proceeds of such real property, from the referees, if the committee, before the money is paid into court, shall have executed, with sufficient sureties, an undertaking, approved by a judge of the court, or if the action be in the supreme court, by a county judge, that he will faithfully discharge the trust reposed in him, and will render a true and just account to the person entitled, or to his legal representative.

§ 992. The general guardian of an infant, and the committee entitled to the custody and management of the estate of an insane person, or other person adjudged incapable of conducting his own affairs, who is entitled to real estate held in joint tenancy, or in common, or in any other manner, to authorise his being made party to an action for the partition thereof, may consent to a partition without action, and agree upon the share to be set off to such infant, or other person entitled, and may execute a release in his behalf, to the owners of the shares of the parts to which they may be respectively entitled, upon an order of the court.

§ 972. The people of this state may be made a party to an action, for the sale or partition of real property, in which case the summons and complaint must be served upon the attorney general, who must appear on behalf of the people.

973. The costs of partition, including fees of referees and other disbursements, must be paid by the parties respectively entitled to share in the lands divided, in proportion to their respective interests therein, and may be included and specified in the judgment. In that case, they are a lien on the several shares, and the judgment may be enforced by execution against the parties separately. Where, however, a litigation arises between some of the parties only, the court may require the expense of such litigation to be paid by the parties thereto, or any of them.

CHAPTER V.

ACTIONS RESPECTING CORPORATIONS.

The provisions of this chapter afford substantially the same remedies as are provided for in articles 1 and 2, title 4, chapter 8, part 3 of the revised statutes, changed so as to conform to the uniform system of procedure under the code in actions. The necessity of some parts of those articles is dispensed with by other parts of the code applicable to such cases. This chapter was prepared before the publication of the Session Laws of 1849, and consequently without adverting to the provisions of the act of that session, chapter 226, making provisions to enforce the liabilities of banks under the article of the constitution on that subject. On examination of that article, it is found, that its provisions, which are not confined to banking corporations, do not conflict with those of this chapter, but that its special provisions are entirely in harmony with the rules of more general application here prescribed. Considering the recent enactment of that statute, and that it is not only confined to banks and banking associations, but to debts contracted after 1st January, 1850, the commissioners have not deemed it necessary or expedient either to attempt a revision of it, or to introduce it into the code, but rather to leave it as a special law applicable to the particular cases embraced within it.

§ 974. This chapter embraces all corporations, including in such designation, all associations having any corporate rights, whether created by special acts of legislation, or under general laws; except that no part of the chapter, other than the next section, extends to a municipal, or religious corporation, or to a corporation for a public library, a cemetery, an academy, or a society for literary or charitable purposes, or for the encouragement of the fine arts, unless such corporation has by its charter, or the law of its organization, shares or stock, from which, in some contingency, a dividend may be made.

The term corporation as used in the constitution and laws of this state in general, includes municipal bodies with corporate powers. These and the other corporations specially exempted in this section, are not clearly within the policy of the provisions of this chapter, though by the terms of the Revised Statutes. vol. 2, p. 466, sec. 57, only religious societies, incorporated libraries, and Lancasterian schools are specially exempted.

§ 975. A foreign corporation cannot maintain an action in this state, upon an obligation or liability, arising out of, or in consideration of an act, which is contrary to the law or policy of this state, or which is thereby forbidden, in respect to corporations or associations therein, whose general business is similar to that of such foreign corporation.

§ 976. When judgment is rendered against a bank, or banking association, for any bill or other contract, for the absolute payment of money, payment of which has been refused, on presentment at the bank, or place of business of the defendant, the plaintiff may recover interest, at the rate of ten per cent a year, from the time of such refusal, unless in the act of incorporation, a different rate of interest, or measure of damages, has been prescribed.

§ 977. A corporation may be restrained by injunction, provisional or final, from exercising any function or doing any act not allowed by law. Such injunction may be granted upon the application of the attorney general, or other officer authorized by statute, on satisfactory evidence that the corporation has usurped, exercised or claimed a franchise, privilege, or other corporate right, not authorized by law, or has done or suffered some other act, by which its corporate existence or rights have become forfeited, or may by authority of law, be terminated.

§ 978. The supreme court has jurisdiction over all corporations, and the directors, managers, trustees and other officers thereof,

1. To compel an officer to account for his official conduct in the management and disposition of its business or property:

2. To suspend an officer from exercising his functions, when it appears that he has abused his trust:

3. To compel the payment, or delivery, by an officer to such corporation, or to its creditors, of any money

or property of such corporation, or the avails thereof, in his hands, or to pay the value of, or to deliver over, any property he may have misapplied, or wasted, or acquired to himself, or withheld, in violation of his duty:

4. To remove an officer from his office on proof of gross misconduct:

5. To direct a new election to be held, to supply a vacancy, occasioned by such removal or otherwise:

6. In case such vacancy cannot be filled by the corporation, then to report the facts to the governor, who is hereby authorized to fill it:

7. To set aside alienations of property made by an officer contrary to the provisions of law, or for purposes foreign to the business of the corporation, in cases where it may be done, without injustice to the purchaser or holder:

8. To prevent the improper alienation or disposition of property, where there is reason to apprehend it will be made.

But this jurisdiction does not deprive any corporate body, or public officer, of visitatorial power over any corporation.

§ 979. The jurisdiction conferred by the last section can only be exercised on the application of an authorized public officer, or of a creditor or stockholder, and the proceedings must be by action, in all proper cases; in other cases, by motion.

§ 980. Whenever the affairs of a corporation are closed by the supreme court, (except on a judgment, obtained by a creditor for the satisfaction of a debt,) the creditors are entitled to be paid rateably in proportion to the amount of their respective demands, as ascertained under the direction of the court, except, that, in case of the insolvency of a bank or banking association, the bill-holders thereof are entitled to preference in payment over other creditors.

§ 981. A corporation may be adjudged to have forfeited its corporate rights, in either of the following cases:

1. When it has for one year neglected to pay its notes, or other evidences of debt, or has, for that period, suspended its ordinary and lawful business:

2. When, having banking powers, or authority to make loans on pledges or deposits, or to make insurance, it violates any of the provisions of the act under which it is incorporated, or of any other law.

§ 982. Any corporation mentioned in the last section, may be restrained by injunction from the further exercise of its corporate rights, and from receiving, paying, transferring, or delivering any money or other property, until the court otherwise order; and in that case, a receiver of the corporate property may be appointed. Such injunction may be granted in an action brought by the attorney general, in behalf of the state, to close the business of the corporation, or by a creditor or stockholder, in an action to have such forfeiture adjudged.

§ 983. If the action be brought by a creditor of a corporation, whose directors, officers or stockholders are, by law, personally liable for its debts, either absolutely or in any contingency, they may be made parties to the action, either at its commencement or subsequently, for the purpose of enforcing such liability.

§ 984. When a judgment has been rendered in such action, whether brought by the attorney general, or by a stockholder or creditor, and the directors, officers or stockholders are personally liable for the debts, and have not been made parties, any creditor may commence an action, founded upon such judgment, to enforce the liability; and in such action, the former judgment is conclusive evidence of the matters therein adjudged.

§ 985. Whenever an execution, issued on a judgment against a corporation, is returned unsatisfied in whole or in part, by the sheriff of the county, where the principal office or place of business of the corporation is situated, and whenever a corporation is adjudged to have forfeited its corporate rights, the court must cause its affairs to be closed, its debts collected, its property converted into money, and its creditors paid in proportion to the amount of their respective debts, in the order provided in the case of a voluntary dissolution of a corporation, except that the bill holders of an insolvent bank or banking association, must be preferred, as provided in section 980.

§ 986. When the property of the corporation is insufficient to discharge its debts, the court may compel each stockholder to pay any amount, that may remain unpaid, on the shares of stock held by him, or so much thereof, as is necessary to satisfy the debts, and when the officers or stockholders are personally liable for the debts, and the property of the corporation, together with the amount unpaid on the stock, is insufficient to discharge its debts, the court may compel contribution from the officers or stockholders, who may be liable to satisfy the balance of the debts, from each according to his liability.

§ 987. In any proceeding, pursuant to this chapter, to close the affairs of a corporation, the court may, on application of a stockholder, officer or creditor, restrain further proceedings by any creditor, in an action against the corporation, so far as may be proper, in order to prevent the waste of the funds by unnecessary litigation; and may by a notice, served or published as the court may direct, require all creditors to present and prove their claims, or become parties to the action, within a reasonable time, or be precluded from the benefit of any distribution, which may be made before such claim is proved.

§ 988. An action against a corporation, created by, or under the laws of, any other state, government or country, and having property in this state, or an agency established therein, may be brought in the supreme court, the superior court of the city of New-York, or the court of common pleas of the city of New-York, in the following cases:

1. By a resident of this state, for any cause of action:

2. By a plaintiff not a resident of this state, when the contract, on which the action is brought, was made or delivered in this state, or when any other cause of action has arisen, or the subject of the action is situated, within this state.

Amended Code, § 427.

CHAPTER VI.

ACTIONS BY OR AGAINST EXECUTORS, ADMINISTRATORS, LEGATEES, HEIRS OR DEVISEES.

§ 989. A cause of action, arising out of an injury to the person, dies with the person of either party, except as provided in section 991.

§ 990. All other causes of action, by one against another, whether arising on contract or not, survive to the personal representatives of the former, and against the personal representatives of the latter. Therefore the executors or administrators may maintain the action against the party, against whom the cause of action accrued, or after his death against his representatives.

§ 991. When the death of one is caused by the wrongful act or omission of another, the personal representatives of the former may maintain an action therefor against the latter, if the former might have maintained an action, had he lived, against the latter, for an injury caused by the same act or omission. But the action must be commenced, within two years after the act or omission, by which the death was caused; the damages thereon cannot exceed five thousand dollars; and the amount recovered is to be for the exclusive benefit of the widow and next of kin, to be distributed to them in the same proportions as the personal property of a deceased person.

§ 992. In an action against several executors or administrators, they are all considered as one person representing their testator or intestate, and judgment may be taken, and execution issued against all who are named as defendants in the summons, although it be served only on part of them, in the same manner as if served on all, except as provided in the next section.

§ 993. When a judgment is taken against an administrator or executor upon failure to answer, it is not to be deemed evidence of assets in his hands, unless it appear that the complaint alleged assets, and was personally served on him.

§ 994. The time which shall have elapsed between the death of a person, and the granting of letters testamentary or of administration, on his estate, not exceeding six months, and the period of six months after the granting of such letters, are not to be deemed any part of the time limited for the commencement of actions, by executors or administrators.

§ 995. An executor of an executor, has no authority as such to commence or maintain an action or proceeding, relating to the property of the testator of the first executor, or to take any charge or control thereof.

§ 996. The real property, which belonged to a deceased person, is not bound, or in any way affected, by a judgment against his executors or administrators, nor liable to be sold, by virtue of an execution issued upon such judgment.

§ 997. In an action against executors or administrators, in which the fact of their having administered the estate of their testator or intestate, or any part thereof, comes in issue, and the inventory of the property of the deceased, filed by them is given in evidence, the same may be repelled by evidence:

1. That any property has been omitted in such inventory, or was not returned therein at its full value:

2. That such property has perished or been lost, without the fault of such executors or administrators; or that it has been fairly sold by them at private or public sale, at a less price than the value so returned; or that, since the return of the inventory, such property has deteriorated or increased in value. In such action, the defendants cannot be charged for any things in action, specified in their inventory, unless it appear that they have been collected, or might with due diligence, have been collected.

§ 998. No person is linble to an action as executor of his own wrong, for having taken, received, or interfered with, the property of a deceased person; but is responsible to the executors, or general or special administrators, of such deceased person, for the value of all property so taken or received, and fcr all damages, caused by his acts, to the estate of the deceased.

§ 999. The next of kin of a deceased person are liable to an action by a creditor of the estate, to recover the distributive shares, received out of such estate, or so much thereof, as may be necessary to satisfy his debt. The action may be against all the next of kin jointly, or against any one or more of them severally.

§ 1000. In such action, the plaintiff may recover the value of all the assets received by all the defendants in the action, if necessary to satisfy his demand; and the amount of the recovery must be apportioned among the defendants, in proportion to the value of the assets received by each; and no allowance or deduction can be made from such amount, on account of there being other relatives to whom assets have also been delivered.

§ 1001. Any one of the next of kin, against whom a recovery is had pursuant to the last section, may maintain an action against all the other relatives of the testator, to whom any such assets have been paid, jointly, or against any of them separately, for a just and equal contribution, and may recover of cach defendant such an amount as shall be in the same proportion to the whole sum collected of the plaintiff, as the value of the assets delivered to such defendant bore to the value of all the assets delivered to all the relatives of the deceased.

§ 1002. Legatees are liable to an action by a creditor of the testator to recover the value of any legacy received by them. The action may be brought against all or only one of the legatees. In such action the plaintiff cannot recover unless he shows:

1. That no assets were delivered by the executor or administrator of the deceased, to his next of kin: or

2. That the value of such assets has been recovered by some other creditor: or

3. That such assets are not sufficient to satisfy the demand of the plaintiff:

And in the last case, he can recover only the deficiency. The whole amount which the plaintiff can recover, must be apportioned among all the legatees of the testator, in proportion to the amounts of their legacies respectively, and his proportion can only be recovered of each legatee.

§ 1003. If an action be brought against several next of kin of jointly, or against several legatees jointly, for assets delivered to them, and a recovery be had against them, the costs of such action must be apportioned among the several defendants, in proportion to the amouut of the debt or damages recovered against each of them.

§ 1004. In case of a judgment against several next of kin of a testator, or against several legatees, the payment or satisfaction of the amount recovered against any one of the defendants, discharges such defendant, and exonerates him and his property from the judgment.

§ 1005. Heirs and devisees are liable to an action by a creditor of a deceased person, to recover the debt, to the extent of the value of any real property inherited by, or devised to, them. If such action be against the heirs, all the heirs who may be liable must be made parties to the action.

§ 1006. But the heirs are not liable for the debt, unless it appear that the personal assets of the deceased were not sufficient to discharge it, or that after due proceedings before the proper surrogate's court, the creditor has been unable to collect the debt, from the personal representatives of the deceased, or from his next of kin or legatees. If the personal assets were sufficient to pay a part of the debt, or in case a part thereof shall have been collected, as mentioned, in the last section the heirs of such deceased person are liable for the residue.

§ 1007. But the last section does not affect the liability of heirs for a debt of their ancestor, where such debt was, by his will, expressly charged exclusively on the real property descended to such heirs, or where such debt is by the will expressly directed to be paid out of the real property descended, before resorting to the personal property.

§ 1008. In cases where the next of kin, legatees, heirs, and devisees are liable for the debts of their ancestors, as herein provided, they must give preference in the payment of the same, and are liable therefor, in the following order:

1. Debts entitled to a preference under the laws of the United States:

2. Judgments against the ancestor or testator according to the priority thereof respectively:

3. Recognizances, bonds, sealed instruments, notes, bills, and unliquidated demands and accounts.

§ 1009. No preference can be given by any next of kin, legatee, heir or devisee, to one debt over another of the same class, except one specified in the second subdivision of the last section; nor is a debt, due and payable, entitled to a preference over a debt not due; nor does the commencement of an action against any next of kin, legatee, heir or devisee, for the recovery of a debt, entitle it to a preference over others of the same class.

§ 1010. The next of kin, legatees, heirs and devisees, may show that there are debts of a prior class unsatisfied; or that there are unpaid debts of the same class with that on which the action is brought; and if it appear, that the value of the personal property delivered to them, or of the real estate descended or devised to them, does not exceed the debts of a prior class, judgment must be rendered in their favor.

§ 1011. If the personal property delivered to such next of kin or legatees, or if the real estate descended or devised to such heirs and devisees, exceed the amount of debts which are entitled to a preference over the debt for which the action is brought, judgment must be rendered against them only for such a sum as shall be a just proportion to the other debts, of the same class with that on which the action is brought.

§ 1012. If a debt of a class prior to that on which the action is brought, or of the same class, shall have been paid by any next of kin, legatees, heirs or devisees, they may prove such payment, and the amount of the debts so paid must be estimated in ascertaining the amount to be recovered, in the same manner as if such debts were outstanding and unpaid, as prescribed in the last two sections.

§ 1013. If it appear that the real property so descended, was not aliened by the heir, at the time of the commencement of the action, or if the heir confess the claim, and show what real property has descended to him, the court must order that the debt of the plaintiff, or the proportion thereof which he is entitled to recover, be levied of the real property so descended, and not otherwise; and every judgment rendered in such action has preference, as a lien on the real property descended, to any judgment obtained against such heir personally, for a debt or demand in his own right.

§ 1014. When it appears, in the action, that before the commencement thereof, the heir has aliened the real property descended to him, or any part thereof, he shall be personally liable for the value of the property so aliened, and judgment may be rendered therefor and execution awarded, as in actions for his own debts. But no real property aliened in good faith by an heir, before action commenced against him, is liable to execution, or in any manner affected by a judgment against him.

§ 1015. In actions brought against several heirs jointly, or several devisees jointly, the amount, which the plaintiff recovers, must be apportioned, among all the heirs of the ancestor, or among all the devisees of the testator, in proportion to the value of the real property descended or devised, and such proportion only can be recovered of each heir or legatee.

§ 1016. Devisees made liable, by the foregoing provisions of this chapter, to the creditors of their testator, are not so liable, unless it appear that his personal assets and the real property of the testator descended to his heirs were insufficient to discharge the debt; or unless it appear, that after due proceedings before the surrogate, the creditor has been unable to recover the debt, or any part thereof, from the personal representatives of the testator, or from his next of kin or legatees, or from his heirs.

§ 1017. In either of the cases specified in the last section, the amount of the deficiency of the personal assets, and of the real property descended, to satisfy the debt of the plaintiff, and the amount which such plaintiff may have failed to recover from the personal representatives of the testator, his next of kin, legatees and heirs, may be recovered of the devisees of such testator, to the extent of the real property devised to them respectively.

§ 1018. But the last two sections do not affect the liability of devisees, for a debt of their testator, where such debt was, by his will, expressly charged exclusively upon the real property devised, or by the terms of the will made payable exclusively by such devisee, or made payable out of the real property devised, before resorting to the personal property or to any other real property descended or devised.

§ 1019. The provisions of this chapter, with regard to heirs, and to proceedings by and against them, and to judgments and executions against them, are applicable to actions and proceedings against devisees; and they must, in like manner, be sued jointly.

§ 1020. In cases where, by the provisions of any statute, a child born after the making of a will, is entitled to succeed to a portion of the testator's real and personal property, such child shall have the same rights and remedies to compel a distribution of the personal property and a partition of the real property, as are provided for next of kin and for heirs; and shall, in all respects, be liable, in the same manner and to the same extent, to the creditors of his ancestor, in respect to the personal property delivered to him, and the real property descended to him, as are herein prescribed in relation to next of kin and heirs; and such child may recover of the legatees and devisees, who may have received or taken any real or personal property of the testator, the share or portion thereof to which he may be entitled.

§ 1021. The provisions of the last two sections relative to a child, born after the making of a will, apply equally to every person, who being a witness to a will, is entitled, by the provisions of any statute, to recover a portion of the real or personal property of the testator, from the legatees and devisees named in such will.

CHAPTER VII.

ACTIONS ON OFFICIAL SECURITIES, AND FOR FINES AND FORFEITURES.

This chapter differs from the Revised Statutes, chiefly in making the rules applicable to all official securities uniform, and in allowing a prosecution upon them, directly in the name of the party aggrieved, instead of doing the same thing indirectly in the name of the people. As in most of the other special cases in this title, the change in the system of procedure has enabled the Commissioners to condense the subject into less than half its length in the Revised Statutes. *See* 2, *R. S.*, 476-483.

§ 1022. The official bond, or other security, of a public officer, to the people of this state, whether with or without sureties, is to be construed as security to the people of the state, as a government, and also to all persons severally, for the official delinquencies, against which it is intended to provide. If it be to a county, town, city, village or other municipal body, it is, in like manner, to be construed as security severally to all persons intended to be secured, as well as tothe body politic named therein.

§ 1023. When a public officer, by official misconduct or neglect of duty, forfeits his official bond, or renders his sureties liable upon an official security, any person injured thereby, or who is, by law, entitled to the benefit of the security, may bring an action thereon, in his own name, against the officer and his sureties, to recover the amount to which he may be entitled, by reason of the delinquency.

§ 1024. Before an action can be brought by a plaintiff, other than the people, or body politic named in the security, leave must be obtained of the court or a judge thereof, or a county judge, within the district or county where the action is triable; and leave can only be granted, on a production of the copy of the bond, and an affidavit showing the delinquency: and if the delinquency be such, as that if established on the trial, it would entitle the party applying to recover in the action, leave must be granted.

§ 1025. A judgment in favor of a party for one delinquency, does not preclude the same, or another party, from an action on the same security, for another delinquency.

§ 1026. If it appear in an action against a surety, on an official security, that he has already been obliged, by reason of prior recoveries against him on the same, to pay amounts, which, in the aggregate, are equal to the extent of his undertaking, or that, by reason of the insolvency of his principal, he will be obliged to pay to that extent on judgments already recovered against the surety. And the recovery against a surety must, in all cases, be limited by the amount of his undertaking.

§ 1027. Upon the execution issued on a judgment, recovered upon the official security of a public officer against him and a surety, there must be endorsed a direction to the officer, to whom the execution is delivered, to collect the same out of the property of the principal, if sufficient can be found, and if not, then to collect it out of the property of the surety.

§ 1028. If there be several judgments on which executions are, at the same time, in the sheriff's hands, against a public officer and his sureties, amounting in the aggregate to a sum greater than that, for which the sureties are liable, the court must, on their application, limit the amount to be collected of them, to the amount of their respective liabilities, and may cause the same to be applied on the judgments or executions, in proportion to such amounts.

§ 1029. Actions for fines and forfeitures, may be prosecuted by the officers or persons, to whom they are by law given, or who, by special provision of law, are authorised to recover them; and whether prosecuted by public officers, or by private persons, are governed by the same rules as other civil actions, except as otherwise specified in this chapter.

§ 1030. When an action is brought for a penalty, which is limited by law, not to exceed a certain amount, the action may be brought for that amount; and upon the trial, the amount recovered, must be determined in proportion to the offence.

§ 1031. A recovery of a judgment, for a penalty or a forfeiture, by collusion between the parties, with intent to save the defendant from the consequences contemplated by law, in a case where the penalty or forfeiture is given, wholly or partly, to the prosecutor, does not prevent the recovery of the same by another person.

§ 1032. Fines and forfeitures, not specially granted or appropriated by law, must be paid into the treasury of the state; and whenever by the provisions of law, any property, real or personal, is forfeited to the people of this state, or to any officer for their use, an action for the recovery of such property, alleging the grounds of the forfeiture, may be brought by the proper officer, in the supreme court.

CHAPTER VIII.

ACTIONS BY AND AGAINST CERTAIN PUBLIC OFFICERS AND PUBLIC BODIES.

This chapter is substituted for the provisions of the Revised Statutes, on the same subject, (art. 4, title 4, ch. 8, part 3,) adapting them to the new system of procedure. It, however, embraces a class of officers, who by special statutes in city charters, are authorized to sue, and contains some new features for the better attainment of the same remedies.

§ 1033. The following officers may prosecute actions in their official capacity:

The board of supervisors of a county;

The loan officers and commissioners of loans of a county;

The superintendents of the poor of a county;

The supervisor of a town;

The overseers of the poor of a town;

The commissioners of highways of a town;

The commissioners of common schools of a town;

The trustees of a school district;

The trustees of gospel and school lots; and

Any organized department of a municipal corporation having a board of officers, in charge of a particular branch public service, and specially authorized by statute to of prosecute. In such action, the plaintiffs may be designated by their official name, or the action may be brought in the name of the body, in whose behalf the action is brought.

§ 1034. Every such action must be either,

1. On a contract made with them in their official capacity; or,

2. To enforce a liability, or a duty enjoined by law, in favor of such officers, or the body represented by them; or,

3. To recover a penalty or forfeiture given to such officers or body; or,

4. To recover damages for an injury to their official rights or property.

§ 1035. When an organized department of a municipal corporation is authorized by statute to sue, it shall, for purposes of the action, be deemed the real party in interest, though the corporation, of which it is a department, be the party ultimately to be benefited by the action, or responsible for any loss incurred therein.

§ 1036. An action may be brought against the officers mentioned in section 1033, in their official capacity, or against the body they represent, either upon a contract made by such officers, in their official capacity, and within the scope of their authority, or for an injury to the rights of the plaintiff, arising from some act or omission of such officers, or of the body represented by them.

§ 1037. The actions authorised by this chapter may be brought by or against the officers mentioned in section 1033 upon a cause of action, which accrued during the term of their predecessors, as well as during their own term of office, and when brought, may be continued by, or against, the successors in office of the parties, whose names may, for that purpose, be substituted in the action.

§ 1038. If judgment, for the recovery of money, be rendered against a county, or the board of supervisors, or superintendents of the poor, of a county, or against a town, or the supervisor or overseers of the poor of a town, on account of the liability of such county or town, and the judgment be not satisfied, or proceedings thereon stayed by appeal or otherwise, before the next annual meeting of the board of supervisors of the county, a certified copy of the docket of the judgment, may be presented to the board of supervisors at their annual meeting.

§ 1039. The board of supervisors must thereupon cause the amount due on the judgment, with interest, from the time of the recovery, until the first Monday in February after such meeting, to be added to the tax of the town or county, for whose liability the same was recovered, and the same must be collected as other contingent charges of the town or county.

§ 1040. The treasurer of a county, against which, or against whose officers, a judgment has been recovered, for a liability of the county, the execution of which has not been stayed upon appeal, must, upon demand, and the delivery to him of a certified copy of the docket of the judgment, pay the amount due thereon, if there be sufficient money of the county in his hands, not otherwise specifically appropriated. If he fail to do so, he shall be personally liable for the amount, unless the collection thereof be afterwards stayed upon appeal.

§ 1041. The supervisors, or overseers of the poor, of a town, against which or against whose officers, a judgment has been recovered for a liability of the town, the execution of which has not been stayed upon appeal, must in like manner, upon demand, and the delivery of a certified copy of the docket of the judgment, pay the amount due thereon, if there be sufficient money of the town in his hands, not otherwise specifically appropriated. If he fail to do so, he shall be personally responsible for the amount, unless the collection thereof be afterwards stayed upon appeal.

§ 1042. Execution cannot be issued on a judgment, mentioned in sections 1038 and 1040 without leave of the court, nor must leave be granted, until the court is satisfied that payment has been demanded of the proper county, or town officers, as provided in the last two sections, and that the board of supervisors have wrongfully omitted to include the amount in the tax list, as provided in section 1039. When execution is issued, the property of the county, or town, only is liable thereon.

§ 1043. Judgments, for the recovery of money, rendered against loan officers, commissioners of loans, commissioners of common schools, commissioners of highways, trustees of school districts, and trustees of gospel and school lots, or other town or county officers, on account of a liability of such county or town, may be enforced by execution, or otherwise, against such officers personally, and the amount collected of them must be allowed to them in their official accounts.

CHAPTER IX.

ACTIONS TO VACATE CHARTERS AND LETTERS PATENT, AND TO PREVENT THE USURPATION OF AN OFFICE OR FRANCHISE.

§ 1044. The writ of scire facias, the writ of quo warranto, and proceedings by information in the nature of quo warranto, are abolished, and the remedies heretofore obtainable in these forms, may be obtained by civil actions, under the provisions of this chapter. But nothing contained in this section affects any right already acquired, or any judgment or order already made, or any proceeding already taken.

Amended Code, §428. See also 2 *R. S.* 579—586.

§ 1045. An action may be brought by the attorney general, in the name of the people of this state, whenever the legislature so directs, against a corporation, for the purpose of vacating or annulling the act of incorporation, or an act renewing its corporate existence, on the ground, that such act or renewal was procured, upon some fraudulent suggestion or concealment of a material fact, by the persons incorporated, or by some of them, or with their knowledge and consent.

Amended Code, § 429.

§ 1046. An action may be brought by the attorney general, in the name of the people of this state, on leave granted by the supreme court, or a judge thereof, for the purpose of vacating the charter or annulling the existence of a corporation, other than munipical, whenever such corporation;

1. Offends against any of the provisions of the act or acts creating, altering, or renewing, such corporation; or

2. Violates the provisions of any law, by which such corporation forfeits its charter, by abuse of its powers; or

3. Whenever it has forfeited its privileges or franchises, by failure to exercise its powers; or

4. Whenever it has done or omitted any act, which amounts to a surrender of its corporate rights, privileges, and franchises; or

5. Whenever it exercises a franchise or privilege, not conferred upon it by law.

And it is the duty of the attorney general, to apply for leave, and upon leave granted, to bring the action in every case of public interest, whenever he has reason to believe, that any of these acts or omissions can be proved, and also in every other case, in which satisfactory security is given, to indemnify the people of this state, against the costs and expenses to be incurred thereby.

Amended Code, § 430.

§ 1047. Leave to bring the action may be granted, upon the application of the attorney general; and the court or judge may, at discretion, direct notice of such application to be given to the corporation or its officers, previous to granting such leave, and may hear the corporation in opposition thereto.

Amended Code, § 431.

§ 1048. An action may be brought by the attorney general in the name of the people of this state, upon his own information, or upon the complaint of a private party, against the party offending in the following cases:

1. When any person usurps, intrudes into, or unlawfully holds or exercises any public office, civil or military, or any franchise within this state, or any office in a corporation created by the authority of this state: or,

2. When any public officer, civil or military, has done or suffered an act which, by the provisions of law, makes a forfeiture of his office: or,

3. When any association, or number of persons, act within this state as a corporation, without being duly incorporated.

And it is the duty of the attorney general to bring the action, whenever he has reason to believe that any of these acts can be proved, or when he is directed to do so, by a judge of the supreme court.

Amended Code, § 432, with the last sentence added.

§ 1049. An action may be brought by the attorney general, in the name of the people of this state, for the purpose of vacating or annulling letters patent, granted by the people of this state, in the following cases:

1. When he has reason to believe, that such letters patent were obtained by means of some fraudulent suggestion or concealment of a material fact, made by a person to whom the same were issued or made, or with his consent or knowledge: or,

2. When he has reason to believe, that such letters patent were issued through mistake, or in ignorance of a material fact: or,

3. When he has reason to believe, that the patentee, or those claiming under him, have done or omitted an act, in violation of the terms and conditions on which the letters patent were granted, or have, by any other means, forfeited the interest acquired under the same.

Amended Code, § 433.

§ 1050. When an action is brought by the attorney general, by virtue of this chapter, on the complaint or information of a person having an interest in the question, the name of such person must be joined with the people, as plaintiff.

Amended Code, § 434.

§ 1051. Whenever such action is brought against a person for usurping an office, the attorney-general, in addition to the statement of the cause of action, may also set forth in the complaint, the name of the person rightfully entitled to the office, with a statement of his right thereto, and in such case, upon proof by affidavit, that the defendant has received fees or emoluments belonging to the office, and by means of his usurpation thereof, an order may be granted by a judge of the supreme court, for the arrest of such defendant, and holding him to bail, and thereupon he may be arrested and held to bail, in the same manner, and with the same effect, and subject to the same rights and liabilities, as in other civil actions, where the defendant is subject to arrest.

Amended Code, § 435.

§ 1052. In every such case, judgment may be rendered upon the right of the defendant, and also upon the right of the party, so alleged to be entitled, or only upon the right of the defendant, as justice requires.

Amended Code, § 436

§ 1053. If the judgment be rendered upon the right of the person so alleged to be entitled, and the same be in favor of such person, he shall be entitled, after taking the oath of office and executing such official bond as may be required by law, to take upon himself the execution of the office, and it is his duty, immediately thereafter, to demand of the defendant in the action, all the books and papers, in his custody or within his power, belonging to the office.

Amended Code, § 437.

§ 1054. If the defendant refuse or neglect to deliver over such books or papers, pursuant to the demand, he is to be deemed guilty of a misdemeanor, and the same proceedings may be had, and with the same effect, to compel delivery of such books and papers, as are prescribed in article five, title six, chapter six, of the first part of the Revised Statutes.

Amended Code, § 438.

1055. If judgment be rendered, upon the right of the person so alleged to be entitled, in favor of such person, he may recover, by action, the damages which he shall have sustained, by reason of the usurpation of the office by the defendant.

Amended Code, § 439.

§ 1056. Where several persons claim to be entitled to the same office or franchise, one action may be brought against all such persons, in order to try their respective rights to such office or franchise.

Amended Code, § 440.

§ 1057. When a defendant, whether a natural person or a corporation, against whom such action has been brought, is adjudged guilty of usurping or intruding into, or unlawfully holding or exercising any office, franchise or privilege, judgment must be rendered, that such defendant be excluded from the office, franchise or privilege, and also that the plaintiff recover costs against such defendant. The court may also, in its discretion, impose upon the defendant a fine not exceeding two thousand dollars; which fine, when collected, must be paid into the treasury of the state.

Amended Code, § 441.

§ 1058. If it be adjudged, that a corporation, against which an action shall have been brought, pursuant to this chapter, has by neglect, abuse, or surrender, forfeited its corporate rights, privileges and franchises, judgment must be rendered, that the corporation be excluded from such corporate rights, privileges and franchises, and that the corporation be dissolved.

Amended Code, § 442.

§ 1059. If judgment be rendered in such action, against a corporation or against persons claiming to be a corporation, the court may cause the costs therein to be collected, by execution against the persons claiming to be a corporation, or by process against the directors or other officers of such corporation.

Amended Code, § 443.

1060. When such judgment is rendered against a corporation, the court has the same power to restrain the corporation, to appoint a receiver of its property, and to take an account, and make distribution thereof among its creditors, as are given in the chapter upon actions respecting corporations, and in the chapter upon the voluntary dissolution of corporations, and it is the duty of the attorney-general, immediately after the rendition of such judgment, to institute proceedings for that purpose.

Amended Code, § 444.

§ 1061. Upon the rendition of such judgment against a corporation, or for the vacating or annulling of letters patent, it is the duty of the attorney-general, to cause a copy of the judgment roll to be forthwith filed in the office of the secretary of state.

Amended Code, § 445.

§ 1062. Such secretary must thereupon, if the record relate to letters patent, make an entry in the records of the commissioners of the land office, of the substance and effect of the judgment, and of the time when the record thereof was docketed; and the real property granted by the letters patent, may thereafter be disposed of by such commissioners, in the same manner as if the letters patent had never been issued.

Amended Code, § 446.

CHAPTER X.

ACTIONS IN JUSTICES' COURTS.

ARTICLE I.

SUMMONS, ARREST AND ATTACHMENT.

It was no part of the original design of the Commissioners to review the system of procedure in justices' courts; but further reflection and observation, as their work advanced, satisfied them that it was indispensable to the proper and harmonious arrangement of the entire system. Many statutes equally applicable to proceedings in that court as to those of higher jurisdiction, are rendered useless in regard to the latter, by the new system of procedure, and must be either repealed so far as they apply to one tribunal, and left to stand in their relation to another, or justices' courts must be included in the revision.

The Commissioners are of opinion, that the records in justices' courts are of a character requiring preservation. Their decisions are final, unless appealed from, in the same manner as judgments in higher courts. Their dockets have long been declared to be evidence, and ought to be secured by provisions for their preservation as public records. They therefore determined to classify these courts as courts of record, and in this view, are required by law to include them in the code.

The business of this court is larger in the aggregate, and more intimately connected with the ordinary transactions of the people, than that of any other, and there is a manifest propriety in providing for it the very best system of procedure which can be devised. An uniformity through all the courts, as far as practicable, not only secures stability in the administration of justice, but it gives to inferior courts the benefit of the learning and construction which would be otherwise confined mostly to the higher tribunals. The justice's court is the school, in which many of our most eminent lawyers and judges have taken their first lessons; lessons which have often beneficially influenced the opinions and conduct of the lawyer, the judge and the statesman, in his later and more elevated sphere.

§ 1063. Parties in justices' courts may prosecute or defend in person or by attorney, and any person may act as attorney, except that the constable by whom the summons or jury process was served, cannot appear or act on the trial in behalf of either party. He may however act, in any other stage of the action, as agent or attorney for a party, and the authority of a person to act for another as attorney, may be oral or written, but unless admitted by the adverse party must be proved by the oath of the attorney or otherwise.

§ 1064. Actions in justices' courts are commenced by summons, or by the voluntary appearance and pleadings of the parties without summons. In the latter case, the action is deemed commenced, at the time of appearance.

In analogy to proceedings in the supreme court and to secure uniformity in all cases as far as practicable, it is deemed best to make the summons the only process by which actions can be commenced, and when an arrest of the defendant or attachment of his property is proper, to require an order of the justice for that purpose to be endorsed.

§ 1065. When a guardian is necessary, he must be appointed by the justice as follows:

1. If the infant be plaintiff, the appointment must be made before the summons is issued, upon the application of the infant, if he be of the age of fourteen years or upwards, if under age, upon the application of some relative or friend. The consent in writing of the guardian to be appointed, and to be responsible for costs, if he fail in the action, must be first filed with the justice.

2. If the infant be defendant, the guardian must be appointed at the time the summons is returned, or before the pleadings. It is the right of the infant to nominate his own guardian, if the infant be over fourteen years of age, and the proposed guardian be present, and consent in writing to be appointed. Otherwise the justice may appoint any suitable person who gives such consent.

§ 1066. The summons must be addressed to the defendant by name, or if his name be unknown, by a description of him, and must summon him to appear before the justice, at his office in a town or ward, and at a time specified therein, to answer the complaint of the plaintiff, for a cause of action therein described in general terms, sufficient to apprise the defendant of the nature of the claim against him, and must state the amount for which the plaintiff will take judgment, if the defendant fail to appear and answer. It must be subscribed by the plaintiff, or by the justice before whom it is returnable.

The principle changes in practice required in this description of the summons are:

1. Its address to the defendant instead of a constable:

2. The direction to state the amount for which judgment will be claimed if the defendant fails to appear and answer. This is analogous to the summons in the supreme court; and subsequent provision is made by which the plaintiff will be induced to state his claim no higher than he can establish it by evidence;

3. The permission to the plaintiff to issue his own summons if he chooses to do so. The summons in the supreme court is always issued by the party or his attorney. Provision is made for regular return days of process issued by the party, at which times the justice is required to be in attendance, and the system of costs is also made applicable to this mode of proceeding.

§ 1067. The time mentioned in the summons, for the appearance of the defendant, and the time of service must be as follows:

1. Where the summons is accompanied by an order to arrest the defendant, or to attach property under sections 1071 and 1076, it must be returnable immediately:

2. When the defendant is not a resident of the county, or where the plaintiff is not a resident, and gives the security required by section 1082, it must be returnable not more than three days from its date, and must be served at least two days before the time for appearance:

3. In all other cases it must be returnable, not more than twelve days from its date, and must be served at least six days before the time for appearance.

§ 1068. The summons must be served by a constable of the county, as follows:

1. If the action be against a corporation, by delivery of a copy to the president, or other head of the corporation, or to the secretary, cashier, or managing agent thereof, or when no such officer resides in the county, to a director resident therein:

2. If against a minor under the age of fourteen years, by delivery of a copy to such minor, and also to his father, mother, or guardian, or if there be none within the county, then to any person having the care or control of such minor, or with whom he resides, or in whose service he is:

3. If against a person, judicially declared to be of unsound mind, or incapable of conducting his own

affairs in consequence of habitual drunkenness, or for any other cause, and for whom a committee has been appointed, by delivery of a copy, to such committee and to the defendant personally:

4. If an order to attach property be endorsed on the summons, by leaving a copy, as prescribed in section 1079.

5. In all other cases by delivery of a copy to the defendant personally.

By this section, the manner of service of the summons is defined, where a corporation or a minor, an insane person or an habitual drunkard, is a defendant. The law has heretofore been defective in this respect. The service by copy at the defendant's residence is omitted. The summons, when served in that manner, was formerly followed by a warrant to arrest the defendant; but that mode having been superseded by the act to abolish imprisonment for debt, and a new summons required to be served personally before judgment can be taken, this mode of service by copy is no longer necessary.

§ 1069. When the action is on a promissory note, bill of exchange, or other obligation for the payment of money only, or for a specified amount of property, at a valuation fixed in the contract, or on an account, the plaintiff may serve, with the summons, a copy of his complaint, together with a copy of such obligation or account. In such case, unless the defendant, in his answer, specifically deny the note, bill of exchange, or other obligation or account, he is to be deemed to have admitted it.

This section is in conformity with the practice introduced by the code in higher courts, where its effects have been very satisfactory. It saves the trouble of proof in those cases, where the demand has been presented to the defendant, and he sees fit not to appear and deny it. In all other cases the demand must be proved, whether the defendant fail to appear or not, unless he puts in an answer, and in that does not deny the allegations in the complaint.

§ 1070. The parties are entitled to one hour in which to appear, after the time mentioned in the summons for appearance, but are not bound to remain longer than that time, unless both parties have appeared, and the justice, being present, is actually engaged in the trial of another action, or of a special proceeding. In such case, he may postpone the time of appearance until the close of such trial.

§ 1071. An order to arrest the defendant may be endorsed on a summons issued by the justice, and the defendant may be arrested thereon, by the constable, at the time of serving the summons, and brought before the justice, and there detained until duly discharged, in the following cases:

1. In an action for the recovery of damages, on a cause of action not arising on contract, when the defendant is not a resident of the county, or is about to remove therefrom, or when the action is for a wilful injury to person, or to property knowing it to belong to another:

2. In an action against a person who does not reside in the state:

3. In an action for a fine or penalty, or for money or property, embezzled or fraudulently misapplied or converted to his own use, by a public officer, or an officer of a corporation, or an attorney, factor, broker agent or clerk,, in the course of his employment as such or by any other person in a fiduciary capacity, or for misconduct or neglect in office, or in a professional employment:

4. When the defendant has been guilty of a fraud in contracting the debt, or incurring the obligation, for which the action is brought, or in concealing or disposing of the property for the taking, detention or conversion of which the action is brought:

5. When the defendant has removed, concealed or disposed of his property, or is about to do so, with intent to defraud his creditors:

6. When an arrest is authorised by special statute, in an action for a fine or penalty, or for a wilful violation of duty.

But no female can be arrested, except for a wilful injury to person or to property knowing it to belong to another.

An order to arrest a defendant is substituted for a warrant, in analogy to the practice in the higher courts. The order to arrest is properly a judicial act, to be granted only in certain cases, and upon compliance with certain conditions, whereas a process to commence an action is matter of right, and does not depend on judicial discretion. The party has a right to his summons or process to commence the action, but not to arrest a defendant, unless his case, when presented to an o fficer, is adjudged to be one entitling him to that remedy. The process is his own act, the order to arrest that of the court.

The cases in which an order for arrest may be made are defined. They are those contained in the act to abolish imprisonment for debt, modified so as to conform to the provisions of the code, and to those cases in which an arrest is allowed in actions in the supreme court. They embrace the cases also in which an order to attach property may be granted.

§ 1072. Before an order for an arrest can be made, the party applying must prove, to the satisfaction of the justice, by the affidavit of himself, or some other person, the facts on which the application is founded, and the amount of his debt or claim over all payments and set-offs. The plaintiff must also execute and deliver to the justice a written undertaking, with or without sureties, to the effect that if the defendant recover judgment the plaintiff will pay to him all costs that may be awarded to the defendant, and all damages which he may sustain by reason of the arrest, not exceeding the sum specified in the undertaking, which must be double the amount claimed, not exceeding one hundred dollars. If the undertaking be executed by the plaintiff without sureties, he must annex thereto an affidavit, that he is a resident and householder or freeholder, within the county, and worth double the sum specified in the undertaking, over all his debts and liabilities.

That part of this section which requires the plaintiff to give security, is new in its application to justices' courts. It is in conformity with the existing law in relation to arrests in the higher courts, in which no man can be arrested by an order of a judge even, without first giving security to pay costs and damages in case the alleged cause of arrest should turn out to be unfounded. Since the justices' act, as contained in the revised statutes, was passed, the policy of the law has been materially changed by abolishing imprisonment for debt; but the law regulating proceedings in this court has never been revised to make it conformable to the spirit of that act. In order to have an attachment against the property of a defendant, stronger proofs were required than to procure a warrant by which the defendant was restrained of his liberty, besides the securities that are required to be given to the defendant for the payment of damages in case the plaintiff shall fail to make out his case. Abuses by the arrest of the defendant without good cause, are of common occurrence, and it is deemed right to throw about the personal liberty of the party safeguards equal to those by which the possession of property is protected.

§ 1073. The defendant, immediately upon being arrested, must be taken to the office of the justice who made the order, and if he be absent, or unable to try the action, or if it be made to appear to him, by the affidavit of the defendant, that he is a material witness in the action, the constable must immediately take the defendant before the next justice of the city or town, who must take cognizance of the action, and proceed thereon, as if the summons had been issued, and the order of arrest made by him.

§ 1074. The constable, making the arrest, must immediately give notice thereof to the plaintiff, and endorse on the summons and subscribe a certificate, stating the time of serving the same, the time of the arrest, and of his giving notice to the plaintiff.

§ 1075. The constable making an arrest, or another constable, by direction of the justice, must keep the defendant in custody until duly discharged by order of the court, but in no case, can such detention exceed twelve hours from the time of his being first brought before the justice, unless, within that time, the trial of the action be commenced, or unless it be delayed at the request of the defendant.

§ 1076. When the cause of action arises upon a judgment rendered within this state, or an order of a court of competent jurisdiction, to pay a sum of money, or upon any other contract, an order to attach the property of the defendant, may be endorsed upon a summons issued by the justice, in the following cases:

1. When the defendant has departed, or is about to depart, from the county of his residence, or where the action is brought, with intent to defraud his creditors, or to avoid the service of process, or when he keeps himself concealed therein with the like intent:

2. When the defendant has concealed, removed or disposed of his property, or is about to do so, with intent to defraud his creditors.

§ 1077. Before an order to attach property can be made the plaintiff must prove to the satisfaction of the justice, by the affidavit of himself, or another person, the facts on which the application is founded; he must also prove in the same manner, the amount, as near as may be, of his debt or claim, over all payments and set-offs. He must also execute, and deliver to the justice, a written undertaking approved by him, with sufficient sureties, to the effect that he will pay to the defendant, all damages which he may sustain by reason of the attachment, if the plaintiff fail to recover judgment; and that if judgment be recovered, the plaintiff will restore so much of the property, or the avails thereof, if any, as may remain after satisfying the judgment and the subsequent costs.

§ 1078. The order of attachment, must state the amount shown by the affidavit to be due, and must direct that the property of the defendant liable to execution, sufficient to satisfy the same, be attached and kept, in order to satisfy any judgment that may be recovered in the action.

§ 1078. The constable, to whom the summons with the order is delivered, must take into his possession, the property of the defendant liable to execution in the action, and keep the same as directed in the order, and make an inventory thereof, and deliver the same to the defendant, if he can be found in the county. If not found, the constable must leave a copy of the summons, the order and the inventory certified by him, at the residence of the defendant, with some person of suitable age and discretion, if any such person be found there, otherwise, he must post the same on the outer door of such residence. If the defendant have no place of residence in the county, then the constable must leave the copy with the person, in whose possession the property is found.

By the act to abolish imprisonment for debt, an attachment may be issued in some cases, when the defendant is neither absent from the county nor concealed; but no provision is made for serving the process by which the action is commenced personally on the defendant. In such cases it might happen that the defendant's property attached is so situated that he would get no notice of the proceedings, and have no opportunity of defending on its return. This defect is remedied in this section.

§ 1080. The property, attached by a constable, must not be removed by him, if an undertaking with sufficient surety, be executed and delivered to him, to the effect, that if judgment be rendered against the defendant in the action, and execution issued thereon, within thirty days after the judgment, the property shall be produced to satisfy the execution. If any person claim the property attached, the same must be delivered to him, if at any time, after the seizure, and before a sale on the execution, upon his executing, and delivering to the constable, in whose custody the property may be, an undertaking, with sufficient surety, to the effect, that if any action be brought thereon within three months, he will establish that he was the owner of the property, at the time of the seizure, or pay the value thereof to the plaintiff.

§ 1081. The constable serving a summons must endorse thereon a certificate of the time and manner of service. If property has been attached, that must be stated in the return, and an inventory of the property annexed. If an undertaking have been given, it must be returned to the justice, with the summons, and mentioned in the return.

§ 1082. A plaintiff, who resides out of the state, before commencing his action, must file or deposit with the justice security approved by him, for the payment to the defendant of any judgment that may be recovered by him in the action.

§ 1083. When property is attached and delivered to a claimant upon an undertaking as provided in section 1080, if the value of the property recovered from him upon the undertaking, exceed the judgment recovered in the action, on which the property was attached, with interest thereon, the defendant in such original action is entitled to the excess. Or if such defendant satisfy the claim and costs, or the judgment against him, he shall be entitled to the benefit of the undertaking of the claimant, and may bring an action thereon in his own name.

ARTICLE II.

PLEADINGS AND TRIAL.

§ 1084. The pleadings must take place at the time the summons is returned served, or at such other time, not exceeding five days thereafter, as the justice may appoint for the convenience of parties, and by their consent.

§ 1085. The pleadings in justices' courts are,

1. The complaint by the plaintiff, stating the cause of action:

2. The answer by the defendant, stating the grounds of the defence:

3. When the answer sets up a counter-claim, the reply by the plaintiff.

§ 1086. The pleadings may be oral, except when the title to real property is brought in question, or they may be in writing; if oral, the substance of them must be entered by the justice in his docket; if in writing, they must be filed in his office, and a reference to them made in the docket. They are not required to be in any particular form, but must be such, as to enable a person of common understanding to know what is intended.

§ 1087. The complaint must state in a plain and direct manner, the facts constituting the cause of action.

§ 1088. The answer may contain a denial of any of the material facts stated in the complaint, which the defendant believes to be untrue, and also a statement, in a plain and direct manner, of any other facts, constituting a defence, or a counter-claim upon which an action might be brought by the defendant against the plaintiff in a justice's court.

§ 1089. When the answer contains a counter-claim, the plaintiff may reply, denying any of the material allegations relating thereto.

§ 1090. A statement in an answer or reply, that the party has not sufficient knowledge or information in respect to a particular allegation in the previous pleading of the adverse party, to form a belief, is equivalent to a denial.

§ 1091. When the cause of action or counter-claim arises upon an account or instrument for the payment of money only, it is sufficient for the party to deliver the account or instrument to the court, and to state, that there is due to him thereon, from the adverse party, a specified sum, which he claims to recover or set off. The court may at the time of the pleading, require that such writing or account be exhibited to the inspection of the adverse party, with liberty to copy the same; or if not so exhibited, may prohibit its being afterwards given in evidence.

§ 1092. Every complaint, answer, or reply, must be verified by the oath of the party pleading, or if he be not present, by the oath of his agent or attorney, to the effect that he believes it to be true. The verification must be oral or in writing, in conformity with the pleading verified.

§ 1093. Every material allegation in a complaint, or relating to a counter-claim in an answer, not denied by the pleading of the adverse party, must, on the trial be taken to be true, except, that when a defendant, who has not been served with a copy of the complaint with the summons, fails to appear and answer, the plaintiff cannot recover, without proving his case.

§ 1094. Either party may object to a pleading of his adversary, or to any part thereof, that it is not sufficiently explicit to enable him to understand it, or that it contains no cause of action or defence, although it be taken as true.

If the court deem the objection well founded, it must order the pleading to be amended, and, if the party refuse to amend, the defective pleading must be disregarded.

§ 1095. A variance between the proof on the trial, and the allegations in a pleading, must be disregarded as immaterial, unless the court be satisfied, that the adverse party has been misled to his prejudice thereby

§ 1096. The pleadings may be amended, at any time before the trial, or during the trial, or upon appeal, to supply any deficiency or omission in the allegations or denial, necessary to support the action or defence, when, by such amendment, substantial justice will be promoted. If the amendment be made after the issue, and it be made to appear to the satisfaction of the court, by oath, that an adjournment is necessary to the adverse party, in consequence of such amendment, an adjournment must be granted. The court may also, in its discretion, require as a condition of an amendment, the payment of costs to the adverse party, to be fixed by the court, not exceeding three dollars; but such payment cannot be required, unless an adjournment is made necessary by the amendment; nor can an amendment be allowed after a witness is sworn on the trial, when an adjournment thereby will be made necessary.

§ 1097. When, by the defendant's answer, the title to real property is brought in question, such answer must be in writing, subscribed by the defendant or his attorney.

§ 1098. If the defendant have been arrested, such answer must be disregarded, unless the defendant also immediately deliver to the justice a written undertaking, executed by the defendant, and one sufficient surety; or if the defendant be absent, by two sufficient sureties, approved by the justice; to the effect, that the defendant will always render himself amenable, within such county, to the process of the supreme court, during the progress of the action, and to such as may be issued to enforce the judgment, which may be given therein; and in case of default, to pay all damages, not exceeding one hundred dollars.

In the next section, the mode of transferring the cause to the supreme court, is changed to a simple order of transfer by the justice. This change renders a change in the undertaking also necessary, as contained in this section.

§ 1099. Upon the defendant's making such an answer, or if he have been arrested, upon such answer and undertaking, the justice must enter an order in his docket transferring the action to the supreme court; and the proceedings must thenceforth be conducted in that court, in all respects as if the action had been first commenced therein; and costs shall there be given without regard to the amount recovered; the costs before the justice being added as disbursements. The plaintiff may, however, by a notice served within twenty days thereafter, decline to prosecute his action in the supreme court; in such case, the claim shall be deemed abandoned, and no costs shall be recovered against him in the supreme court.

§ 1100. The defendant is not at liberty to give evidence, by which the question of title to real property is raised on the trial before a justice. And when from the plaintiff's own showing, on the trial, it appears that the determination of the action will necessarily involve the decision of a question of title to real property, the justice must dismiss the action, with costs, stating on his docket the reason therefor; but such dismissal shall not preclude the plaintiff from an action in the supreme court for the same cause.

§ 1101. When the title to real property is set forth in the answer as provided in section 1097, or appears on the trial as provided in the last section, and there are other causes of action in the complaint, not affected by the question of title, the order to transfer or to dismiss the action, shall not include such other causes; but as to them, the action must be severed, and tried before the justice in the same manner, as if the question of title had not been raised.

§ 1102. Upon the return day, if a jury be required, or if the justice be actually engaged in other official business, he may adjourn the trial without the consent of either party, as follows:

1. Where a party, who is not a resident of the county, is in attendance; or where the defendant is in attendance under arrest; the adjournment not to exceed twenty-four hours; and the defendant, if under arrest, to continue in custody:

2. In other cases, not to exceed five days, unless by consent of parties.

If the trial be not adjourned, it must take place immediately upon the return of the summons.

§ 1103. The trial may be adjourned by consent, or upon application of either party, without the consent of the other, for a period not exceeding eight days, as follows:

1. The party asking the adjournment must, if required by his adversary, prove by his own oath or otherwise, that he cannot, for want of material testimony, which he expects to procure, safely proceed to trial:

2. If the application be on the part of the plaintiff, and the defendant be under arrest, an adjournment for more than twenty-four hours, discharges the defendant from custody, but the action may proceed notwithstanding: and the defendant shall be subject to arrest on the execution in the same manner as if he had not been so discharged:

3. If the application be on the part of a defendant under arrest, before it can be granted, he must execute an undertaking, with one or more sufficient sureties to be approved by the justice, as follows: If the arrest be for a cause specified in the first four subdivisions of section 1071, or in the sixth, the undertaking must be to the effect, that he will appear at the return day, and not depart from the court until duly discharged, or until after the trial and judgment, and after a reasonable opportunity to arrest him on execution issued upon the judgment, if any be obtained against him. If the arrest be for a cause specified in subdivision 5, of that section, the undertaking must be to the effect, that no part of the property of the defendant, liable to be taken on execution, shall be removed, secreted, assigned, or otherwise disposed of, except for the necessary support, for the time, of himself and family, until the plaintiff's demand be satisfied, or until the expiration of ten days after the judgment, if any be obtained against him in the action:

4. Either party applying for an adjournment, must also, if required by the adverse party, consent that the testimony of any witnesses of such adverse party who are in attendance, be then taken by deposition before the justice, which must accordingly be done; and the testimony so taken may be read on the trial with the same effect, and subject to the same objections, as if the witness were produced.

The various provisions for adjournment in the justice's act, are embodied in this section and the two following, with some modification. Under the existing law, an adjournment upon joining the issue, is a matter of course; this section requires that cause for an adjournment should be shown, when moved for, by a party at any time, and imposes the further condition, that any witness on the adverse side may be sworn and examined and that his deposition mny afterwards be read on the trial.

§ 1104. An adjournment may be had, either at the time of joining the issue, or at any subsequent time to which the cause may stand adjourned, on application of either party, for a period longer than eight days, but not to exceed ninety days from the time of the return of the summons, upon compliance with the provisions of the last section, and upon proof, by the oath of the party or otherwise, to the satisfaction of the justice, that such party cannot be ready for trial before the time to which he desires an adjournment, for the want of material evidence, describing it, that the delay has not been made necessary by any act or negligence on his part, since the action was commenced, and that he expects to procure the evidence at the time stated by him.

§ 1105. If the plaintiff fail to appear at the return day of the summons and make his complaint, the action must be dismissed. If the defendant fail to appear at the return day of the summons, or if either party fail, to attend at a day to which the trial has been adjourned, or fail to make the necessary pleading or proof on his part, the case may nevertheless proceed at the request of the adverse party; and judgment must be given in conformity with the pleadings and proofs.

§ 1106. A trial by jury must be demanded at the time of joining issue; and is waived, if neither party then demand it. When demanded, the trial of the case must be adjourned, until a time and place fixed for the return of the jury. If neither party desire an adjournment, the time and place must be determined by the justice, and must be on the same day or within the next two days. The jury must be immediately drawn and summoned, and a return thereof made as prescribed in sections 317, 318, and 319.

Important changes are made in relation to a jury trial in justices' courts:

1. The demand of a jury trial must be made at the time issue is joined:

2. The jury fees are increased to twenty-five cents each, for all who are summoned and attend, whether sworn or not, and must be deposited with the justice at the time a jury is demanded:

3. The jury is drawn from a jury-box, and summoned as in the higher courts, and not left to be chosen by a constable, as heretofore, often to the great scandal of the institution.

4. If, upon the attendance of a jury, the cause is adjourned, the jury fees for attendance must be paid by the party moving the adjournment, and they must again attend at the time to which the trial is adjourned.

These provisions, it is believed, will prove salutary in securing good juries, and in preventing the unnecessary call of juries in trifling cases. Provision is also made for determining the competency of a juror; and the causes of challenge, which are defined in the Code, apply to justices' courts as well as others.

§ 1107. At the time appointed for the trial, and on the return of the order, if the trial be not further adjourned, and if adjourned, then at the time to which the trial is adjourned, the justice must proceed to draw from the jurors summoned the names of persons to constitute the jury for the trial of the issue. Six jurors constitute a jury, but, by consent of parties, a less number may act.

§ 1108. If a sufficient number of competent and indifferent jurors do not attend, the justice must direct others to be summoned by a constable, from the vicinity, sufficient to complete the jury.

§ 1109. The ballots containing names of jurors not summoned, if any, and of those summoned, but not drawn, must be returned by the justice to the drawn jury box, except that such of them as contain the names of persons, not liable to serve as jurors, must be destroyed. The ballots containing the names of the jurors, who serve, must not be returned to the same box from which they were taken, until all the names have been drawn out. As often as that happens, the whole number must be returned to the undrawn jury box, to be drawn as in the first instance.

§ 1110. Before a party can be entitled to a jury, he must deposit with the justice the sum of three dollars, for jury fees, from which the justice must refund to the party the fees of all jurors who do not attend, and those not refunded must be included in the judgment as part of the costs, in case the party calling the jury recover judgment.

§ 1111. No adjournment can be granted after the return of the jury, unless the party requiring the same, in addition to the other conditions imposed on him, deposit with the justice, to be immediately paid to the jurors attending, the sum of twenty-five cents each, which amount is in no case to be included as part of the costs in the judgment. After the adjournment the jurors must attend at the time and place appointed, without further notice, and the fees deposited when the jury was demanded, with the justice, may remain in his hands until the jury are impanelled, and must be then paid over to them.

§ 1112. If either party object to the competency of a juror the question thereon must be tried in a summary manner by the justice, who may examine the juror or other witnesses on oath.

§ 1113. The verdict of the jury must be general, for the plaintiff, for a specified sum, or for the defendant; or when there is a counter-claim proved, exceeding the demand of the plaintiff as proved, for the defendant for a specified sum. But where there are several plaintiffs or defendants, the verdict may be for, or against one, or more, of them.

ARTICLE III.

JUDGMENT AND EXECUTION.

§ 1114. Judgment that the action be dismissed, without prejudice to a new action, may be entered with costs, in the following cases:

1. When the plaintiff voluntarily dismisses the action, before it is finally submitted:

2. When he fails to appear at the time specified in the summons, or upon adjournment, or within one hour thereafter:

3. When it is objected at the trial, and appears by the evidence, that the action is brought in the wrong county or town or by a plaintiff not a resident of the county, without giving security, as provided in section 1082; but if the objection be taken and overruled, it is

cause only of reversal on appeal, and does not otherwise invalidate the judgment, if not taken, at the trial, it is waived, and is no cause of reversal.

By this section, the cases are defined where the action may be dismissed. The plaintiff cannot be non-suited nor can the action be dismissed without his own consent. If he insist on having his case decided finally in the action, it is his right to do so. If he finds his proof defective, or for any other cause chooses to dismiss his own action before it is finally submitted, he reserves his right of action; but if he submits it to either court or jury, it is at his peril, and conclusive.

§ 1115. When the defendant fails to appear and answer, judgment must be given for the plaintiff, as follows:

1. Where a copy of the complaint and account, or instrument, has been served personally with the summons, as prescribed in section 1069, judgment must be given without further evidence for the sum specified in the summons:

2. In other cases the justice must hear the evidence of the plaintiff, and render judgment for such sum only as shall appear by the evidence to be just; but in no case to exceed the amount specified in the summons.

§ 1116. Upon issue joined, if a jury trial be not demanded, the justice must hear the evidence, and decide all questions of fact and of law, and render judgment accordingly.

§ 1117. Upon a verdict, the justice must immediately render judgment accordingly. When the trial is by the justice, judgment must be entered immediately after the close of the trial, if the defendant has been arrested, or his property attached; in other cases, it must be entered either at the close of the trial, or, if the justice then desire further time to consider, on the fourth day thereafter, both days inclusive.

§ 1118. When the amount found due to either party exceeds the sum, for which the justice is authorized to enter judgment, such party may remit the excess, and judgment may be entered for the residue.

§ 1119. In an action arising on contract, when there is no counter-claim, if the plaintiff fail to recover judgment for an amount equal to that stated in his summons, he cannot recover costs.

This section is introduced to prevent plaintiffs from setting up claims for a larger amount than is really due where a cause of action exists. It sometimes happens that a plaintiff (wishing to try a doubtful claim at the expense of his adversary,) buys a small note, commences an action, and litigates his other claim, in the consciousness that the costs must at all events fall upon the defendant. This section also affords security to a defendant who is sued for a debt which he is not disposed to controvert. He is enabled to know, from the copy of summons in his possession, the extent of the judgment that can be taken against him. Instances of fraud upon a defendant have occurred under the present system, where the summons in all cases lays the plaintiff's damage at fifty dollars or under, as expressed in the printed blank forms. When the defendant failed to appear, the plaintiff, instead of declaring on the debt, which the defendant expected, has taken advantage of his absence, and produced perhaps some purchased note, barred by the statute of limitations, or to which the defendant had some other good defence.

§ 1120. If the defendant, at any time before the trial, offer in writing to allow judgment to be taken against him, for a specified sum, the plaintiff may immediately have judgment therefor, with the costs then accrued. But if he do not accept such offer before the trial, and fail to recover in the action a sum equal to the offer, he cannot recover costs accrued after the offer; but costs must be adjudged against him, and if he recover, deducted from his recovery. But the offer, and failure to accept it, cannot be given in evidence, to affect the recovery, otherwise than as to costs, as above provided.

This section introduces a practice analagous to that under the Code in the supreme court, and is calculated to prevent unreasonable claims being set up, and to induce fair offers and liberal compromises. Of its useful effects the Commissioners entertain no doubt.

§ 1121. When a judgment is rendered, in a case where the defendant is subject to arrest and imprisonment thereon, it must be so stated in the judgment, and entered in his docket.

§ 1122. The justice, on the demand of a party in whose favor judgment is rendered, must give him a transcript thereof, which may be filed and docketed in the office of the clerk of the county where the judgment was rendered. The time of the receipt of the transcript by the county clerk, must be noted by him thereon, and entered in the docket; and from that time, the judgment creates a lien in the same manner, as a judgment of the supreme court. Upon a transcript of such docket, certified by the clerk of the county, and filed in any other county, the judgment may be there docketed with the same effect, from the time of filing and docketing in that county. The judgment so docketed, and the enforcement thereof, are subject to the control of the county court of the county where it was first docketed, as a judgment of that court. But a judgment for less than twenty-five dollars, so docketed, is not a lien upon, and cannot be enforced against real property.

§ 1123. Execution for the enforcement of a judgment in a justice's court, except when it has been docketed in the county clerk's office, may be issued by the justice before whom the judgment was rendered, or by his successor in office, on the application of the party entitled thereto, at any time within five years from the entry of judgment.

The existing law changed so as to allow execution to be issued immediately after judgment according to the practice in the higher courts. When a debt is justly due, and has been so adjudged by a court, it seems a perversion of right still to extend the time for its collection. The delay is less necessary since the exemption of property has been extended.

§ 1124. The execution must be directed to a constable of the county, and subscribed by the justice by whom the judgment was rendered, or by his successor in office, and must bear date the day of its delivery to the officer to be executed. It must intelligibly refer to the judgment, by stating the names of the parties, and the name of the justice before whom, and of the county and town where, and the time when, it was rendered; the amount of the judgment; and, if less than the whole is due, the true amount due thereon. It must re require the constable substantially as follows:

1. If it be a case where the defendant cannot be arrested, it must direct the officer to collect the amount of the judgment out of the personal property of the debtor, and to pay the same to the party entitled thereto:

2. If it be a case where the defendant may be arrested, in addition to the foregoing, it must direct the officer, if sufficient property of the defendant, liable to the execution, cannot be found to satisfy the judgment, that he arrest the debtor, and commit him to the jail of the county, until he pay the judgment, or be discharged according to law:

3. It must further, in all cases, direct the officer to make return of the execution, and a certificate thereon, showing the manner in which he has executed the same, in sixty days from the time of his receipt thereof.

§ 1125. Upon an execution on a judgment against joint debtors, upon one or more of whom the summons was not served, the execution must contain a direction to collect the amount out of the joint property of all the defendants, or the separate property of the persons upon whom the summons was served, to be specified by name. If such judgment be also such that the defendants are subject to arrest thereon, the justice must further specify the names of those defendants, served with the summons, who may be arrested for want of property.

§ 1126. A constable may at his peril, omit to arrest a debtor; or after arrest, suffer him to go at large before the return day; subject only to his liability for an escape, or for omitting to arrest, if he fail to have either the money or the person of the debtor in custody at the expiration of the sixty days.

§ 1127. When an execution directs the arrest of the debtor for want of sufficient personal chattels, if there be not sufficient subject to levy, known to the officer, or if upon demand by the officer of the debtor, he fail to produce sufficient property, the officer may without further delay arrest the defendant. When arrested, the defendant must be conveyed to the common jail of the county, and there be kept in custody until the execution with costs be paid, or he be discharged by due course of law.

§ 1128. The debtor committed as provided in the last section, may be held in prison ten days; and if he be a person without a family, for which he provides, one day in addition, for every dollar over ten due on the execution: or, if he have a family for which he provides, one day in addition, for every two dollars over twenty due on the execution.

§ 1129. The affidavit of an imprisoned debtor, that he has a family for which he provides, specifying by name one or more persons, members of such family, and the place of their residence, is sufficient evidence thereof, to authorise his discharge by the jailor.

The last four sections contain some new provisions, calculated to soften the harshness of judicial arrests, when allowed, and yet to secure all the benefits to be expected from them.

§ 1130. An execution may at the request of the plaintiff be renewed before the expiration of sixty days from the time of its issue, by the word "renewed" written thereon, with the date thereof, and subscribed by the justice. Such renewal has the effect of an original issue; and may be repeated as often as may be necessary. If an execution be returned unsatisfied, another may be afterwards issued.

§ 1131. A debtor cannot be arrested, nor his property sold on execution, after sixty days from its issue or renewal; but property levied on within the sixty days, may be sold after a renewal.

§ 1132. A constable is liable to the party in whose favor an execution is issued to him, for the amount thereof, in the following cases:

1. When he suffers sixty days to elapse, without making a true return thereof to the justice, and paying to him or to the party entitled, the money collected thereon by him:

2. When he wilfully or carelessly omits to levy upon property; or if the debtor be liable to arrest, to arrest and imprison him, within sixty days; or having arrested the debtor, fails to commit him to the county jail, within the sixty days.

§ 1133 Upon a justice's judgment docketed in a county clerk's office, execution can only be issued by the clerk, with whom the transcript is filed, or by the plaintiff in person: and it may be sent to one or more counties where the judgment is docketed. It must conform substantially to the execution issued by a justice, except that it must state the time when the judgment was docketed in the county from which it is issued, and must be directed to the sheriff; and may direct, that for want of sufficient personal property, the debt be made out of the real property of the debtor.

Until the adoption of the code in 1848, the county clerk alone could issue executions in these cases. The practice since then of issuing them by the party does not seem well adapted to this class of judgments, when the parties generally act in person, and are not conversant with the forms of process.

ARTICLE IV.

GENERAL PROVISIONS.

§ 1134. Justices' courts being courts of peculiar and limited jurisdiction, only those provisions of this code, which are in their nature applicable to the organization, powers and course of proceeding in justices' courts, and in respect to which no special provision is made in this chapter, are applicable to justices' courts and the proceedings therein.

With a view to promote as far as practicable, a uniform course of proceeding in all courts, it has been deemed best to make the provisions of the code generally applicable to justices' courts as far as the nature of the case and their peculiar jurisdiction and organizations admit. This chapter contains all that is peculiar to the court, and a few rules that are common to all; but these for the most part are contained in other parts of the code.

§ 1135. Every justice must keep a book, denominated a docket, in which must be entered by him,

1. The title of every action in which the summons is returned served, or when the parties voluntarily appear:

2. The date of the summons, and the time of its return; and if an order to arrest the defendant or attach property was made, such fact must also be stated:

3. The time when the parties, or either of them, appeared; a minute of the pleadings; if in writing, referring to them; if not in writing, a concise statement of the material parts of the pleadings:

4. Every adjournment; stating on whose application, whether on oath, evidence, or consent, and to what time:

5. When a trial by jury is demanded, the demand must be stated, and by whom made, the names of the

jury drawn, and the time appointed for the trial and return of the jury:

6. The names of the jury who appear, and of those sworn; the names of all witnesses sworn, and at whose request; the objection, if any, made to testimony, and the decision thereon:

7. The verdict of the jury, and when received; if the jury disagree, and are discharged, that fact must be stated:

8. The judgment of the court; specifying the items of costs included, and the time when rendered:

9. The issuing of execution; when issued, and to whom; the renewals thereof, if any, and when made; the return, and when made; and a statement of any money paid to the justice, and when, and by whom:

10. The giving of a transcript to be filed in the county clerk's office, and when given:

11. The receipt of a notice of appeal, or order to make or amend a return, stating the time of the receipt, and the fees therefor.

§ 1136. The several particulars in the last section specified, must be entered under the title of the action to which they relate, and at the time when they occur. Such entries in a justice's docket, or a transcript thereof, certified by the justice, or his successor in office, are primary evidence to prove the facts so stated therein.

§ 1137. A justice must keep an alphabetical index to his docket, in which must be entered the names of the parties to each judgment, with a reference to the page of the entry. The names of the plaintiffs must be entered in the index, in the alphabetical order of the first letter of the family names.

§ 1138. It is the duty of every justice, upon the expiration of his term of office, to deposit with his successor his official dockets, as well his own as those of his predecessors, which may be in his custody; there to be kept as public records. If the offiee of a justice become vacant, by his death, or removal from the town, or otherwise, before his successor is elected and qualified, the dockets, in possession of such justice, must be deposited with the supervisor of the town, to be by him delivered to the successor in office of the justice.

§ 1139. Any justice, with whom the docket of his predecessor is deposited, may issue execution on a judgment there entered and unsatisfied, and not docketed in the county clerk's office, in the same manner and with the same effect, as the justice, by whom the judgment was rendered, might have done.

§ 1140. The justice elected to fill a vacancy, or when elected, chosen by lot to fill a vacancy for less than a full term, is deemed the successor of the justice whose office became vacant before the expiration of a full term. When a full term expires, the same or another person elected to take office in the same town, from that time is deemed the successor.

§ 1111. When two or more justices are equally entitled, under the last section, to be deemed the successors in office of a justice, the supervisor of the town must by a certificate subscribed by him, and filed in the office of the town clerk, with a duplicate attached to the last docket, designate which justice is to be deemed the successor of a justice going out of office or whose office has become vacant.

The provisions of the last five sections are new, but it is believed that their propriety will be at once generally concurred in. A justice's docket, containing the records of many hundred judgments, and perhaps proof of their satisfaction, ought surely to be provided by law with a place of deposite, where it may be found.

§ 1142. The summons, execution, and every other paper made or issued by a justice, must be filled up, without a blank left to be filled by another; otherwise it is void.

§ 1143. Every justice now in office and every justice hereafter elected, before entering upon the duties of his office, must, by appointment in writing, filed with the town clerk, assign a day of the week, and a place at which, a summons, issued by a plaintiff himself, may be made returnable before him. It is the duty of the justice to attend at his office, thus designated, on the day assigned for returns, from nine o'clock in the morning until four o'clock in the afternoon.

§ 1144. The day so appointed must not be the same, specified in the appointment of another justice of the same town previously filed. The place so designated may be known as the justice's office and may be afterwards changed by him, on filing a new appointment, and posting notices thereof in three public places of the town.

§ 1145. In case of the sickness, other disability, or necessary absence of a justice, at the time appointed, another justice of the same town may, at his request, attend in his behalf, and shall thereupon become vested with the power, for the time being, of the justice before whom the summons was returnable. In that case the proper entry of the proceeding before the attending justice, subscribed by him, must be made in the docket of the justice before whom the summons was returnable. If the case be adjourned, the justice before whom the summons was returnable, must resume jurisdiction.

The last four sections provide for a systematic arrangement of the time at which a summons may be made returnable before a justice when issued by a party. The Commissioners are satisfied that it will be found convenient and beneficial both to the justices' themselves, and to those who do business in their courts. It is not designed to prevent a justice from issuing a summons returnable before himself on another day if he sees fit.

§ 1146. A justice may at the request of a party, and on being satisfied that it is expedient, specially depute any discreet person, of suitable age, and not interested in the action, to serve a summons or execution, with or without an order to arrest the defendant, or to attach property. Such deputation must be in writing on the process.

§ 1147. The person so deputed has the authority of a constable in relation to the service, execution and return of such process, and is subject to the same obligations, but can not receive a fee for the service.

§ 1148. When the sureties of a constable make complaint to a county judge, that such constable has unlawfully converted to his own use, or misapplied, money collected by him as constable, for which they have been sued, or are liable to be sued, such application being verified by oath that they believe it to be true, the county judge must immediately make an order, suspending such constable from the further exercise of his official powers, until he give new security. Such order must be served on the constable, and filed in the office of the town clerk.

§ 1149. When an execution is delivered to a constable, within the last sixty days of his term of office, he may, notwithstanding the expiration of his term, proceed thereon, in the same manner as if he still continued in office, and his sureties shall be liable to the same extent.

§ 1150. A justice may punish, as for a criminal contempt, persons guilty of the following acts, and no others:

1. Disorderly, contemptuous or insolent behaviour toward the justice while holding the court, tending to interrupt the due course of a trial, or other judicial proceeding:

2. A breach of the peace, boisterous conduct, or violent disturbance, tending to interrupt the due course of a trial or other judicial proceeding:

3. Wilful resistance, in the presence of the justi e, to the execution of a lawful order or process made or issued by him.

§ 1151. A warrant of arrest may be issued by such justice, on which the person so guilty may be arrested, and brought before the justice, on the same day, or the next judicial day, when an opportunity to be heard in his defence or excuse must be given. The justice may thereupon discharge him, or may convict him of the offence, and adjudge a punishment by fine or imprisonment, or both; such fine not to exceed twenty dollars, and such imprisonment, ten days.

§ 1152. The conviction, specifying particularly the offence and the judgment thereon, must be entered by the justice in his docket. A warrant of commitment to the jail of the county until the fine be paid, or for the term of the imprisonment, may then be issued. Such warrant must contain a transcript of the entry in the docket; and the same must be executed by any constable to whom it may be given, and by the jailer of the county.

§ 1153. If a person summoned as a juror or witness fail to attend, the justice may issue a warrant to arrest the delinquent for the purpose of compelling his attendance and punishing his disobedience.

§ 1154. When the person arrested is brought before the justice, or when a person in attendance refuses to serve as a juror or to testify as a witness, and no valid excuse be show the justice may impose a fine upon him, not exceeding five dollars. An entry of such fine, stating the reason thereof, must be made by the justice in his docket, and thereupon shall have the effect of a judgment, in favor of the overseers of the poor of the town against the delinquent, and may be enforced as well against his person as his property.

§ 1155. The term "justice," as used in this chapter, includes justice of the peace and justices of justice's courts in cities; the term "town," includes ward or district, in reference to justice's courts in cities; and whenever other sections of the code are made applicable to justice's courts, the terms "judge" and "court" therein, are to be deemed to include justice and justices' courts; and the term "sheriff," to include constable.

§ 1156. For services rendered pursuant to the provisions of this chapter, fees may be charged, and included in the judgment, as follows:

For Justice's Fees.

1. For all proceedings when the defendant does not answer, including judgment, transcript and execution, one dollar:

2. For all proceedings to, and including the issue, if an order to arrest a defendant, or to attach property, be made, one dollar; if there be no order to arrest, or to attach property, fifty cents:

3. For all proceedings after issue, to and including trial by jury, if there be one, one dollar and fifty cents. If there be no jury, one dollar:

4. For judgment upon the issue and any proceedings afterwards, including transcript, executions, returns, and all other proceedings and entries, fifty cents:

5. Postage actually paid, on sending or receiving a commission to take testimony.

§ 1157. Constables are entitled to receive, from the party in whose favor the services are rendered, the following fees; of which those rendered before judgment may be included therein, when it is in favor of the party liable therefor:

1. For serving a summons or execution, and making return, including a copy, when there is no arrest or attachment of property, for each defendant served, twenty cents:

2. When the defendant is arrested; for serving the summons, making the arrest, and giving notice to the plaintiff, including copies and return, forty cents for one defendant, and twenty cents for each defendant, more than one, arrested:

3. When property is attached; for serving summons, attaching property, including copies, inventories and return, fifty cents for one defendant, and ten cents for each defendant more than one:

4. For travel; going to serve a summons, or give notice to the plaintiff, or to arrest a debtor on execution, or to summon a jury, six cents for each mile more than one; to be computed for one person only, from the justice's office to the place where the service is made; but when there is more than one defendant included in the same summons or execution, and in the case of summoning a jury, the constable must certify in his return the number of miles actually and necessarily travelled to make the service on all the persons served, and his fees shall be accordingly; when a debtor is arrested on execution and committed to jail, ten cents for each

mile, from the place where the arrest is made, to the jail:

5. For collecting money on execution, and paying it over where property is not sold: four cents for every dollar collected to fifty dollars, and two cents for every dollar above fifty. For advertising property, twenty-five cents; for selling property, fifty cents:

6. When an execution is settled by the parties while in the constable's hands, he is entitled to receive from the party in whose favor it was issued, his fees for travel, and service actually performed, and one half the fees he would have been entitled to for collecting and paying over.

§ 1158. A witness, is entitled to receive from the party in whose behalf he attends, to be included in a judgment in favor of the party liable therefor, as follows:

If a resident of the city, village or town where the trial is had, twelve and a half cents; in other cases, twenty-five cents; also, four cents for each mile's actual travel, going from his residence to the place of trial and returning.

§ 1159. Jurors are entitled to receive fees from the party who demands a jury trial, to be included in a judgment in his favor, twenty-five cents for attending, whether sworn or not, and the same fee for another attendance pursuant to adjournment, from the party applying therefor.

§ 1160. Upon an execution issued on a justice's judgment docketed in a county clerk's office, the same fees are allowed as on executions issued by a justice; except that when real property is sold, the printer's fees for advertising may be charged in addition, and also, the same fees for a certificate of sale, and for a sheriff's deed, as are allowed in the supreme court.

§ 1161. If a justice, constable, witness or juror receive greater fees than are allowed by law, the excess may be recovered back, even though they may not be included in the judgment.

The changes made in the fees are considerable, and are adjusted like those in the higher courts by the result attained, and the state of the action rather than by the numbers of steps taken to arrive at any particular stage. The items are few in number, but respectable in the amount of compensation for the average services required. Whether they are too large or too small, the legislature can determine quite as well or better than the Commissioners. But recollecting a resolution of the assembly in 1848, in relation to filling the blanks in sections regulating costs in the higher courts, the Commissioners have deemed it their duty to specify sums here leaving it to the legislature to adopt or change them as it may seem fit.

TITLE XII.

OF APPEALS IN CIVIL ACTIONS.

CHAPTER I.

APPEALS IN GENERAL.

§ 1162. A judgment, or order, in a civil action, may be reviewed as prescribed by this title, and not otherwise.

Amended Code, § 323.

§ 1163. An order, made out of court, without notice to the adverse party, may be vacated or modified, without notice, by the judge who made it, or may be vacated or modified on notice, in the manner in which other motions are made.

Amended Code, § 324.

§ 1164. Any party aggrieved may appeal in the cases prescribed in this title.

Amended Code, § 325.

1165. The party appealing, is known as the appellant, and the adverse party as the respondent. But the title of the action is not to be changed, in consequence of the appeal.

Amended Code, § 326.

§ 1166. An appeal must be made by the service of a notice in writing, on the adverse party, and on the clerk with whom the judgment or order appealed from is entered, stating the appeal from the same, or some specified part thereof. When a party gives, in good faith, notice of appeal from a judgment or order, and omits, through mistake, to do any other act necessary to perfect the appeal or to stay proceedings, the court may permit an amendment on such terms as may be just.

Amended Code, § 327.

§ 1167. Upon the appeal, allowed by the second and third chapters of this title, being perfected, the clerk with whom the notice of appeal is filed, must, at the expense of the appellant, forthwith transmit to the appellate court a certified copy of the notice of appeal and of the judgment roll.

Amended Code, § 328.

§ 1168. Upon an appeal from a judgment, the court may review any intermediate order, involving the merits, and necessarily affecting the judgment.

Amended Code, § 329.

§ 1169. Upon an appeal from a judgment or order, the appellate court may reverse, affirm or modify the judgment or order appealed from, in the respect mentioned in the notice of appeal, and as to any or all of the parties, and may, if necessary or proper, order a new trial. When the judgment is reversed or modified, the appellate court may make complete restitution of all property and rights lost by the erroneous judgment.

Amended Code, § 330.

§ 1170. The appeal allowed by the second and third chapters of this title, must be taken within two years after the judgment, if heretofore rendered, and within one year after a judgment hereafter rendered.

Amended Code, § 331, changed so as to reduce the time for appealing from judgments rendered hereafter, see next note.

1171. The appeal allowed by the fourth chapter of this title, must be taken, within sixty days after written notice of the judgment or order shall have been given to the party appealing.

Amended Code, § 332, changed so as to extend the time from thirty to sixty days.

Two years after judgment are deemed too long a time, producing unnecessary delay in the final settlement of the rights of parties. On the other hand, thirty days are too short a limitation for appeals, requiring the same security and the same delibeliberation.

§ 1172. The appellant must furnish the court with copies of the notice of appeal, and of the order or judgment roll. If he fail to do so, the appeal may be dismissed.

Original Code, § 281.

CHAPTER II.

APPEALS TO THE COURT OF APPEALS.

§ 1173. An appeal may be taken to the court of appeals, in the cases mentioned in section 28.

Amended Code, § 333.

§ 1174. To render an appeal effectual for any purpose, a written undertaking must be executed, on the part of the appellant, by at least two sureties, to the effect that the appellant will pay all damages, costs and charges, which may be awarded against him on the appeal, not exceeding two hundred and fifty dollars; or that sum must be deposited with the clerk, with whom the judgment or order was entered, to abide the event of the appeal. But such undertaking or deposit may be waived by a written consent on the part of the respondent.

Amended Code, § 334.

§ 1175. If the appeal be from a judgment directing the payment of money, it does not stay the execution of the judgment, unless a written undertaking be executed on the part ef the appellant, by at least two sureties, to the effect that if the judgment appealed from, or any part thereof, be affirmed, the appellant will pay the amount directed to be paid by the judgment, or the part of such amount as to which the judgment shall be affirmed, if it be affirmed only in part, and all damages which shall be awarded against the appellant, upon the appeal.

Amended Code, sec. 335.

§ 1176. If the judgment appealed from, direct the assignment or delivery of documents, or personal property, the execution of the judgment is not stayed by appeal unless the things required to be assigned or delivered, be brought into court, or placed in the custody of such officer or receiver as the court may appoint, or unless an undertaking be entered into, on the part of the appellant, by at least two sureties, and in such amount as the court or a judge thereof, or county judge may direct, to the effect that the appellant will obey the order of the appellate court, upon the appeal.

Amended Code, § 336.

§ 1177. If the judgment appealed from, direct the execution of a conveyance, or other instrument, the execution of the judgment is not stayed by the appeal, until the instrument is executed and deposited with the clerk with whom the judgment is entered, to abide the judgment of the appellate court.

Amended Code, § 337.

§ 1178. If the judgment appealed from, direct the sale or delivery of possession of real property, the execution of the same is not stayed, unless a written undertaking be executed on the part of the appellant, with two sureties, to the effect, that during the possession of such property by the appellant, he will not commit, or suffer to be committed, any waste thereon, and that if the judgment be affirmed, he will pay the value of the use and occupation of the property, from the time of the appeal until the delivery of possession thereof, pursuant to the judgment, not exceeding a sum to be fixed by a judge of the court by which the judgment was rendered, and which must be specified in the undertaking. When the judgment is for the sale of mortgaged premises, and the payment of a deficiency arising upon the sale, the undertaking must also provide for the payment of such deficiency.

Amended Code, § 338.

§ 1179, Whenever an appeal is perfected, as provided by sections 1175, 1176, 1177, and 1178, it stays all further proceedings in the court below, upon the judgment appealed from, or upon the matter embraced therein; but the court below may proceed, upon any other matter included in the action, and not affected by the judgment appealed from. And the court below may, in its discretion, dispense with, or limit, the security required by sections 1175, 1176, and 1178, when the appellant is an executor, administrator, trustee, or other person acting in another's right; and may also in all cases limit such security to an amount not less than fifty thousand dollars.

Amended Code, § 339, modified by the addition of the last sentence.

§ 1180. In an action arising on contract, notwithstanding an appeal and security given for a stay of proceedings thereon, if the respondent give adequate security to make restitution, in case the judgment is reversed or modified, he may, upon leave obtained from the court below, proceed to enforce the judgment. Such security must be an undertaking, executed to the appellant, by at least two sufficient sureties, to the effect, that if the judgment be reversed or modified, the respondent will make such restitution as the appellate court may direct.

The object of this section is to secure to a party, who has obtained a judgment, the benefit of it, notwithstanding an appeal, if he will give adequate security to make restitution, in case the judgment is reversed. This appears to be reasonable, inasmuch as the recovery of the judgment creates a strong presumption, that the amount of it is due to the creditor. If parties are equally willing to give security to abide by the judgment of an appellate court, he, whose right to the subject of the litigation has been affirmed by the decision of a competent court, has the better claim to the benefit of it, during the appeal. The adoption of the section will do much to discourage unfounded appeals, which are now not unfrequently brought for delay.

§ 1181, The undertakings prescribed by sections 1174, 1175, 1176 and 1178, may be in one instrument or several, at the option of the appellant; and a copy, including the names and residence of the sureties, must be served on the adverse party, with the notice of appeal, unless a deposit is made as provided in section 1174 and notice thereof given.

Amended Code, § 340.

§ 1182. An undertaking upon an appeal is of no effect, unless it be accompanied by the affidavit of the sureties, that they are each worth double the amount specified therein. The adverse party may, however, except to the sufficiency of the sureties, within ten days after notice of the appeal; and unless they or other sureties justify before a judge of the court below, or a county judge, as prescribed by sections 691 and 692, within ten days thereafter, the appeal must be regarded as if no such undertaking had been given. The justification must be upon a notice of not less than five days.

Amended Code, § 341.

§ 1183. In the cases not provided for in sections 1175, 1176, 1177, 1178 and 1179, the perfecting of an appeal, by giving the undertaking mentioned in section 1174, stays proceedings in the court below, upon the judgment appealed from, except, that where it directs the sale of perishable property, the court below may order the property to be sold, and the proceeds thereof to be deposited or invested, to abide the judgment of the appellate court.

Amended Code, § 342.

CHAPTER III.

APPEALS TO THE SUPREME COURT FROM AN INFERIOR COURT.

§ 1184. An appeal may be taken to the supreme court, from the judgment rendered by a county court, or by a city court.

Amended Code, § 344. The amendment restricting the right omitted.

1185. Security must be given npon such appeal, in the same manner, and to the same extent, as upon an appeal to the court of appeals.

Amended Code, § 345.

1186. Appeals in the supreme court must be heard at a general term, either in the district embracing the county where the judgment or order appealed from was entered, or in a county adjoining that county, except that where the judgment or order was entered in the city and county of New-York, the appeal must be heard in the first district.

Amended Code, § 346.

§ 1187. Judgment upon the appeal must be entered and docketed with the clerk in whose office the judgment roll is filed. When the appeal is heard in a county other than that where the judgment roll is filed, the judgment upon the appeal must be certified to the clerk with whom the roll is filed, to be there entered and docketed.

Amended Code, § 347.

CHAPTER IV.

APPEALS IN THE SUPREME COURT, AND IN THE SUPERIOR COURT AND COURT OF COMMON PLEAS OF THE CITY OF NEW-YORK, FROM A SINGLE JUDGE, TO THE GENERAL TERM.

1188. In the supreme court, the superior court of the city of New-York, and the court of common pleas of the city of New-York, an appeal, upon either the law or the fact, may be taken to the general term, from a judgment entered upon the report of referees or the direction of a single judge of the same court. Security must be given upon such appeal, in the same manner as upon an appeal to the court of appeals. In the supreme court, the appeal must be heard in the same manner as if it were an appeal from an inferior court; but the decision at the general term upon the facts separately from the law, is final.

Amended Code, § 348.

Under the former practice, all questions, whether of fact or law, in equity suits, were the subjects of appeal, even to the court of last resort. The amendment made in 1849 by the legislature to section 348, confined an appeal to questions of law only, and in effect made the decision of a single judge on the first trial conclusive. There is a propriety in not subjecting the verdict of a jury on the facts, to the review of a court; to allow which would much impair the value of a jury trial. Not so, however, with respect to the decision of a single judge, where a due regard to the rights of parties seems to us to require, that at least one opportunity should be afforded to review such a decision more especially when we consider that in the class of cases, where the trial of facts is by the court, it is sometimes difficult to separate the law and fact. To meet this view, we propose to modify the amendment of last year as provided in this section.

§ 1189. An appeal may in like manner, and within the same time, be taken from an order made by a single judge of the same court, and may be thereupon reviewed in the following cases:

1. When the order grants or refuses a provisional remedy:

2. When it grants or refuses a new trial:

3. When it involves the merits of the action, or some part thereof:

4. When the order affects a substantial right, and involves the construction of the constitution or of a provision of this code:

5. When the order is made, upon a summary application in an action after judgment, and affects a substantial right.

Amended Code, § 349.

§ 1190. The last section includes an order made out of court upon notice; but in such case, the order must be first entered with the clerk. And for the purpose of an appeal, any party, affected by such order, may require it to be entered with the clerk, and it must be entered accordingly.

Amended Code, § 350.

CHAPTER V.

APPEAL TO THE COURT OF COMMON PLEAS OF THE CITY OF NEW-YORK, OR TO A COUNTY COURT, FROM AN INFERIOR COURT.

§ 1191. Judgments in civil cases, rendered by justices' courts, and by the marine court of the city of New-York, may be reviewed, as prescribed by this chapter, and not otherwise,

Amended Code, § 351.

§ 1192. When the judgment has been rendered by the marine court of the city of New-York, or by a justice's court in that city, the appeal must be to the court of common pleas of the city of New-York; and when rendered by any of the other courts mentioned in the last section, to the county court of the county where the judgment was rendered.

Amended Code, § 352.

§ 1193. The appellant must, within twenty days after the judgment, make, or cause to be made, an affidavit, stating the substance of the testimony and proceedings before the court below, and the grounds upon which the appeal is founded.

Amended Code, § 353.

§ 1194. A copy of the affidavit must, within the same time, be served on the respondent, if he be a resident of the city or county, or can be found therein, personally, or by leaving it at his residence with some person of suitable age and discretion, or if he be not a resident, on the attorney or agent, if any, who appeared for him on the trial, and is a resident of such city or county, with a notice, stating that the appellant appeals from the judgment, and that the appeal will be heard by the appellate court, at a time and place therein designated, not less than six nor more than twenty days thereafter; which time may be in or out of term. When the notice cannot be thus served, the service may be made on the justice.

Amended Code, § 354.

§ 1195. If the appellant desire a stay of execution of the judgment, he must give security as provided in the next section.

Amended Code, § 355.

§ 1196. The security must be a written undertaking, executed by one or more sufficient sureties, approved by the county judge, or by the court below, to the effect, that if judgment be rendered against the appellant, and execution thereon be returned unsatisfied, in whole or in part, the sureties will pay the amount unsatisfied.

Amended Code, § 356.

§ 1197. The delivery of the undertaking to the court below stays the issuing of execution; or if it have been issued, the service of a copy of the undertaking, certified by the court below, upon the officer holding the execution, stays further proceedings thereon.

Amended Code, § 357.

§ 1198. Where, by reason of the death of a justice, or his removal from the county, or any other cause, the undertaking on the appeal cannot be delivered to him, it must be filed with the clerk of the appellate court, and notice thereof given to the respondent, or his attorney or agent, as provided in section 1194, and it shall, thereupon, have the same effect as if delivered to the justice.

Amended Code, § 358.

§ 1199. When the affidavit and notice of appeal have been served, the respondent may supply or correct material omissions or mis-statements therein by an affidavit on his part, a copy of which must be served on the attorney, if any, who prosecutes the appeal, or if there be none, on the appellant, if to be found in the county, at least one day before the time for hearing the appeal.

Amended Code, § 359.

§ 1200. The appellate court must proceed to hear the appeal, at the time and place mentioned in the notice, or at such other time as the court may appoint, and may decide the same upon the affidavits; or if they be contradictory or defective in material points, may order the court below to make a return of the testimony and proceedings before it, within ten days after the service of the order and affidavits, or of copies thereof.

Original Code, § 310.

§ 1201. The court below must thereupon, within the ten days, make a return to the appellate court of the testimony, proceedings and judgment, and file the same, with the order and affidavits, in the appellate court, and may be compelled to do so by the appellate court. But a justice is not bound to make a return, unless the fee prescribed by the last section of this chapter be paid on service of the order.

Original Code, 311. *Amended Code*, § 360.

§ 1202. If the return be defective, the appellate court may direct a further or amended return, as often as may be necessary, and may compel a compliance with its order.

Amended Code, § 362.

§ 1203. When a justice of the peace, by whom a judgment appealed from was rendered, shall have gone out of office, or removed to another county, before a return is made, he must, nevertheless, make a return, in the same manner, and with the same effect, as if he were still in office, and may in the same manner be compelled to do so.

Amended Code, § 361.

§ 1204. If a justice of the peace, whose judgment is appealed from, die, become insane, or remove from the state, the appellate court may examine witnesses on oath, respecting the facts of the trial or judgment, and determine the appeal, as if the facts had been returned by the justice.

Amended Code, § 363.

§ 1205. If a return be made, the appeal may be brought to a hearing at a general term of the appellate court, upon a notice by either party, of not less than eight days. It must be placed upon the calendar and continue thereon without further notice, until finally disposed of; but if neither party bring it to a hearing before the end of the second term, the court must dismiss the appeal, unless it continue the same, by special order, for cause shown.

Amended Code, § 364.

§ 1206. The appeal whether heard on the affidavits or return, must be heard on the original papers; and no copy thereof need be furnished for the use of the court.

Original Code, § 316. *Amended Code*, § 365.

§ 1207. Upon the hearing of the appeal, the appellate court must give judgment upon the law and the facts, according to the justice of the case, without regard to technical errors or defects, which do not affect the merits. In case of a reversal, the court may allow another action for the same cause.

Amended Code, § 366, modified at the end.

§ 1208. To every judgment upon an appeal there must be annexed the affidavits or return on which it was heard, which must be filed with the clerk of the court, and constitute the judgment roll.

Amended Code, § 367.

§ 1209. When upon a reversal, another action is allowed the rights of the parties stand unaffected by the former action. If another action be allowed, a concise statement of the reasons therefor must be filed with the clerk.

The first part of this section is new; the last is the same as in original code, § 319.

§ 1210. If the judgment below, or any part thereof, be collected, and be afterwards reversed, the appellate court must order the amount collected to be restored with interest from the time of collection. The order may be obtained upon proof of the facts made at or after the hearing, upon a previous notice of six days.

Amended Code, § 369.

§ 1211. If, upon an appeal, a recovery be had by one party, and costs be awarded to the other, the appellate court must set off the one against the other, and render judgment for the balance.

Amended Code, § 370.

§ 1212. The following fees and costs, and no other, except fees of officers, are allowed on appeals;

To the appellant, on reversal, if upon affidavits, ten dollars, if upon a return, fifteen dollars.

To the respondent, on affirmance, if upon affidavits, seven dollars, if upon a return, twelve dollars.

To a justice of the peace, for his return, one dollar.

If the judgment appealed from be reversed in part, and affirmed as to the residue, the amount of costs allowed to either party, is such as the appellate court may award, not exceeding ten dollars.

If the appeal be dismissed for want of prosecution, as provided by section 1205, no costs are allowed to either party.

Amended Code, § 371.

TITLE XIII.

OF THE MISCELLANEOUS PROCEEDINGS, IN CIVIL ACTIONS, AND GENERAL PROVISIONS.

CHAPTER II.

PROCEEDINGS AGAINST JOINT DEBTORS, HEIRS, DEVISEES, LEGATEES AND TENANTS HOLDING UNDER A JUDGMENT DEBTOR.

§ 1213. When a judgment is recovered against one or more of several persons, jointly indebted upon an obligation, by proceeding as provided in section 632, those who were not originally summoned to answer the complaint, may be summoned to show cause why they should not be bound by the judgment, in the same manner as if they had been originally summoned.

Amended Code, § 375.

§ 1214. In case of the death of a judgment debtor after judgment, the heirs, devisees, legatees or personal representatives of the judgment debtor, or the tenants of real property, owned by him and affected by the judgment, may be summoned to show cause why the judgment should not be enforced, against the estate of the judgment debtor in their hands respectively. The proceedings thereon are subject to the provisions of the chapter upon actions by or against executors, administrators, legatees, heirs and devisees.

Amended Code, § 376.

§ 1215. The summons provided in the last two sections, must be subscribed by the judgment creditor, his representatives, or attorney, describe the judgment, and require the person summoned, to show cause, within twenty days after the service of the summons; and must be served in the same manner as the original summons.

Amended Code, § 377.

§ 1216. The summons must be accompanied by an affidavit of the person subscribing it, that the judgment has not been satisfied, to his knowledge, or information and belief, and must specify the amount due thereon.

Amended Code, § 378.

§ 1217. Upon such summons, the party summoned may answer within the time specified therein, denying the judgment, or setting up any defence which may have arisen subsequently; and in addition thereto, if he be proceeded against according to section 1213, he may make the same defence which might have been originally made to the action, except the statute of limitations; if he be proceeded against according to section 1214, he may make the same defence, which he might have made to an action upon the judgment.

Amended Code, § 379.

§ 1218. The party issuing the summons, may reply to the answer, if a counter-claim be set up therein, and the issue may be tried and judgment may be given, in the same manner as in an action, and enforced by execution, or the application of property charged, to the payment of the judgment, may, if necessary, be compelled by attachment.

Amended Code, § 380.

§ 1219. The answer and reply must be verified in the same manner, and are subject to the same rules, as the answer and reply in an action.

Amended Code, § 381.

CHAPTER II.

OFFER OF THE DEFENDANT TO COMPROMISE THE WHOLE OR A PART OF THE ACTION.

§ 1220. The defendant may, at any time before the trial or judgment, serve upon the plaintiff, an offer to allow judgment to be taken against him, for the sum or property, or to the effect therein specified. If the plaintiff accept the offer, and give notice therof, within ten days, he may file the summons, complaint and offer, with an affidavit of notice of acceptance, and the clerk must thereupon enter judgment accordingly. If the notice of acceptance be not given, the offer is to be deemed withdrawn, and can not be given in evidence, and if the plaintiff fail to obtain a more favorable judgment, he cannot recover costs, but must pay the defendant's costs, from the time of the offer.

Amended Code, § 385, extended so as to embrace every action, instead of confining it to an action arising on contract.

§ 1221. In an action for the recovery of money only, the defendant may, with his answer, serve upon the plaintiff an offer in writing, that if he fail in his defence, the amount of the recovery be assessed at a specified sum; and if the plaintiff signify his acceptance thereof in writing, with or before the notice of trial, and on the trial have a verdict, the amount must be assessed accordingly.

Amended Code, § 386, extended.

§ 1222. If the plaintiff do not accept the offer, he must prove the amount to be recovered, as if the offer had not been made, and cannot be permitted to give it in evidence. And if the amount assessed in his favor do not exceed the sum mentioned in the offer, the defendant may recover his expenses, incurred in consequence of any necessary preparation or defence in respect to the question of amount. Such expense must be ascertained at the trial.

Amended Code, § 387.

CHAPTER III.

ADMISSION OR INSPECTION OF WRITINGS.

SECTION 1223. A party may be required to admit a paper to be genuine, or pay expense of proving it.
1224. A party may demand inspection and copy of a paper.

§ 1223. Either party may exhibit to the other, or to his attorney, at any time before the trial, any document or paper, material to the action, and request an admission in writing of its genuineness. If the adverse party or his attorney fail to give the admission, within four days after the request, and if the party exhibiting the document or paper, be afterwards put to expense, in order to prove its genuineness, and the same be finally proved or admitted on the trial, such expense to be ascertained at the trial, must be paid by the party refusing the admission; unless it appear to the satisfaction of the court, that there were good reasons for the refusal.

Amended Code, § 388.

§ 1224. The court before which an action is pending, or a judge thereof, or if the action be in the supreme court, a county judge, may order either party to give to the other, within a specified time, an inspection and copy, or permission to take a copy, of any book, document or paper in his possession, or under his control, containing evidence relating to the merits of the action, or the defence therein. If compliance with the order be refused, the court may exclude the book, document or paper from being given in evidence, or if wanted as evidence by the party applying, may direct the jury to presume it to be such as he alleges it to be; and the court may also punish the party refusing. This section is not to be construed to prevent a party from compelling another to produce books, papers, or documents, when he is examined as a witness.

Amended Code, § 388, modified.

CHAPTER IV.

MOTIONS AND ORDERS.

§ 1225. Every direction of a court or judge, made or entered in writing, and not included in a judgment, is denominated an order.

Amended Code, § 400.

§ 1226. An application for an order is a motion.

Amended Code, § 401.

§ 1227. All motions may be made to the court at a special term, except upon appeals. Motions may likewise be made to a judge out of court, as provided in othe parts of this code.

Original Code, § 359, modified.

§ 1228. Motions must be made within the district in which the action is triable, or in a county adjoining that in which it is triable, except that where the action is triable in the first judicial district, the motion must be made therein. Orders made out of court, without notice, may be made by any judge of the court, in any part of the state; and if the action be in the supreme court they may also be made by a county judge of the county where the action is triable, except to stay proceedings after a verdict. No order to stay proceedings for a longer time than twenty days can be granted by a judge out of court, except upon previous notice to the adverse party.

Original Code, § 361.

§ 1229. When a notice of a motion is necessary, it must be served eight days before the time appointed for the hearing; but the court or judge may, by an order to show cause, prescribe a shorter time.

Amended Code, § 402.

§ 1230. In an action in the supreme court, a county judge, in addition to the powers conferred upon him by this code, may exercise, within his county, the powers of a judge of the supreme court out of court as provided in section 222. And in all cases where an order is made by a county judge, it may be reviewed in the same manner, as if it had been made by a judge of the supreme court.

Amended Code, § 403.

§ 1231. When a notice of a motion is given, or an order to show cause provides for a motion, before a judge out of court, and at the time fixed for the motion, he is unable to hear it, the same may be transferred, by his order, to some other judge, before whom the motion might originally have been made.

Amended Code, § 404.

§ 1232. Whenever an order for the payment of a sum of money is made by a court pursuant to a provision of this code, the same may be enforced by execution, in the same manner, as if it were a judgment, except that the person cannot be arrested unless specially directed in the order, nor can real property be sold thereon, except in the cases where the same is by law a charge upon real property.

New.

§ 1233. Upon a motion, any person present in court, whose affidavit or deposition would be admissable thereupon, may be orally examined.

New.

§ 1234. When the answer of the defendant admits part of the plaintiff's claim to be just, the court, on motion, may order such defendant to satisfy that part of the claim, and may enforce the order, as it enforces a provisional remedy.

New. To prevent defendants from keeping plaintiffs out of what is admtted to be due, while litigating as to the rest.

CHAPTER V.

NOTICES, AND FILING AND SERVICE OF PAPERS.

§ 1235. Notices must be in writing; and notices and other papers may be served on the party or attorney, in the manner prescribed in the next three sections, where not otherwise provided by this code.

Amended Code, § 408.

§ 1236. The service may be personal, or by delivery to the party or attorney on whom the service is required to be made, or it may be as follows:

1. If upon an attorney, it may be made during his absence from his office, by leaving the paper with his clerk therein, or with a person having charge thereof; or when there is no person in the office, by leaving it, between the hours of six in the morning and nine in

the evening, in a conspicuous place in the office, or if it be not open, so as to admit of such service, then by leaving it at the attorney's residence, with some person of suitable age and discretion.

2. If upon a party, it may be made by leaving the pape rat his residence, between the hours of six in the morning and nine in the evening, with some person of suitable age and discretion.

Amended Code, § 409.

§ 1237. Service by mail may be made, where the person making the service, and the person on whom it is to be made, reside in different places, between which there is a regular communication by mail.

Amended Code, § 410.

§ 1238. In case of service by mail, the paper must be deposited in the post office, addressed to the person on whom it is to be served, at his place of residence, and the postage paid. And in such case, the time of service must be increased one day for every fifty miles distance between the place of the deposit and the place of the address.

Amended Code, §§ 411 and 412, modified so as not to discourage service by mail.

§ 1239. A defendant appears in an action when he answers, demurs, or gives the plaintiff written notice of his appearance. After appearance, otherwise than by answer, a defendant is entitled to notice of all subsequent proceedings, in the same manner as if he had answered. But where a defendant has not appeared, service of notice or papers, in the ordinary proceedings in an action, need not be made upon him, unless he be imprisoned for want of bail.

Amended Code, § 414. The first sentence is new.

§ 1240. Where a plaintiff, or a defendant who has appeared, resides out of the state, and has no attorney in the action, the service may be made by mail, if his residence be known, if not known, on the clerk for him. But where a party has an attorney in the action, the service of papers must be upon the attorney, instead of the party.

Amended Code, § 415 and 417.

§ 1241. The foregoing provisions of this chapter do not apply to the service of a summons or other process, or of any paper to bring a party into contempt.

Amended Code, § 418.

§ 1242. A notice or other paper is valid and effectual though the title of the action in which it is made, be omitted, or be defective either in respect to the court or parties, if it intelligibly refer to such action or proceeding, and, in furtherance of justice, upon proper terms, any other defect or error in any notice, or other paper or proceeding, may be amended by the court, and any mischance relieved within one year thereafter.

§ 1243. The various undertakings required to be given by this code and the affidavits and other written proceedings in an action, must be filed or entered in court, or with the clerk thereof, unless the court expressly provide for a different disposition thereof, except that the undertakings provided for by the chapter on the claim and delivery of personal property, must after the justification of the sureties, be delivered by the sheriff to the parties respectively, for whose benefit they are taken. The summons, and the several pleadings in an action, must be filed with the clerk within ten days after the service thereof, respectively, or the adverse party, on proof of the omission, is entitled, without notice, to an order from a judge that the same be filed within a time specified in the order, or be deemed abandoned.

CHAPTER IX.

GENERAL PROVISIONS.

§ 1244. If an original pleading or paper be lost or withheld by any person, the court may authorise a copy thereof to be filed and used instead of the original.

Amended Code, § 422.

§ 1245. Successive actions may be maintained upon the same contract, or transaction, whenever after the former action, a new cause of action arises therefrom.

New.

§ 1246. Whenever two or more actions are pending at one time, between the same parties, and in the same court, upon causes of action which might have been joined, the court may order the actions to be consolidated into one.

2 *R. S.* 383, § 36 and 38.

§ 1247. An action is deemed to be pending, from the time of its commencement, until its final determination upon appeal, or until the time for an appeal has passed, and the judgment has been satisfied.

New.

§ 1248. An action may be brought by one person against another, for the purpose of determining an adverse claim, which the latter makes against the former, for money or property, upon an alleged obligation; and also against two or more persons, for the purpose of compelling one to satisfy a debt due to the other, for which the plaintiff is bound as surety.

New.

§ 1249. No natural person is subject to the jurisdiction of a court of this state, unless he appear in the court, or be found within the state, or be a resident thereof, or have property therein; and in the last case only to the extent of such property at the time the jurisdiction attached.

New.

This section and the next two are intended to define the extent of the jurisdiction which our courts may exercise. This seems the more necessary to be done, since legal fictions are abolished. It is a curious fact in legal history, that the jurisdiction, as well as the practice of courts, has depended in a considerable degree upon fictions. In the case of Mostyn vs. Fabrigas, Cowp. 161, it became a question, whether the defendant was responsible in England for a false imprisonment in the island of Minorca, and Lord Mansfield, delivering the judgment of the court, placed his reason principally upon the venue being laid in England, that is, the plaintiff had averred that the defendant imprisoned him *at Minorca, to wit, at London aforesaid in the parish of St. Mary le Bow in the ward of Cheap.* Upon such reasons, was the doctrine established that trespasses abroad might be sued for in courts at home.

The qualification, in section 1251, with respect to actions concerning real property, is proper in itself, and conformable to the decisions of our courts. Livingston vs. Jefferson, 1 Brockenb, 203—Watts vs Kinney, 6 Hill 82.

§ 1250. No corporation is subject to the jurisdiction of a court of this state, unless it appear in the court, or have been created by, or under the laws of this state, or have an agency established therein for the transaction of some portion of its business, or have property therein, and in the last case only to the extent of such property at the time the jurisdiction attached.

New.

§ 1251. When the court has jurisdiction of the parties, it may exercise it, in respect to any cause of action, wherever arising, except for the specific recovery of real property, situated out of this state, or an injury thereto, and except also as provided in section 988.

New.

§ 1252. When a cause of action has arisen in a sister state, or in a foreign country, and by the laws thereof, an action thereon cannot there be maintained against a person by reason of the lapse of time, an action thereon cannot be maintained against him in this state, except in favor of a citizen thereof, who has had the cause of action from the time it accrued.

It is a general principle of our jurisprudence, that the law of the place, where a contract is made, determines its validity and construction, but that the remedy is to be administered according to the law of the place where the action is brought. The prescription of actions, or the time within which they may be brought, is, however, placed in the latter category, 13 Peters, 312,—6 Wend., 475. Hence, it happens, that a person who, by the lapse of time, is absolved from prosecution in his own state, is held liable the moment he passes it, even though the liability may be to his neighbor, who follows him for a remedy which he has lost at home. Now, as a general principle, it appears most consonant with right, that where, by the law of the domicil of the debtor, the debt is barred, it should be barred everywhere, except in favor of a domestic creditor.

Take, for example, the case of two persons living in the same town in Georgia. They had transactions twenty years ago, and one claimed a balance from the other, but time gradually closed over the claim, without any attempt by the creditor to enforce it in his own courts. At length, the debtor takes a journey to this state, and the creditor follows him and sues in our courts. The defendant cannot defend himself upon our rule of limitations, because a person absent from the state is excepted from its operation, and, thus, our courts are compelled to investigate this ancient claim. It is to provide for such a contingency, that this section is proposed.

1253. The clerk must keep, among the records of the court, a register of actions. He must enter therein the title of the action, with brief notes under it, from time to time, of all papers filed, and proceedings had, therein.

New. Necessary for many purposes, and especially for procuring hereafter full and accurate statistics of litigation.

§ 1254. When there are three referees, all must meet, but two of them may do any act which might be done by all; and whenever any authority is conferred on three or more persons, it may be exercised by a majority, upon the meeting of all, unless expressly otherwise provided by this code or by some other statute.

Conformable to the existing law.

§ 1255. The time within which an act is to be done, as herein provided, must be computed, by excluding the first day and including the last. If the last day be Sunday, it must be excluded.

Amended Code, § 407.

§ 1256. The publication of legal notices, required by law, or by an order of a judge or court, to be published in a newspaper once in each week, for a specified number of weeks, must be made on the first day of each week, in which such newspaper is published; and if required to be published oftener than once in each week, the second publication must be made on Thursday of each week, or if the paper be not issued and published on Thursday, then on any other day in the week on which such paper is issued. And in all eases, where a municipal corporation is required to publish legal notices, and may designate the papers in which the publication is to be made, it must make such designation annually, by ordinance, for one year, and after such designation, all such legal notices must be published in the papers so designated.

The time for publication of legal notices must be computed so as to exclude the first day of publication, and to include the day on which the act or event, of which notice is given, is to happen, or which completes the full period required for publication.

Amended Code, § 425, modified.

§ 1257. No counsel can be permitted to speak on the argument of any case, more than one hour, without the special leave of the court, granted before the argument begins.

Conformable to the rule of the supreme court of the United States, lately adopted, substituting one hour for two.

§ 1258. A person, who, without probable cause, prosecutes an action or makes a defence, or takes any legal proceeding against another, is guilty of a contempt, and is also liable to an action therefor, at the suit of the party aggrieved.

Intended to prevent or punish sham actions and defences.

§ 1259. Rights of action, given or secured by existing laws, may be prosecuted in the manner provided by this code. If a case ever arise, in which an action for the enforcement or protection of a right, or the redress or prevention of a wrong, cannot be had under this code, the practice heretofore in use may be adopted, so far as may be necessary to prevent a failure of justice.

Amended Code, § 468.

TITLE XIV.

PROVISIONS RESPECTING SUITS HERETOFORE COMMENCED.

§ 1260. The provisions of this code apply to future proceedings in actions or suits heretofore commenced and now pending, as follows, and not otherwise:

1. If there have been no pleading therein, to the pleadings and all subsequent proceedings:

2. When there is an issue of law or of fact, or any other question of fact to be tried, to the trial and all subsequent proceedings:

3. After a judgment or order, to the proceedings to enforce, vacate, modify or reverse it, including the costs of an appeal.

§ 1261. Whenever the judges of the supreme court, in any district, find, that the court, at any term or circuit, has not been or will not be able to dispose of all the cases upon the calendar, it shall be their duty to request the governor to assign other judges, and if necessary appoint extraordinary terms and circuits, for the purpose of disposing of such cases. The governor must thereupon make such assignment, and the judges assigned must hold the courts accordingly. This provision shall last, so long as any of the actions and suits now pending remain undetermined.

PART III.

OF SPECIAL PROCEEDINGS.

PRELIMINARY PROVISIONS.

§ 1262. The party prosecuting a special proceeding, may be known as the plaintiff, and the adverse party as the defendant.

§ 1263. A judgment in a special proceeding is the final determination of the rights of the parties therein. The definitions of a motion and an order in a civil action are applicable to similar acts in a special proceeding.

TITLE I.

OF STATE WRITS.

CHAPTER I.

STATE WRITS IN GENERAL.

§ 1264. The writs heretofore known as prerogative writs, so far as they are hereafter to be recognized, shall be denominated state writs. They are issued out of the supreme court at the instance of the state, sometimes on behalf of private persons, for the protection of private rights, and sometimes for purposes of state. They are issued in the name of the people, under the seal of the court, and the signature of the clerk.

This title is the same, as that contained in our third report, with slight variations.

§ 1265. When issued on behalf of a private person, such person must be named as a party in the proceedings jointly with the people.

§ 1266. These writs, four in number are defined and regulated in this title in the following order:

1. The writ of review of inferior jurisdictions:
2. The writ of mandate:
3. The writ of assessment of damages:
4. The writ of deliverance from imprisonment.

The writ of quo warranto, the writ of scire facias, and writ of prohibition, are abolished.

The act, under which the Commissioners were appointed, contained this provision; "it shall be the duty of the said Commissioners to provide for the abolition of the present forms of actions and pleadings in cases at common law; for a uniform course of proceedings in all cases, whether of legal or equitable cognisance, and for the abandonment of all Latin and other foreign tongues, so far as the same shall by them be deemed practicable, and of any form and proceeding not necessary to ascertain or preserve the rights of the parties."

It has been our inflexible determination to conform to this provision in letter and in spirit. In seeking English substitutes for the Latin names of prerogative writs, we have endeavored to find such as are really significant of the purposes of the writs. The writ of *habeas corpus* being mentioned in the constitution, we provide simply that it may also be known as the writ of deliverance, or of deliverance from imprisonment. When the novelty of these names has worn off, the old ones will probably appear as uncouth as they really are. Custom only has made them tolerable to the profession, while they have always been a jargon to the mass of the people. Our own language is rich enough to express all our ideas, and, especially in the construction of a new system of law, it should seem in better taste and wiser to make it wholly in the mother tongue of those who are to read it and be governed by it.

§ 1267, The allowance of the writ of review, the writ of mandate, and the writ of assessment, rests in the sound discretion of the court. The writ of deliverance, when regularly applied for, cannot be refused.

§ 1268. The application for a state writ must be made to the supreme court, at a special term, except as provided in the next section.

§ 1269. The writ of deliverance from imprisonment, commonly known as the writ of habeas corpus, may be allowed, not only by the supreme court at a special term, but, out of court, by a judge of the supreme court, a judge of the superior court of the city of New-York, a judge of the court of common pleas of the city of New-York, a county judge, or the city judge of the city of New-York.

§ 1270. After the allowance of the writ of deliverance, all the proceedings thereon, to the judgment, inclusive, are had in the supreme court. But the orders and judgment, respectively, may be entered, in the manner hereinafter provided, upon the certificate out of court, of any judge designated in the last section.

CHAPTER II.

THE WRIT OF REVIEW OF INFERIOR JURISDICTIONS.

§ 1271. The writ of certiorari, whether at common law or by statute, shall hereafter be known as the writ of review of inferior jurisdictions.

§ 1272. The writ of review must command the defendant to certify fully to the supreme court, at a specified time and place, and annex to the writ, a transcript of the record and proceedings, (describing or referring to them, with convenient certainty,) that the same may be reviewed by the supreme court; and requiring the party, in the mean time, to desist from further proceedings in the matter to be reviewed.

§ 1273. If a stay of proceedings be not intended, the words requiring the stay, may be omitted from the writ. These words may be inserted, or omitted, in the sound discretion of the court.

§ 1274. The effect of the writ is to remove, not the record, but the transcript thereof; therefore, the power of the inferior court or officer is not suspended, nor the proceedings stayed, unless an order to that effect be inserted in the writ.

§ 1275. The writ may be granted, wherever specially authorised by this code, and also in all cases where an inferior tribunal, board, or officer, exercising judicial functions, is alleged to have exceeded the jurisdiction of such tribunal, board, or officer; and where there is no appeal, nor, in the judgment of the court, any other plain, speedy and adequate remedy.

§ 1276. Except where otherwise expressly provided by this code or another statute, the review upon this writ cannot be extended further, than to determine whether the inferior tribunal, board, or officer, has regularly pursued the authority of such tribunal, board or officer.

§ 1277. The writ may be directed to such tribunal, board, or officer, or to any other person having the custody of the record or proceedings to be certified.

§ 1278. The motion for the writ must be made upon affidavit, and the court may require a notice of the application to be given to the adverse party, or may grant an order to shew cause why it should not be allowed, or may grant the writ without notice.

§ 1279. The allowance of the writ must be endorsed thereon, signed by the judge granting it, and the writ must be served in the same manner, as a summons in a civil action, except where otherwise expressly provided.

§ 1280. If the return to the writ be defective, the court may order a further return to be made. When a full return has been made, the court must proceed to hear the parties, or such of them as may attend for that purpose, and may thereupon give judgment, either affirming or annulling the proceedings below.

§ 1281. A copy of the judgment, signed by the clerk, entered upon, or attached to, the writ and return, constitute the judgment roll. From the judgment, an appeal may be taken to the general term, and thence to the court of appeals, in the same manner and upon the same terms, as from a judgment in a civil action.

CHAPTER III.

THE WRIT OF MANDATE.

§ 1282. The writ, heretofore known as the writ of mandamus, shall be hereafter denominated the writ of mandate. Such writ is defined and regulated as in this chapter prescribed.

§ 1283. It may be issued to any inferior tribunal, corporation, board, or person, to compel the performance of an act, which the law specially enjoins, as a duty resulting from an office, trust, or station. But though it may require an inferior tribunal to exercise its judgment, or proceed to the discharge of any of its functions, it cannot control judicial discretion.

See 2 *R. S.*, 586, § 54–60.

1284. This writ ought not to be issued, in any case where there is a plain, speedy and adequate remedy, in the ordinary course of the law. It is issued, on the information of the party beneficially interested.

§ 1285. The writ is either alternative or peremptory. The alternative writ mnst state concisely the facts showing the obligation of the defendant to perform the act, and his omission to perform it, and command him, that immediately after the receipt of the writ, or at some other specified time, he do the act required to be performed, or show cause before the supreme court, at a specified time and place, why he has not done so; and that he then and there return the writ, with his certificate of having done as he is commanded. The peremptory writ must be in a similar form, except that the words requiring the defendant to show cause why he has not done as commanded, must be omitted.

§ 1286. When the right to require the performance of the act is clear, and it is apparent, that no valid excause can be given for not performing it, a peremptory mandate may be allowed in the first instance. In all other cases, the alternative writ must be first issued.

§ 1287. The motion for the writ, the allowance, and the service thereof, and the enforcement of obedience thereto, must be in the same manner, as in case of the writ of review.

§ 1288. On the return day of the alternative writ, or such further day as the court may allow, the party, on whom the writ shall have been served, may show cause, by answer made, in the same manner as an answer to a complaint in a civil action.

§ 1289. If no answer be made, a peremptory mandate must be allowed against the defendant. If an answer be made, containing new matter, the same shall not in any respect conclude the plaintiff, who may on the trial or other proceedings avail himself of any valid objection to its sufficiency, or may countervail it by proof, either in direct denial or by way of avoidance.

§ 1290. No other pleading, or written allegation, is allowed than the writ and answer. These are the pleadings in the case, and have the same effect, and are to be construed and may be amended, in the same manner, as pleadings in a civil action, and the issues thereby joined must be tried, and the further proceedings thereon had in the same manner, as in a civil action.

§ 1291. Issues joined in the case, must be tried in the connty where the material facts set forth in the mandate are alleged to have occurred.

§ 1292. If judgment be given for the plaintiff, he shall recover the damages which he shall have sustained, to be ascertained by the court or a jury, or by referees, as in a civil action, together with costs and charges; and a peremptory mandate must also be awarded without delay.

§ 1293. A recovery of damages by virtue of this chapter, against a party, who shall have made a return to a writ of mandate, is a bar to any other action against the same party, for the making of such return.

§ 1294. Whenever a peremptory mandate is directed to a public officer, body, or board, commanding the performance of any public duty, specially enjoined by law, if it appear to the court that such officer, or any member of such body, or board, has, without just excuse, refused or neglected to perform the duty so enjoined, the court may impose a fine, not exceeding two hundred and fifty dollars, upon every such officer or member of such body or board. Such fine, when collected, must be paid into the treasury; and the payment thereof is a bar to an action, for any penalty incurred by such officer or member of such body or board, by reason of his refusal or neglect to perform the duty so enjoined.

CHAPTER IV.

THE WRIT OF ASSESSMENT OF DAMAGES.

§ 1295. The writ heretofore known as the writ of ad quod damnum, shall be hereafter denominated the writ of assessment of damages.

See 2 *R. S.*, 566, § 66–76.

§ 1296. Whenever the governor of this state is authorized by law to take possession of real property, within this state, for the use of the people of the state, and he cannot agree with the owner for the purchase thereof, he must cause application to be made for a writ of assessment, which shall thereupon be issued to the sheriff of the county, where such real property is situated, unless the court direct such damages to be assessed by a jury of another county, commanding him to summon a jury to inquire whether the owners of the property, describing it, will sustain any, and what damage, by the taking of the property for the use of the state.

§ 1297. Upou such writ being delivered to the sheriff, he must give at least three weeks notice of the time and place of executing the same, by publishing a notice thereof in a newspaper printed in his county.

§ 1298. The sheriff must summon twelve qualified jurors in his county, to attend at such time and place, and must then and there administer to each of the jurors an oath, that he will diligently inquire, concerning the matter specified in the writ, and will give a true verdict, according to the best of his judgment.

§ 1299. After the jury shall have been duly sworn, they must proceed to view the property specified in the writ, and having heard the evidence offered, and duly considered the value of the property, they must assess the damages which the owner, or if there be several, which the respective owners, will sustain by being deprived thereof. They must make an inquisition signed by themselves, and by the sheriff, in which they must set forth the names of the several owners of the property, and the rights of each owner respectively, so far as the same can be ascertained by them, together with the amount to be paid therefor by the people of this state, and to whom particularly; which inquisition the sheriff must forthwith return, together with the writ, to the supreme court.

§ 1300. The court must examine the inquisition, and if the same be partial or defective, may set the same aside, either wholly or in part, and may direct a new inquisition to be taken, to supply such defect.

§ 1301. Whenever the writ appears to have been duly executed, an order must be entered, declaring that the people of this state, on paying to the owner or into the supreme court, the amount assessed in the inquisition for damages, and also the costs and charges of the proceedings, shall be entitled to an absolute estate in such real property, as fully and effectually, as if the same had been conveyed to the people by the owner thereof; and immediately after the payment of such amount, the absolute title to such real property shall be vested in the people of this state.

§ 1302. The amount which may be necessary to pay the damages assessed, and the costs and expenses incurred under the provisions of this chapter, must be paid out of the treasury.

§ 1303. Upon the damages so assessed being paid into the supreme court, the court must make an order for the investment thereof and of the interest thereon, in permanent securities, for the benefit of the owners of the property taken, and must cause such securities to be transferred to them, or the amount of the money paid over to them, their guardians or legal representatives, whenever their rights are established.

§ 1304. Such owners may, at any time, apply to the supreme court, for the payment to them of such money, or the transfer of such securities: and such proceedings must be had thereon, as are necessary to ascertain the respective rights of the applicants, and to give notice to all persons who may be interested in the property taken, or in the money paid into court.

1305. Whenever any real property shall be taken for the use of the United States, by the consent of the legislature of this state, and it becomes necessary to issue a writ of assessment, the like proceedings must be had, as are provided in this chapter.

CHAPTER V.

THE WRIT OF DELIVERANCE FROM IMPRISONMENT.

§ 1306. The writ of habeas corpus ad subjiciendum, known in the constitution and statutes of this state as the writ of habeas corpus, is herein designated, and may hereafter be known, as the writ of deliverance from imprisonment. Every other writ of habeas corpus is abolished.

See 2 *R. S.* 563–576, § 21–86.

§ 1307. Every person, imprisoned or restrained of his liberty, within this state, for any criminal or supposed criminal matter, or under any pretence whatsoever, except in the cases specified in the next section, may prosecute a writ of deliverance, according to the provisions of this chapter, to inquire into the cause of such imprisonment or restraint; and if illegal, to be delivered therefrom.

§ 1308. The following persons are not entitled to prosecute the writ:

1. Persons committed or detained by virtue of process issued by a court of the United States, or a judge thereof, in cases where such courts or judges have exclusive jurisdiction, under the laws of the United States, or have acquired exclusive jurisdiction by the commencement of suits in such courts:

2. Persons committed or detained by virtue of the judgment of a competent tribunal, of civil or criminal jurisdiction, or by virtue of an execution issued upon such judgment, but no order of commitment for contempt, is to be deemed a judgment nor an warrant or other process, issued upon such an order, an execution, within the meaning of this section.

§ 1309. Application for the writ must be made in writing, signed, either by the party for whose relief it is intended, or by some person in his behalf, as follows:

1. To the supreme court at a special term:

2. To any one of the judges of the supreme court, or any county judge, being or residing in the county where the party is detained: or, if there be no such officer within the county, or if he be absent, or for any cause incapable of acting, or have refused to grant the writ, then to such officer residing in an adjoining county;

3. In the city and county of New-York, to a judge of the superior court of the city of New-York, or a judge of the court of common pleas of the city of New-York, or the city judge of that city.

§ 1310. Whenever application for the writ is made to an officer, not residing within the county where the party is detained, he must require proof, by the oath of the applicant, or by other sufficient evidence before granting the writ, that there is no officer in the county authorised to grant the writ, or if there be one that he is absent, or has refused to grant it, or for some cause to be specially set forth, is incapable of acting.

§ 1311. The application must state, in substance,

1. That the party, in whose behalf the writ is applied for, is imprisoned, or restrained of his liberty, the place where, and officer or person by whom, he is imprisoned or restrained, naming both parties, if their names be known, or describing them, if not known:

2. That such person is not imprisoned or restrained, by virtue of any order, judgment, or process, specified in section 1308.

3. The cause or pretence of such imprisonment or restraint, according to the best of the knowledge or belief of the applicant:

4. If the imprisonment or restraint be in virtue of an order, warrant, or process, a copy thereof must be annexed, or it must be alleged, that by reason of the removal or concealment of the party before the application, a demand of such copy could not be made, or such demand was made, and the legal fees therefor tendered to the person having the party in his custody, and that a copy was refused:

5. If the imprisonment be alleged to be illegal, the application must also state in what the alleged illegality consists:

6. That the legality of the imprisonment has not been already adjudged, upon a prior writ of deliverance, to the knowledge or belief of the applicant:

7. It must be verified by the oath of the applicant, to the effect, that he believes it to be true.

§ 1312. Any court or judge, empowered to grant the writ, to whom such application is presented, must grant the writ, without delay, unless it appear from the application itself, or from the documents annexed, that the person applying therefor, is, by the provisions of this chapter, prohibited from prosecuting the writ.

§ 1313. The writ of deliverance must command the defendant to produce the person imprisoned or restrained, by whatsoever name he may be called or charged, and certify and return therewith the time and cause of his imprisonment or restraint, before the supreme court, at a special term to be held at a specified time and place, or before the judge allowing the writ, or another judge as provided in the next section, at a specified time and place, or immediately after the receipt of the writ, to do and receive what shall then and there be considered concerning the person so imprisoned or restrained;

Or when, for the reason hereinafter mentioned, the

body need not be produced, the writ, instead of requiring the production of the person, may require the defendant to certify and return, the time and cause of the imprisonment or restraint.

1314. If application for the writ be made to the supreme court, or a judge thereof, in a county other than that where the party is imprisoned, the writ may be made returnable before any officer authorised to grant the writ, in the county of the imprisonment.

1315. The writ must not be disobeyed for any defect of form.

It is sufficient,

1. If the person, having the custody of the party imprisoned or restrained, be designated either by his name of office, if he have any, or by his own name, or if both such names be unknown or uncertain, he may be described by an assumed appellation; and any one who may be served with the writ, is to be deemed the person to whom it was directed, although it may be directed to him by a wrong name or description, or to another person;

2. If the person, who is directed to be produced, be designated by name, or if his name be uncertain or unknown, he may be described in any other way, so as to designate the person intended.

§ 1316. Whenever the supreme court, or a judge thereof, has evidence from a judicial proceeding before such court or judge, that any person within the county where the court or judge may be, is illegally imprisoned or restrained of his liberty, it is the duty of such court or judge, to issue a writ of deliverance for his relief, although no application be made for such writ.

§ 1317. The person, on whom the writ is served, must state in his return plainly and unequivocally,

1. Whether he have, or have not, the party in his custody, or power, or under his restraint:

2. If he have the party in his custody or power, or under his restraint, the authority and true cause of such imprisonment or restraint, setting forth the same at large:

3. If the party be detained, by virtue of a writ, warrant, or other written authority, a copy thereof must be annexed to the return, and the original must be produced and exhibited, on the return of the writ, to the court or judge to whom the same is returnable:

4. If the person on whom such writ shall have been served, shall have had the party in his custody or power, or under his restraint, at any time prior or subsequent to the date of the writ, but has transferred such custody or restraint to another, the return must state particularly to whom, at what time, for what cause, and by what authority such transfer took place.

The return must be signed by the person making the same, and, except where he is a sworn public officer, and makes his return in his official capacity, it must be verified by his oath.

§ 1318. If the writ of deliverance require it, the person or officer on whom the writ shall have been served, must also produce the person in his custody or power, according to the command of the writ, except in the case of the sickness of such party, as provided in section 1332.

§ 1319. If the person, on whom the writ shall have been duly served, refuse or neglect to obey the same, by producing the party named therein, and making a full and explicit return thereto, within the time required, and no sufficient excuse be shown therefor, it is the duty of the court or judge, before whom the writ was returnable, upon proof of the service thereof, forthwith to issue a warrant of arrest against such person, directed to the sheriff of any county within this state, and commanding him forthwith to arrest such person and to bring him before the court or judge; and on his being so brought, he must be committed to close custody, in the jail of the county, without being allowed the liberties thereof, until he makes return to the writ, and complies with any order that may be made in relation to the person, for whose relief the writ was issued.

§ 1320. If a sheriff shall have neglected to return the writ, the warrant may be directed to the coroner, or any other person designated therein, who shall have full power to execute the same; and the sheriff, upon being brought up, may be committed to the jail of any county other than his own.

§ 1321. The court or judge, by whom the warrant is issued, may also, at the same time, or afterwards, issue a precept to the sheriff, or other person to whom the warrant was directed, commanding him, to bring forthwith the party for whose benefit the writ of deliverance was granted; and he shall thereafter remain in the custody of such sheriff or person, until discharged or remanded.

§ 1322. The court or judge, before whom the party is brought, on the writ of deliverance, must immediately, after the return thereof, examine into the facts contained in the return, and into the cause of the imprisonment or restraint of the party, whether the same shall have been upon commitment for any criminal, or supposed criminal, matter or not.

§ 1323. If no legal cause be shown for the imprisonment or restraint, or for the continuance thereof, the party must be discharged from the custody or restraint under which he is held.

§ 1324. The party, must be forthwith remanded, if it appear that he is detained in custody:

1. By virtue of process issued by a court or judge of the United States, in a case where such court or judge has exclusive jurisdiction:

2. By virtue of the judgment, of a competent court of civil or criminal jurisdiction, or of an execution issued upon such judgment; or

3. By virtue of a warrant of commitment for a contempt, specially and plainly charged therein, and issued by a court, officer or body, having authority to commit for the contempt so charged, and

4. That the time, during which such party may be legally detained, has not expired.

§ 1325. If it appear on the return, that the party is in custody by virtue of an order or civil process, from a court legally constituted, or issued by an officer in the course of judicial proceedings before him, authorised by law, the party can be discharged in one of the following cases only:

1. Where the jurisdiction of such court or officer has been exceeded, either as to matter, place, sum, or person:

2. Where, although the original imprisonment was

lawful, yet by some subsequent act, omission, or event, the party has become entitled to his discharge:

3. Where the order or process is defective in some matter of substance required by law, rendering it void:

4. Where the order or process, though in proper form, has been issued in a case not allowed by law:

5. Where the person, having the custody of the prisoner under such order or process, is not the person empowered by law to detain him; or

6. Where the order or process is not authorised by a judgment, or order of a court, or by any provision of law.

§ 1326. But no court or judge, on the return of a writ of deliverance, has power to inquire into the legality or justice of any order, judgment, or process, specified in section 1308, nor into the justice or propriety of any commitment for a contempt, made by a court, officer, or body, according to law, and charged in such commitment, as provided in this code.

§ 1327. If it appear, that the party has been legally committed for a criminal offence, or if he appear by the testimony offered with the return, or upon the hearing thereof, to be guilty of such an offence, although the commitment be irregular, he may be forthwith remanded to the custody, or placed under the restraint, from which he was taken, if the person under whose custody or restraint he was, be legally entitled thereto; if not so entitled, he must be committed, to the custody of the officer or person so entitled.

§ 1328. Until judgment be given upon the return, the party may be either committed to the custody of the sheriff of the county or placed in such care or under such custody, as his age and other circumstances may require.

§ 1329. When it appears from the return to the writ, that the party is in custody on an order or process, under which another person has an interest in continuing his imprisonment, or restraint, no order can be made for his discharge, until the party so interested, or his attorney, has had the same notice of the return as is required to be given of motions in the supreme court.

§ 1330. When it appears from the return, that the party is detained upon a criminal accusation, the court or judge can make no order for his discharge until sufficient notice of the return is given to the district attorney of the county, where the party is detained.

§ 1331. The party produced, on the return of a writ of deliverance, may deny any of the material facts set forth in the return, or may allege any fact, to show, either that his imprisonment or restraint is unlawful, or that he is entitled to his discharge; which allegation or denial must be on oath; and, thereupon, the court or judge must proceed in a summary way, to hear such evidence as may be produced, in support of the imprisonment or detention, or against the same, and to dispose of the party, as the justice of the case may require.

1332. Whenever, from the sickness or infirmity of the party, he cannot, without danger, be produced, the person in whose custody he is, may state that fact in his return to the writ, verifying the same by his oath; and if satisfied of the truth of the allegation, and the return be otherwise sufficient, the court or judge must proceed to decide on the return, and to dispose of the matter in the same manner, as if the party had been produced.

§ 1333. Whenever an application is made for a writ of deliverance, according to the provisions of this chapter, if it appear, upon the face of the application, that the cause, or offence, for which the person is imprisoned or restrained, is not bailable, the production of the party, may be dispensed with though such production be asked, and the writ be issued accordingly.

§ 1334. If it appear, that the party detained is illegally imprisoned or restrained of his liberty, judgment must be given that he be forthwith discharged: otherwise the application must be dismissed.

§ 1335. Notwithstanding the issuing of the writ of deliverance without requiring the production of the person, the court or judge before whom the same was returnable, may, before final decision, issue a new writ, requiring the production of the person.

§ 1336. Obedience to a judgment, for the discharge of a person restrained of his liberty, pursuant to the provisions of this chapter may be enforced by the court or judge, by proceedings for a contempt, in the same manner, and with the same effect, as for a neglect to make return to a writ of deliverance; and the person found guilty of such disobedience, shall forfeit to the party aggrieved, one thousand dollars, in addition to any special damages which he may have sustained.

§ 1337. No sheriff or other officer is liable to a civil action, for obeying such judgment of discharge.

§ 1338. No person, who has been discharged, upon a writ of deliverance, pursuant to the provisions of this chapter, can be again imprisoned, restrained, or kept in custody, for the same cause; but it is not to be deemed the same cause,

1. If he have been discharged from a commitment on a criminal charge, and be afterwards committed for the same offence, by the legal order or process of the court, wherein he is bound, by recognizance or undertaking, to appear, or in which he is indicted or convicted for the same offence: or,

2. If, after a discharge for a defect of evidence, or for a material defect in the commitment, in a criminal case, the party be again arrested, on sufficient evidence, and committed by legal process, for the same offence: or,

3. If, in a civil action, the party have been discharged for any illegality in the judgment or process, herein before specified, and be afterwards imprisoned by legal authority, for the same cause of action: or,

4. If, in a civil action, he have been discharged from commitment on an order of arrest, and be afterwards committed on execution, in the same action, or on an order of arrest in another action, after such first action has been dismissed.

§ 1339. If any person, either solely or as a member of a court, in the execution of a judgment, order, or process, knowingly recommit, imprison, or restrain of his liberty, for the same cause, except as provided in the last section, any person so discharged, or knowingly direct or assist therein, he shall forfeit to the party aggrieved one thousand dollars, and be also guilty of a misdemeanor.

§ 1340. Any person, having in his custody or power, or under his restraint, a party, who, by the provisions of this chapter, would be entitled to a writ of deliverance or for whose relief a writ of deliverance has been issued, who, with intent to elude the service of the writ, or to avoid the effect thereof, transfers the party to the custody, or places him under the power or control, of another, or conceals or changes the place of his confinement, is guilty of a misdemeanor.

§ 1341. Every person who knowingly assists, in the violation of the last section, is guilty of a misdemeanor.

§ 1342. Every person, convicted of an offence under either of the last four sections, may be punished by fine and imprisonment, or both, in the discretion of the court, in which he is convicted; but such fine cannot exceed one thousand dollars, nor such imprisonment six months.

§ 1343. Whenever it appears by satisfactory evidence that any person is held in illegal confinement, and that there is reason to believe, that he will be carried out of the state, or suffer irreparable injury before he can be relieved, by the issuing of a writ of deliverance, any court or judge, authorised to issue such writ, may issue a warrant, directed to any sheriff, constable or other person, reciting the facts, and commanding such officer or person to take the party and forthwith to bring him before the court or judge.

§ 1344. When the evidence, mentioned in the last section, is also sufficient to justify an arrest of the person having the party in his custody, as for a criminal offence committed in the taking or detaining of the party, the warrant must also contain an order for the arrest of such person for the offence.

§ 1345. Any officer or person, to whom the warrant is directed, must execute the same, by bringing the prisoner therein named, and the person who detains him, if so commanded by the warrant, before the court or judge issuing it; and thereupon the person, detaining the party, must make a return in the same manner, and the same proceedings must be had thereon as if a writ of deliverance had been issued in the first instance.

§ 1346. If the person, having the party in his custody, be brought before the court or judge, as for a criminal offence, he must be examined, committed, bailed or discharged, by the court or judge in the same manner as in other criminal cases of the like nature.

§ 1347. Any officer or other person refusing to deliver a copy of an order, warrant, process, or other authority, by which he detains a person, to any one who demands it, and tenders the fees therefor, shall forfeit two hundred dollars to the person so detained.

§ 1348. Whenever a writ of deliverance is required, in any action or matter, civil or criminal, to which the people of this state are a party, the application therefor may be made by the attorney general, or by the district attorney having charge thereof, and whenever so issued, the court or judge allowing it, must state in the endorsement of the allowance, that it was issued on such application.

§ 1349. A writ of deliverence must be served by an elector of this state, and the service thereof is not deemed complete, unless the person, serving it, tenders to the person, in whose custody the prisoner may be, if such person be a sheriff, coroner, constable or marshal, the fees allowed by law for bringing up the party, nor unless he also give an undertaking to such officer, to the effect that the charges of carrying back the party, if remanded, shall be paid, and that he shall not escape by the way, either in going to or returning from the place to which he is to be taken. But this section does not apply to a case, where the writ is issued on the application of the attorney general, or by the district attorney.

§ 1350. The writ of deliverance may be served, by delivering the same to the person to whom it is directed, or if he cannot be found, by leaving it at the jail, or other place, in which the party is confined, with any under officer or other person of proper age, having charge for the time, of such party.

§ 1351. If the person, on whom the writ ought to be served, conceal himself, or refuse admittance to the person attempting to serve it, it may be served by affixing it, or a copy thereof, in some conspicuous place on the outside, either of his dwelling house, or of the place where the party is confined.

§ 1352. It is the duty of every sheriff, coroner, constable or marshal, upon whom a writ of deliverance has been served, whether such writ be directed to him or not, upon payment or tender of the fees allowed by law, and the delivery or tender of the undertaking herein prescribed, to obey and return the writ, according to the exigency thereof; and it is the duty of every other person, upon whom the writ is served, having the custody of the person, for whose benefit it is issued, to obey and return it according to the command thereof, without requiring any undertaking, or the payment of any fees, unless the payment of such fees has been required by the judge issuing the writ.

§ 1353. Every judge, allowing a writ of deliverance directed to a person other than a sheriff, coroner, constable or marshal, may, in his discretion, require in order to render the service effectual, that the charges of bringing up party, be paid by the applicant; and in such case he must, in the allowance of the writ, specify the amount of such charges, which cannot exceed the fees allowed by law to sheriffs for similar services.

§ 1354. If the writ be returnable at a certain time, such return must be made, and the party produced, at the time and place specified therein; if it be returnable forthwith, and the place be within twenty miles of the place of service, the return must be made and the party produced within twenty-four hours, and the same time is allowed for every additional twenty miles.

§ 1355. No question once finally adjudged upon a writ of deliverance, can be re-examined upon a subsequent writ of deliverance.

CHAPTER VI.

APPEALS.

§ 1356. An appeal may be taken to the general term of the supreme court from an order refusing a state writ. For that purpose, if the order have been made by a judge out of court, it must be first entered with the clerk.

§ 1357. An appeal may be taken to the general term of the supreme court from the judgment after the allowance of a state writ.

§ 1358. The appeal, mentioned in the last two sections, must be taken within sixty days after written notice of the judgment or order is given to the party appealing. The appeal is made by the service of a notice in writing on the adverse party, and on the clerk with whom the judgment or order appealed from is entered, stating the appeal from the same or some specified part thereof.

§ 1359. Upon the appeal being perfected, the clerk, with whom the notice of appeal is filed, must, at the expense of the appellant, forthwith transmit to the appellate court, a certified copy of the notice of appeal, and of the judgment or order appealed from, with all papers relating thereto.

§ 1360. Upon an appeal from a judgment, the appellate court may review any intermediate order, involving the merits, and necessarily affecting the judgment.

§ 1361. Upon an appeal from a judgment or order, the appellate court may reverse, affirm, or modify the judgment or order appealed from, in the respect mentioned in the notice of appeal, and may, when it is necessary or proper, order a new trial.

§ 1362. The appellant must furnish the appellate court with copies of the notice of appeal, and of the judgment or order appealed from, and of all other papers transmitted with it, to the appellate court. If he fail to do so, the appeal may be dismissed.

§ 1363. To render an appeal effectual for any purpose, a written undertaking must be executed, on the part of the appellant, by at least two sureties, to the effect that the appellant will pay all costs and damages that may be awarded against him on the appeal, not exceeding two hundred and fifty dollars, or that sum must be deposited with the clerk, with whom the judgment or order appealed from was entered, to abide the event of the appeal. The undertaking must be filed with the clerk.

TITLE II.

OF SUMMARY PROCEEDINGS.

CHAPTER I.

CONFESSION OF JUDGMENT, WITHOUT ACTION.

§ 1364. A judgment by confession may be entered, without action, either for money due, or to become due, or to secure any person against contingent liability on behalf of the defendant, or both, in the manner prescribed by this chapter.

Amended Code, § 382.

§ 1365. A statement in writing must be made, signed by the defendant and verified by his oath, to the following effect:

1. It must authorise the entry of judgment for a specified sum:

2. If it be for money due or to become due, it must state concisely the facts out of which it arose, and must show that the sum confessed therefor is justly due, or to become due:

3. If it be for the purpose of securing the plaintiff against a contingent liability, it must state concisely the facts constituting the liability, and must show, that the sum confessed therefor does not exceed the same.

Amended Code, § 383.

§ 1366. The statement may be filed with a county clerk, or with the clerk of the superior court of the city of New-York, or the clerk of the court of common pleas of the city of New-York, who must endorse upon it, and enter in the judgment book, a judgment of the supreme or superior court or court of common pleas, for the amount confessed, with five dollars costs. The statement and affidavit with the judgment endorsed, thereupon become the judgment roll.

Amended Code, § 384.

§ 1367. In a justice's court where the court has authority to enter the judgment, the statement may be filed with the justice, who must thereupon enter in his docket, a judgment of his court, for the amount confessed, with one dollar costs. If a transcript of such judgment be filed with the county clerk, a copy of the statement must be filed with it.

New.

§ 1368. Upon a bond and warrant of attorney executed and delivered before the first day of July, 1848, judgment may be entered in the manner provided by sections 1364, 1365, and 1366, upon the plaintiff's filing such bond and warrant of attorney, and a statement signed and verified by himself, in the form prescribed be section 1365, the amount of the judgment to be limited to the sum mentioned in the plaintiff's statement, with five dollars costs.

Amended Code, § 424.

CHAPTER I.

SUBMITTING A CONTROVERSY, WITHOUT ACTION.

§ 1369. Parties to a question in difference, which might be the subject of a civil action, may, without action, agree upon a case containing the facts upon which the controversy depends, and present a submission of the same, to any court which would have jurisdiction, if an action had been brought. But it must appear by affidavit, that the controversy is real, and the proceeding in good faith, to determine the rights of the parties. The court must thereupon hear and determine the case, at a general term, and render judgment thereon, as if an action were depending.

Amended Code, § 372.

§ 1370. Judgment must be entered in the judgment book, as in other cases, but without costs, for any proceeding prior to notice of trial. The case, the submission, and a copy of the judgment constitute the judgment roll.

Amended Code, § 373.

§ 1371. The judgment may be enforced in the same manner, as if it had been rendered in an action, and is in the same manner subject to appeal.

Amended Code, § 374.

CHAPTER III.

SUMMARY PROCEEDINGS FOR COLLECTING DEBTS IN CERTAIN CASES.

§ 1372. The summary proceeding provided in this chapter may be taken for a sum of money actually due, upon a contract hereafter made, in the following cases:

1. Upon a bond conditioned for the payment of money only, against the obligor, and in favor of the obligee:

2. Upon a negotiable promissory note, against the maker, endorser, or guarantor, and in favor of the holder, who has received the same in good faith before maturity, for a valuable consideration, and without notice of any defence:

3. Upon a negotiable draft or bill of exchange, against the drawer, endorser, acceptor, or guarantor, and in favor of the holder, who has received the same in good faith, before maturity, for a valuable consideration, and without notice of any defence:

4. Upon a judgment of a sister state, against the judgment debtor, and in favor of the judgment creditor:

The provisions of this chapter have been framed upon the idea, that there is a certain class of obligations, admitting of a more summary remedy than the ordinary cases. They are those whose demands have either been liquidated by the parties, or settled by the decision of a judicial tribunal; where the defences possible to be made are few; where the securities are chiefly commercial, and credit requires that the remedy should be speedy. If the rights of the parties be sufficiently protected, and we think they are so by these provisions, it should seem, that a reasonable objection could hardly be made to them.

There are judges and lawyers, we know, greatly prejudiced against summary proceedings of all kinds. They like the regular course, as it is called; but to our view, those cases to which summary proceedings are applied in this code, are as safely disposed of in this way, and with far greater dispatch, than it is possible to have in the ordinary mode of proceeding, though that were the most expeditious ever yet known.

In every country, we believe, there is a well recognised distinction between ordinary and summary remedies, and to some minds the summary appears the most natural and rational. Among others, Mr. Bentham, a writer to whom the world is indebted for some of the profoundest disquisitions on the philosophy of law, which have ever seen the light, looks upon summary proceedings with much favor. His observations are so striking and original, that we insert a portion of them in this note, as better than any thing of our own.

"What are natural *systems*, and what are technical?"

"It is among the characteristics of technical procedure, all over the world, to abound in rules and formalities. In process of time,—as occasion presented itself, and irresistible necessity urged inquiry,—spite of all prejudices, a discovery was made, that, with little or no exception, these rules and formalities, instead of being necessary, were repugnant to the ends of justice: that an option was to be made between the sacrifice of these rules and formalities, and the sacrifice of certain portions of substantive law, necessary to the existence of the state. Accordingly, certain portions of the field of judicature were marked out, and a course prescribed for the appointment of judges, with authority to proceed and inquire, to hear and determine, as they would do in the bosom of their respective families, paying no sort of regard to any of these rules and formalities. For distinctions sake, the courts thus constituted may be termed *courts of natural procedure* or judicature: of natural procedure *restored*, or (if, in any odd nooks of the field of judicature, discovery should in any instance be made of any little spot, which happened to have escaped the fangs of the technical system,) natural procedure *preserved*.

The character of the natural system of procedure, (it may already be perceived) is little more than negative. Health is the absence of disease. Liberty, in its original sense, is the absence of coertion. Natural procedure is the absence of those rules and formalities of which technical procedure is composed. But for verse, prose would not have had a name. But for technical, natural procedure would not have had› would not have needed one.

In concurrent nomenclature, the distinction nearest to a coincidence with that between technical procedure and natural, as here explained, is that between *regular* and *summary*; but the coincidence is far short of being complete. Thus far, it is true, they agree,—that, in comparison of all technical procedure, all natural is always summary. But technical procedure has its branches which are called *summary*, as well as its branches which are called *regular*: for designating that which is not technical, the word *summary* has therefore been unfitted. Moreover, summary means *short*: and wherever one course is shorter than another, it may, in comparison of that other, be termed *summary*. But, in a series of infinite length, the number of degrees is infinite, and in all that number there is no one that can have any exclusive pretension to the epithet of summary.

The final cause of this article of jurisprudential nomenclature, is not difficult to divine. The use of *regularity* is recognised by every body: the term *regular* is eulogistic. Get people to believe that *summary* procedure is something opposite to regular procedure, you may prevail with them and accustom them to regard the more expeditious procedure with a jealous eye. In an underhand way, you may thus insinuate and get them to believe (what you durst not assert), that there is a sort of incompatibility between the superior despatch observable in the summary mode, and the superior regularity observable in the regular (that is in the technical, mode. The utility of dispatch,—its title to be regarded as one of the ends of justice,—is too plain to be denied: in the technical mode, as compared with the natural, the want of dispatch is also too plain to be denied. To reconcile men, as well as may be, to the repugnancy of the technical system in relation to this end of justice, you thus take the best chance that in so few words can be taken, for getting them to fancy, on the part of the natural course, a repugnancy to the direct and ultimate ends of justice: a conception, the exact reverse of which is the true one.

In every country (so I imagine it would be found,) men of law, unable to find the shadow of an argument, have trusted to the power of this prejudice, preserving a prudent or rather necessary silence. Blackstone, in the fertile soil of England, has been fortunate enough to find another and still stronger prejudice, applicable to the same purpose. Summary procedure is a mode of procedure to be regarded with jealousy, and with such a degree of jealousy as shall prevent as much as possible the extension of it. With jealousy? Why? Because in summary procedure there is no jury. No jury?—and what then? Is the use of trial by jury to be regarded as an end, or only as a means? Taken altogether, are the ends of justice more completely fulfilled by regular procedure with its jury, than by summary procedure without a jury ?—another inquiry in which no lawyer ever ventured to engage, and from which Blackstone knew better than not to start. No : where prejudice reigns, everything is to be lost by inquiry, nothing to be gained : by prejudice the same business is done (when it is done) upon much easier terms.

But, in the very word *summary*, may be seen an indication which, if it does not of itself afford, at least points out the path to, a complete demonstration of the incongruity of that mode to which it stands opposed. What is a summary mode ? It is a mode, in and by which an efficient decision is obtained, with a less quantity of delay, expense and vexation, than that which is attached to the other mode, termed the regular. To the use, then, of the regular mode, a quantity of collateral inconvenience attaches, which does not attach upon h e summary mode. From this single statement, admiting it to be true, follows a necessary consequence : viz : that unless under the summary there be some deficiency in respect of the security against misdecision, and that deficiency such that the mischief of it is of a magnitude to outweigh the advantage obtained by the defalcation from the mass of collateral inconvenience in the shape of delay, expense, and vexation,—the existence of the regular mode, be it what it will, is an enormous nuisance. Is the summary mode then attended with any such disadvantage ? If so, in what particular respect ? What are the arrangements which, being necessary to the giving the completest security that can be given against misdecision, are to be found in the regular, and not to be found in the summary mode ? The question is a conclusive one : no answer has ever been nor ever will be, given to it. Rationale of Judicial evidence, vol. 4, p. 8.

§ 1373. If in any of the cases mentioned in the last section, the obligee, holder, judgment creditor, or prevailing party be dead, the proceeding may be taken by his personal representatives.

§ 1374. A complaint must be made and verified, as in an action, showing that the case is one of those mentioned in section 1372. The original instrument, or a copy of the record, if the proceeding be upon a judgment, must be annexed to the complaint, or if already filed in a court of this state, a copy thereof may be annexed, instead of the original.

§ 1375. If the complaint be against the endorser of a promissory note, or the drawer or endorser of a draft or bill of exchange, there must also be annexed to the complaint an original notarial certificate, showing the due presentment of the note, draft, or bill of exchange to the maker or acceptor thereof, and due notice of non-payment to the defendant, or a written waiver by the defendant of the presentment and notice.

§ 1376. A copy of the complaint and annexed papers must be served by the sheriff, on the defendant, or on any of several defendants jointly indebted, by delivering as in the service of a summons in a civil action, with a notice in writing from the plaintiff or his attorney, that the complaint will be presented, for judgment thereon, to a judge of the court, or, if the complaint be entitled in the supreme court, to a county judge, at a specified time and place; the time to be not less than forty-eight hours after the service, and the place to be within the county, where the service is made, and where the defendant has his place of residence or business.

§ 1377. At the place and time specified, on presenting to the judge the complaint and notice, with a certificate of the service thereof, mentioning the time and place of the service, the judge must endorse on the complaint, an order that judgment be entered for the amount appearing to be due, specifying it; unless the defendant then present a sufficient answer to the complaint, made as in an ordinary action, and verified by himself.

§ 1378. At any time within three days after the making of such order, the complaint and annexed papers may be filed with the clerk, who must endorse upon it and enter in the judgment book a judgment of the court, for the amount ordered, with five dollars costs. The complaint, affidavit, and papers annexed with the judgment endorsed upon the complaint, thereupon become the judgment roll.

§ 1379. If a sufficient answer be presented, the judge must endorse on the complaint an order that, within five days, the same be filed with the answer, and any reply that the plaintiff may desire to make to any counter-claim in the answer, and that the issue thus joined be forthwith placed upon the calendar for trial, if a circuit or term of the court be then in session, or if not, then at the next session thereof. Upon the filing of the pleadings, the proceeding becomes an action pending in the court, to be tried, without further notice, and all subsequent proceedings therein must be the same as in other actions.

§ 1380. If a part only of the claim be denied by the answer, the judge may make an order that the reridue be forthwith paid; and that the issue as to the residue be tried, as prescribed in the last section.

§ 1381. Notwithstanding such answer, the plaintiff may have an attachment against the property of the defendant, to be granted by the judge, upon an undertaking executed on the part of the plaintiff, by at least two sufficient sureties, who must justify as bail are required to justify, and be approved by the judge, to the effect, that the plaintiff will pay to the defendant such damages as he may sustain by reason of the attachment, if it finally appear upon a defence by the defendant, that he was not liable to the plaintiff, in any amount, or if it appear that he was not liable to the amount of the attachment, then such damages as he may sustain by reason of the excess of the judgment.

§ 1382. The defendant, however, may prevent the issuing of such attachment, by delivering to the plaintiff or to the judge, an undertaking, executed and approved as provided in the last section, to the effect, that the sureties will pay to the plaintiff the amount of any judgment, that may be rendered in the action, upon the cause of action mentioned in the complaint.

§ 1383. Such attachment must be issued and executed in the same manner as attachments issued pursuant to the chapter on attachment, and all the provisions of that chapter, apply to the attachment issued, under section 1381.

CHAPTER II.

SUMMARY PROCEEDINGS FOR FORECLOSING MORTGAGES OF REAL PROPERTY.

§ 1384. A mortgage of real property, to secure the payment of money only, and duly recorded in the county where the property is situated, may, at any time after default in the payment of principal or interest, be enforced by foreclosure and sale, as provided in this chapter. In all other cases the foreclosure of mortgages of real property, must be by action; and nothing in this section takes away the right of a party to foreclose by action in every case, at his option.

The summary foreclosure, by the revised statutes, may be had, whatever be the condition of the mortgage, and applies equally to a mortgage for the performance of covenants, or to indemnify for unliquidated damages, as for the payment of money only. We regard the latter class of cases only as the proper subjects of a foreclosure without action. This section, however, goes beyond the revised statutes by including a mortgage for the payment of money, whether it contain a power of sale or not. The pledge of specific property, for the payment of a sum of money, necessarily implies a right to sell in case of default.

We have aimed in this chapter, to unite the simplicity and cheapness of the summary foreclosure by advertisement, with the security of right to the debtor, and the safety of title to the purchaser under the old procedure. The execution and acknowledgment before a public officer, and delivery of a mortgage upon specific real property to secure the payment of a sum of money, and its formal entry upon the public records, constitute a case where the law's delays ought not unneccessarily, to extend the time limited by the parties themselves, for the performance. There appears to be no good reason why the holder of a specific lien by mortgage, should not be entitled to a remedy as summary as if he were a judgment creditor. It is therefore provided in this chapter, that the holder of a mortgage may, upon default in payment, proceed at once to advertise the property for sale, by a notice to be published the same length of time as required for a sale on execution. The provisions to guard the rights of the debtor, and the security of the purchaser, are believed to be ample, and are so arranged as not necessarily to delay the sale.

The provisions of the revised statutes for foreclosure by advertisement, wants the important requisite of a judicial determination precluding absolutely the subsequent redemption of the property. The evidence necessary to sustain the purchaser's title is only presumptive, and may be rebutted at any time afterwards. We therefore propose the submission of the proceeding, in all cases, to a judge of competent jurisdiction, and, upon his order of confirmation, the foreclosure is to become absolute. The system of foreclosure by advertisement, as heretofore established, has been rarely used in cities, or in reference to important mortgages in the country, in consequence of the defect above referred to. It will be observed, that the provisions which it has been found necessary to incorporate, to provide for various possible cases, have no application to ordinary cases where those peculiarities do not exist.

§ 1385. A notice that the mortgage will be foreclosed and the property therein described sold, must be given, as hereinafter prescribed, and must specify,

1. The names of the mortgagor and mortgagee, and of the several assignees, if any:

2. The date of the mortgage, the county where, and the time when it was recorded:

3. The amount due thereon, at the time of the first publication thereof, and if the whole be not then due, the amount of principal to become due thereafter:

4. A description of the mortgaged property, conforming substantially to that contained in the mortgage:

5. The time and place of sale, specifying the day and hour, the town, city, or village and the particular house or place therein. The notice must be subscribed with the name of the party who is the owner of the mort-

gage, or to whom the payment is due, in respect to which default has been made.

1386. The notice must be published and served as follows:

1. By publishing the same for six weeks successively, once in each week, in a newspaper printed and published in the county where the property, or some part thereof, is situated; if the property lie in a city or village, and a newspaper be published therein, the publication to be made in such a paper;

2. By serving a copy of the notice on the mortgagor, and on persons having an interest or lien in the mortgaged premises, subsequent to the mortgage, or their personal representatives, by delivery in the manner of serving a summons in a civil action; or, if the person upon whom the service is to be made, does not reside in this state, or cannot on due diligence be found therein, but his place of residence is known, or can on diligent inquiry be ascertained, by delivery thereof to some person of suitable age and discretion, at the dwelling house of such persons respectively, or by depositing the same in the post office properly enveloped and addressed to such persons, at their several places of residence; the service in all cases to be at least three weeks before the time appointed for the sale:

3. By posting copies of the notice in three public places of the town, city or village where the property, or some

portion thereof is situated, at least five weeks before the time specified therein for the sale.

This section reduces the time of publication from twelve weeks to six, but requires a personal notice to be served and posted in the town, omitting also as useless, the posting on the court house door. When the property is situated in a city or village, it requires the publication in a newspaper therein, if any.

§ 1387. At the time and place specified in the notice, the sale may be postponed on the request of any person claiming an interest in the premises, or for want of bidders, by a public announcement of the postponement, and publishing notice thereof, as soon as practicable, in the same newspaper, at the foot of the original notice, specifying the time and place to which the postponement is made, and continuing the notice until the time appointed therein for the sale. It may be again postponed, and from time to time in the same manner, but no costs or fees for making such postponement, or publishing or continuing the notice, can be a charge on the mortgaged property.

§ 1388. The sheriff of the county must, upon request, attend either in person or by deputy, at the time and place of sale, to superintend the sale, and to receive and keep the money or securities paid or deposited thereon.

§ 1389. The sale must be by public auction, between the hours of nine in the forenoon, and four in the afternoon. If the mortgaged property be situated in a city or village, the sale must be therein, otherwise it may be in any part of the county where the property lies. If the property be a farm, or distinct lot, lying partly in two or more counties, the sale must be in the county where the mansion house, or chief building on the pro perty is situated, or if there be none, or two or more in different counties, the sale may be in either county. If the property consist of distinct farms or parcels, they must be sold separately, but when a part has been sold for sufficient to satisfy the amount due and costs, another parcel cannot be sold.

§ 1390. Immediately after the last parcel is struck off, the sheriff or auctioneer must give public notice of the time and place at which application will be made to a judge to confirm the sale, which time must be not less than three nor more than ten days thereafter.

This is deemed a sufficient notice to all who have had notice of the sale, to attend and protect their rights. Parties having junior liens will be likely to attend the sale, to see that the property is sold for its value.

§ 1391. The mortgagee, or his assignee, may prescribe the terms of sale, and may give time for the payment of the whole or part of the purchase money due him, and may become the purchaser on such sale. In place of payment of the purchase money to the sheriff, the purchaser may deliver to him the receipt of the owner of the mortgage therefor, to the extent of the amount due him thereon, which receipt must be returned with the papers to the judge, on the application for confirmation.

The sheriff, and his sureties, shall be responsible for all moneys paid to him on such sale, in the same manner as for money collected on execution, and he must dispose of such money as the judge may direct.

§ 1392. Upon the application for confirmation, there must be produced before the judge the original mortgage, and any bond or collateral contract for the payment of the same money, or proof of their loss or destruction, together with evidence:

1. Of the amount due on the mortgage at the time of the sale, after allowing all payments thereon:

2. Of the publication, service and posting of notices, as provided in sections 1385 and 1386, and every postponement, and notice thereof, and its publication, as provided in section 1387, and also the service of the copies of the notice, specifying upon whom, and when and how made:

3. That the property was fairly sold to the highest bidder, by public auction, at the time and place specified in the notice of sale or postponement, specifying the several parcels sold, the person to whom sold, rhe amount at which each parcel was struck off, and the order in which they were sold, the amount paid by such purchaser, and the receipt, if any, given by the holder of the mortgage, and the fact, that notice was publicly

given of application for the confirmation, at a specified time and place.

§ 1393. The proof mentioned in subdivisions one and two of the last section, must be by affidavit of the party foreclosing: that of publication, by affidavit of the printer of the newspaper, or his foreman: that of posting and serving notices, and of postponing the sale, by affidavit of the person who performed the service; or if made by any other person, reasons satisfactory to the judge, why they were not made by the persons above designated, must be shown in the affidavits.

§ 1394. Upon the application for confirmation, or upon a day to which it may be adjourned, the judge may correct any error that may appear in the statement of the amount due on the mortgage; and for that purpose may examine witnesses, or receive other evidence.

If it appear to his satisfaction, by the evidence, and by inspection of the mortgage, or other collateral contract, that the holder was entitled to foreclose by reason of default in payment, and that all the proceedings have been in conformity with this chapter he must confirm the foreclosure and sale, by an order indorsed on or attached to, the affidavits or certificate and to be filed and recorded therewith in the office of the county clerk.

Ample power is given to the judge to correct errors, and it is made his duty to investigate and examine the proceedings, and either give or withhold his judicial sanction to them.

§ 1395. The order of confirmation must show:

1. The names of all the persons upon whom it appears that the notice was duly served:

2. The amount due, and the amount of costs to which the party foreclosing is entitled:

3. The whole amount for which the property was sold, stating the surplus, if any, or the deficiency, if any, remaining due on the mortgage, and unsatisfied by the sale:

4. If there be payments to become due, unsatisfied by the sale, and also other property mortgaged and not sold, it must be so stated:

5. It must direct that the foreclosure and sale be confirmed, and that the evidence with the order, be filed and recorded.

This order constitutes the judgment, and the insertion in it of the names of the persons upon whom the notice has been served, as established by evidence, together with the other facts necessary to ascertain the rights of parties and give validity to the transaction, secures an enduring record by which the rights of persons holding under the sale are rendered safe.

§ 1396. If the evidence be defective it may be amended or supplied. If it appear, that one or more parcels were sold, after a sum had been raised sufficient to satisfy the amount due with costs, the sale as to those parcels may be vacated, and in other respects confirmed. The omission to serve notice on persons other than the mortgagor, and his personal representatives, shall not affect the validity of the foreclosure and sale, in respect to the persons upon whom the notice was served. But a sale not confirmed as provided in this chapter is void, any money paid thereon must be restored, and the judge by order may enforce the restoration.

§ 1397. When a person, upon whom notice is required to be served, as provided in section 1386, cannot be found, and his place of residence is unknown, and cannot on diligent inquiry be ascertained, and that fact is upon the application, to confirm the sale,made to appear, by affidavit, to the satisfaction of the judge, the publication and posting of the notice, shall, be deemed a good service on such person and his name must be inserted in the order of confirmation accordingly.

§ 1398. The evidence with the order endorsed or attached, must be filed and recorded at length in the office of the clerk of the county, where the land was sold, and thereupon operates as a conveyance of the title of both the mortgagor and mortgagee to the purchaser, and, as a foreclosure of the equity of redemption of every person, upon whom the notice was served as determined in the order of confirmation, whose interest is derived from the mortgagor subsequent to the mortgage, or from a lien attached since that time.

Laws 1844, *ch.* 346, § 4.

§ 1399. The right of a party to enforce or foreclose a mortage, as provided in this chapter, or the validity of the mortgage, or the amount due thereon, may be contested by action, brought at any time before the sale in favor fo any party interested, against any party who may attempt or threaten such foreclosure. In such action proceedings on the summary foreclosure may be stayed by injunction on such terms, as the court may direct, and in the action the court may complete the foreclosure, or not, in its discretion.

Although this right has hitherto been recognized upon existing laws, its enactment here is deemed necessary under the provisions of this chapter.

§ 1400. At any time prior to the sale, any person having an interest or lien upon the property, subsequent to the mortgage, may assume the same, by paying to the holder the amount secured and interest, with the costs already incurred, together with the amount of any lien of the same holder subsequent to the mortgage, and prior to that of the person offering to assume it; and he shall thereupon be entitled to an assignment of the mortgage and of such subsequent lien, and may proceed in the foreclosure or discontinue it, at his option.

This section is in conformity with the decisions of the courts in relation to the equities between the holders of consecutive liens, though the decisions have not been entirely uniform, as to the extent of the right or the means to be used to acquire the rights of the senior incumbrancer. It is a case of common occurrence, and usually arises after the foreclosure has been commenced. A statutory recognition of the principle, making it available without the interference of the court, is believed to be proper.

§ 1401. Upon the application to confirm the sale, or at such other time as the judge may then appoint, he must proceed to determine in a summary manner, the right of any person entitled to an interest in surplus money arising on the sale. He must also make such order, as may be necessary, for the disposition of any money in the sheriff's hands. His orders in the case may be enforced in the same manner as orders in actions, and disobedience thereof may be punished in the same manner.

§ 1402. The order of a judge, respecting the payment or distribution of money arising upon the sale of mortgaged property, pursuant to this chapter, is subject to appeal to the supreme court, in the same manner, as an order refusing a state writ.

§ 1403. When a part of the money secured by the mortgage only is due, and part of the property remains unsold, the mortgage may, for any subsequent default, be again foreclosed, as to the remainder of such property, and a sale thereof made as at first.

Under a foreclosure pursuant to a power of sale by advertisement, when part of the money only is due, and a part of the property sold, it is doubtful whether another sale can be had. This section obviates any question on that point.

§ 1404. When there is a surplus, arising on the sale, beyond the amount due, with costs, and there remains a sum, secured by the mortgage, yet to become due, the holder of the mortgage is entitled to receive such surplus, to be applied to the amount next to become due, the proper rebate of interest being made, If he refuse to receive the surplus, it may, by order of the judge, be paid to the person next entitled.

§ 1405. Mortgages to the people of the state, may be foreclosed as provided in this chapter.

See 1 *R. S.*, 236, *tit.* 4, *ch.* 9, *part* 1, § 1.

§ 1406. The costs of summary foreclosure, pursuant to this chapter, and to be retained out of the proceeds of the sale, are as follows:

1. The printer's fees allowed by law for publishing notices;

2. The clerk's fees allowed by law for necessary searches to ascertain interests and liens subsequent to the mortgage;

3. For posting and filing notices, one dollar;

4. For service, otherwise than through the post office, of a copy of notice on the mortgagor and other persons, not exceeding five, one dollar each; for all over five, fifty cents each;

5. For service on each person served only through the post office, twenty-five cents;

6. For all other services, prior to the day of sale, five dollars;

7. For attending the sale, and all services to the day of application for confirmation, five dollars;

8. For attending the judge for confirmation, and all subsequent services, five dollars;

9. The clerk's fees allowed by law for recording evidence and order of confirmation;

10. Sheriff's fees upon the sale, for the first parcel sold, three dollars; for every subsequent parcel, separately sold, one dollar; for attending before the judge on the application for confirmation with money received on the sale, two dollars; and for all money actually received by him on the sale and paid over, one-half of one per cent.

The Commissioners feel some delicacy in fixing the amount of costs for legal proceedings, but under the former construction of their duty by the legislature, they nevertheless feel bound to insert them, and in doing so, they are mindful that the people have a right to expect a low rate of legal fees, while they can say to the profession, that there is no restraint on their right to make such agreement for compensation as they see fit.

CHAPTER IV.

SUMMARY PROCEEDINGS FOR OBTAINING POSSESSION OF REAL PROPERTY IN CERTAIN CASES.

§ 1407. Entry upon real property can only be made, where entry is given by law, and then it must not be made forcibly; and an entry peaceably made, must not be forcibly maintained, against one who is entitled to the possession. A forcible entry or detention, within the meaning of this section, is one made with weapons, an unusual number of persons, or threats of violence, or attended with any other breach of the peace.

This chapter is intended as a substitute for 2 R. S., 507–517, and renders the course of proceeding in the different cases, uniform.

§ 1408. In case of a forcible entry or detention, the person dispossessed or excluded may, upon application made within one month thereafter, be placed in possession, if entitled thereto, as provided in this chapter.

§ 1409. If a tenant, who is in arrear for rent, desert the property, leaving the same unoccupied, the landlord may be put in possession thereof, as provided in this chapter.

§ 1410. A tenant of real property, for a term less than for life, may be removed from such property, as provided in this chapter, in the following cases:

1. Where he continues in possession of the property, or any part thereof, after the expiration of his term, without the permission of the landlord but in case of a tenancy at will or sufferance, it must be first terminated by notice, in the manner prescribed by law;

2. Where the tenant continues in possession, without such permission, after default in the payment of rent pursuant to the agreement under which the property is held, and three days notice in writing requiring payment of the rent or possession of the property, shall have been served on the tenant, in the manner prescribed by section 1412, for the service of an order;

3. Where a person continues in possession of real property, which has been sold upon execution against him, or against the person under whom he claims by

a title subsequent to the lien on which it was sold, after a title under such sale shall have been perfected, and possession thereunder has been demanded;

4. Where a person continues in possession of real property, which has been sold upon summary foreclosure of a mortgage, executed by him, or by the person under whom he claims by a title subsequent to the mortgage, after a title under such sale shall have been perfected, and possession thereunder has been demanded.

§ 1411. A complaint must be made, and verified, as in an action, stating plainly and concisely the facts necessary to establish the rights of the plaintiff, and thereupon either,

1. A copy of the complaint must be served upon the defendant, with a notice from the plaintiff that unless the defendant previously surrender to the plaintiff possession of the premises, application will, at a specified time and place, be made to a justice of the town or justices' district where the property is situated, for a warrant of possession in favor of the plaintiff; or,

2. The complaint must be delivered to such justice, who shall make an order, requiring the defendant to surrender possession of the property to the plaintiff, or show cause before the justice, at a specified place and time, why a warrant of possession should not be issued in favor of the plaintiff.

§ 1412. The notice or order, with a copy of the complaint, must be served by a sheriff or constable at least two days before the dav of appearance, either,

1. By delivering it to the defendant personally; or

2. If he be absent from his place of residence, and from his usual place of business, by leaving it with some person of suitable age and discretion at either; or,

3. If such place of residence and business cannot be ascertained, or a person of suitable age and discretion there cannot be found, then by affixing it, in a conspicuous place, on the property, respecting which the proceeding is had, and also delivering a copy to a person there residing, if such person can be found.

The officer must make a return certifying the time and manner of service.

§ 1413. If at the time appointed, the defendant do not appear and defend, the justice, upon production of the complaint, and a certificate of service of a copy thereof and of the notice or order, must give judgment that the defendant be removed from the property, and the plaintiff be put into the possession thereof.

§ 1414. The defendant may at the time for appearance, make and deliver to the judge an answer to the complaint, verified as in an action, denying any of the material allegations thereof, or alleging any defence he may have.

§ 1415. The qustions arising on the complaint and answer must be tried by the justice, or, if either party demand it, a jury must be summoned to try the question of fact, if any. The jury must be formed as in justices' courts, and the provisions of this code, respecting trials by jury in justices' courts, apply to trials by jury under this chapter.

§ 1416. If the justice find, or the verdict of the jury be rendered, in favor of the plaintiff, the justice must give judgment, that the defendant be removed from the property, describing it, and the plaintiff put in the possession thereof, and also that the defendant pay the costs specified in the order.

§ 1417. For the execution of a judgment of removal, a warrant must be signed by the justice and delivered to the sheriff of the county, or to the marshal or constable of the city or town in which the property is situated, commanding him to remove the defendant from the property, and put the plaintiff into possession thereof, and to collect the costs of the proceedings specified in the warrant. The officer to whom the warrant is directed and delivered, must execute the same as prescribed in section 1426, and must collect the costs in the same manner, as upon a judgment in a justices' court.

§ 1418. Upon the request of either party, the justice may adjourn the trial, for the purpose of enabling such party to procure his witnesses, whenever it appears to be necessary, and due diligence has been already used; but such adjournment cannot, without the consent of both parties, exceed ten days in the whole.

§ 1419. When a warrant is issued for the removal of a tenant, the contract under which he holds, if any, is thenceforth, terminated, and the relation of landlord and tenant between the parties, ceases, except as provided in section 1422.

§ 1420. The tenant can stay the issuing of the warrant, when the application grows out of the failure to pay rent, if, before the warrant be actually issued, he pay the rent due, with costs, or give to the landlord security, approved by the justice, for the payment thereof in ten days.

§ 1421. Proceedings must be stayed, when the application grows out of a sale by execution or foreclosure of a mortgage, if, at any time before the issuing of the warrant, the occupant:

1. Pay the costs of the proceedings:

2. File with the justice an affidavit, that he claims the possession of the property, by virtue of a title acquired after the sale, which defeats the plaintiff's right of possession, or that he claims as guardian or trustee of another not made a defendant: and

3. Deliver to the plaintiff an undertaking, with sureties approved by the justice, to the effect, that he will

commit no waste during his occupancy of the property, and that if an action be brought by the plaintiff, within three months, for the recovery of the possession thereof, he will pay the costs, and such damages as may be recovered therein for withholding the possession.

§ 1422. When the application is under the second subdivision of section 1410, if the unexpired term of the lease, under which the property is held, exceed one year at the time of issuing the warrant, and the notice or order was not personally served upon the tenant, he, or his successor in interest, or one having a lien upon the property, may, within sixty days after the execution of the warrant, pay or tender to the lessor or his successor in interest, or to the justice, the rent in arrear to that time, with interest and costs, and thereupon the premises must be restored to the tenant, or his successor in interest, who shall hold the same according to the terms of the original lease.

§ 1423. The warrant cannot issue until twenty-four hours after the judgment of removal, and during that time the defendant may appeal from the judgment. The appeal must be made, in the same manner, and to the same court, as from a justice's judgment, and the proceedings upon the appeal are the same.

§ 1424. If the appellant desire a stay of the proceedings, he must give security, by an undertaking executed by one or more sureties, approved by the justice or the county judge, to the effect, that if the judgment be affirmed, the appellant will obey the judgment of removal, pay the value of the use of the property during the appeal, the costs specified in the warrant, and the costs of the appeal.

§ 1425. Upon an affidavit that the defendant is the tenant of another under a subsisting lease, the landlord may defend the proceeding either with or without the tenant.

§ 1426. A warrant of removal can only be executed in the day time. The officer must execute it, by removing the defendant and any other person occupying, by his permission, any part of the property, as his tenant or otherwise, and putting the plaintiff into possession. But when the premises are underlet, the under-tenant can not be removed, unless the summons has either been served upon him or posted in a conspicuous place on the property.

§ 1427. The justice must make an entry, in his docket, of the proceedings, and such entry is evidence thereof.

§ 1428. Upon the conviction of a defendant on an indictment, for forcible entry or forcible detention, in a court of sessions or a court of oyer and terminer, the court may award restitution, in the same manner as a justice upon a verdict pursuant to this chapter.

TITLE III.

OF THE ENFORCEMENT OF LIENS.

This title is proposed as a substitute for various provisions of the revised statutes and several special statutes.

CHAPTER I.

LIENS IN GENERAL.

1429. A lien is a right to have satisfaction of a claim out of a particular thing, or to retain possession of it until the claim is paid.

§ 1430. The liens, of which the enforcement is provided in this title, are of four kinds:

1. Liens on buildings:

2. Liens on vessels:

3. Liens on cargoes for wharfage.

4. Liens on things doing damage upon real property:

CHAPTER II.

LIENS ON BUILDINGS.

§ 1431. A person who, under the authority of the owner, performs labor, or supplies materials, towards the erection, alteration, or repair of a building, in a city or incorporated village of this state, may create a lien on the building and on the interest of the owner in the lot of land upon which it stands, for the price or value of such labor or materials, as provided in this chapter.

See laws of 1830, chap. 330; 1832, chap. 120; 1844, chap. 220–305; 1845, chap. 205. The system is extended by this chapter to all the cities and incorporated villages of this state. It is at this time a prevailing and wise policy to make laws, as far as possible, general throughout the state.

§ 1432. The aggregate of such liens cannot exceed the amount, which the owner of the building would be otherwise liable to pay, for such erection, alteration or repair.

§ 1433. The lien must be registered with the clerk of the county where the building is situated, or in the city of New-York, with the register of that city and county, as follows:

The claimant must deliver to the clerk a statement in writing, verified by affidavit, setting forth briefly the following particulars:

1. The situation of the building, designating it by the street on which it is situated, and the number of the lot, if the street be named, and the lot numbered, or otherwise by some certain or known designation:

2. The owner of the building, under whose authority the lien was created:

3. The particulars of the claim and the amount thereof, which amount, if the claim be made before the labor has been performed, or the materials supplied, and the amount payable therefor has become due, must be the amount payable by the terms of the contract with the claimant, or capable of being ascertained therefrom by computation, if afterwards, the amount actually due: and,

4. A copy of the contract with the claimant, if it be in writing, and if not in writing, a statement of its substance.

§ 1434. The clerk must thereupon register the lien, in a book to be kept by him for that purpose, called the "book of liens." The entries must be arranged alphabetically, under the name of the owner, and of the street, separately. It must contain the name of the claimant and of the person against whom the claim exists, the amount of the lien, the time when filed, and a brief description of the property. A copy of the statement must be served on the owner, by delivering it to him personally, or by leaving it at his residence with a person of suitable age and discretion, or by depositing it in the post office, directed to him at his place of residence. From the time of filing the statement, and serving the copy, the claimant shall have a lien on the land and building, for the amount then actually due to him for work and materials, or which afterwards becomes due, pursuant to the contract referred to in the statement; but such statement must be made and filed, before the expiration of thirty days after the completion of the work or the supply of the materials.

§ 1435. The lien may be discharged, as follows:

1. By filing a certificate of the claimant or his successor in interest, acknowledged or proved in the same manner as the satisfaction of a mortgage, stating that the lien is discharged: or

2. By the deposit with the clerk, of a sum of money equal to the amount claimed, which money shall thereupon be held subject to the lien: or

3. By an entry of the clerk, made in the book of liens, after one year has elapsed since the filing of the claim, stating that no notice has been given to him of legal steps to enforce the lien: or

4. By a notice from the owner to the claimant, after the amount has become payable, requiring him to commence an action, for the enforcement of his lien, and the lapse of thirty days thereafter, without the commencement of such action: or

5. By satisfaction of the lien, upon an action for the enforcement thereof.

§ 1436. After the registry of a lien, and the performance of the work, or the supply of the materials, the claimant or the owner may either serve personally upon the other, a notice in writing, requiring him to appear before a justice of the peace of the county, at a specified time, not less than five days from the time of service, and submit to an accounting for the amount due for such labor or materials. At the time mentioned in the notice, or at such other time as the accounting may be adjourned to, the parties appearing must each deliver to the justice, an account in writing of his claim or offset, if any, verified by affidavit, and submit to examination thereupon, under the direction of the justice. If both parties appear, and there arise a question of fact, a jury may be demanded by either, and such question must be tried by a jury in the same manner, as an issue joined in an ordinary action in a justice's court. In like manner, a contractor, that is a person who contracts with the owner for labor and materials, and who employs persons under him to do work, or furnish materials, may serve on such persons, and receive from them a similar notice with the like effect; and a payment made by the owner, to a person employed by a contractor must be allowed by such contractor, in his account with the owner, to the extent of any judgment which may be recovered by such person against such contractor, pursuant to this section.

§ 1437. Upon the accounting mentioned in the last section, whether a jury be called or not, witnesses may be produced by either party, and judgment must be rendered upon the amount found by the jury or the justice; which judgment has the same effect, is subject to appeal, and may be enforced in the same manner, as a judgment in an ordinary action in a justice's court.

§ 1438. After the performance of the work, or the supply of the materials, and the expiration of any credit stipulated for the payment, the lien mentioned in this chapter may be enforced, by an action. In such action, all persons whose liens are registered, as provided in section 1433, may be made parties, and the court may, by the judgment, direct a sale of the land and building for the satisfaction of the liens and costs; such sale to be without prejudice to the rights of any prior incumbrancer, owner or other persons not parties to the action. If several such actions be brought by different claimants, and be pending at the same time, the court may order them to be consolidated into one.

CHAPTER III.

LIENS ON VESSELS.

§ 1439. A debt, amounting to at least fifty dollars, contracted in this state by the owner, master, agent or consignee of a vessel, is a lien upon the vessel, her tackle, apparel and furniture, when contracted for either of the following purposes:

1. Work done, or materials furnished in this state, towards the building, repairing, equipping and furnishing thereof;

2. Provisions and stores furnished in this state, proper for the use of the vessel at the time they were furnished;

3. Wharfage and keeping the vessel in port, including the expense of employing persons to watch her.

This lien has preference over every other lien, except for mariners' wages. But it ceases in twelve days after the vessel leaves the port where the debt was contracted for another place in this state, and immediately upon her leaving this state.

4. Damage, occasioned to a vessel by collision with another, through the negligence or wilful misconduct

of its navigator, if it exceed fifty dollars, is also for thirty days after the collison, a lien upon the vessel doing the injury.

See 2 *R. S.*, 493, 500, *and Laws of* 1831, *chap.* 318.

§ 1440. The lien mentioned in the last section, may be enforced by an action; in which the court may order the sale of the vessel and the tackle, apparel and furniture thereof, or the tackle, apparel and furniture alone, and the application of the proceeds for the purpose of satisfying the liens thereon. Upon a judgment of sale, the sale must be made by the sheriff, and his bill of sale, made in pursuance thereof, vests in the purchaser a valid title to the property sold, as against all the parties to the action.

§ 1441. Every person having an interest in, or lien upon the vessel whose name is known to the plaintiff, must be made by name, a party to the action, either as plaintiff or defendant, and all other persons having such interest or lien, are to be deemed parties defendants.

§ 1442. The summons must be directed by name to the known defendants, and generally to all other persons unknown having an interest in the vessel or a lien thereon, and must contain a brief description of the vessel, stating, if contained in the complaint, its name, the port to which it belongs, the name of its last commander, and briefly the object of the action, The summons must be served upon the defendants named therein as prescribed in section 628, and upon the unknown defendants as prescribed in sections 629 and 630.

§ 1443. In such action, the plaintiff, at the time of filing the complaint, may have the vessel attached as a security for the satisfaction of such liens as shall thereon be adjudged valid. The mode of proceeding to obtain such attachment, to execute and discharge it, is the same as upon the ordinary provisional remedy by attachment.

§ 1444. If several such actions be brought by different persons having liens upon the same vessel, and be pending at the same time, the court may order them to be consolidated into one.

§ 1445. No proceeding under this chapter can be had against a vessel which shall have been seized by virtue of process from a court of the United States, having admiralty jurisdiction, while such vessel is actually held under such seizure, nor against a vessel which shall have been sold by order of such court, except for debts contracted after the sale. But nothing in this section impairs the validity of any lien created by this chapter, the payment of which shall be decreed by a court of the United States.

CHAPTER IV.

LIENS ON CARGOES FOR WHARFAGE.

§ 1446. When a vessel has lain twenty-four hours at a wharf in this state, for which wharfage is due, and the same has been demanded of the master or owner, by notice left on board with one of the company of the vessel, and neither payment is made nor security given therefor, the owner of the wharf may distrain any chattels on board the vessel for the amount; and so, from time to time as often as twenty-four hour's wharfage becomes due. The distress must be made by a constable or marshal.

§ 1447. The officer making the distress, must immediately give notice thereof, with the cause of the distress, the amount of wharfage due, and an inventory of the property taken, by leaving it on board with one of the company of the vessel.

§ 1448. If, at the expiration of five days after the notice, the wharfage due, with the costs of the distress, be not paid, and the property distrained, be not legally reclaimed, the officer must summon two disinterested householders, who shall be sworn by him, fairly to appraise the property distrained. They must thereupon make and certify the appraisement.

§ 1449. The officer must, thereupon, give six days public notice of the sale of the property distrained, by affixing it on a conspicuous part of the wharf for which the wharfage was due, and also in two public places in the town or ward. On the day and at the place appointed, he must sell the property by public auction, and apply the proceeds to the satisfaction of the wharfage due, and costs, and pay the surplus, if any, to the owner of the property.

CHAPTER V.

LIEN ON THINGS DOING DAMAGE UPON REAL PROPERTY.

§ 1450. A person, having an interest in real property, or entitled to its use or produce, who may find beasts, or inanimate things, unlawfully thereon doing damage, unless they are at the time in the immediate use or manual possession of another, has a lien upon them for such damage, which he may enforce by distress.

§ 1451. A distress is the taking of personal property into the custody of a party by his own act, without legal process, for the enforcement of a lien.

§ 1452. When a distress is made, the distrainer must keep the property safely, until the appraisement of his damage, and, within twenty-four hours after the distress, unless it was made on a Saturday, and then before the Tuesday morning thereafter, he must apply to two fence viewers of the town to make the appraisement.

See 2 *R. S.* 517, § 1—25.

§ 1453. The fence viewers must immediately repair to the place, view the damage, and thereupon ascertain and certify the amount thereof, with their fees. They must also determine any dispute which may arise, respecting the sufficiency of a fence around the property, where the damage was done, and may take the testimony of witnesses, and for that purpose may administer oaths.

§ 1454. When the distress is of beasts, and the damage and fees are not paid, the distrainer, within twenty-four hours after the appraisement must cause the beasts distrained to be put into the nearest pound in the city or town, if there be one, there to remain till the payment of the damages and fees, or the sale of the beasts as prescribed in section 1462, or until the beasts are legally reclaimed. He must also deliver the certificate of the fence viewers to the pound master.

§ 1455. The pound master must receive, and keep in the pound, the beasts so delivered, and, unless the same be reclaimed or discharged according to law within six days, sell them, or so many of them as may be necessary, by auction, giving forty-eight hours notice thereof, by advertisement posted at the pound and at the nearest public place. While the beasts remain in the pound their owner may feed them without disturbance. From the proceeds of the sale the pound master, after deducting the amount of his fees and charges for keeping the beasts, and the charges of sale, must pay to the distrainer the damages so certified, with the fees of the fence viewers, and the surplus, if any, to the owner of the beasts. If no owner appear to claim the surplus, within a year after the sale, it must be paid to the overseers of the poor of the city or town, for the use of the poor.

§ 1456. A pound master, with whom beasts are impounded, must discharge them, on being paid:

1. The amount of damage certified by the fence viewers:

2. The fees of the fence viewers:

3. The fees of the pound master, with his reasonable charges for feeding the beasts, if fed by him, not ex-

ceeding six cents for each beast every twenty-four hours, and

4. In the city of New-York fifty cents a day each, for every day they remain in the pound.

§ 1457. When distress is made of inanimate things doing damage, or, when distress is made of beasts and there is no pound in the city or town, the distrainer must keep the things or beasts in a safe and convenient place, until the damage is appraised, and they are sold or otherwise disposed of.

§ 1458. In the cases provided for in the last section, the distrainer must affix a notice in three public places of the town six days before the sale, as follows:

1. Specifying the property distrained, and the amount of damage certified:

2. Requiring the owner of the property to redeem, and remove, it before the day appointed for the sale:

3. Stating that the property will be sold at a specified time and place, to pay the damage and the charges of the proceedings.

§ 1459. If the value of the property distrained, as certified by the appraisers, exceed fifty dollars, the distrainer must also publish a similar notice, in the nearest newspaper, once a week for four weeks, but in such case, the time of sale must be at least thirty days from the first publication of the notice.

1460. If the owner of the property be known to the distrainer, or if any person be known to him as claiming an interest therein, and such owner or person be found or reside within the county, the distrainer must also serve a copy of the notice, at least six days before the sale, either personally on such owner or person, or in case of his absence from his last place of residence, by leaving the same at such residence with a person of suitable age and discretion: or if the owner or claimant reside out of the county and his residence be known, and he be not served personally, by sending a copy of the notice by mail properly enveloped to his addresss.

§ 1461. If the property be not removed, and the damage so certified, with the fees of the appraisers and the expense of the notice, be not paid at the time appointed for the sale, the distrainer must apply to the sheriff of the county or a constable of the town, to sell the property, and for that purpose must deliver to the officer the original certificate of the appraisers, and an affidavit, showing his compliance with the provisions of this chapter.

§ 1462. The officer must thereupon sell the property, in the same manner as on execution against personal property in civil actions, and out of the proceeds of the sale, after deducting his own fees, pay to the distrainer, the amount of the damage certified, the expense of the notice and also all other expense, that may have been reasonably incurred in the safe keeping and preservation of the property, to be ascertained and certified by the county judge, or by a justice of the peace of the county, and the balance, if any, pay to the owner of the property; or if he be unknown, to the county treasurer for the owner, to be paid to him upon the order of the county court upon making application and proof of property.

§ 1463. If upon such application, the court entertain a doubt of the ownership of the property, it may, before ordering the payment, require the claimant to execute an undertaking, with sureties to be approved by the court, to the effect, that he will pay the amount established to any person who, in an action on such undertaking, commenced within two years from its date, shall establish his right to such balance, or any part thereof; and any person claiming such balance, or any part thereof, may prosecute the undertaking.

CHAPTER VI.

GENERAL PROVISIONS.

§ 1464. When an officer is authorized by statute to distrain property for any purpose whatever, and no special provision is otherwise made, he must give at least six days' notice of the sale of the property, by posting the same in three public places, of the town where the sale is to be made; and he must, also, before making the sale, require three disinterested freeholders of the town to appraise the property distrained, and they must thereupon make the appraisal on oath, and certify it with an inventory of the property.

§ 1465. Within ten days after the sale, the officer making it must file with the clerk of the town or city where it was made:

1. His own affidavit, specifying the cause of the distress and the amount of the penalty, tax, duty, or other sum for which it was made:

2. Proof by affidavit of the requisite notice:

3. The inventory and certificate of the appraisers:

Which papers thus filed are primary evidence of the facts therein stated.

The officer failing to comply with this section, within the time therein required, forfeits twenty-five dollars to the owner of the property sold besides the damage sustained by him in consequence of the failure.

§ 1466. Out of the proceeds of the sale, the officer may retain the reasonable expense of the appraisal, certificate, notice, affidavits and filing, to be certified by a judge or justice, and the balance, after satisfying the penalty, tax, duty or other sum for which the same was made, must be disposed of as provided in section 1462.

TITLE IV.

OF THE PUNISHMENT OF CONTEMPTS.

§ 1467. The following acts, or omissions, in respect to a court of justice, or proceedings therein, are deemed to be contempts of the authority of the court:

1. Disorderly, contemptuous or insolent behaviour toward the judge while holding the court, tending to interrupt the due course of a trial, or other judicial proceeding:

2. A breach of the peace, boisterous conduct, or violent disturbance, tending to interrupt the due course of a trial or other judicial proceeding:

3. Misbehavior in office, or other wilful neglect or violation of duty, by an attorney, counsel, clerk, sheriff, coroner or other person appointed or selected to perform a judicial or ministerial service:

5. Deceit, or abuse of the process or proceedings of the court, by a party to an action or special proceeding:

6. Disobedience of any lawful judgment, order or process of the court:

7. Assuming to be an officer, attorney, counsel of a court, and acting as such without authority:

8. Rescuing any person or property, in the custody of an officer by virtue of an order or process of such court:

9. Unlawfully detaining a witness or party to an action, while going to, remaining at, or returning from the court, where the action is on the calendar for trial;

10. Any other unlawful interference with the process or proceedings of a court;

11. Disobedience of a subpœna duly served, or refusing to be sworn or answer as a witness;

12. When summoned as a juror in a court, improperly conversing with a party to an action to be tried at such court, or with any other person in relation to the merits of such action, or receiving a communication from a party or other person in respect to it, without immediately disclosing the same to the court;

13. Disobedience by an inferior tribunal, magistrate, or officer, of the lawful judgment, order or process of a superior court, or proceeding in an action or special proceeding, contrary to law, after such action or special proceeding shall have been removed from the jurisdiction of such inferior tribunal, magistrate, or officer.

Disobedience of the lawful order or process of a judicial officer, made in the cases specified in section 228, is also deemed to be a contempt of the authority of such officer.

2 *R. S.*, 278, § 10, 15; 534, § 1—37.

§ 1468. Every court of justice, except a court of conciliation, and every judicial officer, has power to punish contempts by fine or imprisonment, or both. But when the contempt, is not one of those mentioned in the first or second sub-divisions of the last section, or in the first sub-division of section 228, it must appear that the right or remedy of a party to an action, or special proceeding, was defeated or prejudiced thereby, before the contempt can be punished by imprisonment, or by a fine exceeding fifty dollars. Contempts of justices' courts are punishable in the manner provided by sections 1150, 1151, 1152, 1153 and 1154.

§ 1469. When a contempt is committed in the immediate view and presence of the court or officer, it may be punished summarily, for which an order must be made reciting the facts as occuring in such immediate view, and presence, adjudging that the person proceeded against, is thereby guilty of a contempt, and that that he be punished as therein prescribed. Such punishment, however, cannot exceed that prescribed by section 1478. Where the contempt is not committed in the immediate view and presence of the court, an affidavit must be presented to the court, or officer, of the facts constituting the contempt.

§ 1470. In cases, other than those mentioned in the last section, the court or officer may either issue a warrant of arrest, to bring the person charged to answer, or without a previous arrest, may, upon notice or upon an order to show cause, grant a warrant of commitment. But no warrant of commitment can be issued without such previous arrest to answer, or upon such notice or order to show cause.

§ 1471. If the party charged be in the custody of an officer, by virtue of a legal order or process, civil or criminal, except upon a sentence for felony, an order may be made for the production of such person, by the officer having him in custody, that he may answer, and he shall thereupon be produced and held, until an order be made for his disposal.

§ 1472. Whenever a warrant of arrest is issued, pursuant to this chapter, the court or officer must direct, whether the person charged may be let to bail for his appearance upon the warrant, or detained in custody without bail, and if he may be bailed, the amount in which he may be let to bail. The directions, given in this respect, must be specified in the warrant.

§ 1473. Upon executing the warrant of arrest, the sheriff must keep the person in actual custody, bring him before the court or officer, and detain him until an order be made in the premises, unless the person arrested entitle himself to be discharged, as provided in the next section.

§ 1474. When the warrant contains the direction to let the person arrested to bail, he must be discharged from the arrest, upon executing and delivering to the officer, at any time before the return day of the warrant, a written undertaking, with two sufficient sureties, to the effect that the person arrested will appear on the return of the warrant, and abide the order of the court or officer thereupon, or pay, as may be directed, the sum specified in the warrant.

§ 1475. The officer must return the warrant of arrest, and the undertaking, if any, received by him from the person arrested, by the return day specified therein. If he fail to make the return, a warrant of arrest not bailable may be issued against him specifying therein the cause of issuing it.

§ 1476. The officer to whom the warrant mentioned in the last section is delivered, must execute it, by arresting the person proceeded against, bringing him personally before the court or officer, and detaining him in custody until otherwise ordered.

§ 1477. When the person arrested has been brought up, or appeared, the court or officer must proceed to investigate the charge by examining him and witnesses for or against him, for which an adjournment may be had from time to time, if necessary.

§ 1478. Upon the evidence so taken, the court or officer must determine, whether the person proceeded against is guilty of the contempt charged, and if it be adjudged that he is guilty of the contempt, a fine must be imposed upon him, not exceeding two hundred and fifty dollars, or he must be imprisoned not exceeding six months, or both. But in the discretion of the court or officer, (in case of inability to pay the fine, or endure the imprisonment,) he may be relieved in such manner and upon such terms as may be just.

§ 1479. If an actual loss or injury, to a party in an action or special proceeding prejudicial to his rights therein, have been caused by the contempt, the court or officer, in addition to the fine or imprisonment imposed for the contempt, may order the person proceeded against to pay to the party aggrieved a sum of money sufficient to indemnify him, and to satisfy his costs and expenses, which order, and the acceptance of the money under it, is a bar to an action by the aggrieved party for such loss or injury.

§ 1480. When the contempt consists in the omission to perform an act which is yet in the power of the person to perform, he may be imprisoned, until he shall have performed it, and in that case the act must be specified in the warrant of commitment.

§ 1481. Persons proceeded against, according to the provisions of this chapter, are also liable to indictment for the same misconduct, if it be an indictable offence, but the court before which a conviction is had on the indictment, in passing sentence, must take into consideration the punishment before inflicted.

§ 1482. When the warrant of arrest has been returned served, if the person arrested do not appear on the return day, the court or officer may issue another warrant of arrest, or may order the undertaking to be prosecuted, or both. If the undertaking be prosecuted, the measure of damages in the action, is the extent of the loss or injury sustained by the aggrieved party, by reason of the misconduct for which the warrant was issued, and the costs of the proceedings.

§ 1483. Whenever, by the provisions of this chapter, an officer is required to keep a person arrested in actual custody, and to bring him before a court or officer, the inability, from illness or otherwise, of the person to attend is a sufficient excuse for not bringing him up. Nor can the officer be required to confine a person arrested upon the warrant in a prison, or otherwise to restrain him of personal liberty, except so far as may be necessary to secure his personal attendance.

TITLE V.

ASSESSMENTS.

CHAPTER I.

ASSESSMENTS FOR LOCAL IMPROVEMENTS.

The subject of assessments upon private property, for what are called local improvements, has been very much agitated, particularly of late years, and opens a much larger field of discussion, than lies within the scope of this code. How far the government may interfere with property; what are the limits of the right of eminent domain, which it is agreed on all hands, belongs to the sovereign authority; and whether the compulsory improvement of one's property, in a manner disagreeable to him, be ever a fair exercise of such authority, are questions, which it will be necessary to enter upon, before any wise and comprehensive scheme of assessments can be adopted.

Our duties do not lead us into the subject, further than to provide the mode of proceeding in the courts, where their interposition is necessary. This interposition in some form is contemplated by the constitution. When the convention met, the abuses of assessments in our cities had excited so loud remonstrances, that two provisions were made in that instrument looking to their remedy. By the 7th section of the first article it is provided, that, "when private property shall be taken for any public use, the compensation to be made therefor, when such compensation is not made by the state, shall be *ascertained by a jury, or by not less than three commissioners appointed by a court of record, as shall be prescribed by law. Private roads may be opened, in a manner to be prescribed by law; but in every case the necessity of the road, and the amount of all damages to be sustained by the opening thereof, shall be first determined by a jury of freeholders*, and such amount, together with the expenses of the proceeding, shall be paid by the persons to be benefited;" and by the 9th section of the eighth article, that "it shall be the duty of the legislature to provide for the organization of cities and incorporated villages, and to restrict their power of taxation, *assessment*, borrowing money, contracting debts and loaning their credit, *so as to prevent abuses in assessments*, and in contracting debt by such municipal corporations."

These provisions of the constitution for the most part remain yet to be acted on. Seeing therefore that laws on this subject must speedily be made; that whenever made they must prescribe a course of proceeding in the courts; we could not submit to the legislature a complete code of procedure, without including this subject also.

It will not be supposed, that the few provisions which follow, provide for the whole subject of assessments. On the contrary there are many others necessary, to specify the kind of improvements for which assessments may be made, the persons who may be assessed, the extent of the assessments, and the rules by which the commissioners are to be governed, in their estimates. These must be the subject of particular legislation.

The law passed in the session of 1848, on the subject of private roads, (chap. 77,) and the 10th section of an act passed in 1847, (chap. 455,) will of course be repealed, upon the adoption of these provisions. The title of the Revised Statutes on the draining of swamps, marshes and other low lands (2 R.

S. § 548,) has not been incorporated into this, because it has been declared by the supreme court to be unconstitutional.

§ 1484. Assessments, whether for benefit or damage, authorised by any statute of this state, must, in the first instance, be made by three commissioners appointed by the county court of the county, in the following cases:

1. When specific property, real or personal, is taken from the owner and appropriated to public purposes:

2. When the owner of property is required to use, or dispose of, it in a particular manner, for the public benefit; and

3. When a contribution in money is required, towards the expense of local improvement.

Though, as has been said in the last note, it would be leading us too far to enter upon an examination of the right of government, to impose some of the assessments, which are laid under existing laws, about which, however, grave doubts have been expressed, yet the remark may not be out of place, that the cases enumerated in this section are all in effect, whatever they may be in name, cases of appropriation of private property. There should seem to be little difference in principle, between a direct sequestration of property for the use of the state, or the compelling of the owner to use or change it himself for a similar purpose, or what is the same thing, compelling him to pay for it, when others do it. It matters little to the proprietor of a city lot, whether he is required to surrender half of it to public officers for public purposes, or to sink half of it in making a change, by the orders of the same officers.

Two things are certain: that private property may be assumed by the state, by virtue of the right of eminent domain, when the state requires it; and also that whenever the owner of property cannot have the full enjoyment of it, without reaching beyond it upon his neighbor's property, the state may authorize a qualified interference with his neighbor, applying to him in his turn the same rule. This last rule applies in the case of fences, roads, bridges, aud sewers. No man can enjoy his property wholly by himself. The full enjoyment of his own requires, that he should give to his neighbor and take from him, to a certain extent. Upon this ground, contribution between coterminous or joint owners, is required. So far as assessments are covered by these principles, they are rightful beyond dispute; whether they are defensible, if they go further, is a question into which we cannot go.

§ 1485. The appointment of commissioners must be made upon a previous notice from the party, in whose name the application is made; and none but freeholders of the county can be appointed.

§ 1486. The notice must be given by advertisement, published in a newspaper of the county, not less than once a week for three weeks.

1487. From the time of their appointment, the commissioners, and all their proceedings, shall be under the control of the court, which may, in its discretion, direct the time and place of meeting of the commissioners, and the time of making their report. The court also has control over all the proceedings subsequent to the report of the commissioners including the sale for the assessment, if a sale be made.

§ 1488. Any person, interested in the assessment, may make himself a party to the proceedings, by giving to the commissioners written notice of his wish to be made a party, stating his name and address; and thereafter is entitled to have at least six days notice of the meeting of the commissioners, of the time of presenting their report, and of the sale, if any. The notice must be served by delivering it to him personally, or sending the same through the post office to his address; except that when a party comes in after notice already given to the existing parties, a new notice to him is not necessary. But the failure to give the notice required by this section, does not affect the jurisdiction of the court.

§ 1489. The report of the commissioners may refer to a map annexed, accurately tracing the boundaries of property taken or assessed, and need not otherwise describe such property in detail. On receiving the report, the court may confirm or modify it, or may reject it, and order a new report to be made by the same or other commissioners.

§ 1490. Any person interested, may present in writing objections to the report, the facts stated in such objections being verified by oath. The court must decide upon the objections, but if it appear to the court, that there is a fact in dispute between the parties, whether such fact be the amount of damages or otherwise, and a trial thereof by jury be demanded by either party, such trial must be ordered.

§ 1491. When there is a trial by jury, the court may exercise the same control over the jury and the verdict, that is exercised in civil actions, and may thereupon make a final order in the case.

§ 1492. Any sale or lease made for the purpose of satisfying the assessments, mentioned in the third subdivision of section 1484, must be made within three year after the confirmation of the report of the commissioners. Such sale must be reported to the court, which may confirm it, or for good cause order a re-sale, but no sale can in any case be made, or lease granted, for a longer period than twelve years.

§ 1493. The commissioners are entitled for their services, to the same fees as referees, but such fees, in the aggregate, can never exceed one hundred dollars to each commissioner. Necessary surveyor's fees, no texceeding two hundred dollars, and clerk's fees, for copies of papers, at the rate of five cents for every hundred words, may also be included in the assessment. No other fees, costs or expenses of any kind, for any local improvement, or upon any assessment, or for proceedings in relation thereto, can be made a charge upon the property.

CHAPTER II.

OPENING OF PRIVATE ROADS.

§ 1494. Any person desiring a private road to be opened over the land of another, may make application therefor to the county court of the county.

§ 1495. Such application must state briefly the circumstances which make the road desirable to the applicant, and must be verified by him. It must state the names and places of residence of the owners and occupants of the land upon which the road is proposed, and must be accompanied by a map or plan of the road proposed, and of the adjacent lands.

§ 1496. Upon receiving the application, the court must make an order that the persons interested show cause, if they have any, at a specified time and place, why the road should not be opened, and in such order must direct the manner of serving the notice, as may appear most likely to reach the persons interested, such service to be not less than ten days before the time specified.

§ 1497. Upon proof of service of the order, if no sufficient cause to the contrary be shown, the court may make an order, directing the sheriff to summon a jury of freeholders, to appear at a specified time and place, to determine the necessity of the road, and the amount of all damages to be sustained by the opening thereof.

§ 1498. The sheriff must execute the order by drawing from the undrawn jury box of a justice in the town, where the property lies, and summoning eighteen jurors, not interested in the question, and indifferent between the parties to appear at the time and place specified in the order; and upon the appearance of the jurors, twelve of them must be drawn, and sworn to make a true inquisition in the premises.

§ 1499. The jury must thereupon go upon the land proposed to be laid out for a road, and the adjacent land, and after examining the application, maps, and plans, and hearing such evidence as may be offered, must make their inquisition and return the same to the court.

§ 1500. If the jury determine, that the road is necessary, it must determine the proper width and location thereof, and the amount of all damage to be sustained by the opening and continued use thereof. The court may thereupon make an order, describing the road, and declaring it a private road for the applicant, and his assigns, and for travel to and from the property, in respect to which it was applied for. A copy of the order must be filed with the records of roads, in the city or town, where the property is situated.

§ 1501. The court must fix the expense of the proceeding, at such sum as may seem to it reasonable, not exceeding in the whole one hundred dollars, and must direct the payment by the applicant of the same, together with the damages found by the jury, before proceeding to open the road.

§ 1502. The provisions of the statutes, regulating the proceedings of commissioners, or other persons, appointed to estimate or assess the expense of local improvements, in the several cities and villages of this state, or relating to such assessments, or to the sale or lease of real property, for the failure to pay assessments, so far as the same are consistent with the provisions of this chapter, remain in force; the term "commissioners," being taken to include all persons appointed to estimate or assess such damages.

TITLE VI.

OF THE VOLUNTARY DISSOLUTION OF CORPORATIONS.

§ 1503. This title embraces the corporations intended by section 974, and embraced in the chapter on actions respecting corporations.

This title is proposed as a substitute for 2 R. S. 467—473, and Laws of 1832, chap. 295.

§ 1504. A corporation may be dissolved by the supreme court, or the county court, of the county where its office, or principal place of business, is situated, upon the voluntary application for that purpose of a majority of its trustees, directors, or other officers having the management of its affairs.

§ 1505. The application must be in writing, and must set forth, either the insolvency of the corporation, or other sufficient reason for terminating its corporate existence, and must contain the following particulars:

1. An inventory of all the property, and of the books, vouchers and securities of such corporation, as far as the same are known to the applicant, or can be ascertained by him;

2. A statement of the capital stock, the number of shares, and their nominal value, the names of the stockholders, the number of shares belonging to each, the amount paid in, and the amount remaining unpaid;

3. An inventory of the debts and liabilities of the corporation, including contracts not completed or satisfied, specifying the names and residence of the creditors respectively, as far as known, the nature of each debt, and the cause and consideration of each: and,

4. A statement of all the liens, or incumbrances outstanding, unsatisfied, on property of the corporation, and the amount actually due, or to become due thereon.

§ 1506. The application must be verified by affidavit, in the same manner as a complaint in an action, and may be presented to a judge of the court either in or out of court.

§ 1506. If the judge be satisfied, that the application and schedule are in conformity with this chapter, and if there appear sufficient ground for the application, but not otherwise, he must order notice to be given to all the stockholders, creditors and others interested, to show cause, if they have any, at a specified time and place, why the corporation should not be dissolved. He may also, if the nature of the case require it, restrain, by injunction, the sale or transfer of any property, or the transaction of any business, by or on behalf of such corporation, until the further order of the court, and may also, then, or afterwards, appoint a receiver, if, in his opinion, it be necessary.

§ 1507. A copy of the order must be served personally on all the members of the corporation residing and to be found, in the same county, at least ten days before the time appointed, in the same manner as a summons in an action. It must be served on all other persons interested, either personally or by publication thereof, for three weeks successively, next before the time of appearance, in a newspaper printed in the county. The judge may also require its publication in one or more other newspapers, if he deem it necessary, in order to give notice to the persons interested.

§ 1508. At the time and place specified, or at another time and place to which the hearing may be then adjourned, the court must hear the allegations and evidence of the applicant, and of any other party interested. The original application and schedules may be used on the hearing, adjournments may be had, and testimony taken, from time to time, in the discretion of the court, and if it become necessary to take an account, a reference for that purpose may be ordered.

§ 1509. If the court be satisfied that the corporation is insolvent, or that for any other reason, the dissolution thereof will be beneficial to the stockholders, and not injurious to the public, an order of dissolution may be made, and a receiver appointed Such corporation shall thereby cease to exist, and its property shall be applied in satisfaction of its debts, and in discharge of its liabilities, and the residue distributed among the stockholders, according to their respective interests therein. No action or special proceeding shall abate by such dissolution, but the receiver may, on motion, be substituted therein, for the corporation.

§ 1510. All conveyances, sales, transfers, and mortgages of real or personal property of such corporation, in payment of, or security for, an antecedent debt, or otherwise, in violation of the injunction are void against the receiver and the creditors.

§ 1511. The receiver must, by public notice, appoint a general meeting of all the creditors, and others interested in the corporation, at a time within three months after his appointment, when all accounts and demands for and against the corporation, and all open and subsisting contracts, must be liquidated and classified as far as practicable. A statement showing the condition of the funds, and of the affairs gen·rally in the hands of the receiver, must be then prepared and exhibited by the receiver. All books and papers in the hands of the receiver, are also at all timessubject to the examination of the creditors and stockholders.

§ 1512. After such meeting, and within four months from the time of his appointment, the receiver must pay all outstanding just claims against the corporation, to the extent of the funds in his hands, (except such as he is by law authorized to reserve,) or if the funds are insufficient, must make payment and distribution in equal proportions, according to their priority.

§ 1513. If any money remain in the hands of the receiver, or be received by him, after the first dividend, he must within a year thereafter, and as much sooner as the condition of the assets will permit, after giving due notice thereof, make a second, and, if possible, final payment to the creditors, and distribution of the residue to stockholders, or others entitled, of the remaining assets in his hands. If after the second distribution, there still remain any part of the estate not collected or distributed, a third distribution must be made in like manner, and so on, as often as may be necessary; but no distribution among the stockholders can be made within one year after the appointment of the receiver, nor until after all the known debts are paid and liabilities discharged, or a sufficient fund set apart for that purpose.

§ 1514. Notice of every distribution must be published at least once a week, for three weeks next before the time appointed therefor, in a newspaper printed in the county, where the principal place of business of the corporation was situated, and also in the state paper.

§ 1515. Any person having a just claim, who has not been included in the list of creditors, or of persons entitled to distribution, or has not had his just share of the assets at any former distribution, may appear and establish his claim, before the final dividend, and shall thereupon be entitled to his full share out of the remaining assets, if sufficient remain to make his payment or distributive share, equal, in proportion to its amount, to that of other claims of the same class at all former dividends, and may thereafter receive with others his just proportion.

§ 1516. Immediately after all the funds in the hands of the receiver have been paid out and applied, he must make a report to the court, containing a full and accurate account of his proceedings; which report must be filed with the clerk of the court in the county where the principal place of business of the corporation was situated.

§ 1517. Previous notice, of the time and place of filing the account, must be published once a week for three weeks, in a newspaper printed in the county, and also in the state paper, and a copy of such notice must also be served on every party, who has previously, in writing, requested notice of the final account. Such notice must also state, that the account will remain on file for the examination of all persons interested, for two weeks from the time of filing the same, and if no objection be made to it by the service of notice, in writing, on the receiver, within that time, that an order closing the account and discharging the receiver, will be entered.

§ 1518. Upon satisfactory proof, produced to the court, showing that such account has been filed after due notice thereof, in the manner for the time prescribed in the last section, and that no objection has been made thereto, by notice served on the receiver, an order may be made that the account of the receiver be confirmed, and he be thereupon discharged.

§ 1519. An objection taken to such account, must state generally in what respect it is erroneous or defective, and the parties objecting are thereupon entitled to five days notice of the time and place of presenting the account, with the objection, to the court for decision.

§ 1520. The judge must proceed to examine the account and the objection, pursuant to the notice, on the day specified, or on some other day to which the examination may be adjourned, and may, when it involves the taking of oral testimony, or the examination of numerous vouchers, refer the same to a referee, to hear the parties and their evidence, and if necessary, restate the account. Upon filing the report of a referee on a receiver's account, an opportunity must be given to the parties interested to be heard.

§ 1521. The court must make an order, allowing, disallowing or modifying such account, according to the report of the referee or otherwise, as may be just, and must direct the proper payment and distribution of the balance, if any be found in the receiver's hands. Such order is final as to all parties receiving notice, pursuant to the provisions of this title.

§ 1522. Every receiver, appointed pursuant to this title, must close the affairs of the corporation, and render his final account to the court, by filing the same within sixteen months from the time of his appointment, or within such further time as the court, on application and cause shown, may allow.

TITLE VII.

OF PROCEEDINGS IN THE COURTS OF CONCILIATION.

This title is the same as that reported by us, in our third report. The provisions are few and simple; but they appear to us sufficient for the purpose. In the French code of civil procedure, eleven sections only are devoted to the proceedings in conciliation; and that they are not found defective in details is proved by the fact, that in a single year 726,556 cases were settled in that way. (See note to section 350.)

It was a question with us, whether justices of the peace should hold courts of conciliation. Upon much reflection it appeared best to begin the experiment with judges of the county courts, because the advice and influence of such judges would have great effect in bringing parties to a settlement. It strikes us as indispensible, that the officers before whom the parties appear, should be able to give them advice respecting their rights, in which they can confide. If they are not sent before such persons, in fact the proceeding will become a mere form. The experiment is altogether new in this country, and we desire it may be tried under the most favorable auspices.

The experience of other countries is not without its use to us. In Norway it is said, the proceeding is a mere form, because the judges are inferior magistrates, without influence over litigants. In France, we have this account:—"This institution owes its existence to the law of the 24th of August, 1790. It produces much good in the country; but its advantages are almost entirely lost in the large towns, and especially in Paris, where the justices of the peace, having in general little knowledge of the persons who come before them, can exercise but a feeble imfluence."—Les Codes Français Expliques, by Rogron.

§ 1523. A court of conciliation is held in each of the counties of this state. In the city and county of New-York, it is held by the city judge of the city of New-York; in every other county, it is held by the county judge.

§ 1524. The court may be held on any judicial day, wherever in his county, the judge may happen to be.

§ 1525. Any person, claiming to have a cause of action against another, in any of the cases mentioned in section 1527, may serve on him a written notice, mentioning the alleged cause of action, and requiring him to appear in relation thereto, before the court of conciliation of the county, where the notice is served, at a specified time, not less than five days from the time of service.

§ 1526. Such notice must be served in the manner prescribed for a summons, in a civil action.

§ 1527. The causes of action, of which this court has cognisance, are libel, slander, malicious prosecution, breach of promise of marriage, assault, battery, false imprisonment, and personal violence of any kind.

§ 1528. At the time specified in the notice, or at such other time as the hearing may be adjourned to by the court, the parties appearing must be received by the judge, apart from all other persons, except as is provided in section 1537, and thereupon, it is the duty of the judge to hear the allegations and explanations of the parties, to inform them of their respective rights, and to endeavor to reconcile their differences.

§ 1529. Parties may voluntarily appear before the court, without notice, and such appearance is as effectual as if notice had been previously served.

§ 1530. If a reconciliation be had, a memorandum thereof, stating the nature of the controversy, or alleged cause of action, the appearance of the parties, and the fact of the reconciliation, without specifying the terms thereof, unless it be agreed by the parties to specify them, must be entered in a book of records, to be kept by the judge, and such entry must be signed by the respective parties. The reconciliation thus effected, shall be the final determination of the matter in controversy.

§ 1531. If the parties agree to a judgment, in favor of one against the other, in settlement of their differences, the judge may make, at the foot of the entry of reconciliation, a memorandum, stating the judgment agreed upon. A transcript of such memorandum, certified by the judge, may be filed in the office of the county clerk, and shall thereupon have the same effect, and may be enforced in the same manner, as the judgment of a county court.

§ 1532. If, instead of a reconciliation, the terms of which are settled between the parties, they voluntarily submit their matters in difference to the court, and agree to abide the judgment, or assent thereto, in the presence of the court, such submission and agreement, or assent, must be entered in the book of records, and signed by the respective parties; and thereupon the judgment of the court, made pursuant to the submission, shall have the same effect, and may be enforced in the same manner, as the judgment mentioned in section 1531.

Conformable to the provision of the constitution, which is in these words: "Tribunals of conciliation may be established, with such powers and duties as may be prescribed by law, but such tribunals shall have no power to render judgment, to be obligatory on the parties, except they voluntarily submit their matters in difference, and agree to abide the judgment or assent thereto, in the presence of such tribunal, in such cases as shall be prescribed by law."

§ 1533. If, after the service of the notice prescribed in section 1525, either party fail to appear, or if the parties appearing be not reconciled as mentioned in sections 1530 and 1531, or do not enter into the submission and agreement mentioned in section 1532, it is the duty of the judge to make an entry in his book of records, stating in a summary manner the nature of the charge, the notice given, the proof of service thereof, the failure to appear of either party, or the appearance of the parties and their failure to be reconciled.

§ 1534. The entries in such book of records, or certified copies thereof signed by the judge, are evidence of the facts therein stated; and it is the duty of the judge to give a transcript of the entries in any case, certified by him, from his records, to either party on request.

§ 1535. In any action hereafter brought for the recovery of damages, for a cause of action mentioned in section 1527, the plaintiff cannot recover costs, unless he produce at the trial the certified copy mentioned in the last section, and unless it thereby appear that the notice was duly served, and that he appeared pursuant thereto, or that both the parties appeared without notice, as mentioned in section 1529.

The defendant cannot recover costs in such action, when it appears that after service of the notice, he failed to appear pursuant thereto.

§ 1536. If, however, the case be one requiring a provisional remedy, and of such urgency as not to justify the delay arising from a previous notice to appear before the court of conciliation, the action may be commenced without such appearance or notice, and if the plaintiff afterwards give the notice, and appear before the court of conciliation pursuant thereto, he may recover costs accruing subsequent to such appearance.

§ 1537. When an infant, or a woman is a party to a proceeding before the court of conciliation, such infant or woman may be attended by the guardian, or husband, of such party, or if there be none, then by some friend approved by the court.

§ 1538. In an action between partners, or between principal and agent, if either party make it appear to the court, that previous to his complaint or answer, he made an offer in writing to his adversary, to submit the matter in difference between them to arbitration, as in the next section prescribed, no costs can be awarded against the party making such offer.

§ 1539. The arbitrators, required by the last section, must be three competent and disinterested persons, one to be chosen by each party, and the third to be either chosen by those two, or by the judge of the court of conciliation of the county.

§ 1540. It is the duty of the judge of the court of conciliation, so far as may be compatible with his duties as judge, to give to every person, who may ask it, advice respecting his differences with another.

§ 1541. No party to any admission or declaration, made before the court of conciliation, is bound thereby or responsible therefor, in any other judicial proceeding whatever, except as provided in this title.

1542. No fee can be received by the judge, for any services rendered in the court of conciliation.

TITLE VIII.

OF ARBITRATIONS.

§ 1543. Persons, capable of contracting, may submit to arbitration any controversy, which might be the subject of a civil action between them, except a question of title to real property, in fee or for life, or for an existing term of more than twelve years. This qualification does not include questions relating merely to the partition, or boundaries of real property, or to the admeasurement of dower.

§ 1544. The submission to arbitration must be in writing, and may be to one or more persons.

§ 1545. It may be stipulated in the submission that it be entered as an order of the county court, for which purpose it must be filed with the clerk of the county, where the parties or one of them reside. The clerk must thereupon enter in his register of actions, a note of the submission, with the names of the parties, the names of the arbitrators, the date of the submission, when filed, and the time limited by the submission, if any, within which the award must be made. When so entered, the submission cannot be revoked without the consent of both parties, the arbitrators may be compelled by the court to make an award, and the award may be enforced by the court, in the same manner as a judgment. If the submission be not made an order of the court, it may be revoked at any time before the award is made, or if unrevoked, the award can be enforced by action only.

§ 1546. Abitrators have power to appoint a time and place for hearing, to adjourn from time to time, to administer oaths to witnesses, to hear the allegations and evidence of the parties, and to make an award thereon.

§ 1547. All the arbitrators must meet and act together during the investigation, but when met a majority may determine any question. Before acting, they must be sworn, before an officer authorized to administer oaths, faithfully and fairly to hear and examine the allegations and evidence of the parties, in relation to the matters in controvesy, and to make a just award, according to their understanding.

§ 1548. The award must be in writing, signed by the arbitrators, or a majority of them, and delivered to the parties. When the submission is made an order of court, the award must be filed with the clerk, and a note thereof made in his register, after the expiration of ten days from the entry upon the application of a party, and on filing an affidavit, showing that a copy of the award and notice of filing the same, has been served at least eight days prior to the application, and that no order staying the entry of judgment has been served, the award may be entered in the judgment book, and shall thereupon have the effect of a judgment.

§ 1549. The county court, on motion, may vacate the award, upon either of the following grounds, and may order a new hearing before the same arbitrators, or not, in its discretion:

1. That it was procured by corruption or fraud:

2. That the arbitrators were guilty of misconduct, or committed gross error in refusing, on cause shown, to postpone the hearing, or in refusing to hear pertinent evidence, or otherwise acted improperly in a manner by which the rights of the party were prejudiced:

3. That the arbitrators exceeded their powers in making their award, or that they refused, or improperly omitted,

to consider a part of the matters submitted to them, or that the award is indefinite, or cannot be performed.

The court may, on motion, modify or correct the award, where it appears:

1. That there was a miscalculation in figures, upon which it was made, or that there is a mistake in the description of some person or property therein:

2. When a part of the award is upon matters not submitted, which part can be separated from other parts, and does not affect the decision on the matters submitted:

3. When the award is imperfect in form, and if it had been a verdict could have been amended, or those imperfections disregarded.

§ 1550. Upon such motion, the costs thereof, may, in the discretion of the court, be added to the award, but no other costs or charges.

§ 1551. The decision upon the motion, is subject to appeal in the same manner as an order which is subject to appeal in a civil action; but the judgment, entered before a motion is made, is not subject to appeal.

§ 1552. If a submission to arbitration be revoked, and an action be brought therefor as provided in section 1545, the amount to be recovered can only be the costs, expenses and damages sustained, in preparing for and attending the arbitration, nor can the recovery be increased by any penalty or sum fixed as damages in the submission or otherwise, in case of revocation.

§ 1553. The provisions of this title must not be construed to prevent a recovery in an action upon the written award of one or more arbitrators, to whom a matter in controversy may be submitted in writing, to decide upon their own knowledge, with or without testimony.

TITLE IX.

OF PROCEEDINGS IN SURROGATES' COURTS.

CHAPTER I.

PROCEEDINGS IN GENERAL.

§ 1554. There are no pleadings in surrogates' courts. The proceedings are those prescribed by special statutes in the cases not provided for in this chapter, except that letters of administration and letters testamentary may be known as the appointment of administrators, or executors. Those proceedings are had upon the application of a party, verbal or written; and when verbal, entered in the minutes or otherwise; when written they are filed. The surrogates' powers are exercised by means of

1. A citation to a party;

2. An affidavit, deposition, or the statement of a party;

3. A subpœna to witness;

4. Orders and judgments; and,

5. An execution or warrant to enforce them.

§ 1555. The surrogate must keep an office open at all reasonable hours, suitable and convenient for the transaction of the business, and for the deposit and safe keeping of the public books and papers under his charge. If such office be not provided by the supervisors of the county, the surrogate must provide it, at his own expense. He may also hold his court at any other place in his county, which he may from time to time appoint. He must also provide suitable cases for the books and papers of his office, the expense of which is a county charge. They belong to the county, and must be delivered by the surrogate to his successor in office.

§ 1556. The following books must be kept by the surrogate:

1. A register, in which must be entered a memorandum of all official business transacted in his office;

appertaining to the estate of each person deceased, under the name of such person; that pertaining to the general guardian of an infant, under the name of such infant; that pertaining to an insane person or drunkard, under his name;

2. A record of wills, in which must be recorded all wills proved before the surrogate with the certificates of probate thereof; and of all wills proved elsewhere, upon which letters of administration are issued by him;

3. A record of appointment of administrators, whether general or special, and of executors;

4. A record of the appointment of general guardians of infants, and of committees of insane persons and drunkards;

5. A record of accounting and of distribution, in which must be entered a summary balance sheet, of the accounts of administrators, and guardians and committees before him, with his orders and judgments relating to the same; a memorandum of executions issued thereon, with a note of satisfaction when satisfied; also, orders relating to the sale of real estate, and to the distribution of the proceeds thereof; and notices of all money or securities received by him, as proceeds of such sales, or otherwise; and a statement, showing the names of creditors, and the debts established and entitled to distribution, the amount to which each person is entitled out of the funds, and the amount actually paid by him to each person, and when paid;

6. A record of the appointment of admeasurers of dower; with all orders relating to the same, and the admeasurers' reports;

7. An order book, in which must be entered orders made by him directing the conduct of executors, administrators, guardians or committees; orders for publication of notice to creditors; orders in behalf of creditors, directing debts to be paid, or allowing an action to be commenced, or an execution to be issued; appointments of special guardians, appraisers, referees and arbitrators; orders relating to the production of a will, to removal of administrators, committees or guardians; in relation to sureties for executors, administrators, committees or guardians; and all other orders which he is required to make in writing, and not required to be recorded in some other book;

8. A book of fees, in which must be entered the items of all fees for services in each particular proceeding, or estate, and when and by whom paid.

§ 1557. To each of such books, there must be attached an index, securely bound in the volume, referring to the entries in alphabetical order, under the name of the person, to whose estate or business they relate, and indicating the page of the book where the entry is made.

§ 1558. The successor in office of a surrogate has power to complete any unfinished business commenced by his predecessor.

§ 1559. A surrogate cannot be counsel or attorney in a civil action, for or against any executor, administrator, guardian or minor, committees or other person over whom or whose accounts he would by law have jurisdiction; whether such action relate to the business of the estate or not.

§ 1560. Costs may be awarded in favor of one party against another, to be paid personally out of the estate or fund, in any proceedings contested adversely before the surrogate; but such costs cannot exceed those allowed in the supreme court, for a trial in civil actions. Witnesses' fees, and other disbursements similar to those allowed in the supreme court, may also be allowed.

§ 1561. Orders for the payment of money may be enforced by execution, or otherwise, in the same manner as judgments for the payment of money in the supreme court; except, that in the surrogate's court, all process is issued by the surrogate.

§ 1562. Executions, warrants, and other process issued by a surrogate, must be executed by the sheriff or coroner of the county, to which they are sent to be executed, in the same manner, and with the same powers, responsibilities and fees, as process issued from the supreme court.

CHAPTER II.

PROCEEDINGS IN CASES OF INSANITY AND HABITUAL DRUNKENNESS.

§ 1563. The surrogate of the county has the care and custody of the person and property of idiots, lunatics, and other persons of unsound mind, and of persons, who, in consequence of habitual drunkenness, or for any other cause, are incapable of the proper care and management of their own property; all of whom are known in this code as insane persons, or habitual drunkards.

§ 1564. For the purpose of exercising these powers, the court may appoint a committee, or if necessary, two or three in each case, whose duty it is,

1. To take possession of the property of the person, and manage the same in a manner proper to produce income, and to prevent its being wasted or destroyed:

2. To take the care and custody of such person, and so far to hold him in restraint, as may be necessary to prevent injury to the person or property of himself or others:

3. To provide out of his property for the maintenance of such person and his family, and the education of his children:

4. To make an inventory of his property, real and personal, and to file the same in the surrogate's office, immediately after his appointment, and to keep and annually file in the surrogate's office, an account of all sums received and expended for the year, verified by his oath.

§ 1565. The overseer of the poor of the town, or the superintendent of the poor of the county, where the insane person or habitual drunkard resides, or any member of the family of such insane person or drunkard, or any person related to him by blood or marriage, who, in case of his death, intestate, would be entitled to any portion of his property, may apply to the surrogate for the appointment of the committee.

§ 1566. Such application must be in writing, stating the facts upon which it is founded, and verified by the affidavit of the applicant, to the effect that he believes it to be true.

§ 1567. Upon receiving the application, the surrogate must immediately appoint a time and place in the town or city, where the insane person or drunkard resides, to investigate the truth of the allegations made in the application, which time must not be less than eight nor more than sixteen days thereafter.

§ 1568. The surrogate must also issue a citation to the insane person, to appear at the time and place specified, and show cause, if he have any, against the application. Such citation with a copy of the application must be served by the sheriff, at least six days before the time of appearance, on the insane person or drunkard, and on some member of the family of such person, or of the family in which he resides, of suitable age and discretion, other than the applicant.

§ 1569. The surrogate must also issue to the sheriff an order, directing him to summon a jury of eighteen persons, to be drawn from a justice's jury box, of the town or city where the trial is to be had, to appear at the time and place appointed for the investigation, and to determine the truth of the allegations made in the application.

§ 1570. The jury must be drawn by the sheriff, in the presence of the justice, and summoned pursuant to the surrogate's order, and a return thereof made, at the time and place specified, stating the time and manner of summoning each juror.

§ 1571. At the time and place appointed, or at such other time as the hearing may be adjourned to for cause shown, the surrogate must attend and draw and empanel a jury of twelve persons, in the same manner as a jury is drawn by a justice, for the trial of civil actions. When the jury is completed, it must be sworn by the surrogate, to investigate the truth of the matters stated in the application, and to find a true inquisition thereon, according to the evidence.

§ 1572. The surrogate must preside at the trial, and decide all questions of law arising therein, and the trial must be conducted in all respects like a trial in a civil action, except as otherwise provided in this chapter.

§ 1573. Upon such trial, the alleged insane person or drunkard may appear by counsel, and may produce witnesses on his part. But whether he appear or not, the applicant must prove the truth of the allegations made in his application.

§ 1574 The inquisition of the jury must be in writing, subscribed by at least nine of the jurors, and must declare that there exists no sufficient reason for a committee, or that the person is in one of the conditions mentioned in section 345, specifying which of them. The surrogate must instruct the jury, as to the form of the inquisition, and it may be found and subscribed in his presence, but he can take no part in the deliberation of the jury, nor advise them in respect to their decision, except on questions of law.

§ 1575. If the jury find that the person is in one of the conditions mentioned in section 1563, the surrogate must immediately appoint a committee, for him. When the application is for a cause other than habitual drunkenness, the jury must state in the inquisition, whether or not, in their opinion, the disability is likely to be permanent. If the jury find that there exists no sufficient reason for a committee, the application must be dismissed.

§ 1576. The appointment must be in writing, and must define the general duties of the committee, as prescribed in section 1564. It must be recorded in the surrogate's office, in the book where the appointment of general guardians is recorded. The committee must also give public notice of his appointment, by advertisement in a newspaper printed and published in the county.

§ 1577. The committee must be sworn to execute faithfully the duties of his trust, according to the best of his ability. He must also give security in the same manner, and to the same effect as the general guardian of an infant. The oath and undertaking must be filed in the surrogate's office.

§ 1578. The surrogate must also appoint appraisers; and an inventory and appraisal of all the personal property of the insane person, must be taken, verified and returned in the same manner and with the same effect, as in the case of administration of the estate of a deceased person, except that it must contain also a description of the real property, and a valuation by the appraisers of the annual income of each parcel thereof.

§ 1579. The powers and responsibilities of a committee, in the execution of the trust reposed in him as prescribed by section 1564, are in all respects like those of a general guardian, in respect to an infant and his estate, except as in this chapter otherwise provided.

§ 1580. In the payment of debts, the committee must be governed by the same rules, as those which regulate the conduct of administrators.

§ 1581. When there is not personal property, sufficient with the income of the real property, for the payment of the debts, or for the proper maintenance of the insane person or drunkard person and his family, the surrogate may upon a proper accounting by the committee, of the personal, and of the income of the real, property, order the real property or such part thereof as he may deem necessary, to be sold or mortgaged to procure the necessary funds therefor.

§ 1582. When the inquisition does not state, that the disability is likely to be permanent, the surrogate must, before ordering a sale, ascertain the probable necessary expenditure over the annual income, for a period not exceeding three years in advance, and must limit the sale or mortgage, to so much of the real property as can be sold or mortgaged separately, without material injury to the residue of the property, and as may be sufficient to raise such sum, and in all cases he must first ascertain by evidence the present condition of the person. Further sales or mortgages may be ordered from time to time, as may be necessary.

§ 1583. The proceedings for a sale or mortgage, must be conducted in all respects in the same manner, as for a sale by administrators, except as herein otherwise provided; but the proceeds of sales, instead of being paid to the surrogate, are to be placed in the hands of the committee.

§ 1584. The committee may be required to give new or additional security, or to render an account, and may be removed. He is also subject, in all other respects, to the control and direction of the surrogate, in the same manner as the general guardian of an infant.

§ 1585. The committee has power, under the direction of a court of competent jurisdiction, to execute a conveyance of real property, or to do any other act, in the specific performance of a contract made by the insane person or drunkard, when he was capable to contract.

§ 1586. The power of a committee ceases, upon the death of the insane person, and also when the disability, in respect to which he was appointed, has been adjudged by the surrogate to have ceased, or when he has been removed for any cause as provided in the next two sections.

§ 1587. Upon application to the surrogate to remove a committee or to revoke appointment, made upon the affidavits of at least two respectable persons, showing misconduct of the committee, or that the disability, in respect to which the commitete was appointed, has ceased, a citation must be issued to the committee, to the person upon whose application he was appointed, if living within the county, and to the next of kin, if any, within the county, who are of full age, to show cause, if they have any, why the appointment of the committee should not be removed or his appointment revoked.

§ 1588. The citation must be served at least fourteen days before the time appointed for the hearing. Upon its return duly served, or upon another day to which the hearing may be adjourned, the surrogate must hear the evidence offered for and against the application. If sufficient cause for the continuance of the committee be not shown, the surrogate must by an order declare, that the disability, in respect to which the committee was appointed, has ceased, that the powers of the committee are therefore revoked, and that the party for whom he was appointed is restored to his original rights. If misconduct of the committee be established, he must be removed and another appointed in his place.

§ 1589. The fees of the surrogate, on the appointment of a committee, are the same, as on the proof of a will, and for his removal, and the proceedings in relation thereto, the same as for similar services in case of administrators. Upon a trial before him, the surrogate may order costs to be paid, either by a party, or out of the fund or estate, to any other party, not exceeding the costs allowed for the trial of a civil action.

CHAPTER III.

APPEALS FROM SURROGATES' COURTS.

§ 1590. An appeal may be taken to the supreme court from a judgment or order in a surrogate's court, in the following cases:

1. An order admitting a will to record or probate, or refusing the same:

2. An order appointing a person administrator, executor or collector, guardian of an infant, or a committee of an insane person, or removing him, or refusing to make such appointment or removal:

3. An order directing real property to be sold, mortgaged or leased, or confirming the same:

4. An order or judgment by which a debt, claim, legacy, or distributive share is allowed, or payment thereof directed, or such allowance or direction refused:

5. Judgment upon accounting, by an executor, administrator, guardian or committee, including an intermediate order involving the merits and necessarily affecting such judgment.

§ 1591. The appeal can only be taken by a party aggrieved, who appeared and moved for or opposed the order or judgment appealed from, or who being entitled to be heard thereon, had no notice or opportunity to be heard; the latter fact to be shown by affidavit, and filed and served with the notice.

§ 1592. The appeal may be taken upon questions of fact or of law, and must be heard upon a statement of the case, to be made and settled before the surrogate, in the manner provided in section 807, and in giving judgment thereon, the decision upon the facts when separate from the questions of law, is final.

§ 1593. The appeal must be taken within thirty days after notice of the order or judgment appealed from, but such appeal does not affect the order appealed from, unless, upon motion, the supreme court, on cause shown, direct a suspension of the order, until the appeal is determined.

§ 1594. The appeal is made by the service of a notice on the adverse party, stating the appeal from the order or judgment, or some specified part thereof, and filing a copy of the notice in the office of the surrogate, and of the county clerk, together with an undertaking with sufficient surety, approved by the surrogate or county judge, and filed in the surrogate's office, to the effect that the party will prosecute his appeal with due diligence to a determination, and will pay all costs that may be adjudged against him in the supreme court thereon.

TITLE X.

OF PROCEEDINGS IN CASES OF INSOLVENCY.

CHAPTER I.

PROCEEDINGS OF INSOLVENT TO DISCHARGE HIMSELF FROM AN IMPRISONMENT ON EXECUTION.

§ 1595. An insolvent who has been imprisoned on execution for thirty days, may be discharged from the imprisonment, as provided in this chapter.

This title has been prepared as a substitute for the 3d, 4th, 5th, 6th, 7th, and 8th articles of the fifth chapter of the second part of the revised statutes, (2 R. S., 16–51.) By making the proceedings be had in court, and applying to them the machinery of the court, we are enabled to dispense with the great details, made necessary when the proceedings take place before an officer out of court. The provisions explain themselves. The third article provides a means of winding up the affairs of an insolvent, which we think will be found salutary in its effect upon credit.

§ 1596. He must present to the county court of the county where he is imprisoned, an application in writing, verified by his oath, setting forth the fact of his imprisonment, the amount, kind, and particulars of his property, and the amount, nature, and particulars of his debts, with the names and residence of the creditors, so far as they are known or can be ascertained by him, and asking for his discharge from the imprisonment.

§ 1597. He must at the same time prove by affidavit, or admission in writing, that a copy of the application, with notice of presenting the same at a specified time and place, has been served on the judgment creditor, upon whose execution the insolvent is imprisoned, at least ten days before the application, in the same manner as a notice of motion in an action.

§ 1598. The application is to be heard in the same manner as any other motion, and if it be shown to the satisfaction of the court, that the allegations of the application are true, that the applicant is insolvent, that he does not conceal any of his property, and that he has not, after knowing his insolvency, and within six months before his application, given a preference to a creditor for an antecedent debt, by any payment or disposition of his property, the court may make an order, declaring that the applicant is an insolvent debtor, and appointing a receiver of his property.

§ 1599. Upon a certificate of the receiver, upon a copy of the inventory, that the insolvent has transferred and delivered to him all the property specified therein, excepting property exempt from execution, to be therein specified, with all books, instruments and papers relating thereto, and after due notice to the judgment creditor, the court may make an order, discharging the insolvent from his imprisonment; but such discharge shall not affect the judgment, nor any other remedy for the collection thereof, other than against the person of the insolvent.

§ 1600. The receiver must proceed in the conversion of the property into money, and the distribution thereof among the creditors existing at the time of the application, whether their demands are due or not, according to their several rights, giving no preference, except where a preference is required by the statutes of this state or of the United States, and must deliver the surplus to the insolvent, under the direction of the court. The receiver is at all times subject to the control of the court, until his final discharge by its order. If other property of the insolvent, not stated in the inventory, be discovered by the receiver, it must be deemed a part of the property assigned, and the receiver must collect the same and account therefor.

CHAPTER II.

PROCEEDINGS OF INSOLVENT TO DISCHARGE HIMSELF FROM DEBT.

§ 1601. Any insolvent, who, at the time of his application, has resided in this state five years, may present to the county court of the county where he resides, an application in writing, verified by his oath, setting forth the fact of his insolvency, the amount, kind, and particulars of his property, and the amount, nature and particulars of his debts, specifying the residence of his creditors, so far as they are known or can be ascertained by him, alleging that he has not given a preference as specified in section 1598, and asking a discharge from his debts.

§ 1602. Upon receiving the application, the court may make an order, requiring the creditors of the insolvent to show cause, if they have any, before the court, at a specified time and place, not less than three months thereafter, why the application should not be granted, and directing the publication once a week for ten weeks of the application, or a condensed statement thereof, and of the order, in the state paper and in two other newspapers which the court may designate as most likely to give notice to the creditors.

§ 1603. At a time and place specified, upon proof of the publication in conformity with the order, and also that a copy of one of the papers containing the application or statement, and order, was deposited in the post office, at least nine weeks previously, directed to each creditor within the United States, at his residence, when such residence is stated in the application, the court may proceed to hear the application.

§ 1604. If a creditor appear and deny any of the material allegations of the application, or allege that the applicant has fraudulently contracted the debt to such creditor, or that such debt arose from a fraudulent misapplication by the applicant of the property of another, or that since it was contracted, the applicant, if a merchant, has not kept proper books of account; the court may either try the question of fact, or may order it to be tried by a jury or by referees.

§ 1605. If such denial or allegation be not made, or if made, be found on the trial to be untrue, the court may make an order declaring that the applicant is an insolvent debtor, and appointing a receiver of his property not exempt from execution; the receiver must give the certificate, and has the power and is subject to the responsibilities mentioned in section 1600.

§ 1606. Upon the final report of the receiver, shewing the collection and conversion into available assets, of all the property of the insolvent, not exempt from execution, and the proper application and payment thereof, if it appear that at least twenty-five per cent. of each of the insolvent's debts contracted before his application, has been paid, or a dividend to that extent offered and set apart thereon, the court may order that the insolvent be discharged from all such debts of the following kinds:

1. Debts due to persons who were residents of this state at the time of the application:

2. Debts contracted in this state:

3. Debts due to creditors who have received a dividend from the receiver.

But such order in no case discharges a debt arising out of a fraudulent misapplication of the property of another, nor does it affect the liability of another person who is liable jointly with the insolvent.

CHAPTER II.

PROCEEDINGS OF A CREDITOR TO CLOSE THE AFFAIRS OF AN INSOLVENT.

§ 1607. Any creditor residing in this state, having a claim arising on contract, and already due, to the amount of five hundred dollars, against a debtor residing in this state, may apply to the county court, of the county where the debtor resides, to declare him insolvent, and close his affairs, in any of the following cases:

1. When he has fraudulently contracted the debt to such creditor:

2. When he has concealed, removed or disposed of of some part of his property, or is about to do so, with intent to defraud his creditors:

3. When an execution against his property has been returned unsatisfied in whole or in part: or,

4. When a promissory note made by him or a bill of exchange accepted by him, while engaged in the business of a merchant, broker, factor or banker, and owned by the creditor, has fallen due, and has remained unpaid and under protest for at least ten days before the application, without notice from the debtor, that he has a valid defence to such note or bill, accompanied by an offer of good security for the payment of any judgment that may be recovered thereon.

§ 1608. The application must be in writing, verified by the affidavit of the creditor, or another person, and showing that the case is within the last section, and asking that a receiver of the property of the insolvent may be appointed and his affairs closed.

§ 1609. Upon receiving such application, the court may make an order, requiring the defendant to show cause at a specified time and place, why the application should not be granted; and if, then or at any time afterwards, there appear to be danger of the defendant's disposing of property, to the prejudice of the application, the court may grant an injunction against any disposition thereof.

§ 1610. At the time and place specified, upon proof of the personal service of the order to show cause, the court may proceed to hear the application.

If the defendant appear and deny any of the material allegations of the application, the court must order the question of fact to be tried by a jury, or, if the defendant waive a trial by jury, may itself try the question, or may order a trial thereof by referees.

§ 1611. If such denial be not made, or, if made, be found on the trial to be untrue, the court may make an order, declaring that the defendant is an insolvent debtor, within one of the subdivisions of section 1607, specifying which, and appointing a receiver of his property.

§ 1612. The receiver must immediately publish notice of his appointment in the state paper, and in two other newspapers designated by the court, for such time as the court may direct; and, from the time of his appointment he is vested with all the property of the insolvent debtor not exempt from execution. The court may compel the transfer and delivery by the insolvent debtor of any of his property, in the manner mentioned in section And section 1600 is applicable to the receiver appointed under this chapter.

TITLE XI.

OF THE ADMEASUREMENT OF DOWER.

§ 1613. A widow's dower in the real property of her deceased husband, may be admeasured and set off to her, at any time after the death of her husband, by agreement between her and the heirs or other owners in fee thereof, who are of full age and competent to contract; or it may be set off by referees, appointed as hereinafter provided.

§ 1614. The widow may, at any time within twenty years from the death of her husband, by a notice in writing, demand the admeasurement of her dower from the heirs of her husband, or other owners in fee, or persons in possession of real property in which she is entitled to dower; and in like manner, the heirs of the deceased husband, or other owners in fee of real property in which a widow is entitled to dower, may, by notice in writing, offer to set off to her her dower therein.

§ 1615. Such demand or notice must specify the lands in which the right of dower exists or is claimed, in an intelligible manner, and must nominate three disinterested freeholders, who are not of kin to either party, as referees, to admeasure the same; and must designate a place and time, not less than ten nor more than forty days from the time of service, at which application will be made to a court having jurisdiction, for an order appointing the referees. Service thereof may be made and proved, in the same manner as the service of a summons in a civil action, except by publication.

§ 1616. Upon application to the court, at the time and place specified, or at such other time as the court may designate, proof by affidavit of the applicant or other person, must be made to the satisfaction of the court, of the right of the widow to dower in the property, and thereupon the court must appoint three referees to make the admeasurement.

§ 1617. The referees must be freeholders residing in the county where the real property or some part of it lies, and must be persons named by the parties or one of them, unless reasonable objection to them be made. The order of appointment must describe the property, out of which dower is to be admeasured, and specify the time when the report must be made.

§ 1618. The referees, before entering upon their duties, must be sworn, before some person authorised to administer oaths, that they will honestly and faithfully execute the trust reposed in them by the appointment.

§ 1619. If the persons so appointed referees, or either of them, die, resign, or fail to serve, others may be appointed in their places, by the court which appointed the first referees, and must take the same oath.

§ 1620. The referees, so appointed, must execute their duties as follows:

1. They must admeasure and lay off, as speedily as possible, the one-third part of the real property, embraced in the order for their appointment, as the dower of such widow, designating such part by posts, stones, or other permanent monuments;

2. In making such admeasurement, they must take into view, any permanent improvement made upon the property embraced in the order, by any heir, guardian of a minor, or other owner, since the death of the husband, or since the alienation thereof by him; and, if practicable, must award such improvements within that part of the property not allotted to the widow; and if not practicable so to award the same, they must make a deduction from the property allotted to the widow, proportionate to the benefit she will derive from such part of the improvements, as may be included in the portion assigned to her;

3. They must make a full report of their proceedings, with the quantity, and description of the property, admeasured and allotted by them to the widow, mentioning the posts, stones, and other permanent monuments thereof, and the items of their charges, to the court by which they were appointed, at the time specified in the order for their appointment;

4. They may employ a surveyor, with necessary assistants, to aid them in such admeasurement.

§ 1621. The court appointing such referees, may, upon their application, or that of either party, enlarge the time for making their report; and may, by order, compel such report, or discharge the referees neglecting to make the same, and appoint others in their places.

§ 1622. The court to whom the report is made, may, at the time appointed for receiving the same, or at such other time to which the hearing may be adjourned, on good cause shown, set aside the report, and appoint, as often as may be necessary, new referees, who shall proceed in the manner hereinafter directed; and, if not set aside, the court must, by order, confirm the report and admeasurement.

§ 1623. The admeasurement so made and confirmed, shall, at the expiration of twenty days from the date of such confirmation, unless appealed from, be binding and conclusive, as to the location and extent of the widow's right of dower, on the parties who applied for the same, and on all parties to whom notice has been given, as hereinafter directed. But no person shall be precluded thereby from controverting the right of such widow to the dower so admeasured.

§ 1624. The widow to whom dower is admeasured, after the expiration of twenty days from the date of the confirmation, unless the same be appealed from, may, if possession be withheld or her right denied, bring an action to recover the possession of the lands so admeasured to her for her dower, and, upon recovery, may hold the same during her life, subject to the payment of all taxes and charges accruing thereon, subsequent to her taking possession.

§ 1625. The order of a court, confirming the admeasurement of dower, may be reviewed, by appeal in the same manner as a judgment in an action in the same court, and the manner of bringing an appeal, and the security required thereon, must be in conformity with similar proceedings in civil actions.

§ 1626. The appellate court, may, on such appeal, affirm or reverse the order, and may require a new admeasurement by the same or new referees, to be appointed by the appellate court, if the appeal be to the supreme court, or by the court in which the proceedings were originally had, if the appellate court so direct. Proceedings upon a second or other subsequent report may be had in all respects as on the first.

§ 1627. Such reasonable sum, for the costs of the party applying for admeasurement, as may be certified by the court, not exceeding twenty dollars, for each parcel of land out of which dower may be separately admeasured, besides referees' fees and other disbursements, must be paid, one-half by the widow and the other half by the adverse party. The allowance of costs on the appeal is in the discretion of the appellate court, but when allowed, they must be at the rate allowed on appeals, to the same court, in civil actions.

§ 1628. When dower is admeasured pursuant to the provisions of this title, and the right to dower is disputed, if in an action brought by the widow to recover possession, she fail to establish her right, the share of the costs on admeasurement, which may have been paid by the other party, may be added to the costs of the defence in such action; and if the dower be withheld from her and she fail for two years to bring an action for the recovery thereof, she shall be liable in an action to the other party for the expenses of admeasurement paid by him.

TITLE XII.

OF MISCELLANEOUS PROCEEDINGS AND GENERAL PROVISIONS.

CHAPTER I.

DISPOSITION OF THE REAL PROPERTY OF INFANTS.

§ 1629. A conveyance by an infant, of real property, owned or held by him, may be ordered by the supreme court in an action in either of the following cases:

1. When the property is held in trust for another:

2. When an agreement to convey the property has been made, and the agreement ought to be specifically performed by the infant. When so ordered, the conveyance is as effectual as if the infant were of full age. But nothing in this chapter affects a sale of infants' estate when made, as provided in special statutes, by an executor or administrator, upon an order of the surrogate's court.

§ 1630. The real property and leasehold estate of an infant, may be sold or mortgaged under the direction of the supreme court, or the county court of the county in a special proceeding, on the application in writing of the general guardian or some person next of kin of the infant, for him, in either of the following cases:

1. When the sale or mortgage is necessary for the infant's support or education:

2. When the interest of the infant will be promoted by it, by reason of the unproductiveness of the property or its being exposed to waste or for any other peculiar circumstances. But such sale or mortgage can in no case be made contrary to the provisions of the will or conveyance by which the property was devised or granted to the infant. The application must state the grounds therefor and must be verified as a complaint in an action.

§ 1631. A copy of the application must be served by delivery in the manner required for the service of a summons to commence an action against an infant, with a notice stating that the same will be presented to the court at a specified time and place, and that application to appoint a special guardian will then be made. The service must be at least ten days before the time of application, and two days in addition for every fifty miles distance from the residence of the infant to the place specified.

§ 1632. Upon the day specified, or some other day to which the hearing shall be then adjourned, the court must appoint a suitable person to be special guardian for the infant in the proceedings to be had thereon; or two or more such guardians may be appointed.

§ 1633. Before the appointment of the guardian can be effectual, and before any further proceedings can be had, security must be given by the guardian, to the infant, to be approvedby the court, and in such sum as the court may by an order direct, faithfully to perform the trust reposed in him, and to account for and apply all moneys received by him under the directions of the court.

§ 1634. The security must be an undertaking of the guardian, either with one or more sufficient sureties, who must justify, in the manner required for bail on arrest in an action, or with security by mortgage on unincumbered real property in the county where the real property lies, or the infant resides, worth, exclusive of buildings thereon, double the value of the amount of security required.

§ 1635. Upon security being given and upon at least eight days notice to the special guardian, or upon his consent without notice, the court must proceed to hear the evidence for and against the application, or may order a reference, as in an action, to ascertain and report the facts.

§ 1636. Upon the hearing, or in case of reference, upon the report of the referee, the court must by an order grant or refuse the application. If granted, the order may direct either a sale or a mortgage of the whole or any part of the property, and must contain a description of the same.

§ 1637. Upon a report to the court, verified by the oath of the guardian, of an argreement for the sale or mortgage of the property, subject to the approval of the court, it must confirm or disapprove the same; if approved, a conveyance must be given by the guardian under the direction of the court. The report of the agreement may be made at the time of the hearing or afterwards.

§ 1638. The court must make such order for the application and disposition of the proceeds of the sale or mortgage, and for the investment of the same or any part thereof, as it shall deem best for the benefit of the infant, and must require accounts to be rendered periodically by the guardian or other person entrusted with the disposition of the proceeds or its income. Such proceeds shall be deemed real property of the same nature as the property disposed of.

§ 1639. Where property is subject to dower, and the person entitled thereto consents in writing to accept a gross sum in place thereof, or the income during life of a permanent investment of a reasonable sum, the court may ascertain and direct the payment of such sum out of the proceeds of the property, or the investment thereof and the payment of the income, as may be deemed reasonable and may be acceptable to the person entitled. If no such consent be given the sale or mortgage must be made subject to the right of dower. Before any sum shall be paid or investment made, an effectual release of the right of dower must be made.

§ 1640. When there are several infants owning real estate as tenants in common or joint tenants, they may all be united in one application, but the security of the guardian must be to each severally.

§ 1641. The costs and expenses of the proceedings, not to exceed twenty-five dollars when there is but one infant, and ten dollars for each additional one embraced in the same application, may be paid by the order of the court from the proceeds of the property.

CHAPTER II.

DISCOVERING THE DEATH OF A PERSON ON WHOSE LIFE AN ESTATE DEPENDS.

SECTION 1641. Application to produce person on whose life an estate depends.
1642. Contents of application.
1643. Twenty days' notice to be given.
1644. Proceedings on the hearing.
1645. Costs may be allowed.
1646. An estate recovered on presumption of death, to be restored afterwards, if the person be living.

§ 1641. A person entitled to claim real property, or the profits thereof, after the death of another who is entitled to a prior estate, or interest therein, may, once a year, by motion, apply to the supreme court for an order, that the person, upon whose life such prior estate depends, be produced.

§ 1642. The application must be made upon affidavit, showing,

1. The interest of the applicant, in the real property which is the subject of the application, describing it, with the grounds thereof:

2. The belief of the applicant, that the person, upon whose life the prior estate depends, is dead, and that his death is concealed by the party, against whom the application is made.

§ 1643. The motion must be upon previous notice, of at least twenty days, and must be made at a special term, where a motion might be made in an action triable in the county where the real property is situated.

§ 1644. Upon such motion, the court may make an order, requiring the production and proof of the identity of the person, upon whose life the estate depends, and, in default of his production, may require of the party against whom the application is made, proof of his existence, with satisfactory reasons for his absence. Such evidence may be taken in open court, or by reference, or by commission to another state or county, together with any other evidence, which may be necessary to determine the question of the existence of such person. Such order must then be made declaring the existence or death of the person, as may be in the judgment of the court conformable to the fact. This order is primary evidence of the facts therein determined.

§ 1645. Costs on such application, and the proceedings founded thereon, not to exceed twenty-five dollars, may, in the discretion of the court, be ordered to be paid, by either party, to the other.

§ 1646. An estate, which shall have been recovered upon the presumption or proof of the death of a person, pursuant to this chapter, must be restored to the party from whom it was recovered, or to his heirs, or representatives, with the issues and profits in the meantime, if it be established that such person is living.

CHAPTER III.

THE COLLECTION AND REMISSION OF FINES AND FORFEITURES.

§ 1647. Every order imposing a fine, except upon conviction for a public offence, must contain a direction that the delinquent be imprisoned until the fine be paid; not to exceed one day for every two dollars of the fine.

§ 1648. The clerk, immediately after the imposition

of a fine, must deliver to the sheriff a certified copy of the order imposing it, and transmit a copy of the same to the treasurer of the county. One order may provide for the collection of all the fines imposed at the same court.

§ 1649. The sheriff must proceed to collect the fine,s or to imprison the delinquents named in the order, and within sixty days from the time of receiving the copy of the order, must pay over to the county treasurer the fines collected by him, and file his return in the county clerk's office, showing the manner in which he has executed the order, stating the amount paid to the county treasurer, if any. Fines imposed by a city court must be paid into the city treasury.

§ 1650. The sheriff is liable to the county or city for the amount of every fine specified in the order, unless it appear by his return that the person, on whom the fine was imposed, has been arrested, or could not be found. Such liability may be enforced by action in the supreme court or by motion in the county court. The sheriff is liable by action for a false return.

§ 1651. When an undertaking or the condition of a recognisance, in a criminal action, is by any court declared broken, the court in which it is filed, or the county court of the county where it is filed, may order the same to be prosecuted. If judgment be given for the plaintiff in such action, it must be for the penalty or sum specified in the undertaking.

§ 1652. The county court may, except in the cases specified in the next section, remit wholly or partly fines imposed or forfeitures declared by any court in the county, on application and cause shown, and on such terms as may be deemed just. If the fine or forfeiture remitted shall have been paid, the officer in whose hands it may be, must refund the same, or the part thereof remitted, upon an order of the court to that effect.

§ 1653. Fines imposed on conviction of a public offence or for actual contempt of a court, or for disobedience to its orders or process, can only be remitted by the court by which they were imposed, and that on cause shown, upon notice to the district attorney. An undertaking entered into in one county, for the appearance of a person in another, can only be remitted or discharged by the court, in which such person was bound to appear, or by the county court of that county, after the time designated for such appearance, and then only upon notice to the district attorney and on cause shown.

§ 1654. Summary judgment upon an undertaking declared forfeited, may be ordered by the court, without action, on motion of the district attorney, after ten days previous notice to the adverse party, of the application for the forfeiture and for judgment thereon.

CHAPTER IV.

GENERAL PROVISIONS.

§ 1655. From the judgment of a county court, in any special proceeding, except when otherwise expressly prescribed by this code, an appeal may be taken to the supreme court, and thence to the court of appeals.

§ 1656. The appeal must be taken in the same manner, within the same time, and upon the same security, as an appeal from a judgment at a general term of the county court, in a civil action commenced therein, except as otherwise expressly provided by a particular provision of this code.

§ 1657. In special proceedings where the costs are not by this code defined, the court may, in its discretion, require costs to be paid by any party to another, or to be paid from the fund which is the subject of the proceeding. The costs allowed must be a fixed sum, to be determined by the court, on the hearing, or afterwards on motion, and must not exceed the rate of costs allowed for similar services in actions.

§ 1658. Amendments, in furtherance, of justice may be allowed by any court or judicial officer in a special proceeding before him, in every stage thereof, upon such terms as to costs or otherwise, as may be proper; and a substitution may, in the same manner, be allowed of a successor in interest, in place of a party, when by reason of death or other cause it becomes proper.

PART IV.

OF EVIDENCE.

GENERAL DEFINITIONS AND DIVISIONS.

This, the only remaining part of the code, embraces the subject of evidence. Large and difficult as is the subject, we cannot omit it from this work, without presenting to the legislature an incomplete code of procedure. As we interpret the constitutional and statutory provisions, under which we act, our commission includes the whole procedure, in civil and criminal cases. To omit the subject of evidence would therefore imply, either that it did not fall within the scope of a code of procedure, or that it was in its nature incapable of being reduced to a written code.

We have referred to the subject in our communications to both the legislatures, to which we have already reported. In the report of 1848, we took occasion to say, that "the courts of justice and all their officers, the time within which actions must be commenced, the mode of bringing the parties before the court, their respective allegations, the trial of disputed questions of fact and of law, *the summoning of witnesses, and the manner of their examination, including the question of their competency, and the rules of evidence,* the judgment to be rendered, the execution of the judgment, and appeals, together with the immense mass of special proceedings known to our law, prerogative, and remedial writs, arbitrations, the processes against absent and insolvent debtors, and a revision of the practice, pleadings and proceedings in criminal cases, all appear to be embraced in the comprehensive language of the constitution. Acting upon this view, it is the design of the Commissioners to prepare a code of procedure which shall comprehend the whole law of the state, concerning remedies in the courts of justice."

This declaration was reiterated at the last session, in our answer to a resolution of the senate, and in our report to the legislature; and with these views before them, they continued the commission to the present time.

In accordance, doubtless, with the same view of the subject, the legislature of Massachusetts, at their last session, following the example of New-York, passed a resolution, for the appointment of three commissioners, "to revise and reform the proceedings in the courts of justice, in the commonwealth, except in criminal cases," and directed, "that the duties of the commissioners shall embrace the consideration and revision of the mode of bringing the parties before the court; all their respective allegations; the trial of questions of fact and of law;

the summoning of witnesses; the question, also, who may be witnesses, and who may be compelled to give testimony; the manner of their examination, and the competency of the same; the judgment to be rendered, its execution, appeals, arbitrations, prerogative and remedial suits, and all processes against absent and insolvent debtors."

It appears to us that the subject properly belongs to the department of procedure. The great line of division in the law, is between the department of rights, and the department of remedies, of which the latter has been confided to our commission; the former to a different one. A complete code of procedure must furnish a guide to the suitor for every step he takes, from the beginning to the end of his controversy; in short he ought to find in it, the whole law of remedies. How can he do this, unless he find the rules which inform him what witnesses he may bring, the method of producing them, and of the examination to which they may be subjected? Can it be said with any propriety, that the subject of evidence belongs to the code of rights? Then is not its appropriate place in the code of remedies? It is so classed by philosophical and legal writers. Bentham's Rationale of Judicial Evidence, the most profound and original work ever written upon this subject, proceeds upon that classification:

"The system of procedure," says he, "judicial procedure, the system of adjective law, is a means to an end. That end is, or ought to be, the execution of the commands issued, the fulfilment of the predictions delivered, of the engagements taken, by the system of the substantive law: the system composed of all the other branches of the body of law put together.

"The law respecting evidence, is one branch of that system of adjective law: it therefore ought to be, and everywhere in some degree is, one part of the means directed and applied to the attainment of that end. In proportion to the steadiness and consistency with which it does act in subservience to that end, is its congruity, its propriety, its fitness, the claim it has to be approved of, and preserved unchanged. Vol. 4, p. 477.

That the law of evidence is not capable of being reduced into a written code, cannot be admitted, for a moment. Our people but yesterday signified in their constitution, their wish for the formation of "a written and systematic code," not only of the statute, but of the common law. It is too late after the discussions and achievements of the last half century, now to insist, that there is any part of the unwritten law, which cannot be reduced to a written code. Though not written in statutes, it is yet written in books, whether books of reports or elementary writers; it does not depend upon tradition; it is not handed down from memory, through successive generations, as if there were no written language; but it is preserved in writing. Whatever has been once written can be written again; wherever scattered, it can be found, gathered, digested, reconciled and arranged in one book, consisting of a series of propositions. Such a book is a code.

The codes of other countries have been thus framed. It was not expected, it could not be expected, that they would come forth perfect at first; but time and experience wrought the necessary amendments, and the results are great national works.

One of the most distinguished members of the council of state, under Napoleon, and one who bore a part in the revision of the French codes, Count Real, wrote a few years since, to the late eminent reformer, William Sampson of New York, in these terms:

"Courage; persevere in the support of written reason, against precedents and vague traditions. If law had no foundation but precedents, all crimes and injuries would have remained unpunished, and unredressed from the creation, till this day. The first judgment must have been guided by reason. Has reason lost its power? Precedents have been made by lawyers as articles of faith by divines. But whatever respect I may entertain for religion, I have not the same reverence for the decisions of judges. I do not believe that the march of the human mind is retrograde. * * * * *

Do as we did, but do it better, profiting by our mistakes.

Let four or five good heads be united in a commission, to frame in silence the project of a code. It is not so difficult a task. It is only to consult together, and to select. Do with your best authors as we did with ours, and principally with Pothier's treatise on Obligations, which we simply converted into articles of our code. This *project* once formed, submit it *disputationibus eorum*, and you come to a result. As long as nothing is written, nothing will be done; but you will gain something the moment you have a written text for the groundwork of your discussions, how imperfect soever it may be at first. Our code was far from being adopted, as it was originally proposed in the entire. I doubt whether one hundred articles were preserved in the form in which they were presented. It will require ardent hearts, and cool heads, and resolved industry, for such a work. With these, I think, you will not fail of complete success."

With these views of the relation of evidence to the general subject of procedure, of the importance of at least beginning a code of the common law, and of our obligations, under the law of our appointment, we submit to the Legislature the following portion of our work.

§ 1659. Judicial evidence is the means, sanctioned by law, of ascertaining in a judicial proceeding the truth respecting a question of fact.

§ 1660. Proof is the effect of evidence, the establishment of a fact by evidence.

§ 1661. The law of evidence, which is the subject of this part of the code, is a collection of general rules established by law,

1. For declaring what is to be taken as true, without proof:

2. For declaring the presumptions of law, both those which are disputable and those which are conclusive; and

3. For the production of legal evidence:

4. For the exclusion of whatever is not legal:

5. For determining in certain cases the value and effect of evidence.

We are told occasionally of the law of evidence, as of the other branches of the law, that its rules are well defined, well understood, and stable. The entire opposite would be nearer the truth. The books abound with contradictory, fluctuating, and inconsistent opinions. The following may be taken as specimens:

Lord Mansfield said, in the case of Lowe against Joliffe, (1 Bl., 366,): "We do'nt now sit here to take our rules of evidence from Siderfin or Keble."

Lord Kenyon: "All questions upon the rules of evidence are of vast importance to all orders and degrees of men; our lives, our liberty, and our property, are all concerned in the support of these rules, which have been *matured by the wisdom of ages*, and are now *revered* from their *antiquity* and the *good sense* in which they are founded: they are *not rules depending on technical refinements*, but upon *good sense*; and *the preservation of them is the first duty of judges.*" 3 *Term Rep.*, 721, King *vs.* Eriswell.

The same Lord Kenyon, in Bent *vs.* Baker, 3 *Term. Rep.* 32. "I premise with mentioning what was said by Lord Mansfield on this subject, that the old cases, upon the competency of witnesses, have gone upon *very subtle grounds.* I must acknowledge that there have been various opinions upon this subject, and that it is impossible to reconcile all the cases." 33.

Ashhurst, "There is *so great a contradiction* in decisions respecting the boundaries of evidence, that I rather choose to give my opinion on the particular circumstances of the case, than to lay down any general rule on the subject." 3 *Term Rep.* 34.

Buller, on the same occasion: "This case involves in it the question which has been so repeatedly agitated in courts of law, what objections go to the *credit*, and what to the *competency* of the witness: than which *no question is more perplexed.*"

Grose, on another occasion: "The distinction between *competency* and *credit* is *by no means accurately settled*: in many of the books, the shade between them is so light that the boundaries of either can hardly be perceived. But in all the books which treat of evidence, there are certain *technical* rules laid down, which are *highly beneficial* to the public, and ought not to be departed from."

§ 1662. The law does not require demonstration, that is, such a degree of proof as, excluding possibility of error, produces absolute certainty; because such proof is rarely possible. Moral certainty only is required, or that degree of proof, which produces conviction in an unprejudiced mind.

§ 1663, There are four kinds of evidence:

1. The knowledge of the court:

2. The testimony of witnesses:

3. Writings:

4. Other material objects presented to the senses.

§ 1664. There are several degrees of evidence:

1 Original and secondary:

2. Direct and indirect:

3. Primary, partial, satisfactory, indispensible and conclusive.

§ 1665. Original evidence is an original writing or material object introduced in evidence.

§ 1666. Secondary evidence is a copy of such original writing or object, or oral evidence thereof.

§ 1667. Direct evidence is that which proves the fact in dispute, directly, without an inference or presumption, and which in itself, if true, conclusively establishes that fact. For example, if the fact in dispute be an agreement, the evidence of a witness who was present and witnessed the making of it, is direct.

§ 1668. Indirect evidence is that, which tends to establish the fact in dispute by proving another, and which, though true, does not of itself conclusively establish that fact, but which affords an inference or presumption of its existence. For example, a witness proves an admission of the party to the fact in dispute. This proves a fact, from which the fact in dispute is inferred.

§ 1669. Primary evidence is that, which suffices for the proof of a particular fact, until contradicted and overcome by other evidence. For example, the certificate of a recording officer is primary evidence of a record; but it may be afterwards rejected upon proof that there is no such record.

§ 1670. Partial evidence is that, which goes to establish a detached fact, in a series tending to the fact in dispute. It may be received, subject to be rejected as incompetent, unless connected with the fact in dispute, by proof of other facts. For example, on an issue of title to real property, evidence of the continued possession of a remote occupant is partial, for it is of a detached fact, which may or may not be afterwards connected with the fact in dispute.

§ 1671. That evidence is deemed satisfactory, which ordinarily produces moral certainty, or conviction in an unprejudiced mind. Such evidence alone will justify a verdict. Evidence less than this is denominated slight evidence.

§ 1672. Indispensible evidence is that, without which a particular fact cannot be proved.

§ 1673. Conclusive or unanswerable evidence is that, which the law does not permit to be contradicted. For example, the record of a court of competent jurisdiction cannot be contradicted by the parties to it.

§ 1674. Cumulative evidence is additional evidence of the same character, to the same point.

§ 1675. Corroborative evidence is additional evidence of a different character, to the same point.

§ 1676. This part of the code is divided into six titles:

The first contains the general principles of evidence:

The second relates to the kinds and degrees of evidence and contains the rules by which is determined what may be received as evidence:

The third title relates to the production of evidence;

The fourth relates to the effect of evidence:

The fifth relates to the rights and duties of witnesses;

The sixth relates to evidence in particular cases, and contains also miscellaneous and general provisions.

TITLE I.

OF THE GENERAL PRINCIPLES OF EVIDENCE.

§ 1677. The direct evidence of one witness, who is entitled to full credit, is sufficient for proof of any fact, except usage, perjury and treason.

It was at first our intention, whenever the rule stated is the same as that which now prevails, to refer to the authorities in support of them. But upon reflection, we abandoned that intention, because it might lead into an unprofitable discussion, whether the rule was correctly stated, rather than whether the rule was right. There is so much that is new, blended with that which is old, that it was thought better, to leave the provisions to speak for themselves, with the general observations that accompany this report.

§ 1678. A witness can testify of those facts only which he knows of his own knowledge, that is, which are derived from his own perceptions; except in those few express cases, in which his opinions, or inferences or the declarations of others, are admissable.

§ 1679. A witness can be heard only upon oath or affirmation; and, upon a trial, he can be heard only, in the presence, and subject to the examination, of all the parties, if they choose to attend and examine.

§ 1680. A witness is presumed to speak the truth. This presumption, however, may be repelled by the manner in which he testifies, by the character of his testimony, or by evidence affecting his character or motives, or by contradictory evidence; and the jury are the exclusive judges of his credibility.

§ 1681. The rights of a party cannot be prejudiced by the declaration, act or omission of another, except by virtue of a particular relation between them; therefore proceedings against one cannot affect another.

§ 1682. Where, however, one derives title to real property from another, the declaration, act or omission of the latter, while holding the title, in relation to the property is evidence against the former.

§ 1683. Where also the declaration, act or omission, forms part of a transaction, which is itself the fact in dispute, or evidence of that fact, such declaration, act or omission, is evidence, as part of the transaction.

§ 1684. And where the question in dispute between the parties, is the obligation or duty of a third person, whatever would be evidence for or against such person, is primary evidence between the parties.

§ 1685. The declaration, act or omission of a member of a family, who is deceased, or out of the jurisdiction, is also admissible as evidence of common reputation, in cases where, on questions of pedigree, such reputation is admissible.

§ 1686. The declaration, act or omission of a deceased person, having sufficient knowledge of the subject, against his pecuniary interest, is also admissible as evidence to that extent, against his successor in interest.

§ 1687. When part of an act, declaration, conversation or writing, is given in evidence by one party, the whole, on the same subject, may be inquired into by the other; when a letter is read, the answer may be given; and when a detached act, declaration, conversation or writing is given in evidence, any other act, declaration, conversation or writing, which is necessary to make it understood, may also be given in evidence.

§ 1688. There can be no evidence of the contents of a writing, other than the writing itself, except in the following cases:

1. When the original is in the possession of the party against whom the evidence is offered, and he withholds it under the circumstances mentioned in section 1758:

2. When the original cannot be produced, by the party by whom the evidence is offered, in a reasonable time, with proper diligence, and its absence is not owing to his neglect or default:

3. When the original is a record, or other document, in the custody of a public officer:

4. When the original is a record or other document, of which a certified copy is expressly made evidence by this code, or some other statute of this state:

5. When the originals consist of numerous accounts, or other documents, which cannot be examined in court, without great loss of time, and the evidence sought from them, is only the general result of the whole.

In the cases mentioned in subdivisions 3 and 4, a copy of the original must be produced; in those mentioned in subdivisions 1 and 2, either a copy or oral evidence of the contents.

§ 1689. When the terms of an agreement have been reduced to writing by the parties, it is to be considered as containing all those terms, and therefore there can be, between the parties and their representatives, or successors in interest, no evidence of the terms of the agreement, other than the contents of the writing, except in the following cases:

1. Where a mistake or imperfection of the writing is put in issue by the pleadings:

2. Where the validity of the agreement is the fact in dispute. But this section does not exclude other evidence of the circumstances under which the agreement was made, or to which it relates, as defined in section 1693, or to explain an ambiguity, intrinsic or extrinsic, or to establish illegality or fraud. The term agreement includes deeds and wills, as well as contracts between parties.

§ 1690. The language of a writing is to be interpreted, according to the meaning it bears in the place of its execution, unless the parties have reference to a different place.

§ 1691. In the construction of a statute or instrument, the office of the judge is simply to ascertain and declare, what is, in terms or in substance, contained therein, not to insert what has been omitted, or to omit what has been inserted; and, where there are several provisions or particulars, such a construction is, if possible, to be adopted as will give effect to all.

§ 1692. In the construction of a statute, the intention of the legislature, and in the construction of an instrument, the intention of the parties, is to be pursued if possible; and when a general and particular provision are inconsistent, the latter is paramount to the former. So a particular intent will control a general one, that is inconsistent with it.

§ 1693. For the proper construction of an instrument, the circumstances under which it was made, including the situation of the subject of the instrument, and of the parties to it, may also be shown, so that the judge be placed in the position of those, whose language he is to interpret.

§ 1694. The terms of a writing are presumed to have been used in their primary and general acceptation, but evidence is nevertheless admissible, that they have a local, technical or otherwise peculiar signification, and were so used and understood in the particular instance, in which case the agreement must be construed accordingly.

§ 1695. When an instrument consists partly of written words, and partly of a printed form, and the two are inconsistent, the former controls the latter.

§ 1696. When the characters, in which an instrument is written, are difficult to be decyphered, or the language of the instrument is not understood by the court, the evidence of persons skilled in decyphering the characters, or who understand the language, is admissible to declare the characters, or the meaning of the language.

§ 1697. When the terms of an agreement have been intended in a different sense by the different parties to it, that sense is to prevail, against either party, in which he supposed the other understood it; and when different constructions of a provision are otherwise equally proper, that is to be taken which is most favorable to the party, in whose favor the provision was made.

The first part of this section expresses a rule of ethics, which should find a place in these rules of construction. "When the terms of promise admit of more senses than one, the promise is to be performed, in that sense in which the promisor apprehended at the time, that the promisee received it." It is not the sense in which the promisor actually intended it, that always governs the interpretation of an equivocal promise; because at that rate you might excite expectations, which you never meant, nor would be obliged, to gratify. Much less is it the sense, in which the promisee actually received the promise; for, according to that rule, you might be drawn into engagements, which you never designed to make. It must therefore be the sense, (for there is no other remaining,) in which the promisor believed the promisee accepted his promise.

"This will not differ from the actual intention of the promisor, when the promise is given without collusion or reserve; but we put the rule in the close form, to exclude evasion in cases, in which the popular meaning of a phrase, and the strict grammatical construction of the words, differ; or in general wherever the promisor attempts to make his escape through some ambiguity in the expressions which he used.

"Temures promised the garrison of Sebastia, that if they would surrender, *no blood should be shed.* The garrison surrendered, and Temures buried them all alive. Now Temures fulfilled the promise in one sense, and in the same too in which he intended it at the time; but not in the sense in which the garrison of Sebastia actually received it, nor in the sense in which Temures himself knew that the garrison received it; which last sense, according to our rule, was the sense in which he was in conscience bound to have performed it."

* * * * * *

"From the principle established in the last chapter, 'that the obligation of a promisor is to be measured by the expectation, which the promisor any how voluntarily and knowingly excites, results a rule, which governs the construction of all contracts, and is capable from its simplicity, of being applied with great care and certainty, viz: that *whatever is expected by one side, and known to be so expected by the other, is to be deemed a part or condition of the contract.*"—Paley's Moral Philosophy, pp. 85, 97.

§ 1698. A written notice, as well as every other writing, is to be construed according to the ordinary acceptation of its terms. Thus a notice to the drawers or endorsers of a bill of exchange or promissory note, that it has been protested for want of acceptance or payment, must be held to import, that the same has been duly presented for acceptance or payment, and the same refused, and that the holder looks for payment, to the person to whom the notice is given.

§ 1699. Where a statute or instrument, is equally susceptible of two interpretations, one in favor of natural right, and the other against it, the former is to be adopted.

§ 1701. None but a material allegation need be proved.

§ 1702. Evidence must correspond with the substance of the material allegations and be relevant to the question in dispute. Collateral questions must therefore be avoided. It is however within the discretion of the court, to permit inquiry into a collateral fact, when such fact is directly connected with the question in dispute, and is essential to its proper determination, or when it affects the credibility of a witness.

§ 1703. Each party must prove his own affirmative allegations. Evidence need not be given in support of a negative allegation, except when such negative allegation is an essential part of the statement of the right or title, on which the cause of action or defence is founded, nor even in such case when the allegation is a denial of the existence of a document, the custody of which belongs to the opposite party.

§ 1704. In conformity with the preceding provisions, evidence may be given, upon a trial, of the following facts:

1. The precise fact in dispute;

2. The act, declaration or omission of a party as evidence against such party;

3. An act or declaration of another, in the presence and within the observation of a party, and his conduct in relation thereto;

4. The act or declaration, verbal or written, of a deceased person, in respect to the relationship, birth, marriage or death of any person related by blood or marriage to such deceased person; the act or declaration of a deceased person, done or made against his interest in respect to his real property; and also in criminal actions, the act or declaration of a dying person, made under a sense of impending death, respecting the cause of his death;

5. After proof of a partnership or agency, the act or declaration of a partner or agent of the party, within the scope of the partnership or agency, and during its existence; the same rule applies to the act or declaration of a joint owner, joint debtor or other person jointly interested with the party;

6. After proof of a conspiracy, the act or declaration of a conspirator against his co-conspirator, and relating to the conspiracy;

7. The act, declaration or omission forming part of a transaction, as explained in section 1683;

8. The testimony of a witness deceased, or out of the jurisdiction, or unable to testify, given in a former action between the same parties, relating to the same matter;

9. The opinion of a witness respecting the identity or handwriting of a person, when he has knowledge of the person or handwriting; his opinion on a question of science, art or trade, when he is skilled therein;

10. The opinion of a subscribing witness to a writing, the validity of which is in dispute, respecting the mental sanity of the signer, and the opinion of an intimate acquaintance, respecting the mental sanity of a person, the reason for the opinion being given;

11. Common reputation, existing previous to the controversy, respecting facts of a public or general interest, more than thirty years old, and in cases of pedigree and boundary;

12. Usage, to explain the true character of an act, contract or instrument, where such true character is not otherwise plain; but usage is never admissable except as an instrument of interpretation;

13. Monuments and inscriptions in public places, as evidence of common reputation, and entries in family bibles or other family books or charts, engravings on rings, family portraits, and the like, as evidence of pedigree;

14. The contents of a writing, when oral evidence thereof is admissable;

15. Any other facts from which the facts in issue are presumed, or are logically inferrible:

16. Such facts as serve to show the credibility of a witness as explained in section 1680.

TITLE II.

OF THE KINDS AND DEGREES OF EVIDENCE.

CHAPTER I.

KNOWLEDGE OF THE COURT.

§ 1705. There are certain facts of such general notoriety, that they are assumed to be already known to the court. Of those facts evidence need not be produced.

§ 1706. The following facts are assumed to be thus known:

1. The true signification of all English words and phrases, and of all legal expressions:

2. Whatever is established by law:

3. Public and private official acts of the legislative, executive and and judicial departments of this state of the United States:

4. The seals of all the courts of this state and of the United States:

5. The accession to office, and the official signatures and seals of office, of the principal officers of govern-

ment, in the legislative, executive and judicial departments of this state and of the United States:

6. The existence, title, national flag and seal of every state, or sovereign, recognized by the executive power of the United States:

7. The seals of courts of admiralty and maritime jurisdiction, and of notaries public:

8. The laws of nature, the measure of time, and the geographical divisions and political history of the world.

In all these cases, the court may resort for its aid to appropriate books or documents of reference.

CHAPTER II.

WITNESSES.

§ 1707. A witness is a person whose declaration under oath is received as evidence for any purpose, whether such declaration be made on oral examination, or by deposition or affidavit.

§ 1708. All persons, without exception, otherwise than as specified in the next two sections, who, having organs of sense, can perceive, and perceiving can make known their perceptions to others, may be witnesses. Therefore neither parties, nor other persons who have an interest in the event of an action or proceeding, are excluded; nor those who have been convicted of crime; nor persons on account of their opinions on matters of religious belief: although in every case, the credibility of the witness may be drawn in question, as provided in section 1680.

The fundamental difference between this system of evidence and that in common use, consists in this, that the former goes upon the principle of admission, the latter upon the system of exclusion. Admission is the rule here; exclusion is the rule of the common law. Let in all the light possible, we ask. Not so the common law; exclude the light, it says, lest perchance it deceive you; unmindful, as it appears to us, that poor light is better than none. There are many occasions, when you cannot have the pure light of heaven; it sometimes comes through a stained medium; but you should not therefore prefer total darkness.

The code of 1848 abolished incompetency from mere interest, but left *parties* still incompetent, as witnesses in their own favor. In this completed code, we are for abolishing the remaining portion of the rule of exclusion, and for declaring parties competent as well as others. This has been already done in Connecticut, by a section of the Revised Statutes of 1849, as follows:

"No person shall be disqualified as a witness in any suit or proceeding at law or in equity, by reason of his interest in the event of the same, as a party or otherwise, or by reason of his conviction of a crime; but such interest or conviction may be shown for the purpose of affecting his credit." (*Revised Statutes of Connecticut*, 1849, *page* 86, *sec.* 141.)

One of the commissioners has taken occasion to inquire into the operation of this law, and has received the following answer on the subject from the Lieutenant Governor of that state, which we think will serve to remove any apprehension respecting the result of a similar law here:

Lyme, Conn., Dec, 10th, 1849.

DEAR SIR.

I have delayed answering your inquiry, respecting the operation of our law allowing parties in civil causes to testify, partly in consequence of other engagements, but principally for the purpose of enabling me to speak with some confidence on the subject. As the statute is recent, and excepts from its provisions suits pending at its passage, the experiment has not been fully tested. So far, however, as it has been tried, I may safely say, after conversing with eminent gentlemen of the bar, in different parts of the state, and from my own observation, professional and judicial, that the result is highly satisfactory. So important a change in the rules of evidence met of course, at the outset, a very earnest opposition; especially, (with some distinguished exceptions,) from the senior members of the profession. Their fears I believe, are in a great measure quieted, and I am not aware of any intention or desire to attempt a return to the old system.

Many innovations on the principles of the common law, relating to the admissibility of interested witnesses had formerly been made in Connecticut. The most common action with us is book-debt, and in this, the parties and others having an interest in the event of the suit, had always been allowed to testify. The action of account at law is still in constant use here, in which the same rule exists. In other cases special statutes had obviated the difficulties arising from the restrictions of the common law, until it was found that either both of the parties, or one of them, were permitted, or might be required, to testify, in about twenty of the different forms of civil and judicial proceedings. These changes having proved salutary, it was at last deemed safe and expedient to throw open the door entirely. There appears no tendency to go back; and as soon as the new system is firmly established, I think it will be a matter of surprise that any other should ever have obtained.

It would seem to be a principle of natural justice, that a person whose rights are at stake, should at least have the privilege of telling his own story, and making his own explanations—that he should have the right of saying to the law "strike but hear." Generally he must know more of the facts than any body else. The objection of course is, that his testimony is not to be relied upon on account of his interest. But I think the presumption of falsehood from that cause, in the majority of instances, is not warranted by experience. Such a presumption exists no where except in a tribunal of justice. In the daily transactions of life it finds no place. Business could hardly be done, or society be held together, if men in fact lied whenever it was for their interest. The first persons to whom we ordinarily go, in searching for the true facts of an occurrence, are the parties themselves.

I doubt again whether the new rule will lead to an increase of perjury. Men who would be guilty of that crime themselves, can usually find others to commit it for them; especially when there is no danger of a contradiction. This is frequently exemplified in the proof of pretended declarations and confessions.

Nor do I believe it will increase litigation. Many a suit is brought or defended, solely because the mouth is shut, whose voice would be conclusive to defeat or sustain it. Much of the time of courts, and the property of suitors, is spent in settling questions on this subject, and especially the nice distinctions between credibility and competency. The common law is said to be "the accumulated wisdom of a thousand years." In accumulating its wisdom on this branch, it has probably cost millions of money.

The inconsistencies of the common law, on this point, are too palpable to escape notice. A witness is excluded who is interested to the value of a cent *in the event of the suit*, but is not, if interested to the amount of thousands, or his whole estate, in the *question* at issue. The party himself is excluded, but not his father or child, though their bias may be equal, or their interest really identical. A party claiming to be injured may be a witness in a criminal suit instigated by himself, but not in a civil one for the same cause, though his feelings interests and passions may be involved alike in both.

A member of a public corporation, as a town, may testify, but a member of a private one, as a turnpike company, cannot, though each may be interested in the same manner and to the same extent; as for instance, to avoid the liability arising from a defective bridge. There is a large class of cases where a person interested is admitted, from what is called "the necessity of the case." If this means because he is the best or the only witness, why should not the rule be co-extensive with the reason; which would make it universal. But I am expressing opinions and giving reasons, when I suppose you simply expected facts. My excuse is the earnestness of my conviction on the subject. Trusting confidently that here and elsewhere, the change will be found a most important improvement in the administration of justice.

I am very respectfully,

Your friend and obedient serv't,

CHARLES J. McCURDY.

The distinguished judge of the district court of the United States for the district of Missouri, Judge Wells, writes also on the same subject as follows:

"I entirely concur with you in the opinion, that all rules for the exclusion of evidence are rules for the exclusion of light. I am satisfied, that every sensible man trying a cause, would be glad to hear, and would find great advantages in hearing, every thing that could be said upon the subject. Those who object to juries hearing every thing relative to the cause, object wholly upon the ground that *jurors* are unable properly to discriminate, between evidence that is credible and that which ought not to be credited The *objectors* are, however, all perfectly competent to make such discrimination. The truth, however, I believe to be, that jurors, from their business and intercourse with all classes, are much more able to make just discriminations, than are the judges. There is another objection to those rules. In their application, nice distinctions are to be taken, and decisions made, which cause reversals, expense and delay. If I were preparing a *Code*, I would not, therefore, hesitate in permitting the parties to testify in their own favor."

This subject was brought last year before the "Society for promoting the amendment of the law," in England, a society composed of the most distinguished judges and lawyers of that country, and referred to a committee. The report of the committee is so full, and the subject is one of such great interest, that we are led to insert in this place the entire report.

COMMON LAW COMMITTEE.

The following reference was made to the Committee:—

> "To consider whether parties to the record, both at Law and in Equity, should not be competent witnesses in their own favor, and liable to compulsory examination at the instance of their opponents."

REPORT.

Your Committee have considered the above reference, and beg to answer in the affirmative the questions involved therein. When a matter is submitted to the decision of any persons, be they judges or jurors, it is obviously of the last importance, that those persons should be made acquainted with the real circumstances of the case before them; and it is equally obvious, that the real circumstances are usually best known, and are often only known, to the litigating parties themselves. If then, the parties to the record were as willing, as they are able, to narrate events as they really happened, they would of course be the best witnesses that could be produced; but inasmuch as they are often deeply interested in the result of the cause, and are consequently exposed to the temptation of colouring or misstating the facts, it has been hitherto supposed, at least at common law, that their testimony could not be received, without endangering the best interests of morality, and embarrassing the investigation of truth. In other words, the admissibility of the testimony of parties has been objected to, on the twofold ground, that it is calculated to increase the crime of perjury, and to mislead the court or jury.

Let us consider these objections in their order; and first, as to the temptation to commit perjury. The importance of this objection appears to your Committee to be greatly overrated. So long as parties, like other witnesses, are liable to a rigid cross-examination, it matters comparatively little, what amount of interest they may have in withholding or perverting the truth. The dread of detection and of consequent punishment, even in the absence of every moral sentiment, will in the great majority of instances check the commission of perjury. The *party* knows that his testimony will be sifted with more than ordinary care, and this knowledge must have a tendency to restrain any inclination to falsehood. This very objection be it remembered, was urged most loudly, when Lord Denman brought in his bill to admit the testimony of interested witnesses. It did not then prevail, but the bill became the law of the land, and the practical working of that great measure has since amply demonstrated the invalidity of the reasoning, on which the objection rests. Besides, if the admitting parties to be witnesses would sometimes occasion perjury, it cannot be doubted but that at other times its effect would be to prevent the commission of that crime. For, who that practices in courts of law but must acknowledge, that one of the most frequent and dangerous forms of perjury is that which affects to narrate the admissions of one or other of the parties to the record? A witness for the plaintiff, for instance, distinctly swears, that he called upon the defendant on a certain occasion, and that the defendant then acknowledged the justice of the plaintiff's demand. The scene is laid where no third person was present; the defendant cannot himself be called to contradict the statement of the witness. The interview has perhaps taken place to the knowledge of the defendant's servant, and the servant to this extent corroborates the testimony of the witness. Cross-examination is obviously ineffectual. The witness tells his story in a calm and plausible and connected manner; he is believed, and the defendant unjustly loses the verdict.

Now, if in such a case, and there are many such, the defendant were capable of himself giving testimony, not only would the jury be better enabled, by contrasting the manner of the two witnesses and the probability of their opposite statements, to form a correct decision, but the false witness would hesitate much before he would tell a tale which he knew full well would be flatly contradicted ; and even if he did venture to enter the box, the mere knowledge of the fact that he was uttering falsehoods, and that another witness could and would be called to make an opposite statement, would often have the effect of rendering his story incoherent and his manner suspicious, and would thus prevent any credit from being given to his testimony. On the whole, therefore, your Committee consider that the crime of perjury would not to any serious, if indeed to any, extent be increased by a law which should render parties to the record competent witnesses. But even if they have come to an erroneous conclusion on this head, and if the crime of perjury would in point of fact be increased by such law, they are by no means prepared to condemn its introduction on that ground alone. The folding of sheep by night on lands at a distance from the homestead, no doubt affords facilities for sheep-stealing; the exposure of goods in front of shops leads to larceny; nocturnal travelling may tempt to the commission of highway robbery; but no one thinks of prohibiting these innocent acts on the ground that they hold out temptations to crime. Why is this? Because the inconveniences that would result from such a prohibition would be felt far more by the public, than those engendered by a partial increase in the number of offences. So, in the case under discussion, your Committee consider that the advantages derivable to the cause of truth, from the examination of persons best conversant with the facts, would far more than counterbalance any evils, which the cause of morality would be likely to sustain, from the crime of perjury becoming somewhat more frequent. In all cases of this kind, the legislature must be content to decide on a balance of evils; for even the best human measures are not exempt from some inconveniences.

But secondly, it is urged that the testimony of parties should be withheld, because it is calculated to mislead the court and jury. This objection your Committee think entitled even to less consideration than the one already discussed; for, in the first place, they consider, as already intimated, that, as a general rule, parties would be found to tell the substantial truth; and next, they entertain no doubt, but that as, where parties are made witnesses, the motive to deceive is at least as apparent as it is strong, the court and the jury would naturally sift with proportionate suspicion, the testimony of such persons, and, being on their guard, would refrain from giving implicit credit to statements, which, coming from a less suspicious quarter, would demand unhesitating belief.* Besides, the very circumstance of the parties themselves being examined would not unfrequently prevent the jury from being misled; for their examination would afford an opportunity, which is at present,

* See Taylor on Evidence, § 953.

often wanted, of ascertaining the motives, characters, and interests of the witnesses called on their respective behalves, and might thus furnish a clew whereby to deturmine the relative amounts of credit due to such witnesses.

Your Committee, having now answered the two main objections to the plan proposed, beg leave to call the attention of the Society to those cases in which the law at present allows parties to be examined. For instance, at our Police Courts, in Courts-martial, in the new county courts, and in most of the summary proceedings befere magistrates, parties are allowed to tell their own tales, and not only is no inconvenience felt from the prevalence of this practice, but it is unquestionably productive of great advantage. Your committee have sought for information on this subject from several of the judges and officers of the county courts, and the almost uniform answer to their inquiries has been, that the system of examining the parties themselves has in those courts worked extremely well. So also in criminal prosecutions, which, though nominally ininstituted in the name of the Crown, and having for their dedeclared object the satisfaction of public justice, are in fact carried on at the instance of the injured party, who, in some cases, is even entitled to the restitution of his property on conviction of the offender, the prosecutor has ever been admitted as a competent witness.

And there is no pretence for asserting that the fountains of justice have been defiled by the contaminating influence of such testimony. In the Irish Civil Bill Courts parties may be compelled to testify as witnesses for their opponents; and a clause enabling arbitrators to examine at their discretion the litigating parties, is now inserted almost as a matter of course in all orders of reference. Again, in the Superior Courts of law, affidavits sworn by either party, may in general be read in support of, or in opposition to, any *interlocutory* motion; and in Equity, not only is the sworn answer of the defendant admitted as evidence against him in all cases, and for him in some, but however deeply he may be interested in the question involved in the cause, he may, in almost every instance, by the express provision of Lord Denman's Act, be examined as a witness on behalf of the plaintiff or of any co-defendant.

Moreover, a clause is now uniformly introduced in the order of reference to the Master, enabling him to examine both parties on interrogatories.

In considering these exceptions to the general rule which rejects the testimony of parties, one is naturally inclined to ask, how is it possible to reconcile the law with the exceptions; or, in other words, how can both, at one and the same time, be founded on principles of justice and expediency?

If it be right and advisable that parties to the record should be admissible witnesses in the County Courts, on what ground can their testimony be rejected at Nisi Prius? If the law be sound, which enables plaintiffs in equity to appeal to the oaths of defendants, why should not plaintiffs at law have the same powers; and why should not defendants either at law or in equity be authorised to examine their adversaries as witnesses? These questions are far easier asked than answered. Indeed, your committee are of opinion that they do not admit of a satisfactory answer. In practice, nothing can exceed the absurdity and injustice occasioned by the above anomalous state of the law. An action is brought at common law, and the defendant feels that he has no defence unless he can examine the plaintiff on his oath. This he is not allowed to do; and, therefore, if he be a poor man, his case is hopeless, But if he be sufficiently wealthy to bear the costs of a bill in equity, the result may be very different, for what cannot be effected by direct means may be indirectly obtained; and the plaintiff, albeit an inadmissible witness at common law, may be made a defendant to a suit for discovery; and by this cumbrous and costly process, his action may be defeated by his own testimony. Thus the fate of the action will depend on the length of the defendant's purse. Again, a suit is instituted in Chancery, and the defendant, though himself compellable to put in his answer on oath, has no direct means of examining the plaintiff; but his sole remedy, unless the suit be one which admits of a reference to the Master, is to institute, in his turn, proceedings against his opponent, or, in the language of the law, to file a cross-bill. In the one case the merits of the cause cannot be determined rightly without having recourse to two courts; in the other without having recourse to two suits in the same court. Surely these instances of gross defects in the law require no further comment.

Your Committee, therefore, beg merely to convey to the Society their decided opinion, that the time has now arrived when it has become expedient to enact, that, excepting in the case of actions for criminal conversation, which, for obvious reasons, should be excluded from any general rule, all parties to the record, whether at law or in equity, should be competent witnesses in their own favor, and be liable to compulsory examination at the instance of their opponents."

To this array of authority, we will add the names of Livingston and Bentham; and with the following extract from the latter's work already mentioned, we leave the subject to the judgment of the legislature:

"Evidence is the basis of justice: to exclude evidence is to exclude justice.

On the plaintiff's side, in a suit of a criminal nature, an excluding rule, as often as it has the effect of shutting the door against an article of true and unfallacious evidence necessary to conviction, operates as a license for the commission of a crime.

In the exclusionary system, may therefore be seen a fund of encouragement constantly applied to the production of all imaginable crimes.

On the plaintiff's side, in a suit of a non-criminal nature, an excluding rule, as often as it has the effect of shutting the door, against an article of true and unfallacious evidence, necessary to the giving effect to a rightful demand, operates as a denial of justice.

In the exclusionary system may thus be seen a fund of encouragement constantly applied to the production of injustice in all its shapes, to the prejudice of the plaintiff's side: to the destruction of all those private rights which it has been the business of the substantive law to create, and for the efficiency of which it stands pledged.

On the defendant's side, in a suit of a criminal nature, an excluding rule, as often as it has the effect of shutting the door against an article of true and unfallicious evidence necessary to acquittal, (evidence sufficient for conviction having been delivered on the other side), operates as a license for inflicting punishment upon the innocent on a false pretence of criminality.

In the exclusionary system, may thus be seen a fund of encouragement constantly applied, or applicable to the oppression, of the innocent, by the infliction of punishment, in all its shapes, on persons in whose instance it is groundless and undue.

On the defendant's side, in a suit of a non-penal nature, an excluding rule, as often as it has the effect of shutting the door against an article of true and unfallacious evidence, necessary to a decision exempting him from the objection sought by the plaintiff to be imposed upon him, (evidence sufficient for a decision imposing that obligation having been delivered on the other side), operates as a license for imposing undue obligation in general, a license to oppression by all imaginable wrongs other than on the score of punishment."

Rationale of Judicial Evidence.

The section we are considering provides, that a person shall not be excluded, because he has been convicted of crime. To exclude a person as a witness, for that reason, is as much as to say, that it is presumed he will utter a falsehood, or in other words, that it is more likely he will tell what is false than what is true. Now, no person acts in common life upon such a presumption. If he did, he would never ask such a person any question whatever. If, on arriving at a railway station, you desire to know whether you are too late, and the first person you meet is a man who has been in the state prison, you ask him, without hesitation, whether the train has passed; and yet, according to the rule of exclusion you should not ask him, because it is probable he will answer you falsely. To such absurdity does this unnatural rule lead us.

That no person can be excluded, on account of religious belief, is settled by the constitution: "No person shall be rendered incompetent to be a witness on account of his opinions on matters of religious belief."—Article 1, section 3.

§ 1709. The following persons are not admissible:

1. Those who are of unsound mind at the time of their production for examination:

2. Children under ten years of age, who appear incapable of receiving just impressions of the facts, respecting which they are examined, or of relating them truly.

§ 1710. There are, particular relations, in which it is the policy of the law to encourage confidence, and to preserve it inviolate; therefore, a person cannot be examined, as a witness, in the following cases:

1. A husband cannot be examined, for or against his wife, without her consent, nor a wife, for or against her husband, without his consent, nor can either, during the marriage or afterwards, be, without the consent of the other, examined, as to any communication made by one to the other during the marriage. But this exception does not apply to a civil action or proceeding, by one against the other, nor to a criminal action or proceeding, for a crime committed by one against the other;

2. An attorney cannot, without the consent of his client, be examined, as to any communication made by the client to him, or his advice given thereon, in the course of professional employment;

3. A clergyman, or priest cannot, without the consent of the person making the confession, be examined

as to any confession made to him in his professional character, in the course of discipline, enjoined by the church to which he belongs;

4. A licensed physician or surgeon cannot, without the consent of his patient, be examined, in a civil action, as to any information acquired in attending the patient, which was necessary to enable him to prescribe or act for the patient:

5. A public officer cannot be examined as to communications made to him in official confidence, when the public interests would suffer by the disclosure.

Whether even these four exclusions should all be retained, is a question not admitting of an easy solution. Neither Livingston nor Bentham admit the exclusion in the case of husband and wife. The only exclusions which Mr. Livingston admits are those of a lawyer and confessor; the only one allowed by Mr. Bentham is that of a confessor.

§ 1711. If a person offer himself as a witness, that is to be deemed a consent to the examination also, of a wife, husband, attorney, clergyman, physician or surgeon, on the same subject, within the meaning of the first four subdivisions of the last section.

CHAPTER III.

WRITINGS.

ARTICLE I.

WRITINGS IN GENERAL

§ 1712. Writings are of two kinds:

1. Public: and,

2. Private.

§ 1713. Public writings are:

1. The written acts, or records of the acts, of the sovereign authority, of official bodies and tribunals, and of public officers, legislative, judicial and executive, whether of this state, of the United States, of a sister state, or of a foreign country:

2. Public records, kept in this state, of private writings.

§ 1714. All other writings are private.

ARTICLE II.

PUBLIC WRITINGS.

§ 1715. Every citizen has a right to inspect, and take a copy of, any public writing of this state, except as otherwise expressly provided by statute.

§ 1716. Every public officer, having the custody of a public writing, which a citizen has a right to inspect, is bound to give him, on demand, a certified copy of it, on payment of the legal fees therefor, and such copy is primary as evidence of the original writing.

§ 1717. Public writings are divided into four classes:

1. Laws:

2. Judicial records:

3. Other official documents:

4. Public records, kept in this state, of private writings.

§ 1718. Laws, whether organic or ordinary, are either written or unwritten.

§ 1719. A written law is that which is promulgated in writing, and of which a record is in existence.

§ 1720. The organic law is the constitution of government, and is altogether written. Other written laws are denominated statutes. The written law of this state is therefore contained in its constitution and statutes, and in the constitution and statutes of the United States.

§ 1721. Statutes are public or private. A private statute, is one which concerns only certain designated individuals, and affects only their private rights. All other statutes are public, in which are included, statutes creating or affecting corporations.

§ 1722. Unwritten law is the law not promulgated and recorded, as mentioned in section 1719, but which is nevertheless observed and administered in the courts of the country. It has no certain repository; but is collected from the reports of the decisions of the courts and the treatises of learned men.

§ 1723. Books, printed or published, under the authority of a sister state, or foreign country, and purporting to contain the statutes, code, or other written law, of such state or country, or proved to be commonly admitted in the tribunals of such state, or country, as evidence of the written law thereof, are admissible in this state, as evidence of such law.

§ 1724. The public seal of the state or country, affixed to a copy of a written law, or other public writing, is also admissible as evidence of such law or writing.

§ 1725. The oral testimony of witnesses skilled therein, is admissible as evidence of the unwritten law, of a sister state, or foreign country, as are also printed and published books of reports of decisions of the courts of such state, or country, or proved to be commonly admitted in such courts.

§ 1726. The recitals in a public statute, are conclusive evidence of the facts recited for the purpose of carrying it into effect, but no further. The recitals in a private statute, are conclusive evidence between parties who claim under its provisions, but no farther.

§ 1727. A judical record, is the record or official entry of the proceedings in a court of justice, or of the official act of a judicial officer, in an action or special proceeding.

§ 1728. A judicial record of this state, or of the United States, may be proved by the production of the original, or by a copy thereof, certified by the clerk, or other person having the legal custody thereof. That of a sister state, may be proved by the attestation of the clerk, and the seal of the court annexed, if there be a clerk and seal, together with a certificate of the chief judge, or presiding magistrate, that the attestation is in due form.

§ 1729. A judicial record of a foreign country, may be proved by the attestation of the clerk, with the seal of the court annexed, if there be a clerk and seal, or of the legal keeper of the record with the seal of his office annexed, if there be a seal, together with a certificate of the chief judge, or presiding magistrate, that the person making the attestation is the clerk of the court, or the legal keeper of the record, and in either case, that the signature of such person is genuine; and also together with the certificate of the secretary of state, or other officer of the government, under whose authority the record is kept, having the custody of the great or principal seal of such government, to the effect that the court or officer, whose judicial act is certified, had jurisdiction to perform such act, specifying generally the nature of the jurisdiction, and verifying the signature of the clerk, or other legal keeper of the record, and also verifying the signature of the chief judge, or presiding magistrate.

§ 1730. A copy of the judicial record of a foreign country is also admissible in evidence upon proof;

1. That the copy offered has been compared by the witness with the original, and is an exact transcript of the whole of it:

2. That such original was in the custody of the clerk of the court, or other legal keeper of the same: and

3. That the copy is duly attested by a seal, which is proved to be the seal of the court where the record remains, if it be the record of a court, or if there be no such seal, or if it be not a record of a court, by the signature of the legal keeper of the original.

§ 1731. The effect of a judgment, or final order, in an action or special proceeding, before a court or judge of this state, or of the United States, having jurisdiction to pronounce the judgment or order, is as follows:

1. In case of a judgment, or order, against a specific thing, or in respect to the probate of a will or the administration of the estate of a deceased person, or in respect to the personal, political or legal condition or relation of a particular person, the judgment or order is conclusive upon the title to the thing, the will or administration, or the condition or relation of the person:

2. In other cases, the judgment or order is, in respect to the matter directly adjudged, conclusive between the parties, and their successors in interest by title subsequent to the commencement of the action or special proceeding, litigating for the same thing, under the same title, and in the same capacity.

§ 1732. Other judicial orders of a court or judge of this state, or of the United States, create a disputable presumption according to the matter directly determined, between the same parties, and their representatives and successors in interest by title subsequent to the commencement of the action or special proceeding, litigating for the same thing, under the same title, and in the same capacity.

§ 1733. The parties are deemed to be the same, when those, between whom the evidence is offered, were on opposite sides in the former case, and a judgment, or other determination, could in that case have been made between them alone, though other parties were joined with both or either.

§ 1734. That only is deemed to have been adjudged in a former judgment, which appears upon its face to have been so adjudged, or which was actually and necessarily included therein, or necessary thereto.

§ 1735. Whenever, pursuant to the last four sections, a party is bound by a record, and such party stands in the relation of a surety for another, the latter is also bound, from the time that he has notice of the action or proceeding, and an opportunity, at the surety's request, to join in the defence.

§ 1736. The effect of a judicial record of a sister state, is the same in this state as in the state where it was made, except that it can only be enforced here by an action or special proceeding, and except also, that the authority of a guardian or committee, or of an executor or administrator, does not extend beyond the jurisdiction of the government, under which he was invested with his authority.

§ 1737. The effect of the judicial record of a court of admiralty of a foreign country, is the same as if it were the record of a court of admiralty of the United States.

§ 1738. The effect of the judgment of any other tribunal of a foreign country, having jurisdiction to pronounce the judgment, is as follows:

1. In case of a judgment against a specific thing, the judgment is conclusive, upon the title to the thing:

2. In case of a judgment against a person, the judgment is presumptive evidence of a right, as between

the parties, and their successors in interest by a subsequent title, and can only be repelled by evidence of a want of jurisdiction, want of notice to the party, collusion, fraud or clear mistake of law or fact.

§ 1739. Any judicial record may be impeached, by evidence of a want of jurisdiction in the court or judicial officer, of collusion between the parties, or of fraud in the party offering the record, in respect to the proceedings.

§ 1740. The jurisdiction sufficient to sustain a record, is jurisdiction over the cause, over the parties, and over the thing when a specific thing is the subject of the judgment.

§ 1741. Other official documents may be proved as follows:

1. Acts of the executive of this state, by the records of the state department of the state, and of the United States, by the records of the state department of the United States, certified by the heads of those departments respectively; they may also be proved by public documents, printed by order of the legislature or congress, or either house thereof:

2. The proceedings of the legislature of this state, or of congress, by the journals of those bodies respectively, or either house thereof, or by published statutes or resolutions, or by copies certified by the clerk, or printed by their order:

3. The acts of the executive, or the proceedings of the legislature, of a sister state, in the same manner:

4. The acts of the executive, or the proceedings of the legislature, of a foreign country, by journals published by their authority, or commonly received in that county as such, or by a copy certified, under the seal of the country or sovereign, or by a recognition thereof, in some public act of the executive of the United States:

5. Acts of a municipal corporation of this state, or of a board or department thereof, by a copy certified by the legal keeper thereof, or by a printed book published by the authority of such corporation:

6. Documents of any other class in this state, by the original, or by a copy certified by the legal keeper thereof;

7. Documents of any other class in a sister state, by the original, or by a copy certified by the legal keeper thereof, together with the certificate of the secretary of state, judge of the supreme, superior, or county court, or mayor of a city, of such state, that the copy is duly certified by the officer having the legal custody of the original;

8. Documents of any other class in a foreign country, by the original, or by a copy certified by the legal keeper thereof, with a certificate under the seal of the country or sovereign, that the document is a valid and subsisting document of such country, and that the copy

is duly certified by the officer having the legal custody of the original.

§ 1742. A public record of a private writing may be proved by the original record, or, by a copy thereof certified by the legal keeper of the record.

§ 1743. Entries in public, or other official, books or records, made in the performance of his duty, by a public officer of this state, or by another person in the performance of a duty specially enjoined by law, are primary evidence of the facts stated therein.

§ 1744. A transcript from the record, or docket, of a justice of the peace of a sister state, of a judgment rendered by him, of the proceedings in the action before the judgment, of the execution and return, if any, subscribed by the justice and verified in the manner prescribed in the next section, is admissible evidence of the facts stated therein.

§ 1745. There must be attached to the transcript, a certificate of the justice, that the transcript is in all respects correct, and that he had jurisdiction of the action, and also a further certificate of the clerk or prothonotary of the county in which the justice resided at the time of rendering the judgment, under the seal of the county, or the seal of the court of common pleas or county court thereof, certifying that the person subscribing the transcript was, at the date of the judgment, a justice of the peace in the county, and that the signature is genuine. Such judgment, proceedings and jurisdiction may also be proved by the justice himself, on the production of his docket, or by a copy of the judgment and his oral examination as a witness.

§ 1746. Whenever a copy of a writing is certified for the purpose of evidence, the certificate must state that the copy has been compared by the certifying officer with the original, and is a correct transcript therefrom, and of the whole of such original, or of a specified part thereof. The official seal, if there be any, of the certifying officer, must also be affixed to the certificate, except when the certificate of a clerk of a court is used in the same court or before an officer thereof.

§ 1747. The provisions of the preceding sections of this article, applicable to the public writings of a sister state, are equally applicable to the public writings of a territory of the United States.

ARTICLE III.

PRIVATE WRITINGS.

§ 1748. Private writings are either,

1. Sealed; or,

2. Unsealed.

§ 1749. A seal is a particular sign, made to attest in the most formal manner, the execution of an instrument.

§ 1750. A public seal in this state is a stamp or impression made upon wax wafer, paper, or any other substance, upon which a visible and permanent impression can be made. A private seal may be made in the same manner, or it may be made, without an impression, by a wafer or wax attached to the instrument or by a paper attached to it by an adhesive substance. A scroll or other sign, made in a sister state or foreign country, and there recognised as a seal, must be so regarded in this state, except for a transfer of real property, in this state.

§ 1751. The seal affixed to a writing is presumptive evidence of a consideration. In other respects there is no difference between sealed and unsealed writings, except as to the time of commencing actions thereon. A writing under seal may therefore be changed, or altogether discharged, by a writing not under seal, or by an oral agreement otherwise valid.

§ 1752. The execution of an instrument is the subscribing and delivering it, with or without affixing a seal.

§ 1753. An agreement in writing, without a seal, for the compromise or settlement of a debt, is as obligatory, as if a seal were affixed.

§ 1754. The last three sections do not repeal any statute of this state expressly requiring a seal to a deed or other instrument.

§ 1755. A subscribing witness, is one who sees a writing executed, or hears it acknowledged, and, at the request of the party, thereupon signs his name as a witness.

§ 1756. Historical works, books of science or art, and published maps or charts, when made by persons indifferent between the parties, are primary evidence of facts of general notoriety and interest.

§ 1957. The original writing must be produced and proved, except as provided in section 1688. If it have been lost, proof of the loss must first be made, before evidence can be given of its contents. Upon such proof being made, together with proof of the due execution of the writing, its contents may be proved by a copy, or by a recital of its contents in some authentic document, or by the recollection of a witness, as provided in section 1688.

§ 1758. If the writing be in the custody of the adverse party, he must first have reasonable notice to produce it. If he then fail to do so, the contents of the writing may be proved as in case of its loss. But the notice to produce it, is not necessary where the writing is itself a notice, or where it has been wrongfully obtained or withheld by the adverse party.

§ 1759. Though a writing, called for by one party, is produced by the other, and is thereupon inspected by the party calling for it, he is not obliged to produce it as evidence in the case.

§ 1760. If there be a subscribing witness to a writing, produced in evidence, its execution must be proved by him, if he can be produced, and can testify. If there be more than one subscribing witness, the evidence of one is sufficient. If all the subscribing witnesses be dead, or out of the jurisdiction, or incapable of attending or testifying, or cannot be found, the handwriting of one of them, and that of the party must be proved.

§ 1761. If the subscribing witness denies, or does not recollect, the execution of the writing, its execution may still be proved by other evidence.

§ 1762. Where however, evidence is given that the party, against whom the writing is offered, has at any time admitted its execution, no other evidence of the execution need be given, when the instrument is one mentioned in section 1765, or one produced from the custody of the adverse party, and has been acted upon by him as genuine.

§ 1763. The handwriting of a person may be shown, by any one who believes it to be his, and who has seen him write, or has seen writings purporting to be his, upon which he has acted or been charged, and who has thus acquired a knowledge of his handwriting.

§ 1764. Evidence respecting the handwriting may also be given, by a comparison, made by the witness, or the jury, with writings, admitted or treated as genuine by the party against whom the evidence is offered.

§ 1765. Where a writing is more than thirty years old, the comparison may be made with writings, purporting to be genuine, and generally respected and acted upon as such, by persons having an interest in knowing the fact.

§ 1766. The entries and other writings of a person deceased, made at or near the time of the transaction, and in a position to know the facts stated therein, may be read, as primary evidence of the facts stated therein, in the following cases:

1. When the entry was made against the interest of the person making it: or

2. When it was made in a professional capacity, and in the ordinary course of professional conduct:

3. When it was made in the performance of a duty specially enjoined by law.

§ 1767. When an entry is repeated, in the regular course of business, one being copied from another, at or near the time of the transaction, all the entries are equally regarded as originals.

§ 1768. Every private writing, except last wills and testaments, may be acknowledged or proved, and certified, in the manner provided for the acknowledgment or proof of conveyances of real property, and the certificate of such acknowledgment or proof, is primary evidence, of the execution of the writing, in the same manner as if it were a conveyance of real property.

§ 1769. Every county clerk, and the register of the city and county of New-York, must receive and file in his office, any private writing, delivered to him for that purpose, and give a written receipt therefor. Such writing must be properly endorsed, so as to indicate its general nature, the names of the parties thereto, and the time of filing, and must be deposited and kept in such office separate from other papers. It is then subject to the examination of any person, but cannot be withdrawn, except temporarily, upon the written order of the depositor, or his legal representatives, or on the order of a court of record, for the purpose of being read in evidence therein.

§ 1770. Every surrogate must receive, and deposit in his office, any last will and testament, delivered to him for that purpose, and give a written receipt therefor. Such will must be enclosed in a sealed wrapper, so that its contents cannot be read, and be endorsed with the name of the testator, his place of residence, and the precise time of the deposit, and must not be read or opened, until delivered to a person entitled to it, as provided in the next section.

§ 1771. It can be delivered only,

1. To the testator in person:

2. Upon his written order, proved by a subscribing witness: or,

3. After his death, to the person named in the endorsement, if any, or if he be dead, to the person entitled to the papers of the testator: or,

4. If not so delivered, the surrogate must publicly open and examine it, make known its contents, and file it in his office, to remain there until proved, if capable of proof, and then to be delivered to the person entitled to its custody, or until required by the authority of a competent court to be produced therein.

1772. The record of a conveyance of real property, or other record, a transcript of which is admissible in evidence, must not be removed from the office where it is kept, except upon the order of a court, or when temporarily removed by the clerk, having it in custody, to the court of which he is clerk, or to courts held in the city or village, where his office is situated.

CHAPTER IV.

MATERIAL OBJECTS PRESENTED TO THE SENSES OTHER THAN WRITINGS.

§ 1773. Whenever an object, cognizable by the senses, has such a relation to the fact in dispute, as to afford reasonable grounds of belief respecting it, or to make an item in the sum of the evidence, such object may be exhibited to the jury, or its existence, situation and character may be proved by witnesses. The admission of such evidence must be regulated by the sound discretion of the court.

CHAPTER V.

INDIRECT EVIDENCE; INFERENCES AND PRESUMPTIONS.

§ 1774. Indirect evidence is of two kinds:

1. Inferences: and,

2. Presumptions.

§ 1775. An inference is a deduction, which the reason of the jury makes from the facts proved, without an express direction of law to that effect.

§ 1776. A presumption is a deduction which the law expressly directs to be made from particular facts.

§ 1777. An inference must be founded:

1. On a fact legally proved: and,

2. On such a deduction from that fact as is warranted by a consideration of the usual propensities or passions of men, the particular propensities or passions of

the person whose act is in question, the course of business, or the course of nature.

§ 1778. A presumption, (unless declared by law to be conclusive,) may be controverted by other evidence, direct or indirect; but unless so controverted, the jury are bound to find according to the presumption.

§ 1779. The following presumptions and no others, are deemed conclusive:

1. An intent to murder, from the deliberate use of a deadly weapon, causing death within a year.

2. A malicious and guilty intent from the deliberate commission of an unlawful act, for the purpose of injuring another.

3. The truth of the facts recited from the recital in a written instrument, between the parties thereto, or their successors in interest, by a subsequent title, but this rule does not apply to the recital of consideration:

4. Whenever a party has, by his own declaration, act or omission, intentionally, and deliberately led another to believe a particular thing true, and to act upon such belief, he cannot, in any litigation arising out of such declaration, act or omission, be permitted to falsify it:

5. A tenant is not permitted to deny the title of his landlord at the time of the commencement of the relation:

6. The issue of a wife cohabiting with her husband, who is not impotent, is indisputably presumed to be legitimate:

7. The judgment or order of a court, when declared by this code to be conclusive: but such judgment or order must be alleged in the pleadings, if there be an opportunity to do so; if there be no such opportunity, the judgment or order may be used as evidence:

8. Any other presumption, which by statute, is expressly made conclusive.

§ 1780. All other presumptions are satisfactory, if uncontradicted. They are denominated disputable presumptions, and may, be controverted by other evidence. The following are of that kind:

1. That a person is innocent of crime or wrong:

2. That an unlawful act was done with an unlawful intent:

3. That a person intends the ordinary consequence of his voluntary act:

4. That a person takes ordinary care of his own concerns:

5. That evidence wilfully suppressed would be adverse, if produced:

6. That higher evidence would be adverse, from inferior being produced:

7. That money paid by one to another, was due to the latter:

8. That a thing delivered by one to another, belonged to the latter:

9. That an obligation, delivered up to the debtor, has been paid:

10. That former rent, or instalments have been paid when a receipt for later is produced:

11. That things which a person possesses are owned by him:

12. That a person is the owner of property, from exercising acts of ownership over it, or from common reputation of his ownership:

13. That a person in possession of an order on himself, for the payment of money, or the delivery of a thing, has paid the money, or delivered the thing accordingly:

14. That a person acting in a public office, was regularly appointed to it:

15. That official duty has been regularly performed:

16. That a court or judge acting as such, whether in this state, or any other state or country, was acting in the lawful exercise of his jurisdiction:

17. That a judicial record, when not conclusive, does still correctly determine, or set forth the rights of the parties:

18. That all matters, within an issue, were laid before the jury, and passed upon by them, and in like manner, that all matters, within a submission to arbitration, were laid before the arbitrators, and passed upon by them:

19. That private transactions have been fair and regular:

20. That the ordinary course of business has been followed:

21. That a promissory note or bill of exchange, was given or endorsed for a sufficient consideration:

22. That an endorsement of a negotiable promissory note or bill of exchange, was, made at the time and place of making the note or bill:

23. That a writing is truly dated:

24. That a letter duly directed and mailed, was received in the regular course of the mail:

25. Identity of person, from identity of name:

26. That a person not heard from in seven years is dead:

27. That an obligation under seal, to pay money more than twenty years past, has been extinguished:

28. That acquiescence followed from a belief, that the thing acquiesced in was conformable to the right or fact:

29. That things have happened, according to the ordinary course of nature, and the ordinary habits of life:

30. That persons acting as copartners, have entered into a contract of copartnership:

31. That a man and woman, deporting themselves as husband and wife, have entered into a lawful contract of marriage:

32. That a wife, acting with her husband, in the commission of a felony other than murder, acted by coercion and without guilty intent:

33. That a child born in lawful wedlock, there being no divorce from bed and board, is legitimate:

34. That a thing once proved to exist, continues as long, as is usual with things of that nature:

35. That the law has been obeyed:

36. That a document or writing, more than thirty years old, is genuine, when the same has been since generally acted upon as genuine, by persons having an interest in the question, and its custody has been satisfactorily explained:

37. That a printed and published book, purporting to be printed or published by public authority, was so printed or published:

38. That a printed and published book, purporting to contain reports of cases adjudged in the tribunals of the state, or country, where the book is published, contains correct reports of such cases:

39. That an uninterrupted, adverse possession of real property for twenty years, or more, has been held pursuant to a written conveyance:

40. That a trustee or other person, whose duty it was to convey real property to a particular person, has actually conveyed to him, when such presumption is necessary to perfect the title of such person, or of his successor in interest:

41. The uninterrupted use by the public, of land, for, a burial ground, for ten years, with the consent of the owner, and without a reservation of his rights, is presumptive evidence of his intention to dedicate it to the public, for that purpose.

42. Every sale of personal property, capable of immediate delivery to the purchaser, and every assignment of such property, by way of mortgage or security, or upon any condition whatever, unless the same be accompanied by an immediate delivery, and be followed by an actual and continued change of possession, creates a presumption of fraud, as against the creditors of the seller or assignor, during his possession, or as against subsequent purchasers in good faith, disputable only by making it to appear on the part of the person claiming under such sale or assignment, that the same

was made in good faith, and without intent to defraud such creditors or purchasers:

43. When two persons perish in the same calamity, such as a wreck, a battle, or a conflagration, and it is not shown who died first, and there are no particular circumstances from which it can be inferred, survivorship is presumed, from the probabilities resulting from the strength, age, and sex, according to the following rules:

First. If both those who have perished were under the age of fifteen years, the older is presumed to have survived:

Second. If both were above the age of sixty years, the younger is presumed to have survived;

Third. If one be under fifteen and the other above sixty, the former is presumed to have survived:

Fourth. If both be over fifteen and under sixty, and the sexes be different, the male is presumed to have survived; if the sexes be the same, then the older;

Fifth. If one be under fifteen or over sixty, and the other between those ages, the latter is presumed to have survived.

CHAPTER VI.

INDISPENSABLE EVIDENCE.

§ 1781. The law makes certain evidence necessary to the validity of particular acts, or the proof of particular facts.

§ 1782. Usage, perjury, and treason must be proved by the testimony of more than one witness; usage by the testimony of at least two witnesses; treason by the testimony of two witnesses to the same overt act; and perjury by the testimony of two witnesses, or one witness and corroborating circumstances.

§ 1783. A last will and testament, except when made by a soldier, in actual military service, or by a mariner at sea, is invalid, unless it be in writing, and executed with such formalities as are required by law. Evidence, therefore, of such will cannot be received, without the written instrument itself, or secondary evidence of its contents, in the cases prescribed by law.

§ 1784. A written will cannot be revoked or altered, otherwise than by another written will, or another writing of the testator, declaring such revocation or alteration, and executed with the same formalities, required by law for the will itself; or unless the will be burnt, torn, cancelled, obliterated or destroyed, with the intent and for the purpose of revoking the same, by the testator himself, or by another person, in his presence, by his direction and consent; and when so done by another person, the direction and consent of the testator, and the fact of such injury or destruction, must be proved by at least two witnesses.

§ 1785. No estate or interest in real property, other than a lease for a term not exceeding one year, nor any trust or power concerning it, can be created, transferred or declared otherwise than by operation of law, or by a conveyance or other instrument in writing, subscribed by the party creating, transferring or declaring the same, or by his lawful agent, under written authority, and executed with such formalities as are required by law.

§ 1786. The preceding section must not be construed to affect the power of a testator, in the disposition of his real property by a last will and testament; nor to prevent a trust from arising or being extinguished by implication or operation of law, nor to abridge the power of any court, to compel the specific performance of an agreement, in case of part performance thereof.

§ 1787. A transfer of a vessel is not complete, unless it be in writing, and signed by the party making the transfer.

§ 1788. The authority to execute a sealed instrument must be under seal, if the sealing of the instrument be essential to its validity.

§ 1789. In the following cases the agreement is invalid, unless the same, or some note or memorandum thereof, expressing the consideration, be in writing and subscribed by the party to be charged, or by his agent; evidence therefore of the agreement cannot be received without the writing, or secondary evidence of its contents:

1. An agreement that, by its terms, is not to be performed within a year from the making thereof:

2. A special promise to answer for the debt, default or miscarriage of another:

3. An agreement made upon consideration of marriage, other than a mutual promise to marry:

4. An agreement for the sale of goods, chattels, or things in action, at a price not less than fifty dollars, unless the buyer accept and receive part of such goods or chattels, or the evidences, or some of them, of such things in action, or pay at the time some part of the purchase money; but when a sale is made by auction, an entry by the auctioneer, in his sale-book, at the time

of the sale, of the kind of property sold, the terms of sale, the price, and the names of the purchaser and person on whose account the sale is made, is a sufficient memorandum:

5. An agreement for the leasing, for a longer period than one year, or for the sale of real property, or of an interest therein. An agreement relating to real property, made by an agent of the party sought to be charged, is invalid unless the authority of the agent be in writing, subscribed by the party.

ized in writing.

§ 1790. No evidence is admissible to charge a person upon a representation, as to the credit of a third person, unless such representation, or some memorandum thereof, be in writing, and either subscribed by, or in the handwriting of, the party to be charged.

§ 1791. Nothing in this chapter repeals any statute of this state, prescribing the form of any agreement or instrument not herein mentioned.

CHAPTER VII.

CONCLUSIVE OR UNANSWERABLE EVIDENCE.

§ 1792. No evidence is by law made conclusive or unanswerable, unless so declared by this code. Estoppels are therefore abolished.

TITLE III.

OF THE PRODUCTION OF EVIDENCE.

CHAPTER I.

BY WHOM TO BE PRODUCED.

§ 1793. The party holding the affirmative of the issue must produce the evidence to prove it. Therefore the burden of proof lies on the party, who would be defeated, if no evidence were given on either side.

§ 1794. The party producing a writing, as genuine, which has been altered, or appears to have been altered, after its execution, in a part material to the question in dispute, must account for the appearance, or alteration. He may show, that the alteration was made by another without his concurrence, or was made with the consent of the parties affected by it, or otherwise properly or innocently made, or that the alteration did not change the meaning or language of the instrument. If he do that, he may give the writing in evidence, but not otherwise.

CHAPTER II.

MEANS OF PRODUCTION.

§ 1795. The process by which the attendance of a witness is required, is a subpœna. It is a writ or order directed to a person, and requiring his attendance, at a particular time and place, to testify as a witness. It may also require him to bring with him any books, documents, or other things under his control, which he is bound by law to produce in evidence.

§ 1796. The subpœna is issued as follows:

1. To require attendance before a court, or at the trial of an issue therein, it is issued in the name of the court, before which the attendance is required, or in which the issue is pending:

2. To require attendance out of court, in an action or special proceeding pending in court, it is issued in the name of the court, in which the action or proceeding is pending:

3. To require attendance out of court before a judge, justice, or other officer, authorized to administer oaths in a special proceeding, under the authority of this state, and pending in court, it is issued by the judge, justice, or other officer, before whom the attendance is required:

4. To require attendance before a commissioner, appointed to take testimony, by a court of any other state, or country, or before a judge, justice or other person, in any other case allowed by law, it may be issued by a judge of the supreme court, or by a county judge or justice of the peace, in places within their respective jurisdictions.

§ 1797. Any party or attorney of a party, in an action, or special proceeding pending in court, may at any time, issue in the name and on behalf of the court, as many subpœnas for witnesses within the state, pursuant to subdivisions 1 and 2 of the last section, as may be required by such party. Every judge, justice, or other officer, authorized by subdivisions 3 and 4 of the last section to issue subpœnas, may on the application of any party, and such proof, as this code requires in the particular case, issue subpœnas signed by such judge, justice, or other officer, with his name of office for such witnesses, as the party reasonably requires.

§ 1798. The service of a subpœna is made, by showing the original, and delivering a copy or a ticket, containing its substance, to the witness personally, giving or offering to him at the same time, the fees to which he is entitled, for travel to and from the place designated, and one day's attendance there. Such service must be made, so as to allow the witness a reasonable time, for preparation and travel to the place of attendance.

§ 1799. If a witness be concealed in a building or vessel, so as to prevent the service of a subpœna upon him, the court or officer issuing the subpœna, may, upon proof by affidavit, of the concealment, and of the materiality of the witness, make an order, that the sheriff of the county serve the subpœna, and the sheriff must serve it accordingly, and for that purpose may break into the building or vessel, where the witness is concealed.

§ 1800 A witness is not obliged to attend for examination upon a deposition, or for cross-examination upon an affidavit, in any other county than that of his residence, or where he is served with the subpœna; nor is a witness obliged to attend for oral examination, before a court or judge out of the county where the witness resides, or is served with the subpœna; except that in case of an action or special proceeding pending in court, a judge thereof, or a judge of the supreme court, or a county judge, upon an affidavit of a party, or his attorney, shewing that the testimony of the witness is material and his attendance necessary, may endorse on the subpœna an order for the attendance of the witness; in which case, the service of such subpœna and order, and the payment of double fees to the witness, are sufficient to require his attendance, in the same manner as if he resided in the county.

§ 1801. A person present in court, or before a judicial officer, may be required to testify, in the same manner, as if he were in attendance upon a subpœna, issued by such court or officer.

§ 1802. Disobedience to a subpœna, or a refusal to be sworn or to answer as a witness, or to subscribe an affidavit or deposition when required, may be punished as a contempt, by the court or officer issuing the subpœna, or requiring the witness to be sworn; and if the witness be a party, his complaint, answer or reply may be stricken out.

§ 1803. A witness disobeying a subpœna shall also forfeit to the party aggrieved the sum of fifty dollars, and all damages which he may sustain, by the failure of the witness to attend; which forfeiture and damages may be recovered in a civil action.

§ 1804. In case of the failure of a witness to attend, the court, or officer issuing the subpœna, upon proof of the service thereof, and of the failure of the witness, may issue a warrant to the sheriff of the county, to arrest the witness, and bring him before the court or officer where his attendance was required.

§ 1805. Every warrant of commitment, issued by a court or officer, pursuant to this chapter, must specify therein particularly the cause of the commitment, and if it be for refusing to answer a question, such question must be stated in the warrant. And every warrant to arrest, or commit a witness, pursuant to this chapter, must be directed to the sheriff of the county, where the witness may be, and must be executed by him in the same manner as process issued by the supreme court.

§ 1806. If the witness be a prisoner, confined in a prison within this state, an order for his examination in the prison upon deposition, or for his temporary removal and production, before a court or officer, for the purpose of being orally examined, may be made, as follows:

1. By the court itself, in which the action or special proceeding is pending, unless it be a justice's court:

2. By a judge of the supreme court, or county judge of the county, where the action or proceeding is pending, if pending in a justice's court, or before a judge, or other person out of court.

§ 1807. Such order can only be made on the motion of a party, upon affidavits, showing the nature of the action or proceeding, the testimony expected from the witness, and its materiality.

§ 1808. If the witness be imprisoned in the county where the action or proceeding is pending, and for a cause other than a sentence for felony, his production may be required. In all other cases, his examination must be taken upon deposition.

CHAPTER III.

MANNER OF PRODUCTION.

ARTICLE I.

MODE OF TAKING THE TESTIMONY OF WITNESSES.

§ 1809. The testimony of witnesses is taken in three modes:

1. By affidavit:

2. By deposition:

3. By oral examination.

§ 1810. An affidavit is a written declaration under oath, made without notice to the adverse party.

§ 1811. A deposition is a written declaration under oath, made upon notice to the adverse party for the purpose of enabling him to attend and cross-examine.

§ 1812. An oral examination, is an examination in presence of the jury or tribunal, which is to decide the fact, or act upon it, the testimony being heard by the jury, from the lips of the witness.

§ 1813. In all affidavits and depositions, the witness must be made to speak in the first person. Depositions must be taken in the form of question and answer, and the words of the witness must be written down, unless the parties agree to a different mode.

§ 1814. An affidavit or deposition taken in another state of the United States, or in a foreign country, otherwise than upon commission, must be authenticated as follows, before it can be used in this state:

1. It must be certified by a commissioner, appointed by the governor of this state, to take affidavits and depositions in such other state: or

2. It must be certified, by a judge of a court having a seal, to have been taken and subscribed before him, at a time and place specified, and the genuineness of the signature of the judge, the existence of the court, and the fact that such judge is a member thereof, must be certified by the clerk of the court, under the seal thereof.

ARTICLE II.

AFFIDAVITS.

§ 1815. An affidavit may be used, to verify a pleading or a paper in a special proceeding, to prove the service of a summons notice or other paper in an action or special proceeding, to obtain a provisional remedy, the examination of a witness, or a stay of proceedings, or upon a motion and in any other case, expressly permitted by some other provision of this code, exeept as provided in the next section.

§ 1816. Whenever a provisional remedy, had been granted upon affidavit, the party against whom it was granted, may serve upon the party by whom it was obtained, a notice requiring the person making the affidavit to be produced for cross-examination. Thereupon the party making the motion, shall lose the benefit of the affidavit, and of all proceedings founded thereon, unless within eight days, or such other time as the court or a judge thereof may direct, upon a previous notice to his adversary of at least three days, he produce the deponent for examination, before an officer authorized to administer oaths. Upon such production, the deponent may be examined by either party.

§ 1817. Evidence of the publication of a document or notice required by law, or by an order of a court or judge, to be published in a newspaper, may be given by the affidavit of the printer of the newspaper, or his foreman or principal clerk, annexed to a copy of the document or notice, specifying the times when, and the paper in which, the publication was made. But such affidavit must be made within six months after the last day of publication.

§ 1818. If such affidavit be made in an action or special proceeding pending in a court, it may be filed with the court, or a clerk thereof, if not so made it may be filed with the clerk of the county, where the newspaper is printed. In either case the original affidavit, or a copy thereof, certified by the court or clerk having it in custody, is primary evidence of the facts stated therein.

ARTICLE III.

DEPOSITIONS.

§ 1819. In all cases, other than those mentioned in section 1815, where a written declaration under oath is used, it must be a deposition as prescribed by this code.

§ 1820. The testimony of a witness out of the state, may be taken by deposition in an action, at any time after the service of the summons or the appearance of the defendant, and in a special proceeding, at any time after a question of fact has arisen therein.

§ 1821. The testimony of a witness in this state may be taken by deposition, in an action, at any time, after the service of the summons or the appearance of the defendant, and in a special proceeding, after a question of fact has arisen therein, in the following cases:

1. When the witness is a party to the action or special proceeding:

2. When the witness resides more than one hundred miles from the place where his testimony is to be used:

3. When the witness is about to leave the state, and will probably continue absent when the testimony is required:

4. When the witness, otherwise liable to attend the trial, is nevertheless too infirm to attend:

5. When the testimony is required upon a motion, or in any other case where the oral examination of the witness is not required.

ARTICLE IV.

MANNER OF TAKING DEPOSITIONS OUT OF THE STATE.

§ 1822. The deposition of a witness out of the state, may be taken upon commission issued from the court, or, without commission, before a commissioner appointed by the governor of this state to take depositions in other states.

§ 1823. The commission may be issued by the clerk under the seal of the court, or a surrogate, or by a justice in their courts, on the application of either party, upon five days' previous notice to the other. It must be issued to a person agreed upon by the parties, or if they do not agree, to a judge or justice of the peace, selected by the officer issuing it.

Such proper interrogatories, direct and cross, as the respective parties may prepare, to be settled by the clerk or justice in a summary manner, if the parties disagree, may be annexed to the commission, or when the parties agree to that mode, the examination may be without written interrogatories.

§ 1824. The commission must authorise the commissioner, to administer an oath to the witness, and to take his deposition in answer to the interrogatories, or when the examination is to be without interrogatories, in respect to the question in dispute, and to certify the deposition to the court, in a sealed envelope directed to the clerk, or other person designated or agreed upon, and forwarded to him by mail, or other usual channel of conveyance.

§ 1825. A trial or other proceeding must not be postponed by reason of a commission not returned, except upon evidence satisfactory to the court, that the testimony of the witness is necessary, and that proper diligence has been used to obtain it.

§ 1826. The deposition of a witness out of this state, and in any other of the United States, may also be taken before a commissioner, appointed by the governor of this state to take depositions in other states, upon eight days previous notice of the time and place of examination, given to the adverse party, if the distance of the place of examination from the place where the testimony is to be used, do not exceed one hundred miles, and three days in addition for every additional hundred miles.

§ 1827. Either party may attend on such examination, and put such questions, direct and cross, as may be proper, or if either party by written notice to the other, six days before the examination, require it, it must be taken upon written interrogatories. The deposition must be taken, certified to the court, and filed with the clerk in the same manner, as a deposition upon commission.

§ 1828. The deposition mentioned in this article, may be used by either party on the trial or other proceeding, against any other party, giving or receiving the notice, subject to all just exceptions.

ARTICLE V.

MANNER OF TAKING DEPOSITIONS IN THE STATE.

§ 1829. Either party may have the deposition taken of a witness in this state, in either of the cases mentioned in section 1821, before a judge of the court, or any other person authorised to administer oaths, on serving upon the adverse party, previous notice of the time and place of examination, together with a copy of an affidavit, showing that the case is within that section. Such notice must be at least five days, adding also one day for every fifty miles of the distance of the place of examination from the residence of the person, to whom the notice is given, unless for cause shown, a judge prescribe a shorter time.

§ 1830. Either party may attend such examination, and put such questions, direct and cross, as may be proper, and the deposition must be certified by the officer, and filed with the clerk, or if the parties so agree, deposited with some other person, and may thereupon be used by either party upon the trial, motion, or other proceeding, against any party giving or receiving the notice, subject to all legal exceptions. But no objection to the relevancy of testimony can be made at the trial unless the same were stated at the time of the examination. If the deposition be taken under subdivisions 2, 3, and 4, of section 1821, proof must also be made that the witness continues absent or infirm.

§ 1831. Notwithstanding the taking of a deposition mentioned in sections 1826 and 1829, it may be excluded from the case, upon proof that sufficient notice was not given to the party, against whom it is offered, to enable him to attend the taking thereof, or that the taking was not in all respects fair.

§ 1832. When a deposition has been once taken, it may be read in any stage of the same action or proceeding, or in any other action between the same parties, upon the same subject, and is then to be deemed the evidence of the party reading it.

§ 1833. Any party to an action or special proceeding, in a court, or before a judge, of a sister state, may obtain the testimony of a witness residing in this state, to be used in such action or proceeding, in the cases mentioned in the next two sections.

§ 1834. If a commission to take such testimony have been issued from the court or judge, before whom such action or proceeding is pending, on producing the commission, to a judge of the supreme court, or a county judge, with an affidavit, satisfactory to him, of the materiality of the testimony, he may issue a subpœna to the witness, requiring him to appear and testify, before the commissioner named in the commission, at a specified time and place.

§ 1835. If a commission have not been issued, and it appear to a judge of the supreme court, county judge, or justice, by affidavit satisfactory to him:

1. That the testimony of the witness is material to either party:

2. That a commission to take the testimony of such witness has not been issued:

3. That according to the law of the state where the action or special proceeding is pending, the deposition of a witness taken under such circumstances, and before such judge or justice, will be received in the action or proceeding, he must issue his subpœna, requiring the witness to appear and testify before him at a specified time and place.

§ 1836. Upon the appearance of the witness, the judge or justice must cause his testimony to be taken in wriing, and must certify and transmit the same to the court or judge before whom the action or proceeding is pending, in such manner as the law of that state requires.

ARTICLE VI.

GENERAL RULES OF EXAMINATION.

§ 137. The order of proof must be regulated by the sound discretion of the court. Ordinarily the party, beginning the case, must exhaust his evidence before the other party begins.

§ 1838. If either party require it, the judge may exclude from the court room any witness of the adverse party not at the time under examination, so that he may not hear the testimony of other witnesses.

§ 1839. When a witness does not understand and speak the English language, an interpreter must be sworn to interpret for him.

§ 1840. The court may exercise a reasonable control over the mode of interrogation, so as to make it as rapid, as distinct, as little annoying to the witness, and as effective for the extraction of the truth, as may be, but subject to this rule, the parties may put such legal and pertinent questions as they see fit. The court, however, may stop the production of further evidence, upon any particular point, when the evidence upon it is already so full as to preclude reasonable doubt.

§ 1841. The examination of a witness by the party producing him, is denominated the direct examination; the examination of the same witness, upon the same matter, by the adverse party, the cross-examination. The direct examination must be completed before the cross-examination begins, unless the court otherwise direct.

§ 1842. A question, which suggests to the witness the answer which the examining party desires, is denominated a leading or suggestive question. On a direct examination, leading questions are not allowed, except in the sound discretion of the court, under special circumstances, making it appear that the interests of justice require it.

§ 1843. A witness is allowed to refresh his memory, respecting a fact, by anything written by himself, or under his direction, at the time when the fact occured or immediately thereafter, or at any other time when the fact was fresh in his memory, and he knew that the same was correctly stated in the writing. But in such case the writing must be produced, and may be seen by the adverse party, who may, if he choose, cross-examine the witness upon it, and may read it to the jury. So also a witness may testify from such a writing, though he retain no recollection of the particular facts; but such evidence must be received with caution.

§ 1844. The opposite party may cross-examine the witness, as to any facts stated in his direct examination, or connected therewith, and in so doing, may put leading questions, but if he examine him, as to other matters, such examination is to be subject to the same rules as a direct examination.

§ 1845. The party producing a witness, is not allowed to impeach his credit by evidence of bad character, but he may contradict him by other evidence, and may also show that he has made at other times, statements inconsistent with his present testimony, as provided in section 1848.

§ 1846. A witness once examined, cannot be re-examined as to the same matter, without leave of the court, But he may be re-examined as to any new matter, upon which he has been examined by the adverse party. And after the examinations on both sides are once concluded, the witness cannot be recalled without leave of the court. Leave is granted or withheld, in the exercise of a sound discretion.

§ 1847. A witness may be impeached by the party against whom he was called, by contradictory evidence, or by evidence that his general reputation for truth is bad, or that his moral character is such as to render him unworthy of belief, but not by evidence of particular wrongful acts; except that it may be shown by the examination of the witness, or the record of the judgment, that he has been convicted of a felony.

§ 1848. A witness may also be impeached, by evidence that he has made, at other times, statements inconsistent with his present testimony; but before this can be done, the statements must be related to him, with the circumstances of times, places and persons present; and he must be asked whether he has made such statements, and if so, allowed to explain them. If the statements be in writing, they must be shown to the witness, before any question is put to him concerning them.

§ 1849. Evidence of the good character of a party, is not admissible in a civil action, nor of a witness in any action, until the character of such party or witness has been impeached, or unless the issue involve his character.

§ 1850. Whenever a writing is shown to a witness it may be inspected by the opposite party, and if proved by the witness, must be read to the jury before his testimony is closed, or it cannot be read, except on recalling the witness.

§ 1851 The judge himself, or any juror, may be called as a witness by either party; but in such case it is in the discretion of the court or judge, to order the trial to be postponed or suspended, and to take place before another judge or jury.

TITLE IV.

OF THE EFFECT OF EVIDENCE.

§ 1852. The jury, subject to the control of the court, in the cases specified in this code, are the judges of the effect or value of evidence addressed to them, except when it is hereby declared to be conclusive. They are however to be instructed by the court, on all proper occasions;

1. That their power of judging of the effect of evidence is not arbitrary, but to be exercised with legal discretion, and in subordination to the rules of evidence;

2. That they are not bound to decide in conformity with the declarations of any number of witnesses, which do not produce conviction in their minds, against a less number, or against a presumption or other evidence satisfying their minds;

3. That a witness, false in one part of his testimony, is to be distrusted in others;

4. That the testimony of an accomplice ought to be viewed with distrust, and the oral admissions of a party with caution:

5. That in civil cases the affirmative of the issue must be proved, and when the evidence is contradictory, the decision must be made according to the preponderance of evidence; that in criminal cases, guilt must be established beyond reasonable doubt;

6. That evidence is to be estimated, not only by its own intrinsic weight, but also according to the evidence which it is in the power of one side to produce, and of the other to contradict, and therefore,

7. That if weaker and less satisfactory evidence is offered, when it appears that stronger and more satisfactory was within the power of the party, the evidence offered should be viewed with distrust.

TITLE V.

OF THE RIGHTS AND DUTIES OF WITNESSES.

§ 1853. It is the duty of a witness, duly served with a subpœna, to attend at the time appointed, with any papers under his control required by the subpœna, to answer all pertinent and legal questions, and, unless sooner discharged, to remain till the testimony is closed.

§ 1854. A witness must answer questions legal and pertinent to the matter in issue, though his answer may establish a claim against himself. But he need not give an answer, which will have a tendency to subject him to punishment for a felony. Nor need he give an answer, which will have a direct tendency to degrade his character, unless it be to the very fact in issue, or to a fact from which the fact in issue would be presumed. But a witness must answer as to the fact of his previous conviction for felony.

§ 1855. It is the right of a witness to be protected from irrelevant, insulting or improper questions, and from harsh or insulting demeanor; to be detained only so long as the interests of justice require it; to be examined only as to matters legal and pertinent to the issue.

§ 1856. Every person who has been in good faith, served with a subpœna, to attend as a witness before a court, judge, commissioner, referee, or other person, in a case where the disobedience of the witness may be punished as a contempt, is exonerated from arrest, in a civil action, while going to the place of attendance, necessarily remaining there, and returning therefrom.

The arrest of a witness contrary to this section is void, and when wilfully made, is a contempt of the court; and the person making it, is responsible to the witness arrested, for double the amount of the damages which may be assessed against him, and is also liable to an action at the suit of the party serving the witness with the subpœna, for the damages sustained by him in consequence of the arrest.

§ 1857. But an officer is not so liable, unless the person claiming exemption make, if required, an affidavit, stating:

1. That he has been served with a subpœna, to attend as a witness before a court, officer, or other person, specifying the same, the place of attendance, and the action or proceeding in which the subpœna was issued, and:

2. That he has not been thus served by his own procurement, with the intention of avoiding an arrest.

The affidavit may be taken by the officer, and exonerates him from liability for not making the arrest or for discharging the witness when arrested.

§ 1858. The court or officer issuing the subpœna, and the court or officer before whom the attendance is required, may discharge the witness from an arrest made in violation of section 1856. If the court have adjourned before the arrest, or before application for the discharge, a judge of the court, or a county judge, may grant the discharge.

TITLE VI.

OF EVIDENCE IN PARTICULAR CASES AND MISCELLANEOUS AND GENERAL PROVISIONS.

CHAPTER I.

EVIDENCE IN PARTICULAR CASES.

§ 1859. An offer in writing, to pay a particular sum of money, or to deliver a written instrument or specific personal property, is, if not accepted, equivalent to the actual production, and tender of the money, instrument or property.

§ 1860. Whoever pays money, or delivers an instrument or property, is entitled to a receipt therefor, from the person to whom the payment or delivery is made, and may demand a proper signature to such receipt as a condition of the payment or delivery.

§ 1861. The person to whom a tender is made, must at the time specify any objection he may have to the money, instrument or property, or he must be deemed to have waived it, and if the objection be to the amount of money, the terms of the instrument, or the amount or kind of property, he must specify the amount, terms or kind which he requires, or be precluded from objecting afterwards.

§ 1862. The following are the rules, for construing the descriptive part of a conveyance of real property, when the construction is doubtful, and there are no other sufficient circumstances to determine it:

1. Where there are certain definite and ascertained particulars in the description, the addition of others, which are indefinite, unknown or false, does not frustrate the conveyance, but it is to be construed by the first mentioned particulars:

2. When permanent and visible, or ascertained boundaries or monuments, are inconsistent with the measurement, either of lines, angles or surfaces, the boundaries or monuments are paramount:

3. Between different measurements, which are incon-

sistent with each other, that of angles is paramount to that of surfaces, and that of lines, paramount to both:

4. When a road, or a stream of water not navigable, is the boundary, the rights of the grantor to the middle of the road, or the thread of the stream, are included in the conveyance, except where the road or bed of the stream is held under another title;

5. When tide water is the boundary, the rights of the grantor to low water mark are included in the conveyance:

6. When the description refers to a map, and that reference is inconsistent with other particulars, it controls them, if it appear, that the parties acted with reference to the map; otherwise the map is subordinate to other definite, and ascertained particulars.

§ 1863. An offer of compromise is not an admission, that any thing is due; but admissions of particular facts, made in a negotiation for a compromise, may be proved, unless otherwise specially agreed at the time.

§ 1864. In an action for divorce, on the ground of adultery, a confession of adultery, whether in or out of the pleadings, is not of itself sufficient to justify a judgment of divorce.

CHAPTER II.

PROCEEDINGS TO PERPETUATE TESTIMONY.

§ 1865. The testimony of a witness may be taken conditionally and perpetuated, as provided in this chapter.

§ 1866. The applicant must produce to a judge of the supreme court, or to a county judge, an affidavit, stating,

1. That the applicant is a party, or expects to be a party, to an action in a court of this state:

2. That the testimony of a witness, residing in this state, whose place of residence is stated, is necessary to the prosecution or defence of such action: and generally the facts expected to be proved:

3. If the action be not actually commenced, that the party named who is expected to be adverse to the applicant, resides in this state, and is of full age.

The judge may thereupon, in his discretion, make an order, allowing the examination, and prescribing how long before the examination, the order and notice of the time and place therefor must be served.

§ 1867. Upon proof of personal service upon the person, who is, or is expected to be, the adverse party, of the order, copy of the affidavit, and of a notice that the examination will be taken before a judge of the supreme court, or county judge of the county wherein the witness resides or may be at a specified time and place, such judge may take the deposition of the witness conditionally, and the examination may, if necessary, be adjourned from time to time.

§ 1868. Every answer or declaration of the witness must be taken down, unless the parties otherwise agree. The deposition, when completed, must be carefully read to, and subscribed by, the witness, then certified by the judge, and immediately thereafter filed in the office of the clerk of the county where it was taken, together with the order for the examination of the witness, the affidavit on which the same was granted, and the affidavit of service of the affidavit, order, and notice.

§ 1869. The affidavits filed with the deposition, or a certified copy thereof, are primary evidence of the facts stated therein, to show compliance with the provisions of this chapter.

§ 1870. If a trial be had, between the persons named in the affidavit as parties actual or expectant, or their successors in interest, upon proof of the death or insanity of the witness, or of his inability to attend the trial by reason of age, sickness, or settled infirmity, the deposition, or a certified copy thereof, may be given in evidence by either party.

§ 1871. The deposition so taken and read in evidence has the same effect as the oral testimony of the witness, and no other, and every objection to the witness, or to the relevancy of any question put to him, or of any answer given by him, may be made in the same manner, as if he were examined orally at the trial.

CHAPTER III.

ADMINISTRATION OF OATHS AND AFFIRMATIONS.

§ 1872. Every court, judge, justice or other officer, or person, authorised to take testimony, in any action or proceeding, or to decide upon evidence, has power to administer oaths or affirmations to witnesses.

§ 1873. An oath is usually administered as follows: the person, who swears, lays his hand upon the gospels, while the person administering the oath, thus addresses him: "You do swear that the evidence you shall give in this issue, (or matter) pending between —— and ——, shall be the truth, the whole truth, and nothing but the truth, so help you God," and thereupon the person, who swears, assents by kissing the book.

§ 1874. Any person who desires it, may swear by expressing his assent, when addressed, in the following form: "You do swear, in the presence of the everliving God, that the evidence you shall give, &c.," as in the last section, holding up his hand or not, at his option.

§ 1875. Whenever the court, before which a person is offered as a witness, is satisfied that he has a peculiar mode of swearing, connected with, or in addition to, the usual form of administration, which, in his opinion, is more solemn or obligatory, the court may in its discretion adopt that mode.

§ 1876. When a person is sworn, who believes in any other than the Christian religion, he may be sworn according to the peculiar ceremonies of his religion, if there be any such.

§ 1877. Any person who desires it, may, at his option, instead of taking an oath, make his solemn affirmation or declaration, by assenting, when addressed, in the following form: "You do solemnly affirm (or declare) that, &c., as in section 1873.

An important change is made by this section in respect to the administration of oaths, inasmuch as it allows a witness, in any case, to make a declaration or affirmation, instead of taking an oath. By the present law, the oath must be administered, unless the witness declares that he has conscientious scruples against taking an oath. We would not require it, if the witness merely preferred the declaration or affirmation.

That many good men doubt the lawfulness of oaths, and that more are shocked at their frequency, and the levity with which they are taken, are sufficient reasons for dispensing with them, wherever it can be done with safety. It appears to us safe to leave it optional with the witness, whether to take the oath or make the declaration, even though he have no scruple whatever about the lawfulness of an oath.

A bad man will avoid the oath, if he choose, by feigning a scruple he does not feel; a good man does not need it as a sanction for the truth of his declarations.

§ 1878. Whenever, by any provision of this code, an oath is required, an affirmation or declaration, as prescribed in the last section, is to be deemed equivalent thereto, and a false affirmation or declaration is to be deemed perjury, equally with a false oath.

CHAPTER IV.

GENERAL PROVISIONS.

§ 1879. All questions of fact, other than those mentioned in the next section, are to be decided by the jury, and all evidence thereon addressed to them, except when otherwise provided by this code.

§ 1880. All questions of law, including the admissibility of testimony, the facts preliminary to such admission, and the construction of statutes and other writings, and other rules of evidence, are to be decided by the court, and all discussions of law, addressed to it. And whenever the knowledge of the court is, by this code, make evidence of a fact, the court is to declare such knowledge to the jury, who are bound to accept it.

§ 1881. The provisions contained in this part of the code, respecting the evidence on a trial before a jury, are equally applicable on the trial of a question of fact before a court, referees or other officer.

§ 1882. Whenever by special statute, a certificate is expressly made evidence of a fact, or particular evidence is required, such statute remains unaffected by this code.

§ 1883. All the rules and laws of evidence, heretofore existing in this state, in any case provided for by this code, or inconsistent with it, are abrogated and repealed. But, if there be any former law, or rule of evidence, which is both consistent with this code, and not within the scope of any of its provisions, such law or rule is not abrogated by it.

GENERAL PROVISIONS APPLICABLE TO THE WHOLE CODE.

§ 1884. Words used in this code in the past or present tense include the future as well as the past and present; words used in the masculine gender include the feminine and neuter; the singular number includes the plural, and the plural the singular; the word person includes a corporation as well as a natural person; writing includes printing or printed paper; oath includes affirmation or declaration; signature or subscription, includes mark, when the person cannot write, his name being written near it, and witnessed by a person who writes his own name as a witness. The following terms also have in this code the signification attached to them in this section, unless otherwise apparent from the context:

1. The word "property," includes property, real and personal;

2. The words "real property," are co-extensive with lands, tenements, and hereditaments;

3. The words "personal property," include money, goods, chattels, things in action, and evidences of debt;

4. The word "district,,' signifies judicial district;

5. The word "clerk," signifies the clerk of the court where the action is pending, and in the supreme court the clerk in the county mentioned in the title of the complaint, or in another county, to which the court may have changed the place of trial.

6. The word "writ," signifies an order or precept in writing, issued in the name of the people, or of a court or judicial officer; "Process" is a writ or summons issued in the course of judicial proceedings;

7. The word "corporation" includes every association having any corporate rights, whether created by special acts of legislation or under general laws; a "foreign corporation," is a corporation created by, or under the laws of some other state, government or country.

§ 1885. All statutes, laws and rules, heretofore in force in this state, in any case provided for by this Code, or inconsistent with its provisions, are hereby repealed and abrogated, nor is any such statute, law, or rule, to be deemed retained, because it is consistent with provisions upon the same subject in this code; but such repeal or abrogation does not revive any former law heretofore repealed, nor does it affect any right already existing or accrued, or any proceeding already taken, except as in this code provided.

www.ingramcontent.com/pod-product-compliance
Ingram Content Group UK Ltd.
Pitfield, Milton Keynes, MK11 3LW, UK
UKHW041132071026
15587UKWH00009B/449

9 781886 363342